PETER GABRIEL, FROM GENESIS TO GROWING UP

This book is dedicated to the work of Witness http://www.witness.org/

The editors would like to thank Rob Bozas and Real World for permission to reproduce the album covers featured on the front of this book and Peter Gabriel for inspiring this project.

Peter Gabriel, From Genesis to Growing Up

EDITED BY
MICHAEL DREWETT, SARAH HILL AND KIMI KÄRKI

ASHGATE

Published by
Ashgate Publishing Limited
Wey Court East
Union Road
Farnham
Surrey, GU9 7PT
England

Ashgate Publishing Company
Suite 420
101 Cherry Street
Burlington
VT 05401-4405
USA

www.ashgate.com

British Library Cataloguing in Publication Data
Peter Gabriel, from Genesis to Growing up. – (Ashgate popular and folk music series)
1. Gabriel, Peter, 1950– 2. Gabriel, Peter, 1950–
– Influence.
I. Series II. Drewett, Michael, 1965– III. Hill, Sarah, 1966–
IV. Kärki, Kimi, 1976–
782.4'2166'092–dc22

Library of Congress Cataloging-in-Publication Data
Drewett, Michael.
Peter Gabriel, from Genesis to growing up / Michael Drewett, Sarah Hill and Kimi Kärki.
  p. cm. — (Ashgate popular and folk music series)
Includes bibliographical references and index.
ISBN 978-0-7546-6521-2 (hardcover : alk. paper) 1. Gabriel, Peter, 1950–
—Criticism and interpretation. 2. Genesis (Musical group) 3. Rock music—
England—History and criticism. I. Hill, Sarah, 1966– II. Kärki, Kimi. III. Title.
ML420.G107D74 2010
782.42166092—dc22

2010032125

ISBN 9780754665212 (hbk)

Mixed Sources
Product group from well-managed
forests and other controlled sources
www.fsc.org Cert no. SA-COC-1565
© 1996 Forest Stewardship Council
FSC

Printed and bound in Great Britain by
MPG Books Group, UK

Contents

General Editor's Preface   vii
List of Figures   ix
List of Tables   xi
List of Musical Figures   xiii
Notes on Contributors   xv
Abbreviations   xix

1   Peter Gabriel: From Genesis to Growing Up   1
       Michael Drewett, Sarah Hill and Kimi Kärki

PART I   IDENTITY AND REPRESENTATION

2   From the New Jerusalem to the Secret World: Peter Gabriel and
       the Shifting Self   15
       Sarah Hill

3   Peter Gabriel and the Question of Being Eccentric   31
       Kari Kallioniemi

4   How Peter Gabriel Got His Mozo Working   43
       Kevin Holm-Hudson

5   Staging Masculinities: Visual Imagery in Peter Gabriel's
       'Sledgehammer' Video   57
       Brenda Schmahmann

6   Peter Gabriel's Elegy for Anne Sexton: Image and Music in
       'Mercy Street'   71
       Carol Vernallis

PART II   POLITICS AND POWER

7   The Eyes of the World Are Watching Now: The Political
       Effectiveness of 'Biko' by Peter Gabriel   99
       Michael Drewett

8   Musical Markers as Catalysts in Social Revolutions: The Case of
        Gabriel's 'Biko'   113
        Ingrid Bianca Byerly

9   'Nothin' but the Same old Story': Old Hegemonies, New Musics   131
        Timothy D. Taylor

10   'Hand-made, Hi-tech, Worldwide': Peter Gabriel and World Music   141
        Dave Laing

PART III   PRODUCTION AND PERFORMANCE

11   Nursery Crymes and Sirens' Cries: Peter Gabriel's Use of the Flute 159
        Rebecca Guy

12   'I'd Like my Record to Sound Like This': Peter Gabriel and Audio
        Technology   173
        Franco Fabbri

13   'I Need Contact' – Rock'n'Roll and Ritual: Peter Gabriel's Security
        Tour 1982–83   183
        Jeffrey Callen

14   Plasticine Music: Surrealism in Peter Gabriel's 'Sledgehammer'   195
        John Richardson

15   The Introspectionist: The Phonographic Staging of Voice in Peter
        Gabriel's 'Blood of Eden' and 'Digging in the Dirt'   211
        Serge Lacasse

16   Turning the Axis: The Stage Performance Design Collaboration
        Between Peter Gabriel and Robert Lepage   225
        Kimi Kärki

Bibliography   *241*
Index   *263*

General Editor's Preface

The upheaval that occurred in musicology during the last two decades of the twentieth century has created a new urgency for the study of popular music alongside the development of new critical and theoretical models. A relativistic outlook has replaced the universal perspective of modernism (the international ambitions of the 12-note style); the grand narrative of the evolution and dissolution of tonality has been challenged, and emphasis has shifted to cultural context, reception and subject position. Together, these have conspired to eat away at the status of canonical composers and categories of high and low in music. A need has arisen, also, to recognize and address the emergence of crossovers, mixed and new genres, to engage in debates concerning the vexed problem of what constitutes authenticity in music and to offer a critique of musical practice as the product of free, individual expression.

Popular musicology is now a vital and exciting area of scholarship, and the *Ashgate Popular and Folk Music Series* presents some of the best research in the field. Authors are concerned with locating musical practices, values and meanings in cultural context, and may draw upon methodologies and theories developed in cultural studies, semiotics, poststructuralism, psychology and sociology. The series focuses on popular musics of the twentieth and twenty-first centuries. It is designed to embrace the world's popular musics from Acid Jazz to Zydeco, whether high tech or low tech, commercial or non-commercial, contemporary or traditional.

Derek B. Scott
Professor of Critical Musicology
University of Leeds, UK

List of Figures

6.1	Images from Peter Gabriel's 'Mercy Street' video	71
8.1	Diagrammatical Representation of the Music *Indaba*	121
14.1	Image from Frank Zappa's 'City of Tiny Lites' (1979)	196
14.2	'Starkicker' logo from *The Old Grey Whistle Test*	197
14.3	Image from Jan Švankmajer's *Dimensions of Dialogue* (1982)	201
14.4	Opening scene from Salvador Dalí and Luis Buñuel's film *Un Chien Andalou* (1929)	206
15.1	Performance Intensity *Versus* Dynamic Level (Voice) in Peter Gabriel's 'Blood of Eden' (1992)	218
15.2	'Digging in the Dirt'	222
15.3	Hypermetric structure of C_2	222

List of Tables

2.1   Three-Category Summary of Gabriel's First Album,
        Peter Gabriel (1977)   21
2.2   Thematic Reduction of Gabriel's First Four Albums   22
2.3   First Solo Album *Peter Gabriel* (1977)   26
2.4   Second Solo Album *Peter Gabriel* (1978)   26
2.5   Third Solo Album *Peter Gabriel* (1980)   26
2.6   Fourth Solo Album *Peter Gabriel* (1982)   27
2.7   *So* (1986)   27
2.8   *Us* (1992)   28
14.1   Synopsis and Audiovisual Relations in the Music
        Video of 'Sledgehammer'   198
15.1   Phonographic Staging Effects   213

List of Musical Figures

2.1	'Solsbury Hill'	20
2.2	Drum patterns in 'Intruder' and 'Biko'	24
8.1	Syncopated opening drumbeat: The call to arms	126
8.2	Shift of rhythms and semantics	127
8.3	Cross-cultural overlays of style	127
8.4	Vocal audience participation in finale: The taking up of arms	128

Notes on Contributors

Ingrid Bianca Byerly is an interdisciplinary scholar, holding research and teaching affiliations in the Department of Cultural Anthropology and the Pre-Major Advising Center at Duke University, USA. With an advisory focus on the Senior Honors Theses (for students graduating with distinction), and a teaching focus on Freshman seminars, she has offered courses in literature, anthropology, ethnomusicology, study skills, public speaking and intercultural communication in South Africa, England, Russia and the USA. She has also held the position of Course Director of the International Regent Courses in Oxford, UK, for ten summer sessions. A fellow of Sigma Xi and the American Council of Learned Societies, her interests include filmmaking (for which she was awarded the Panasonic Individual Videomakers' Award in London for *When Nations Meet*), and the investigation of protest music in Apartheid South Africa (for which her research received the Charles Seeger Prize in Toronto, Canada from the Society for Ethnomusicology). She is presently completing a book on *The Music Indaba of South Africa* and a guide for students entitled *To a Certain Degree: The Art of Graduating*.

Jeffrey Callen is an ethnomusicologist (Ph.D., UCLA) whose writing on popular music and culture appears in both popular and scholarly publications. DECIPHERING CULTURE is his professional blog that details his work as a researcher, writer, consultant and educator (and items of relevant interest). His blog POP CULTURE TRANSGRESSIONS provides a forum in which he explores the boundaries of style, genre, culture and gender. He is currently completing a book on alternative music in Morocco based on his doctoral dissertation on Moroccan alternative music.

Michael Drewett is an Associate Professor in Sociology at Rhodes University, South Africa. He is co-editor (with Martin Cloonan) of *Popular Music Censorship in Africa* (Ashgate, 2006) and produced the documentary film *Stopping the Music* (2002) about an instance of South African music censorship. He is a member of the Freemuse Advisory Board and is on the executive of the International Association for the Study of Popular Music.

Franco Fabbri, born in Sâo Paulo (Brazil) in 1949, teaches 'Popular music' at the University of Turin, 'Musicologia' at the University of Genoa and 'Economia dei beni musicali' (music economy) at the University of Milan. He served as chairman of IASPM during two terms: 1985–87 and 2005–07. As a musician and music activist, he has been a member of the rock band Stormy Six since 1966, and president of L'Orchestra Co-operative since 1975. Amongst his books are

Elettronica e musica (Fabbri Editori, 1984), *Il suono in cui viviamo* (Arcana, 1996, new editions 2002 and 2008), *L'ascolto tabù* (Il Saggiatore, 2005), *Around the clock. Una breve storia della popular music* (UTET Libreria, 2008). Essays in English were published in the journal *Popular Music*, and (amongst others) in Simon Frith (ed.), *World Music, Politics And Social Change* (Manchester University Press, 1989) and Goffredo Plastino (ed.), *Mediterranean Mosaic. Popular Music And Global Sounds* (Routledge, 2003).

Rebecca Guy studied the role of the flute in progressive rock at the University of Salford under Professor Sheila Whiteley, gaining her PhD in 2008. She previously studied music at Manchester University and the Royal Northern College of Music, making flute her principal study. After several years lecturing in music at the University of Salford and the University of Manchester, she now lives in France, where she continues to pursue her interests in both music research and performance, alongside her work teaching at various universities in Grenoble. She has presented papers on the subject of the flute, progressive rock and semiotic analysis at various conferences around the world.

Sarah Hill is a lecturer in Music at Cardiff University. She is the author of *'Blerwytirhwng?' The Place of Welsh Pop Music* (Ashgate, 2007), and has published articles on female vocality, Otis Redding, and popular music in postcolonial Wales. She is currently working on a cultural history of popular music in San Francisco, 1965–69.

Kevin Holm-Hudson is Associate Professor of Music Theory at the University of Kentucky (USA). He is the author of *Genesis and The Lamb Lies Down on Broadway* (Ashgate, 2008) and editor of *Progressive Rock Reconsidered* (Routledge, 2002). His articles on popular music have appeared in a number of publications including *Popular Music and Society*, *Music Theory Online*, *Genre* and *American Music*. His research interests include progressive rock, musical signification, the work of Lithuanian composer-painter M.K. Ciurlionis and, more recently, the music of Karlheinz Stockhausen.

Kari Kallioniemi is Docent of History of Popular Culture and Researcher in Cultural History at the University of Turku, Finland. He is the author of *Put the Needle on the Record and Think of England: Notions of Englishness in the Post-war History of British Pop Music* (University of Turku, 1998). His contemporary work deals with the eccentricity in British (pop) stardom.

Kimi Kärki works as a coordinator of both Turku Institute for Advanced Studies, a high quality researcher colloquium meant to promote cutting-edge university research in the humanities and social sciences, and an international Master's programme *European Heritage, Digital Media and the Information Society*. He is based in the Department of Cultural History, University of Turku, Finland. He has written articles and edited several books on cultural history, popular music studies, and cultural integration, and is the editor of IIPC Online Series (http://iipc.utu. fi/). He is currently writing his doctoral thesis on stadium rock spectacles, stage designing and performance of Pink Floyd, The Rolling Stones and U2. He is also a practicing popular musician and songwriter.

Serge Lacasse is Professor at Laval University in Quebec City, where he teaches popular music theory and history, as well as songwriting, audio mixing and other popular music-related courses. In addition to his teaching activities, Serge is a researcher and member of the Executive for the Centre de Recherche Interuniversitaire sur la Littérature et la Culture Québécoises (CRILCQ) and the Institut du Patrimoine Culturel de l'Université Laval (IPAC), member of the scientific committee of the Observatoire interdisciplinaire de création et de recherche en musique (OICRM) and a member of the editorial board for *Les Cahiers de la Société Québécoise de Recherche en Musique*. Favouring an interdisciplinary approach, he has published many chapters and articles, and recently co-edited (with Caroline Traube) a special issue of *Les Cahiers de la SQRM* (*Le timbre musical: Composition, interpretation, perception et reception* 9/1–2, 2007). He also co-edited (with Patrick Roy) *Groove: Enquête sur les phénomènes musicaux contemporains* (Presses de l'Université Laval, 2006). Besides his academic career, he is still active in the recording industry as a producer, songwriter and arranger.

Dave Laing is a visiting research fellow at the University of Liverpool. He is associate editor of *Popular Music History* and the author or editor of several books including *One Chord Wonders* (Open University Press, 1985) and *Buddy Holly* (Indian University Press, 2009).

John Richardson is Adjunct Professor of Musicology at the University of Helsinki and Adjunct Professor of Music and Media at the University of Turku. He currently lectures at the Åbo Academy in Turku, Finland. He is the author of *An Eye for Music: Popular Music and the Audiovisual Surreal* (Oxford University Press, 2011) and *Singing Archaeology: Philip Glass's* Akhnaten (Wesleyan University Press, 1999). In addition, he is co-editor with Stan Hawkins of the collection *Essays on Sound and Vision* (Helsinki University Press, 2007). He has published on popular music, contemporary avant-garde music, musical multimedia and Finnish music

Brenda Schmahmann is Professor in the Fine Art Department at Rhodes University in South Africa. An art historian whose primary focus is on issues of gender, her publications include *Material Matters* (Wits University Press, 2000), *Mapula: Embroidery and Empowerment in the Winterveld* (David Krut Publishing, 2006), *Through the Looking Glass: Representations of Self by South African Women Artists* (David Krut Publishing, 2004) for which she won the Vice Chancellor's Book Award 2007, and *Between Union and Liberation: Women Artists in South*

Africa 1910-1994 (Ashgate, 2005) which she co-edited with Marion Arnold. The author of various exhibition catalogues, she has also published articles in journals such as *African Arts*, *Textile: The Journal of Cloth and Culture* and *De Arte*.

Timothy D. Taylor is a Professor in the Departments of Ethnomusicology and Musicology at the University of California, Los Angeles. In addition to numerous articles on various musics, he is the author of *Global Pop: World Music, World Markets* (Routledge, 1997), *Strange Sounds: Music, Technology and Culture* (Routledge, 2001), and *Beyond Exoticism: Western Music and the* World (Duke University Press, 2007), and is currently writing a history of music used in advertising in the USA from early radio to the present. His article 'The Commodification of Music at the Dawn of the Era of Mechanical Music', published in *Ethnomusicology* in 2007, was awarded the Jaap Kunst Prize by the Society for Ethnomusicology in 2008.

Carol Vernallis is Associate Professor of Film and Media Studies at Arizona State University. Her areas of specialization are music video and the contemporary film soundtrack in relation to image; her research deals more broadly with questions of music, image and text in moving media. Her first book, *Experiencing Music Video* (Columbia University Press, 2004), attempts to theorize an aesthetics of the genre, while her second book, *The Art and Industry of Music Video* (Duke University Press, forthcoming) draws on fieldwork and interviews with music video directors and others in the industry to give an account of the production, post-production and distribution of music videos. Her article on *Eternal Sunshine of the Spotless Mind* was published in *Screen* in 2008. Her work appears in *American Music*, *The Journal of Popular Music Studies*, *Journal of the Society for American Music*, *Popular Music*, the *Quarterly Review of Film and Video*, and *Screen*, and has been anthologized in Roger Beebe and Jason Middleton (eds), *Medium Cool: Music Videos from Soundies to Cell Phones* (Duke University Press, 2007) and Allan Moore (ed.), *Critical Essays in Popular Musicology* (Ashgate, 2007). Her videos have been screened nationally and internationally.

Abbreviations

AIDS	Acquired Immune Deficiency Syndrome
BCP	Black Community Programmes
bpm	beats per minute
CCR	Creedence Clearwater Revival
CMI	Computerized Musical Instrument
DIY	do it yourself
DL	dynamic level
EST	Erhard Seminar Training
IASPM	International Association for the Study of Popular Music
MUDDA	Magnificent Union of Digitally Downloading Artists
PC	pre-chorus
PI	performance intensity
Prog	progressive (rock)
RWN	Real World Notes
WOMAD	World of Music and Dance
WOMEX	Worldwide Music Expo

Chapter 1

Peter Gabriel: From Genesis to Growing Up

Michael Drewett, Sarah Hill and Kimi Kärki

Genesis

The idea for this collection stemmed from a casual conversation between Michael Drewett and Sarah Hill outside the Turku Cathedral at the International Association for the Study of Popular Music (IASPM) Conference in 2001. The final session of the conference had just ended, and had featured Serge Lacasse discussing recording techniques in Peter Gabriel's song 'Blood of Eden'. Apart from Umberto Fiori's seminal 'Listening to Peter Gabriel's "I Have the Touch"' (1987), there had been no academic treatments of Gabriel's work in scholarly journals or, to the collective memory, at academic conferences. Michael and Sarah decided to propose a panel session on Peter Gabriel for the IASPM-Montreal conference in 2003, which would allow them to pursue their academic interest in Gabriel's work in tandem with their more personal attachment to it.

Kimi Kärki had been one of the organizers of the Turku conference, and was in the audience for the Gabriel session in Montreal. In a discussion following the session Michael, Sarah and Kimi decided to work towards putting together an edited volume on Peter Gabriel's music. In a curious bit of chronological coincidence, the evening after the Gabriel session was the closing performance of Peter Gabriel's summer tour, at the Bell Arena in Montreal. In a last-minute scramble the editors of this collection were all fortunate enough to secure tickets for the concert. Sarah had seen Peter Gabriel live on a number of occasions in the UK and the USA, but not since the *So* tour; Michael had not previously seen him perform live while Kimi, who was sitting in another part of the stadium, had the opportunity that night of seeing a stripped-down, yet nevertheless affecting, production of the *Growing Up* stage show, with the added attraction of Robert Lepage emerging onstage to be greeted enthusiastically by his hometown crowd. The IASPM conference ended the following day, and, in a further moment of synchronicity, Michael soon found himself at the Montreal airport check-in – and the next morning at the London baggage claim – chatting with Peter Gabriel.

One of the challenges of this project, and one of the joys of its inception, was in the contributors finding the delicate balance between academic interest and their own personal investment. There are recurring themes in the following chapters, about musical production and artistic influence, about political conviction, self-awareness, social activism and cultural investment. Peter Gabriel's career has spanned almost the length of rock music itself, and his continued contributions to technological advancement, to the promotion of 'world musics', and to political awareness have given him a vitality in popular culture that few other musicians can claim.

Growing Up

Peter Gabriel (born 1950) has always been interested in rock music performance as a form of theatre. His stage performances are famous for their theatrical innovations and experiments. As a member of progressive rock band Genesis in the late 1960s and in the first half of 1970s he took unusual personae, stories and costumes to the centre of his performances.

One of the most successful rock acts of the 1970s and 1980s, Genesis has enjoyed an unusual longevity, borne of inauspicious beginnings: the Garden Wall, a band founded in 1965 at Charterhouse School by 15-year-old schoolboys Peter Gabriel, Tony Banks, Johnny Trapman, Chris Stewart and Rivers Job. Fellow student Anthony Phillips was in another group called Anon; Mike Rutherford was in The Climax, alongside Chris Stewart and three others. As members of each group eventually left school, these various groups joined forces; Gabriel, Banks, Rutherford, Phillips and drummer Chris Stewart were soon uniting as the New Anon, and recorded a six-song demo featuring songs primarily written by Rutherford and Phillips. The Charterhouse connection went even deeper: school alumnus Jonathan King, now a recording artist and producer, heard the tape, and began to champion their music, renaming the band Genesis along the way.

In December of 1967 the group had their first formal recording sessions. Their debut single, 'The Silent Sun', was released in February 1968 without attracting much notice from the public. When the members of Genesis – with John Silver now replacing Chris Stewart – left Charterhouse in the summer of 1969 they had just released their first album, *From Genesis to Revelation*. They decided to try their luck as a professional band; John Silver was replaced by John Mayhew; they got their first paying gig in September of 1969, and began the long process of working out new material.

Genesis were soon signed to the new label Charisma, and recorded their second album, *Trespass* (1970). This was followed by even more personnel changes: Phillips left in July of 1970, followed by Mayhew, leaving a vacancy for child-actor-turned-drummer Phil Collins, former member of Hickory and Flaming Youth. Guitarist Steve Hackett completed the new line-up: his presence, and that of Collins, toughened up the group's sound, which became apparent immediately upon the release of their next album, *Nursery Cryme* (1971).

During these formative years Gabriel developed an interest in the theatrical use of masks, make-up and props, and took to telling framing stories for Genesis' more elaborate works. *Foxtrot* (1972) was a landmark album: seminal in creative terms, successful in commercial ones. Genesis's reputation as a live band was soaring, and demand for their live performance to be documented on an official release was satisfied in August 1973 with the Charisma release of *Genesis Live*. 1973 also saw the release of *Selling England by the Pound*, perhaps the group's most sophisticated album to date. *The Lamb Lies Down on Broadway* (1974) was Gabriel's last album with Genesis, though he performed with Genesis one final time, at a 1982 benefit concert for the WOMAD (World of Music and Dance) Festival.

During the late 1970s and first half of 1980s Gabriel released four solo records, each titled *Peter Gabriel*, but known also by the titles *Car* (1977), *Scratch* (1978), *Melt* (1980) and *Security* (1982). In addition he released *Peter Gabriel Plays Live* (1983) and the soundtrack to Alan Parker's film *Birdy* (1985). His fifth solo album, *So*, released in 1986, became a huge mainstream hit, aided by the success of the groundbreaking video for the single 'Sledgehammer'. His interest in non-western music became evident with the 1989 release of *Passion*, the soundtrack to Martin Scorsese's film *The Last Temptation of Christ*.

In the 1990s Gabriel released *Us* (1992), followed by *Secret World Live* (1994), which documented the subsequent ambitious and theatrical tour. At the same time Gabriel became more and more interested in multimedia production, resulting in two CD-Roms, *X-Plora* (1993) and *Eve* (1997). Along with architectural designer Mark Fisher, Gabriel was involved in designing the London Millennium Dome performance, the music and narrative for which was then released as Gabriel's album *OVO* (2000). In 2002 he released *Up*, which was followed by yet another notably theatrical and technologically challenging tour. In 2010 he released *Scratch My Back*, an album of cover versions.

In the twenty-first century Gabriel has been active in promoting digital music delivery, co-founding one of the first online music services, and MUDDA (Magnificent Union of Digitally Downloading Artists), a musicians' union. He has also been continuously active in human rights issues, most notably through the *Witness* programme, and in the production and distribution of artists from around the world with his Real World label..

Identity and Representation

From his school days through his adulthood, a common theme of Peter Gabriel's lyrics has been belonging: the self in society, his self in a rock band, his rock band in England, England in the world, the world itself. Gabriel's innate and ceaseless musical curiosity has provided a rich palette for the exploration of this overriding theme, and his position at the vanguard of music video has constantly supplied compelling, and often uncomfortable, visual representations of it. Yet despite a fluidity of style and myriad influences, Gabriel's own identity is always foregrounded, deconstructed, reassessed, and re-presented to himself and his audience. And this has been the difficulty for audiences and critics alike. In a review for the *New York Times*, Jon Pareles noted that:

since he left the group Genesis in 1975 for a solo career, Mr Gabriel has written about amnesia, about faith healing, about psychosis, about revelations, about torture, about transcendence – all moments when the 'self' disappears. And at a moment in rock when marketing wisdom decrees that a successful musician needs to stick to a recognizable image, or identity, Mr Gabriel avoided one, letting listeners conjure him for themselves. His first four solo albums didn't even have their own titles, just his name. (Pareles 1986)

Of course, Gabriel's most recognizable identity is his voice. It is an instrument of range and complexity, at times sounding restless, battered, life-weary; at others nothing less than a startling organ of screeching emotionalism, a soul voice, the voice of the soul. Gabriel's voice developed on record, from the schoolboy progressive rock of Genesis to the mature ruminations of *Up* (2002), with Gabriel himself leaving tantalizing clues along his journey about that elusive 'self' Pareles pondered in 1986. The opening section of this book attempts to address the many facets of Gabriel's self which he has revealed on record and through his music videos. The first three chapters consider the remnants of the progressive in Gabriel's musical and theatrical personae; the last two consider the shift from self-directed expressions of self into collaborative explorations of the body and psyche in two landmark videos, 'Sledgehammer' and 'Mercy Street', with the musical and performative interlinked in compelling ways.

First, Sarah Hill sketches an outline of Gabriel's solo career, from his first self-titled studio album (1977) to *Us* (1992), by way of 'Supper's Ready', from the Genesis album, *Foxtrot* (1972). She sees Gabriel's subjectivity as a process mappable across his first six solo albums, from the early, tentative moves toward musical independence through to the multicultural tapestry of his later solo work. The fragility of some of Gabriel's lyrical expressions of self and other, especially on his first four, self-titled solo albums, hint at a much larger quest, one which was to find near resolution in the latter albums *So* (1986) and *Us* (1992). Hill considers such individual moments of personal and spiritual release, and relates them to Gabriel's musical development, from progressive to 'world'.

In his chapter, Kari Kallioniemi explores eccentricity as part of the 'normal character-building activities of English self-definition', looking at models from Victorian literature and twentieth-century music, along with Gabriel's early career in Genesis. By tracing some of the general traits of eccentricity through Gabriel's 1980s solo output, Kallioniemi sheds light on some of the more difficult strands of Gabriel's lyrical expression – insanity, nonconformity, primitivism – and connects Gabriel's earliest work with his latest solo album, *Up* (2002). What this reveals is a man sympathetic to a particular cultural lineage, and sensitive to the changing technological needs of the world beyond his own musical core.

Common to Hill's and Kallioniemi's chapters is the mention of fictive identities. Kevin Holm-Hudson continues with this theme, specifically investigating Mozo, the persona Gabriel adopted as a soulful alter ego. Holm-Hudson traces the influence of soul on Gabriel's musical development, from Gabriel's 'pivotal' experience of listening to Otis Redding on a Dansette player at Charterhouse school, to seeing the man in concert in 1966, right through to the overt sexuality of his mainstream hit singles, 'Sledgehammer' (1986) and 'Steam' (1992). In tracing the latent soul elements of some of Gabriel's earlier work, Holm-Hudson uses those later singles to compare the recording processes of Gabriel with those of the Motown and Stax labels. This is the first of many instances in this collection wherein 'Sledgehammer' is invoked as one of Gabriel's significant moments, musically, stylistically and visually, and serves as a useful introduction to the final two chapters of this section.

Brenda Schmahmann's chapter focuses on Gabriel's groundbreaking video for 'Sledgehammer', an artistic collaboration with Stephen R. Johnson, Aardman Animations and the Brothers Quay. She argues that the video for 'Sledgehammer', along with that for 'Mercy Street', subverts gendered conventions, and she analyses the video from that starting point. Schmahmann suggests that one of the pleasures derived from viewing this particular video is in the understanding of the laborious process behind its creation. We are therefore given to the 'glance', rather than the 'gaze', and can understand the processes by which gendered identities are being 'performed' in a video which even now enthrals with its technology, and captivates with its vision.

To conclude this first section, Carol Vernallis offers a very close reading of the visual and musical codes of the video for 'Mercy Street' (1986), questioning the identity of the narrative voice, and also of the viewer's own position. Gabriel's 'elegy' for Anne Sexton provides a fascinating series of problems: Gabriel's increasingly 'confessional' approach to lyrical writing, married with his mid-1980s fascination with Sexton, the American confessional poet, produced one of the most haunting songs in his output. The video, directed by Matt Mahurin, provides the perfect visual complement to Gabriel's own 'hermetic' musical style. Indeed, as Vernallis argues, the unpredictability of the song's structure and harmonic blueprint is similarly mirrored in the often inscrutable imagery, and series of references, in the video.

In each of these chapters, Gabriel's identity in lyrical codes, musical production and visual imagery is of primary consideration. Read together, they present a rounded portrait of an often perplexing, occasionally bewildering, sometimes worrying, unendingly creative mind at work.

Politics and Power

Peter Gabriel's politics are well known, both in terms of his songwriting and the causes he supports through performance, fundraising and other activities. However, throughout the 1970s, both as a member of Genesis and as a solo artist, Gabriel's political convictions, whatever they were, were not directly reflected in his music. It was only in 1980, with the release of the song 'Biko', that Gabriel began a long political journey which has seen him explore human rights abuses, political prisoners, the world's poor, victims of apartheid, women's rights and, more recently, AIDS awareness. In addition, he has provided an important performance and recording platform for musicians from around the world through WOMAD and Real World Studios.

Gabriel's entrance into the arena of music and politics came as a personal response to the news of the death of Stephen Biko, an anti-apartheid activist tortured and killed by the South African security police. Moved by Biko's death, Gabriel researched Biko's life and wrote a song about the incident. The writing of the song coincided with Gabriel's discovery of African music, which influenced the musical direction of his third album (1980), upon which 'Biko' appeared. While 'Biko' was not the only political song on the album, it was certainly the only one which was overtly a protest song (see Laing 2003: 345). The effect of 'Biko' on Peter Gabriel's career was enormous. Although Gabriel had written the song as an isolated musician without formal association with political organizations, the song soon attracted the attention of those concerned with human rights, in particular anti-apartheid organizations and Amnesty International.

Gabriel's alignment with political organizations, together with his status as musical spokesperson for the anti-apartheid movement (see chapters by Drewett and Byerly) provided him with an important context within which to promote his political concerns. While such platforms undoubtedly offered Gabriel the opportunity to promote himself as a popular musician, there is no doubt that his convictions were genuine. He specifically released 'Biko' as both a single and 12-inch single in order to raise awareness (providing background to the song on the cover of the 7-inch single), and donated the proceeds to the Black Consciousness Movement in South Africa. In turn, when in 1985 Little Steven coordinated the Artists United Against Apartheid ('Sun City') project, Gabriel actively lent his weight to it. Gabriel's concern with Biko's death led to his wholehearted support of Amnesty International, an organization set up in the early 1960s to document and campaign against human rights abuses. This instigated Gabriel's involvement in *The Secret Policeman's Third Ball* in 1987 as well as in two Amnesty music tours: *The Conspiracy of Hope* tour of the USA in 1986, alongside U2, Sting, Lou Reed, the Neville Brothers, Bryan Adams and Joan Baez; and then in the more international *Human Rights Now!* tour in 1988, with Bruce Springsteen, Sting, Tracy Chapman and Youssou N'Dour. Gabriel participated in these in order to galvanize support for human rights and Amnesty International, as he firmly believed in the power of concerned individuals to bring about change. As he explained (in Henke 1988):

> In a world of cynicism and pessimism, Amnesty International is a beacon of hope. It is proof that ordinary people have power. Thousands of men and women have been rescued from unfair imprisonment, torture and execution by the simple act of letter writing. Now, more than ever, it is important for each of us to recognize and use the power we have to bring about change.

This has been most dramatically demonstrated in Gabriel's challenge to his audiences every time he sings 'Biko'. At the end of the song, with the audience singing along to the chorus, Gabriel puts forward the challenge 'I've done what I can, the rest is up to you'.

The importance of 'Biko' to Gabriel's career and as a political song more generally is reflected in the inclusion in this volume of two chapters focused on the song. In his chapter, Drewett documents the story of 'Biko' and how the song has met with different responses, from South African government censorship to Little Steven's 'Sun City' project and numerous cover versions, each of which has led to further coverage of Biko's death. Drewett argues that Gabriel's temporary positioning of himself as an activist–performer played an important role in the effectiveness of 'Biko' as a protest song, one which has affected many lives, galvanized support for the anti-apartheid movement and Amnesty International, and ultimately highlighted broader human rights concerns. In her chapter, Byerly also focuses on the political effectiveness of 'Biko', but does so through the notion of waves of protest that spark further protest, culminating in political transformation. Both of these chapters reveal that, whatever the musical analysis, and despite multiple points of reception, the broader political context is crucial to a thorough understanding of protest songs. It is this context, particularly in regions of contest, which provides the framework of reception for many of those who hear the song.

Gabriel's involvement in Amnesty led to invitations for him to participate in other political and charitable concerns, some of which he agreed to support. These include the free Artists Against Apartheid concert on Clapham Common in June 1986; Nelson Mandela's 70th birthday concert at Wembley Stadium in June 1988, when Mandela was still in prison; the 'International Tribute for a Free South Africa' concert to celebrate Mandela's release held at Wembley Stadium in April 1990; and the 46664 concerts in Cape Town, Oslo, Johannesburg and London between 2003 and 2008. He also released the song 'Shaking the Tree' (1990)[1] with Youssou N'Dour, in support of women's rights. Furthermore, in 1992 Peter Gabriel founded Witness, an organization which trains human rights advocates to use video cameras to document human rights abuses. Witness provides video cameras to activists, houses an archive of video material and works with local organizations to lobby for an end to human rights abuses wherever these occur. This initiative developed out of Gabriel's involvement in the 1988 Amnesty tour. Gabriel noted that:

> The experience of meeting people who had been tortured, who had watched their families being killed – suddenly it became real for me and not something I was just reading about. One of the things that was most shocking was that people who had experienced these things then had their stories completely denied,

---

[1]   Originally released on Youssou N'Dour's *The Lion* (1989) album but with a different mix.

buried, and forgotten. Wherever there were good pictures or video material, it was a great deal harder to [deny]. In a way *Witness* grew out of the technical innovation of the video age. Suddenly there was a small [video] camera that was affordable. (Business Week 2006)

For Gabriel, Witness is an important reaction to human rights abuse because it tackles the issue in a considered manner. As he explains,

Celebrities shouldn't take on causes in a trivial way. They should find things that mean something to them and do their homework, so that they can speak as articulately as they are able, and then hand over to the people doing the real work. (Business Week 2006)

Gabriel's commitment to Witness reflects a consistency between his musical message and his activities beyond his recorded work. A similar link can be found in his involvement with musicians from around the world, performers of 'world music'.

In the late 1970s Gabriel began to discover and become enthused by music from around the world, including (especially) Africa, Bali and Australia (Bright 1988: 140). While excited about the idea of working with these sounds himself, he also wanted to create a platform on which he could promote the music so that others could hear it too. After a period of brainstorming and planning beginning in 1980, Gabriel launched the first WOMAD festival at the Royal Bath and West showground near Shepton Mallet, Somerset in July 1982. Although the first festival was a financial disaster and famously led to a Genesis reunion concert when his former band members offered to help Gabriel out of his financial difficulties, the organization went on to become a highly successful one, holding numerous festivals annually in different parts of the world. In 1983 the WOMAD Foundation was established as an educational charity. Its stated aim was 'to promote, maintain, improve and advance education in world cultures and multi-cultural education' (WOMAD 1996: 34). Thus Gabriel sought a way to combine his own interest in music from other parts of the world with his desire to promote this music and share it with listeners in the western world.

However, Gabriel's interest in and promotion of music from around the world has not been without controversy. The most important criticism levelled at Gabriel involves appropriation. In this volume Timothy D. Taylor argues that in his 'world'-music-influenced music (in particular *Passion* [1989] and *Us* [1992]), Gabriel makes assumptions rooted in metropolitan and colonial ideologies, while at the same time attempting to advocate the preservation of 'world' music and the empowerment of peoples from around the world. However much Gabriel attempts to promote and empower 'world' musicians, Taylor argues that Gabriel's position as a westerner and a male star in the music industry results in music which is always in some way appropriative because in the end the sound is Gabriel's, in terms of both how his voice dominates and ownership of the copyright. For Taylor, the incorporation of various sounds under Gabriel's name amounts to a continuation of colonial relationships in which people from around the world become subjects of western Europeans. In his chapter Dave Laing acknowledges that in at least one instance Gabriel might be guilty of the sort of allegation made by Taylor, but he argues that Taylor's critique is too severe and does not take full account of the music industry conventions involved in collaborative work, in which the singer–songwriter does take ownership of collaborative work, whether it be a western or non-western musician. Laing explores both the aesthetic and ethical issues that arise from the process of combining elements of different musical sources in a single track and concludes that each musical instance should be examined in its own context before a general verdict can be made. While Laing does not reach a general verdict in his chapter, he does make the point that the incorporation of elements of 'world' music in Gabriel's solo work is only one aspect, albeit an important one, of Gabriel's engagement with 'world' music and musicians from around the globe. Laing explores Gabriel's relationship to 'world' music in terms of three components, 'as a creator/performer, as an autodidactic ideologue and as a music-business entrepreneur'. While Gabriel's method can be questioned and criticised, Laing concludes that in all three areas Gabriel's approach has been one of celebration rather than anxiety.

Indeed, considering Gabriel's approach to human rights, the risk of appropriation certainly seems to be taken in pursuit of a higher aesthetic goal rather than simply to exploit musicians for financial gain, as has happened elsewhere, in the musical output of less scrupulous musicians. This is in contrast to Gabriel's stated position that musicians can ensure fair exchange by at the very least promoting the source of the music (as discussed in Laing's chapter). Gabriel believes that 'Whatever corner of this planet you happen to be born in, you should have equal opportunity to get yourself heard and seen in terms of music, arts and politics' (St Michael 1994: 64). Certainly, Gabriel's approach to the musicians he works with – both as a musician and record-label owner – speaks of sensitivity rather than exploitation. This is not to suggest that Gabriel always acts altruistically – as is argued by various contributors to this volume (most particularly Hill, Drewett and Taylor), Gabriel does approach his work from a subjective position, reflecting his British identity in terms of musical style and lyrical themes. He does so in pursuit of pushing the barriers, trying to find 'a better way or a more interesting way' (Gabriel cited in St Michael 1994: 69) of expressing himself, with new sounds and lyrical expression. This is true of his approach not only to production, but also to performance, as considered in the following section.

Production and Performance

The theatrical aspects of Peter Gabriel as performing artist have been evident since his early performances as the front man of Genesis. When he left Genesis in 1975, Gabriel took with him his trademark flamboyant persona and flashy stage shows, and his solo concerts allowed the development of his theatrical ideas into some of the most influential stage productions in rock history. One of his stage performance rituals during his early solo years was to dive or fall into the audience during performances, thus showing his trust that the audience members would catch him. He purposefully avoided other theatrical tricks and costumes during the first years as a solo performer, only to revive them in the 1990s with a new eye to technological possibilities and means to create ambitious rock theatre.

Gabriel's collaboration with different media artists and designers during his later solo career established his reputation as one of the most innovative and authentic rock performers. Furthermore, his influence as the producer of many groundbreaking music videos, and his continued use and development of new studio technology in his Wiltshire-based Real World Studios, still keeps him on the cutting edge of entertainment technology. During the 1990s he started to see himself as an 'experience designer' or a 'boat maker who rows in the oceans of telecommunication' (Townsend 1994: 22–5) and helped to change the face of the new information society through entertainment. This techno-optimism has sometimes led him into a corner, most notably with his yet unrealized plans of a 'Real World theme-park'.

Performance is a central element in creating the idea of rock 'authenticity'. Philip Auslander argues that modern techno-spectacles in vast arenas are other than 'live', however, because both the visual representations on the video screens flanking the stage and the pre-recorded sequences in concert audio are rather a version of mechanical reproduction played simultaneously with the concert to enhance its effect on the audience (Auslander 2005: 27, 38, 83–5).

Rock performed in concert, as an art form, is unique in the sense that it must be constantly re-interpreted by the audience, who then give feedback to the band on stage. As a performance tradition, when it comes to playing, progressive rock in its various forms and offshoots is situated between the strict notated structure of classical music and the improvisation of jazz, but the theatrical performing style is what makes it special (Shumway 1999: 188–9). In large arenas bands have to exaggerate their own stage performance and develop a proportionate surrounding spectacle in order to deliver an enjoyable performance for those audience members situated far away from the stage.

A rock star performing live is a ritual actor who, if we embrace anthropologist Victor Turner's influential ideas, is a liminal being, living between two worlds, on the threshold, like poets, monks, shamans, fools and madmen (Turner 1970: 95). Performative acts by liminal people can also be a source of new cultural innovations. This kind of performance needs an influential and charismatic front figure, someone who will act as the centre of the liminal performance, as a technological 'shaman' (Carlson 2006: 36).

Peter Gabriel claimed during his Genesis days that all performances have ritualistic aspects. This follows naturally from the relation of stage and the audience, from the necessary need of the performer to exaggerate even basic gestures. His own goals were very ritualistic indeed:

Sometimes by moving very slowly and deliberately one can pinpoint a mood in a way that draws people into the music. When I go to a concert I want to be moved and excited by the passion or the ideas. That is my aim as a performer. (Gallo 1986: 7)

In other words, the ritual aspect is central for Gabriel when it comes to creating a relationship between the audience and performer.

The final third of the book is concerned with many of these issues of live performance and production, and is divided more or less chronologically. It opens with Rebecca Guy's chapter on Peter Gabriel's flute playing. Gabriel has been known as an artist capable of playing many instruments, such as drums, piano, various synthesizers, and, as emphasized in Guy's chapter, the flute. Gabriel's flute playing was an integral part of Genesis' sound, both on albums and in live performance. Interestingly enough, the flute has rarely appeared in his later solo works, and even then it has not been Gabriel who has played the instrument. Thus Guy focuses on Gabriel's flute playing on Genesis albums from *Trespass* (1970) to *The Lamb Lies Down on Broadway* (1974), and especially in the band's live shows. Guy relates Gabriel's flute playing to other progressive rock flute masters, notably Ian Anderson of Jethro Tull.

Besides being a skilled musician, Gabriel is considered to be a pioneer in many studio production areas. Two prime examples of his innovative use of studio are co-creating inventive 'gated' drum sounds, and the extensive and even pioneering use of Fairlight CMI synthesizers. Franco Fabbri observes the era of the two studio albums when Gabriel's influence as a studio user and owner was perhaps most evident, namely the time of the recordings of his third and fourth solo albums (1980 and 1982). These albums are milestones in audio engineering and the use of new audio technology, in terms of both sound innovation and production quality.

Jeffrey Callen writes about Gabriel's *Security* tour (1982–83, also known as *Playtime 1988*), and the performance history of Gabriel's early solo career. During the late 1970s and first half of the 1980s Gabriel's live performances were fairly stripped-down occasions, especially compared to the flamboyant and eccentric rock theatre of Genesis or Gabriel's own later multimedia spectacles. During the *Security* tour performances, the arty minimalism of his early solo career met indigenous visual influences, coming from African, Asian and Native American cultures, but also reflected Gabriel's increasing fondness for technology. The performances during that tour were a step toward theatrical ideas of his later tours, but still lacked most of the pop-star mannerisms which were incorporated into Gabriel's performances after the success of *So*.

John Richardson analyses how Gabriel's groundbreaking Claymation video 'Sledgehammer' (1986) was constructed. It could be argued that the video and its record-breaking rotation on MTV made *So* Gabriel's biggest financial success. By taking a look at the elements of Gabriel's 'Sledgehammer' video, Richardson reveals different cultural contexts, both musical and visual, which had an effect or influence on it. The history of animation in music videos receives a more focused study, but the complex cultural traces which are explored during the video analysis also cover surrealism, Nietzsche, Sixties soul and *Wallace & Gromit*, to mention but a few.

Serge Lacasse is interested in Gabriel's vocal staging, or, more accurately, how his voice is presented and affected in a studio environment. Lacasse has created new methodological ways for analysing the experience of recorded voice, based on careful listening of several voice-defining elements, such as loudness, space, time and timbre. Lacasse calls the artistic combination of these elements phonographic staging. As his main case studies in this chapter, Lacasse analyses the technological–musical parameters in 'Blood of Eden' and 'Digging in the Dirt', both from Gabriel's *Us* album (1992), and both fine examples of the use of different vocal techniques and dynamic solutions for musical affect.

Like Jeffrey Callen, Kimi Kärki concentrates on live performance, and more accurately the staging collaboration between Gabriel and Canadian director Robert Lepage in the 1990s and in recent years. Their work on the staging of Gabriel's *Secret World* in the early 1990s was a highly original combination of rock and theatre. As Lepage's background was in experimental theatre, he could indeed feed Gabriel's playful imagination with suitable theatrical ideas. Kärki seeks to find the essential forms of this fruitful collaboration, but also looks into the finished stage productions themselves, in order to analyse the various elements that the actual performances contained. On many occasions what was planned was changed, due to budget reasons or simply because some more exciting stage gimmicks or theatrical solutions serving the song narratives were found. The chapter focuses on two of Gabriel's most recent tours, *Secret World* (1993) and *Growing Up* (approximately 2002–04). During these tours Gabriel made a return to very theatrical expression and flamboyant stage productions, something he had consciously avoided after leaving Genesis. The man who had become famous for the masks he wore onstage during the Genesis days had returned to identity plays with added strength, and also brought in a clever use of highly developed technological tools.

Today, Gabriel remains a vital force with a wide area of interests in the entertainment industry and its future role in global media culture. In the summer of 2008, Real World Records released *Big Blue Ball*, a fruit of Gabriel's collaborative 'Recording Weeks' held since the early 1990s. More recently, in 2010, he released *Scratch My Back*, an album of cover versions on which no guitars or drums are used. The idea is that there will be a follow-up, titled *I'll Scratch Yours*, where the artists featured on the former album each cover a Gabriel song. A new studio album, with the provisional title I/O has been long in the making, but there is no certainty about the release date. His work continues to inspire people, be it in the realms of self-exploration, human rights issues or producing new audiovisual experiences for a global audience. This volume offers a variety of insights into Peter Gabriel's body of work so far, but we hope that he will have ambition and means to continue to cross new borders in the future.

PART I
Identity and Representation

Chapter 2

From the New Jerusalem to the Secret World: Peter Gabriel and the Shifting Self

Sarah Hill

> Identities are never unified and, in late modern times, increasingly fragmented
> and fractured; never singular but multiply constructed across different, often
> intersecting and antagonistic, discourses, practices and positions. They are
> subject to a radical historicization, and are constantly in the process of change
> and transformation. (Hall 1996: 4)

Longevity for an artist in the popular music industry requires transformation and
engagement – with history, with contemporary life, and with one's surroundings.
Musical change is one marker of such engagement (the *Freewheelin'* Bob Dylan
is not the Bob Dylan of *Love and Theft*), although a musician's subjective
identity is not always an agent of that change (David Bowie, despite his myriad
character transformations, has nonetheless left on vinyl very little by way of
tangible autobiography). These transformations are also a natural side-effect of
the aging process, but the result can often leave the listener, or the academic,
wondering about the person behind the sound. Peter Gabriel's career has taken
him from British progressive rock of the late 1960s, through the integration of
'world music' into mainstream radio, and onto the soundtracks of major motion
pictures. At times he has laid himself bare, at others he has lain prostrate before the
voices of others. His career is the embodiment of the 'fragmented and fractured',
'multiply constructed', 'often intersecting and antagonistic discourses, practices
and positions' of contemporary identity: Gabriel's musical exploration and self-
awareness have been interlinked, in often radical ways.

Gabriel's musical identity first emerged at the height of British progressive
rock while a member of the group Genesis. Prog rock was a grandiose movement
toward musical maturity, but Genesis' early recordings betrayed the group's youth.
Like many of his peers, as lyricist and lead singer of Genesis Peter Gabriel utilized
the distancing nature of progressive rock to explore issues of personal and cultural
identity, what it meant to be English, and what being English *sounded* like. In part
this involved an exploration of symbols of national pride, expressions of valour,
and depictions of agrarian hope. Many of these ideas had been distilled much
earlier, of course, in William Blake's 1804 poem, 'Jerusalem':

And did those feet in ancient time
Walk upon England's mountains green?
And was the holy Lamb of God
On England's pleasant pastures seen?
And did the Countenance Divine
Shine forth upon our clouded hills?
And was Jerusalem builded here
Among these dark Satanic mills?
Bring me my bow of burning gold!
Bring me my arrows of desire!
Bring me my spear! O clouds unfold!
Bring me my chariot of fire!
I will not cease from mental fight,
Nor shall my sword sleep in my hand
Till we have built Jerusalem
In England's green and pleasant land.

This meditation on the rape of the English countryside was taken into the heart and choirs of the Church of England and public schools across the land; it has provided the punchline for at least one Monty Python sketch and the title for at least one Oscar-winning film; and it has served as the actual and inspirational basis for at least two works in the progressive rock literature.[1] The multisectional epic 'Supper's Ready', which closed Genesis' *Foxtrot* album (1972), is one such work. It embodies many of the traits characteristic of progressive rock which, according to Jerry Lucky (in Holm-Hudson 2002: 3), include 'a mixture of loud passages, soft passages, and musical crescendos to add to the dynamics of the arrangements' and 'a blending of acoustic, electric and electronic instruments where each plays a vital role in translating the emotion of compositions which typically contain more than one mood'. There are a few points I would like to embellish here, notably what Lucky terms 'a mixture of loud [and] soft passages', and 'a blending of acoustic [and] electric instruments'.

In *Rocking the Classics*, Edward Macan (1997: 43–4) states that:

> Clearly, in progressive rock the alternation of electronic and acoustic sections creates a set of dialectical opposites. Acoustic passages suggest the meditative, pastoral, traditional, and 'feminine', electronic passages the dynamic, technological, futuristic, and 'masculine'. The masculine/feminine analogy goes deeper than one might think, since masculine and feminine sections complete each other, contributing to the expansion and contraction, the movement toward and away from climaxes, that was such a central facet of progressive rock structure. Furthermore, this masculine/feminine dialectic … symbolizes how a

---

[1]   Emerson, Lake and Palmer's 'Jerusalem' (*Brain Salad Surgery*, 1973) being one notable example.

whole set of cultural opposites – high and low culture, European and African-American creative approaches, a futuristic technocracy and an idyllic agrarian past, or matriarchal (creative, intuitive) and patriarchal (rational, carefully organized) modes of society – might be integrated into a larger whole.

'Supper's Ready' serves to typify all of the above characteristics.[2] As an example of British progressive rock, it has one identifiable root in William Blake's 'Jerusalem'; it also name checks figures from ancient history (Pythagoras), Greek mythology (Narcissus), and more recent British political life (Churchill); it shines a commercial light on Biblical figures (the Guaranteed Eternal Sanctuary Man); and it views all of these things through the lens of the British public education system. It is, on the most simplistic level, an epic song of good versus evil. The acoustic sections herald the pastoral, emotional verses of the text, the 'good'; the electric sections herald the verses dealing with conflict, danger, the 'bad'. In the final section of 'Supper's Ready', the acoustic and electric combine to build to the revelatory climax which not only reprises the opening lyrical and musical material, but integrates the mythological and the ideological, or, to be fanciful, Gabriel's sexuality ('Can't you feel our souls ignite / Shedding ever-changing colours, in the darkness of the fading night') and his Anglicanism ('Lord of Lords, King of Kings / has returned to lead his children home, / To take them to the new Jerusalem').[3]

Much can be said about someone named Gabriel invoking Biblical passages of angelic proclamations, but 'Supper's Ready' more simply provides a suitable point of departure for the consideration of Gabriel's solo career. Lyrically, 'Supper's Ready' touches on many of the themes which Gabriel was to explore in his later solo work – belonging, love, spirituality; musically, it suggests that the 'prog rock' of Genesis was the basis for Gabriel's ultimate excursions into African and 'world' musics. As a performed piece, it introduced the contemporary prog rock audience to Gabriel's theatricality, to his commitment to the characters which inhabited his musical world. This aspect of Gabriel's persona was highlighted further by his embodiment of Rael, the protagonist of *The Lamb Lies Down on Broadway* (1974), whose journey through subterranean Manhattan and his subconscious mind also suggested Gabriel's own journey to come;[4] indeed, Gabriel's commitment to the theatrical remains a central component of his performing self.

Peter Gabriel left Genesis following the tour to support *The Lamb Lies Down on Broadway*. In announcing his departure, he stated that

---

[2]   This is a topic which I pursue in greater detail in 'Ending It All: Genesis and Revelation' (forthcoming).

[3]   'Supper's Ready', music and lyrics by Genesis.

[4]   For more on *The Lamb Lies Down on Broadway* and the contemporary climate of Gabriel's personal and musical lives, see Bright (1988), Nicholls (2004), and Holm-Hudson (2008).

[as] an artist, I need to absorb a wide variety of experiences. … I felt I should look at/learn about/develop myself, my creative bits and pieces and pick up on a lot of work going on outside music. … I believe the world has soon to go through a difficult period of changes. I'm excited by some of the areas coming through the surface which seem to have been hidden away in people's minds. I want to explore and be prepared to be open and flexible enough to respond, not tied into the old hierarchy. … My future within music, if it exists, will be in as many situations as possible.[5]

This might suggest that Gabriel felt he had exhausted his interest in progressive rock, but the arc of his solo material suggests otherwise. Indeed, it is possible to show a progression in Gabriel's musical and lyrical themes, from an 'Englishness' to an 'otherness', to equate those themes with a shifting sense of identity, and to illuminate the significance of the different musical textures which accompanied his personal evolution.

To return to Macan, the 'masculine' and 'feminine' ideals in progressive rock were defined by stylistic and instrumental distinctions.[6] As controversial a vocabulary as this is, it nonetheless enables a link to be drawn between 'gendered' musical construction and 'gendered' psychology. The point I wish to make here is that, while a member of Genesis, Gabriel's musical and performative personae displayed certain stereotypical attributes of the English character, attributes which developed within the masculine/feminine prog rock opposition. As a solo artist, Gabriel began to depart from this initial repressed public schoolboy construct and embrace the processes of self-realization popular in the 1970s and 1980s. In other words, Peter Gabriel, post-Genesis, expanded on that metaphorical 'feminine' side. As he moved musically from the acoustic/pastoral into the 'other', the Englishness which he explored in Genesis gave way to a more inward-looking quest for a subjective identity. To generalize, that quest for the 'new Jerusalem' of 'Supper's Ready' was ultimately supplanted by an acknowledgement of the 'Secret World' of *Us*.[7]

An analogy could be drawn here between the musical and the visual. The abstract/progressive nature of Gabriel's first four albums is suggested by their various album covers: Gabriel distorts his own image, or hides himself from clear view; the music within gives little away about his own life. In contrast, *So* is

---

[5]   Peter Gabriel's press release stating the reasons for his departure from Genesis is reproduced in full in Bright (1988: 65–6).

[6]   See Rebecca Guy's further exploration of these themes in this collection.

[7]   I should make it clear that I am concerned primarily with Gabriel's studio albums between his first solo release of 1977 and *Us*, released in 1992; *Peter Gabriel Plays Live*, released in 1983, revisited songs from his first four solo albums, with the addition of one previously unreleased track, 'I Go Swimming'; his soundtrack to the film *Birdy*, released in 1985, included tracks based on previously released material; and *Passion*, his soundtrack to the Martin Scorsese film *The Last Temptation of Christ*, is a complete departure, and worthy of its own study.

not only the first of Gabriel's solo albums to be given an actual title,[8] it is the first of his solo albums to provide an unretouched photograph of the man, albeit apparently trying to escape the camera's eye. Going one step further, *Us* shows Gabriel embracing the unembraceable; his stance is open, but not directed toward his audience. He is not hidden, but he seems unaware of the world beyond himself and the other figure. There could be no more accurate picture to represent the music on *Us*; it is at times painfully personal, seemingly addressed entirely to the elusive woman on the cover who, one can only suppose, is representative of one or more of Gabriel's personal relationships.[9] The musical content of *Us* moves further away from 'rock' and into a more all-embracing, multicultural tapestry.[10]

Gabriel's first solo album reflects the beginning of his personal battle between progressive rock and musical independence. Lyrically, this is represented in the single 'Solsbury Hill', generally interpreted as Gabriel's statement of future intent, of a freeing of his individual creativity, as expressed in the second verse:

> I was feeling part of the scenery
> I walked right out of the machinery
> My heart going boom boom boom
> 'Hey', he said, 'grab your things I've come to take you home.'

But 'Solsbury Hill' is a deceptive departure. Returning to Macan, I would summarize the structural, thematic and musical characteristics of progressive rock as follows:

structural:
- multisectional
- 'classical' forms
- acoustic/electric opposition

thematic:
- mythology
- religion/spirituality
- surrealism/fantasy

musical:
- orchestral textures
- extramusical devices
- shifting rhythms/unusual metres

---

[8]   His fourth studio album was titled *Security* for its US release. See Kevin Holm-Hudson's and Jeffrey Callen's contributions in this volume (Chapters 4 and 13) for further analysis.

[9]   For more on Gabriel's first marriage and subsequent relationship with Rosanna Arquette, both of which inflected his solo albums under consideration here, see Bright (1988).

[10]   See Timothy D. Taylor's discussion of *Us* in this volume (Chapter 9) for a more detailed discussion.

'Solsbury Hill' satisfies all three categories: structurally, there is a conflict between the overriding pastoral mood and the 'power chords' of the final verse and outro; thematically, the lyrics may be interpreted as representing an inner, or spiritual quest; musically, the dominant flute and horns cede at the end to a much larger orchestral texture, and the song adheres roughly to a 7/4 metre. 'Solsbury Hill' represents on the one hand the 'safety' of progressive rock, the means by which Peter Gabriel can find his way 'home', back to his subjective self. But the irregular metre projects uncertainty, the ground shifting under the delicate determination to explore his own creative mind. To take this idea one step further, the solid metrical foundation of the instrumental interjections – a nod toward the standard, 4/4 pop song – is offset by the 3/4 vocal ruminations – abbreviated phrases, their relative haste contrasting starkly with the reassuring *urlinie* in the horns and flute:

Example 2.1   Solsbury Hill

As unlikely a single as it was,[11] 'Solsbury Hill' is still a fair representation of Gabriel's first solo album. Many of the other tracks on the album flirt with the 'progressive', though the album as a whole tends generally more toward the electric than the acoustic. Nonetheless, charting the whole of Peter Gabriel's first solo album according to the three-category summary outlined above, it would seem that he still had a few progressive demons to exorcise (see Table 2.1).

'Solsbury Hill' represents perhaps the first attempt by Gabriel at psychological self-assessment; he is describing a process of departure, opening himself up to new experiences and potential loss. But the other songs on his first album follow in the Genesis vein, and allow Gabriel to hide behind the façades of various characters. Rather than rendering himself completely vulnerable, Gabriel expresses emotions through the adoption of other voices, much as he did on Genesis albums such as *Foxtrot* (1972), *Selling England By the Pound* (1973), and *The Lamb Lies Down on Broadway* (1974). Vocally, his first solo album is a natural extension of his recordings with Genesis; structurally, it suggests a faltering motion toward

---

[11]   'Solsbury Hill' reached No. 13 in the UK singles chart, which was a higher placing than any of the singles Genesis released while Peter Gabriel was a member. Following his departure, of course, Genesis enjoyed a rather long string of popular albums and high-placing singles on both sides of the Atlantic.

the more standard, 'predictable', three-minute pop song; but thematically it is a different story altogether.[12]

Table 2.1 Three-category summary of Gabriel's first album, *Peter Gabriel* (1977)

Song title	Structural	Thematic	Musical
Moribund the Burgermeister	✓	✓	✓
Solsbury Hill	✓	✓	✓
Modern Love	✓	✓	✓
Excuse Me			✓
Humdrum	✓	✓	✓
Slowburn	✓	✓	✓
Waiting for the Big One			✓
Down the Dolce Vita	✓	✓	✓
Here Comes the Flood	✓	✓	✓

By isolating structural and thematic characteristics, it is possible to chart similar tendencies in Gabriel's subsequent releases, and to consider his first four solo albums – as he originally intended – as 'four issues of the same magazine'.[13] I have suggested that one of Gabriel's tendencies on his first album was to 'hide behind characters'; I would now suggest that there are – in the most reductive sense possible – four thematic tendencies Gabriel exhibits on his first four solo albums, and that those tendencies predict his eventual shift from 'English' to 'other'. I would define these tendencies as:

- hiding behind characters: using voices or dialogue for dramatic effect;
- exploring the psychology of characters: moving beyond narrative devices or simple dialogue to uncover motivation;
- exploring Gabriel's own psychology: applying some of the same techniques for a clearly subjective outlook; and
- reaching beyond: applying developing self-awareness to the quest for love and spiritual truth.

To illustrate these ideas, I have selected representative songs from each of the first four albums, and indicated to which thematic category they belong. As an aggregate this shows a general trend over Gabriel's first four solo albums toward a 'reaching beyond'. Furthermore, it can be seen from this reduction that Gabriel's third solo album represents the thematic turning point (Table 2.2).

---

[12]   See Kevin Holm-Hudson's contribution to this collection (Chapter 4) for further discussion of Gabriel's identity play in *Security* and *So*.

[13]   See Bright (1988).

Table 2.2   Thematic reduction of Gabriel's first four albums

	1	2	3	4
hiding behind characters	Moribund the Burgermeister Waiting for the Big One	Flotsam and Jetsam A Wonderful Day… Home Sweet Home		
exploring the psychology of characters	Humdrum	On the Air Indigo	Intruder No Self Control I Don't Remember Family Snapshot Not One of Us Lead a Normal Life	I Have the Touch Wallflower San Jacinto
exploring own psychology	Solsbury Hill			Lay Your Hands on Me
reaching beyond				The Rhythm of the Heat Kiss of Life

There were a few important developments in Gabriel's musical and personal life between the recording of his second and third albums which should be mentioned here. His compositional method was altered dramatically by the acquisition of a programmable drum machine, which inspired him to build songs from a rhythmic, rather than a lyrical or melodic, basis; he made pioneering and extensive use of the Fairlight CMI synthesizer; and he stepped outside of his established sonic setting by using the marimba and Kate Bush's voice as textural instruments. All of these elements marked a shift in Gabriel's musical life, moving him more decidedly away from the purely progressive inclinations of the first two solo albums and into a much more measured fusion of his past and his future.

On the personal level, Gabriel and his then-wife Jill were undergoing a period of involvement with Erhard Seminar Training (EST), which encourages participants to confront their emotions and realize their hidden potential. Perhaps because of this, the lyrics on Gabriel's third album began to reflect a greater search for meaning in his life – a motion away from fictive identities and into his own psychological terrain – and offered a few more tangible clues as to Gabriel's (auto)-biographical arc.

> The existential question of self-identity is bound up with the fragile nature of the biography which the individual 'supplies' about herself. A person's identity is not to be found in behaviour, nor – important though this is – in the reactions of others, but in the capacity to keep a particular narrative going. The individual's biography, if she is to maintain regular interaction with others in the day-to-day world, cannot be wholly fictive. It must continually integrate events which

occur in the external world, and sort them into the ongoing 'story' about the self. (Giddens 1991: 54)

The new textures Gabriel was able to incorporate into his music on the third album replaced the acoustic elements of his earlier material; that 'feminine' side of the progressive opposition was thus shifting from an acoustic/pastoral Englishness to a technological/emotional New Self. 'No Self Control' is a good example of this. It serves as the locus of the personal/world intersection, with the directness of lyrical address ('You know I hate to hurt you / I hate to see your pain / But I don't know how to stop') accompanied by an insistent marimba pattern and percussive vocal interjections. The repetition of the line 'I don't know how to stop' as the song's grounding sentiment, adds to the sense that this 'new self' was as yet unfamiliar to Gabriel himself.

The entire third album has an ominous quality. From the opening drum pattern of 'Intruder' to the final percussive gunshot of 'Biko', Gabriel establishes a primordial rhythm to accompany the darker recesses of his own and others' psyches.[14] Indeed, the drums of the opening and final tracks seem to share the same heartbeat.[15]

More significantly, on the third album Gabriel releases his own voice from the shackles of conventional pop singing. The primal wailing at the opening of 'I Don't Remember', for example, immediately precedes the initial lyric, 'I've got no means to show identification'. But the wail becomes Gabriel's identification on the third album. It maps the motion from Gabriel's chest voice to his head voice, from his heart to his brain and back again. While Gabriel allowed the occasional, brief upward hiccup in Genesis, this is the first moment that he has unleashed the power of his primeval cry. Here Peter Gabriel is releasing himself with self-confidence, telling listeners simply and lucidly, 'you'll have to take me just the way that you find me / what's gone is gone and I do not give a damn'.

Moving into the fourth solo album, Gabriel delved still deeper into his subconscious. While it would be tempting to relate all of the songs on the album to the various alternative practices Gabriel embraced in the early 1980s, it is enough to consider the fourth album as representing an overall quest for deeper meaning, an exploration of parallel musical worlds and parallel states of consciousness. 'The Rhythm of the Heat', as just one example, is the result of a long-standing fascination Gabriel had with Carl Jung, but it also touches on the kind of primeval

---

[14]   It is worth noting the lack of hi-hat on the third album. For more, see Franco Fabbri's chapter in this volume (Chapter 12) and Schwarz (1997).

[15]   The grunting in these two songs – in 'Intruder', initially from 0:52–0:56 and in 'Biko', initially from 0:59–1:04 – serve to emphasize each song's pulse: the driving, steady-crotchet pulse in 'Intruder' heightening the sense of suspense implicit in the lyric, and the heartbeat rhythm in 'Biko' suggesting the martyr's final, laboured breath.

Example 2.2   Drum patterns in 'Intruder' and 'Biko'

dream state Gabriel attempted to reach in the flotation tank he had bought in 1981.[16] The song's working title, 'Jung in Africa', provides one indication of the external influences shaping his compositional and lyrical processes. The 'transcendence through healing rituals'[17] at issue begin from the outset – 'drawn into the circle / that dances round the fire' – and the basic desire for physical reassurance is stated clearly in two song titles, 'I Have the Touch' and 'Lay Your Hands on Me'. The final track, 'Kiss of Life', one of the most joyous-sounding songs in Peter Gabriel's output, is still tinged with uncertainty; the shifting 3+3+4 metre recalls 'Solsbury Hill', but at the bridge the lyrical references to resuscitation ('with heat from her skin and fire from her breath / she blows hard, she blows deep / in the mouth of death') again suggest a darker undercurrent.

Perhaps more significantly, the fourth album was recorded as Gabriel was organizing the first festival for the World of Music, Arts and Dance. WOMAD has since developed from a financially insecure venture into an enormous enterprise, sponsoring annual weekend festivals and, of course, prompting Gabriel to launch his Real World label for the promotion of 'world' musics.[18] Because of Gabriel's commitment to WOMAD, it would be useful now to consider how the shift from progressive rock to 'world' was enacted in Gabriel's first four solo albums, particularly in view of his simultaneous and ongoing emotional journey.

I suggested earlier that there were four general thematic tendencies in Gabriel's solo output which accompanied his shift into world music. I would like

[16]   For another take on Gabriel's 'self' and the fourth album, see Fiori (2000). For unique and in-depth coverage of the creation of Gabriel's fourth album see *The South Bank Show*, ITV, 31 October 1982. The flotation tank also calls to mind the contemporary film *Altered States* (Ken Russell, 1980), which one might assume Gabriel had seen. Thanks to Kimi Kärki for suggesting this connection.

[17]   In his review of the album *So*, Jon Pareles (1986) states that 'the characters in … *Security* … found transcendence through healing rituals'.

[18]   For more on WOMAD see Dave Laing's contribution to this volume (Chapter 10). The incorporation of 'world music' into mainstream Anglo-American mainstream pop is often problematic, and one might consider Gabriel's use of 'African' and 'other' musics as inherently reserved and, therefore, 'English'. With the exception of *Passion*, Gabriel does not always allow 'other' musics to determine the direction of the music, and his tight control over the process and end result might, from some perspectives, suggest a problematic relationship between industrialized and developing nations. I am grateful to Michael Drewett for reminding me that the balance of power in these situations is rarely fairly level.

to extrapolate those four categories now and suggest a connection with the earlier notion of fictive identities. Each of the categories outlined above – hiding behind characters, exploring characters' psychology, exploring subjective psychology, reaching beyond – may be interpreted as extensions of Gabriel's 'progressive' persona, in a circuitous journey toward self-knowledge. I would now generalize those four characteristics as follows:

- a caricatured or abstract persona;
- a questioning persona;
- a quest-ing persona; and
- a general holistic awareness of love and/or spiritual truth.

As one axis of a graph, these characteristics represent the thematic or lyrical levels to Gabriel's solo albums. A general thematic tendency toward the isolation of modern existence is palpable across the first four albums and some lyrics ('It's not easy making real friends'; 'Each one drawn to empty spaces / outsiders, border-line cases'; 'Space is what I need / it's what I feed on'; 'If only I could touch you'; 'A sense of isolation inspires me'; 'I need some attention'; 'I'm [only… only] wanting contact'[19]) seem effortlessly to connect them. The other axis of the graph is stylistic, and would include the following four basic musical tendencies of Gabriel's solo material:

- progressive rock (extended or multisectional works);
- rock (more standard structure, a circa-three-minute format);
- 'African' (influence of African rhythmic or textural characteristics); and
- 'other' (influence of 'world' rhythmic or textural characteristics).

Obviously these categories are fallible, and there would be some degree of overlap between some or all of them on both of the axes; but I have summarized the contents of Gabriel's solo albums from his eponymous 1977 debut to 1992's *Us* (Tables 2.3–2.8), and again, as reductive as this process is, I believe it highlights the shift from progressive to 'other', from Englishness to self-awareness, from the abstract to the personal.

---

[19] 'On the Air', 'White Shadow', 'Exposure', 'Flotsam and Jetsam' from second album; 'Intruder' and 'Family Snapshot' from third; 'I Have the Touch' from fourth.

Table 2.3   First solo album *Peter Gabriel* (1977)

	'prog'	'rock'	'African'	'other'
persona / **abstract**	Moribund the Burgermeister Excuse Me Humdrum Slowburn Waiting for the Big One Down the Dolce Vita			
questioning	Here Comes the Flood	Solsbury Hill Modern Love		
questing				
love				

Table 2.4   Second solo album *Peter Gabriel* (1978)

	'prog'	'rock'	'African'	'other'
persona / **abstract**	A Wonderful Day… White Shadow Exposure Flotsam and Jetsam	On the Air D.I.Y. Animal Magic Perspective Home Sweet Home		
questioning	Indigo	Mother of Violence		
questing				
love				

Table 2.5   Third solo album *Peter Gabriel* (1980)

	'prog'	'rock'	'African'	'other'
persona / **abstract**	Intruder	Family Snapshot And Through the Wire Games Without Frontiers	Lead a Normal Life	
questioning			Not One of Us Biko	
questing		Start/I Don't Remember	No Self Control	
love				

Table 2.6   Fourth solo album *Peter Gabriel* (1982)

	'prog'	'rock'	'African'	'other'
persona / abstract		Shock the Monkey Wallflower		
questioning	San Jacinto The Family & the Fishing Net			
questing		I Have the Touch Lay Your Hands on Me	The Rhythm of the Heat Kiss of Life	
love				

Table 2.7   *So* (1986)

	'prog'	'rock'	'African'	'other'
persona / abstract	This is the Picture	Red Rain Big Time		
questioning	We Do What We're Told	That Voice Again		
questing		Sledgehammer Don't Give Up**	Mercy Street*	
love			In Your Eyes	

* This is one instance of fallible categorization. I suggest 'Mercy Street' as 'African' based on the prominent use of non-Western percussion, though the song structure itself is traditionally 'rock'. See Carol Vernallis' analysis of 'Mercy Street' in Chapter 6 of this volume for further exploration of this point.

**'Don't Give Up' is similarly problematic. While Manu Katche's drumming is African-influenced, the keyboards evoke a South-American panpipe-type flute sound. Gabriel's vocal in the verses suggests a particular Englishness, though the middle eight ('got to walk out of here / I can't take any more...'), accompanied by Richard Tee's keyboard playing, is much more soulful, almost gospel in its delivery. Because of this latter point, I have placed 'Don't Give Up' in the 'rock' category, as all of these musical traits mentioned above represent but a few of the many strands of influence which created the hybrid type of pop music Gabriel is here evoking.

Table 2.8   *Us* (1992)

	'prog'	'rock'	'African'	'other'
persona / abstract		Kiss That Frog		
questioning		Steam		14 Black Paintings
questing		Washing of the Water Digging in the Dirt		Come Talk to Me Love to be Loved Blood of Eden
love				Only Us Secret World

With 'No Self Control' as the symbolic turning point between Gabriel's progressive and subjective stages, a motion into the more 'ethnic' sonic pallette of *So* (1986) and *Us* (1992) should not sound surprising. As well as being Gabriel's most successful commercial release, *So* also suggests an unusually even distribution of songs across the two axes. The primeval rhythmic emphasis of the third and fourth solo albums had then been paired with the 'questioning' persona, thus suggesting a separation between mind and body; but on *So* Gabriel marries that rhythmic drive to lyrics of a much more personal or overtly sexual nature than he had previously written, and the album therefore seems to come from a much more subjective standpoint.[20] 'In Your Eyes' is one such example. Here Gabriel marries effortlessly the spiritual and the emotional ('In your eyes / the light, the heat / I am complete / I see the doorway / to a thousand churches'), and the vaulted vocalese of the outro finds Gabriel overcome to the point of wordlessness by the emergence in the texture of Youssou N'Dour. The song is almost a mandala:[21] the ground bass, the static harmonies of the verses lead in their circular way to the chorus – a literal support network of British male voices allowing Gabriel access to his Anglican spirituality – returning to the circularity of the verse and chorus before reaching the blossoming of sound at 4:33, the sanctified space where the

---

[20]   It should be noted that some of the songs which appeared on *So* had been written much earlier. 'Red Rain' was intended as a companion piece to 'Indigo', from the second album; 'We Do What We're Told (Millgram's 37)' was written around the time of the recording of the third album. The songs with more sexually oriented lyrics – 'Sledgehammer', 'Mercy Street' – were contemporaneous with the early recording stages of *So*. For more information see Bright (1988).

[21]   The use of the mandala as a metaphor for a musical journey is one I borrow from Graeme Boone (1997, 2008), whose analyses of the Grateful Dead's 'Dark Star' are at once deeply insightful and profoundly personal.

'other' reflects Gabriel's grasping toward the inexpressible, the wonders of love and spiritual truth. In that last minute of the song, Gabriel reaches enlightenment, and Youssou N'Dour is presented to western ears as signifying, if not the universe, then at least the World.

I cited 'The Secret World', from *Us*, as the logical developmental bookend to Peter Gabriel's career, the flip side of 'Supper's Ready'. To recount briefly, 'Supper's Ready' was a multisectional song, incorporating several attributes of the 'typical' progressive rock style – acoustic/electric opposition; 'classical' textures; references to mythology, an agrarian utopia, and a sense of Englishness. In the 20 years between *Foxtrot* and *Us*, Peter Gabriel went through a process of emotional and compositional maturity, exploring different sides of himself through songs such as 'Solsbury Hill'; his embracing of 'world' music was indicative of a certain freeing of his capacity for lyrical expression, and his overall musical progression from progressive to 'world' was paralleled by his personal journey from imposed theatricality to fully realized subjectivity.

If 'The Secret World' serves as the logical conclusion of that process, it should be made clear that it holds remnants of the progressive traits outlined earlier. In place of the acoustic, here we have 'other', pitted against an increasingly urgent electric guitar; the biblical ('divided in two like Adam and Eve') replaces the mythical; and lyrical references to pastoral England are replaced by a nostalgic mapping of a private terrain ('In our secret world we were colliding / In all the places we were hiding love'). The circuitous musical route around the verses reflects a certain inward psychological focus, and the lyrical and musical release of the bridge transports Gabriel from an initial resignation ('Oh the wheel is turning spinning round and round / And the house is crumbling but the stairways stand') to the acknowledgment of a greater purpose ('With no guilt and no shame, no sorrow or blame / Whatever it is, we are all the same, the same').

The 'new Jerusalem', the hope which closed 'Supper's Ready', could very well have been this 'Secret World'. Gabriel's English character had needed at first to hide behind Genesis' prog rock bombast; a gradual shedding of progressive rock signalled a shedding of Englishness; and an embracing of 'world' music allowed for an embracing of his new self. The final, almost inaudible, lyric of 'The Secret World' and the album *Us* ('Shh, listen') places Gabriel in amongst a world of listeners, the subjective within the collective, moving confidently onward to his next epiphany.

Chapter 3
Peter Gabriel and the Question of Being Eccentric

Kari Kallioniemi

You can have an eccentric temperament and be just a bit stubborn, unpredictable and contrary. (Celebrity Star Horoscope for Peter Gabriel)

During the mid- and late 1990s there were several articles in the British press claiming that original and authentic English rock-stardom had come to an end. It was argued that one of the reasons for this was the British media's convergence with a new national populism of common culture which created a whole new cultural environment for rock-stardom with its cult of celebrity (Gray 2002: 28–30). One of the most outstanding examples of this original English rock-stardom was, and still is, Peter Gabriel, whose career has fearlessly continued to explore different aspects of rock-stardom, his own identity and peculiarities of English culture. This 'investigation' was very much based on ideas created around the 1960s pop-boom, counter-culture, art-schools and individual artistry.

The idea of unique English rock-stardom enjoyed a temporary revival in the form of Britpop, but without the same counter-cultural and eccentric edge. Britpop was castigated for becoming part of a cult of normality. Sean O'Hagan wrote in *The Sunday Times* in 1995: 'Another question begged by Britpop is where are all the great British weirdos, the eccentrics and gender-benders? Forget the shock of the new, Britpop is all about the thrill of the familiar' (O'Hagan 1995: 20). The new conservative Britpop anti-intellectualism was condemned by commentators like O'Hagan, who suggested that British pop-stardom has fallen from grace, maybe permanently. This transition from originality and eccentricity to contemporary populist individuality with its reality TV shows and pop-idol contests interrupted the canonized history of British rock celebrating the golden era of British popular music in the 1960s and early 1970s.

I will begin this chapter by analysing the cultural history of eccentricity and ask how it is connected to this supposed golden era of English rock. Certain ideas involved in eccentricity are often confused with the peculiarities of Englishness, as distinct from the performed eccentricity of the rock-star. In this connection I will ask how the polarities in Gabriel's personality are associated with his background, his star-image and its role in the contemporary cultural milieu.

The Cultural History of Eccentricity

Eccentricity can be defined as 'capriciousness and whimsicality. Eccentric people are impulsive, puerile, child-like and odd' (*Chambers Encyclopedic English Dictionary* 1994: 397). In a positive light, eccentricity can been perceived as a form of forthright enthusiasm which is closely linked to creativity and the presentation of a performance. In a negative light, an eccentric person is represented as an alien or the other. In this case, he or she is associated with madness, fanaticism and extremism, closely related to religious or political fundamentalism and linked to non-conformist actions which may even be manifestations of 'obsession', 'infatuation' and 'monomania'.

The literature on eccentricity tends to concentrate on entertaining characters and their 'wacky' antics from British history (Caufield 2005). However, wackiness could be interpreted as a type of performance, an important factor in understanding eccentricity. Clinical neuropsychologist David Weeks and journalist Jamie James conducted a scientific study of eccentrics in 1995 and placed great emphasis on the performative mind. For Weeks and James, eccentrics are non-conforming, creative, strongly motivated by curiosity, idealistic and happily obsessed with their hobbyhorses. Playfulness and a mischievous sense of humour, which are often linked to artistic, scientific and religious traits, are also important to eccentrics (Weeks and James 1995: 18, 43). Inventing things fascinates eccentrics as much as does founding religions or cults.

Weeks and James see eccentricity mainly as a positive thing and do not talk much about the situation in which the merely eccentric becomes genuinely frightening or alien. The non-conformist behaviour of their case studies suggests that eccentrics are happier, more creative and healthier than average people. Although they found that it was no easy matter to draw a clear boundary between eccentricity and mental illness, they do distinguish it sharply from such pathologies as psychosis, neurosis and schizophrenia (Weeks and James 1995: 3–12, 95). They also take a conservative position against 'popular mass culture', declaring that 'it has promoted so much boredom and such deep feelings of powerlessness, that we would do well if we could exchange our excessive material acquisitiveness for the eccentrics' inner inquisitiveness' (Weeks and James 1995: 178). Given the prevalence of stereotypes associated with eccentricity in art, pop and film culture, it is understandable that attention-seeking conduct in some eccentric performances has attracted a degree of odium to show business. However, it is as difficult to distinguish genuine eccentricity in the legion of performative-eccentric stars as it is to find the thin line between 'healthy' and 'mad' real-life eccentrics.

The eccentrics' unconcealed enthusiasm, free-thinking, non-conformism and altruistic energy were apparent in the liberal thread of Victorian culture. In his classic essay *On Liberty* (1859) the nineteenth-century liberal thinker John Stuart Mill identified eccentricity as crucial to the definition of individual liberties. For Mill the great threat to eccentricity was not the state or society itself, but 'the great public' and its democratic opinions, which might in the name of conformity suppress those eccentric traits and opinions which were to him the true signs of moral courage and spiritual alertness (Mill 2002: 56).

According to historian David Altick, eccentricity was an antidote to Victorian evangelical conformism which tried puritanically to suppress individuality in society (Altick 1973: 185–6). Charles Dickens and the eccentric characters of his novels exemplify this 'eccentric antidote' against protestant fundamentalism. Dickens loved amateur theatrics and was very keen to perform his characters live, such as the benevolent Mr Pickwick, the slightly mad Mr Dick and the awkward but generous Mr Micawber. His characters also often portrayed the obsessive, monomaniacal and cruel side of grim, macabre eccentricity, which worked for Dickens as an element in the articulation of his liberal politics. For example, he was very much against the extreme temperance that was central to Victorian evangelicism, and advocated moderation and toleration towards habits of the 'lower classes' (Ackroyd 2002: 86–99).

The more playful version of Victorian eccentricity is manifested in two fantasists of the nineteenth century, Lewis Carroll (1832–98) and Edward Lear (1812–88), who displayed this trait through their deeply original use of words and imagination (Jolliffe 2001: 121–44). Their surreal stories fascinated both children and adults and they were an important influence among British psychedelic and early progressive rock, notably in the works of Peter Gabriel and early Genesis. The link between Victorian eccentricity and Englishness and its nationalist rhetorics is obvious. Chroniclers and writers dealing with eccentricity tend to imply that only the English, or more broadly Anglo-Saxon nations, can be authentically eccentric. Weeks and James argue that in the English-speaking nations there has been, at least fitfully, a greater tolerance for non-conformist thinking, leading to eccentric traits: England has become known throughout the world as a haven for eccentrics, and the USA provides strong competition (Weeks and James 1995: 178–79).

The connection between eccentricity and the English idea of liberty has survived from the nineteenth century. Edith Sitwell, author of the classic *The English Eccentrics* (1933), explains the nexus between eccentricity and Englishness thus:

> This attitude, rigidity, protest, or explanation, has been called eccentricity by those whose bones are too pliant. Eccentricity exists particularly in the English, and partly, I think, because of that peculiar and satisfactory knowledge of infallibility that is the hallmark and birthright of the British nation. (Sitwell 1971: 3. See also Timpson 1991: 3–6, 70–71)

Sitwell describes classic English 'eccentric' stereotypes, also celebrated by Victorian culture. These include scientists, explorers, Shakespearean actors, music-hall stars, the world of the Victorian freak show, the lonely squire as an aristocratic collector and the rural vicar.

Performative eccentrics and English middle-class rock-bohemians

All of these characters have worked as stereotypes for the popular culture of the twentieth century, especially in cinema, but also in popular music from the nineteenth-century music hall to contemporary rock culture. Modern popular music offered many ways to emphasize both performance and character in popular songs (Middleton 1990: 249–50), at the same time disconnecting it from the physical side of performance in the circus (Attali 2006: 72–7) until the birth of rock'n'roll. The performative element and the mediation between an artist and his or her audience (Frith 1996: 203–225) were strengthened by the theatrics created by rock-culture in the late 1960s. The magical synthesis of stardom, combining 'the exceptional with the ordinary, the ideal with the everyday' (Dyer 2004: 22; see also Mäkela 2004: 15–25) in the 1960s placed an emphasis on the ideal, the exceptional and the eccentric.

The new English rock-star attacked the puritan side of Victorian tradition but embraced its eccentric Englishness. The southern English rural/suburban middle-class background from which Peter Gabriel and Genesis came (Bright 1989: 13–23) is very much the site where 'traditional' English identity is defined, and so its mythology has been familiar to Gabriel from his childhood.

In some writing concerning Englishness, the gentle Dickensian side of eccentricity is associated with the 'normal' character-building activities of English self-definition. This key to Englishness refers to the traditional English identity, which has been generally interpreted as signifying middle-class or suburban identity. According to E.M. Forster, 'the character of the English is essentially middle class' (Forster 1936: 3).

Although English rock culture was seen as predominantly working class, in the late 1960s a certain quirky middle-class eccentricity was superimposed on English pop/rock stardom. Simon Frith finds social and historical foundations for this in the 'suburban dreaming of pop':

> The suggestion that British pop sensibility is essentially suburban is hardly new. … In England suburbanism is, it seems, equally implicated in folk revival and indie ideology, and what is the Last Night of the Proms if not a celebration of a suburban night out? (Frith 1997: 269)

Suburbia is a place between city and countryside. In pop music terms, it is the site of longing for both places, the lure of the city and rural bliss. Michael Bracewell also refers to the relationship between pop music and the English culture of ruralism and suburbanism:

> Certainly, for the young Graham Greene as much as for Betjeman or Waugh, suburbia – the spiritual home of English pop – held a morbid, mesmeric fascination which they could neither ignore nor reject, most probably because they were all suburban sons themselves. (Bracewell 1997: 24)

It is then arguable that middle-class suburbanism contributed to the emergence of eccentric identities in English rock stardom. Simon Frith's and Howard Horne's identification of art-school pop as the product of middle-class suburbanism also emphasizes the importance of class in relation to English pop from the 1960s, through progressive rock, and onwards: 'in doing so [students] inflected pop music with bohemian dreams and Romantic fancies and laid out the ideology of "rock" – on the one hand a new art form, on the other a new community' (Frith and Horne 1987: 73).

Frith and Horne define two basic communities – rock-bohemians and pop-situationists – which could be used to define two different kinds of rock-eccentrics in English pop. Rock-bohemians were the product of the counter-culture, anti-commercialism and avant-garde experimentalism, who despised rock-music as pop-commodity and believed in the artistic integrity of the rock star. Pop-situationists were the product of punk. They theorized about the idea of pop and new market-friendly attitudes in pop-culture and questioned the autonomy of a rock-star indifferent to the machinations of the market-place (Frith and Horne 1987: passim.).

English rock eccentrics before and after early Genesis

Both of these communities produced outsiders, psychedelic unknowns, mad geniuses, punk pioneers and lo-fi mavericks who were often commercial failures and as such maintained their eccentric cult-image (Unterberg 1998: passim.). However, the position of Peter Gabriel is problematic in this context. He never studied in any art-school and his career has always been high-profile in a way that made it hard to see him as a commercial failure by any standards. His pop-sensibility could be interpreted as being both rock-bohemian and pop-situationist. He has always avoided the rock'n'roll-lifestyle, was mostly non-political during his time in Genesis, and could not be seen as a counter-cultural icon in the early 1970s.

But his work in Genesis could be linked to the pop-Englishness of English folk, psychedelia and prog rock as practised by artists like Kevin Ayers, Syd Barrett, Nick Drake, and Ian Anderson of Jethro Tull. This group of rock-bohemians sought inspiration from the fantastic visions of William Blake, Edward Lear's child-like eccentricity and Kenneth Graham's quasi-mystical and bucolic world of the English countryside in *The Wind in the Willows*.

Pop-Englishness was eager to define itself with reference to the English rural myth. Eccentric squires and their excesses sat comfortably with the rock-stars living in country mansions and ritualistically attacking English decency. This decency, with its hints of hidden sinister eccentricity, was mythologized by artists like Peter Gabriel and poet laureate Sir John Betjeman, who in the 1970s was elevated to the status of pop figure because of his spoken-words albums recorded on Genesis' Charisma label.

The connection between eccentricity and pop-Englishness was vividly exemplified by Vivian Stanshall of The Bonzo Dog Doo Dah Band. Stanshall's album *Sir Henry at Rawlinson End* (1978), which was also made into a movie in 1980, was a comic eulogy to the imaginary temperamental English squire Sir Henry. Stanshall's poetic shambles created a vision of the quirkiness of bygone rural England, occupied by eccentric characters, and serving to ridicule English middle- and upper-class stiff-upper-lip attitudes and generally absurd behaviour (Randall and Welch 2002: 198–202).

Vivian Stanshall was also the rock-eccentric teetering on the edge of lunacy and suffering the inevitable tragic end as an alcoholic. Another troubled example, Joe Meek, the maverick and often besotted producer of one of the most innovative pop-songs from the early 1960s, the Tornadoes' *Telstar*, was obsessed with mysticism, and ended his days by killing his landlady and then himself (Repsch 2004: passim.). Meek also worked as the producer for David 'Screaming Lord' Sutch, rock-theatrics pioneer from the early 1960s, who became a beloved British eccentric after founding The Monster Raving Loony Party and serving for several decades as its parliamentary candidate. The spoils of his mania for collecting once filled three houses, floor to ceiling (Sharpe 2005: 100–101, 191–2).

The punk movement centred more on situationist-influenced maverick tactics which targeted the pop industry and capitalist culture. Manager, recording artist and 'all-around art-prankster' Bill Drummond burnt a million pounds of his money as an art-comment, creating a *cinema verité* film about it. With his partner Jimmy Cauty, Drummond also wrote a zenanarchistic manual, providing a step-by-step method in how to have a No. 1 single in the official UK charts regardless of previous musical experience (Timelords 1988: passim.). Situating himself in the long line of eccentric travellers and explorers Drummond formed an obsession with a mythical alternative Atlantis called Mu-land and in 1996 went to Lapland to bury an icon of Elvis Presley believing that it would radiate good vibes down the longitudes, bringing about world peace (Drummond 2000: 5). Drummond's former client, Julian Cope, has also specialized in eccentric exploration. He travelled for several years in Britain and in continental Europe to research prehistoric sites and publish findings (Cope 1998: passim.; 2004: passim.). All of these eccentric traits could be interpreted as rock-follies, commenting on the absurdity of being a pop star, but also simply as a star's way of displaying his or her private obsessions.

However, rock-eccentricity has often been a privileged playing-ground for boys, exclusive of women. General histories of eccentricity often note the importance of non-conformist women as pre-modern feminists (Jolliffe 2001: 93–119), but the conventional role for women in popular music was markedly questioned by the new wave era. In the late 1970s Kate Bush emerged as one of the first quintessential female English rock-eccentrics and collaborated with Peter Gabriel on his third album (1980) and the1986 hit 'Don't Give Up'.

Peter Gabriel and the Formation of his Performative Eccentricity

Bush's star-image is layered with the romantic ideas of mythical Englishness and Victoriana (Sutcliffe 2003: 72–80), which were also incorporated in early material of Genesis and Gabriel, along with biblical and mythological imagery. The ironies and contradictions of Englishness were represented in the form of rock-theatre, which both attacked bourgeois values and celebrated the remnants of Victorian culture. This structured, traditional and conventional side of the Victorian world was questioned by a culture of liminality, in which the outsider, the rebel and the deviant were heroes, the self was exalted, spontaneity was everything, and rules, restrictions, conventions and traditions, both in art and life, were ditched. In popular culture this had the effect of highlighting fantasy and sexuality rather than serious political engagement (Richards 1997: 167).

Eventually there grew a reaction against Romantic excess, with a return to structure and ultimately the rise of Thatcherism. This was reflected in Gabriel's marginalizing of his whimsical performative eccentricity in favour of political activism, concern with the global issues and the disclosure of personal anxieties.

A Google search for the words 'Peter Gabriel' and 'eccentric', made on 19 December 2007, resulted in about 49,800 hits. Unsurprisingly, Gabriel's public image was generally that of a decent, honest and truthful man, concerned about the injustices of the world, and involved in good causes like humanitarian activity in Amnesty International and the anti-apartheid movement. In the late 1980s Gabriel's new superstardom was also associated with his role as a post-colonial English middle-class hero raising consciousness of the developing world. In this connection, in a *New Musical Express* interview from November 1987, Gabriel mentioned that his main concern as a star was to grow up as a human being (Jackson 1987: 28). Unlike an unrestrained eccentric, he wanted to proclaim his political correctness.

But both his correctness and performative eccentricity arise from his background. His middle-class and public-school upbringing formed a basis for the particular forms of integrity and idealism in his world-view:

> Genesis were a literate, educated, upper-middle-class rock band: exclusively male and often emotionally constipated. But there was always an honesty to Genesis: they didn't fake cockney accents or pretend to be the rock world's equivalent of the *sans culottes*. (Buckley 2005: 86)

The link between Gabriel and his highbrow roots defined the attitudes in the music press to the early work of Genesis. An interview from 1972 referred to him as rock's very own schoolboy, 'restless kid Hamlet', somebody taken from the classic nineteenth-century public-school story for youngsters *Tom Brown's Schooldays* (1857):

He cycles to Island Studios to begin a day's work on the new Genesis album, and unpacks a bottle of throat medicine rather like a schoolboy would unload his textbooks. In fact Gabriel personifies a schoolboy rather in the way a schoolboy might be portrayed at some distant point in time. (Gilbert 1972)

His own memories about his school days at Charterhouse reveal the oppressive and sinister side of this Victorian institution:

I hated it. There was this incredible power set-up with the older boys having fags to do all their menial duties, clean their shoes and so on. It was really crazy. I think people that flourish in public schools are either good at sports, work, the arts or gregarious, and I was none of these. So I didn't feel I fitted in. (Collis 2001: 72)

This whole early profile helps to make explicable the connections between Gabriel's childlike demeanour, contempt against Victorian decency and the macabre whimsy of some of Genesis' early songs. Paul Stump describes the cultural roots of Genesis as lying in a distinctive Victorian mystique of bourgeois Olde English romanticism of the nineteenth century and Anglo-Saxonry that lurked behind the band's early music. This is exemplified by the influences of English sacred music, but also by Rachmaninov and Liberace harmonies, all examples of the taste of middle-class Britain in the late 1950s, which led to the generation of progressive musicians of the 1960s and 1970s (Stump 1997: 173).

The 1960s interpretation of Victorian middle-classness and its traditional English values and morals was articulated both through nostalgia and counter-culture. It continued to provide imagery for English culture in both general and popular music, finding its most spectacular expression in the form of The Beatles' *Sgt Pepper's Lonely Hearts Club Band*. This nostalgia for all things Victorian and Edwardian was also expressed in the incorporation of Sir John Tenniel's drawing of the Mad Hatter from Lewis Carroll's *Alice's Adventures in Wonderland* (1865) into The Famous Charisma record label for Genesis and Gabriel.

This whimsical streak, also drawn from English music hall, was always shadowed by more sinister aspects of Victoriana and English culture. Connected to ideas taken from the Theatre of Cruelty and of the Absurd, these formed the core of both the camp and counter-cultural rock-theatrics of early 1970s English rock (Stump 1997: 175–6). Original member of Genesis Anthony Phillips has recalled how Gabriel's early lyrics reflected this: 'He wrote some pretty eccentric things right from the start. There was one called "Masochistic Man" with a line that goes, *Carve the englantine with bitter juices of her body*. I didn't understand half the stuff he was on about' (Bright 1989: 36–7).

Gabriel's songs and performance style gradually moved from the biblical and Blakean visions of *Trespass* (1970) to the darker side of Victoriana and mythology. The strange combination of macabre and whimsy was at the centre of *Nursery Cryme* (1971), and especially its two songs 'The Musical Box' and 'Harold the

Barrel'. The former song, with its macabre references to child molestation and repressed sexuality, centred on a children's fantasy story, provided Gabriel with an opportunity to create one of his revolting stage costumes: an old man mask. The latter song can be interpreted as being about sadism lurking beneath the rosy façade of middle-class rural England. Gabriel once again returned to this territory in 'I Know What I Like (In Your Wardrobe)' from *Selling England by the Pound* (1973). The song suggests transvestism and refers to the subversiveness of English eccentricity in much the same way as Pink Floyd does in their 'Arnold Layne', a music-hall-influenced song about a kleptomaniac collecting women's underwear. Cross-dressing is a crucial aspect of British theatre and pantomime history, and also an important element in English eccentricity. Peter Gabriel invented his own version of it by using bizarre costumes like a fox's head with a woman's full-length red dress (used in performance of the song 'The Musical Box') and dressing as a daffodil (in the 'Willow Farm' section of 'Supper's Ready').

The man without masks and qualities

The ideas on the record *The Lamb Lies Down On Broadway* (1974) and the lavish stage sets of its tour reflected both transformations in Gabriel's personal life and a reassessment and reconstruction of his own identity in his solo career. Flesh-eating snake babies, a cage made of memories, a four-headed female monster and a Puerto Rican street kid, making his 'pilgrim's progress' into this world made up of mythology and emotional traumas, formed the core of *Lamb* (Fielder 2006: 38–43). The album said goodbye to Gabriel's Genesis-era masks, as in the form of his most revolting creature 'The Slipperman', and foreshadowed a more realistic and psychological treatment of identity in his future works.

Gabriel has referred to childhood traumas and domestic problems in many of his songs and interviews. Problems in his personal life following the start of his solo career led to anger therapy, reading of esoteric teachings (especially by C.G. Jung), a growing awareness of world events and a continuous quest for self-improvement (Bright 1989: 110–22). This quest has sometimes been perceived as a tendency toward madness and self-destruction. For example, 'Lead A Normal Life', the song about conformity, led his US record company executive Ahmet Ertegun to ask 'if Peter had any mental problems' (Bright 1989: 105).

Explorations of the fragile boundaries between conformity, collapse of identity and madness have been Gabriel's solo career trademarks. Through these questions, the repressed identity of the (English) middle-class person trying to handle emotional turmoils has been ruthlessly unmasked. His playful use of contact lenses in the publicity shots of the late 1970s also exemplifies a disruption of his rock-stardom identity and its relationship with fans. The whimsical eccentricity of Gabriel's performative persona still emerged in a couple of songs on his first solo album: the mysterious character of 'Moribund the Burgermeister' and the barbershop quartet of 'Excuse Me'. On the second album this disappeared, to be replaced by an attack against consumerism and its 'dumbing down' effects in 'A Wonderful Day In A One-Way World' and in the social critique of housing problems in 'Home Sweet Home'.

The whole spectrum of questions of identity, including the fear of losing one's mind, the questioning of dominant modes of behaviour in society and the longing for a primitive self, stretches across Gabriel's solo works of the 1980s. The telephone-addict and sleeping/eating disorder sufferer of 'No Self Control' ('Got to get some food / I'm so hungry all the time / I don't know how to stop') presaged the freakishness of reality television guests in 'The Barry Williams Show', from *Up* (2002). 'I Don't Remember' ('I've got no means to show identification / I've got no paper to show you what I am / You'll have to take me just the way that you find me / What's gone is gone and I do not give a damn) developed such themes, crying out the anxieties of being 'somebody'.

Songs on Gabriel's fourth solo album, especially 'The Rhythm of the Heat' and 'Shock the Monkey', displayed his interest in the analysis of the atavism of western life, influenced by writings of C.G. Jung. The urge to disappear into a primal or tribal identity by psychic dissolution is vividly evident in the video for 'Shock the Monkey' (1982), in which 'suburban Mr Gabriel' metamorphoses into tribal-Kabuki warrior. Gabriel's interests in the question of normality and the heterogeneity of marginal people were exemplified by his comment that 'there are rapists and murderers in every psyche' (Sullivan 1980: 24). This disturbing eccentricity was illustrated by Gabriel shaving his head and performing in the garb of a motor mechanic. All of this echoes his interest in raw and outsider art – art escaping cultural conditioning and social conformity – made by criminals or mental patients (Gablriel 1987: 38–41).

The covers of Gabriel's first four solo albums in particular portray the abandonment of the performative masks, leading to a preoccupation with and fear of the public gaze, and the effacement of personal characteristics, eventually producing the macabre mask-like security camera photo of his fourth solo album (1982). 'Wallflower', from the same album, was a return to the anthemic form of early Gabriel solo songs and its outspoken lyrics declared human rights for all 'outsiders and borderline cases' in the world. 'We Do What We're Told (Milgram's 37)', from *So* (1986) was based on Professor Stanley Milgram's experiments on teachers willing to 'punish' their students with electric shocks: 63 per cent were willing to administer shocks of the maximum strength (Sullivan 1980: 24).

Peter Gabriel and the age of 'normality'

This search for many layers of himself eventually led Gabriel to admit that 'part of what I discovered was the bastard in me. I was trying to get in touch with that and put it in some of the songs' (Colbert 1992: 24). This revelation obviously helped him to rediscover his whimsical and childlike side and to put its performative eccentricity back to work in his music videos, and in his 'real life' eccentricity as 'friendly boffin' to explore new and unusual modes of life.

Playful inventiveness is especially apparent in Gabriel's videos, in which remnants of Genesis-era whimsy surface, with ideas constructed around relationships and the primitivism of western life. Gabriel's visual imagery alludes to eccentric Britain/Britons but his interests and influences are everywhere in his videos: the images of sperm, big dippers, steam trains and bumper cars of the groundbreaking 'Sledgehammer' video (Bright 1989: 217–19); the 'Burry Man' – a man totally covered with burdock burrs (Le Vay 2000: 18–19), who makes a brief appearance as a lightbulb-man in the end of 'Sledgehammer', as the Flower man, the monsters made of mud and the Mushroom Man in 'Big Time' and 'Digging in the Dirt', respectively.

Gabriel's positive obsessive traits have helped him to create 'new territories' by linking entertainment and exploration in an inventive way. This could be easily associated with Victorian scientific liberalism and its eccentric scientists prophesying a 'new world' equipped with 'devices' (Coleman 1994: 53). Gabriel's desire to remain in touch with new technology obviously comes from his father, who in the 1970s tried unsuccessfully to sell the idea of cable TV and home shopping (Townsend 1994: 23). With similar 'eccentric' inventiveness Gabriel has dreamed of a machine that can interface with plants and has planned an interactive science-entertainment park called Real World Experience Park. He has also played music with bonobo apes at a research centre in Atlanta.

Throughout all this, he sees himself not primarily as a rock-star or a musician, but more as 'an experience designer or boat-builder for the information ocean' (Coleman 1994: 53). This inclination toward non-musical eccentricities has been regularly greeted with hostility in the press since his days in Genesis. He annoyed a *Guardian* journalist in 2004 when he founded the Magnificent Union of Digitally Downloading Artists (MUDDA), dedicated to the transformation of the music business:

> Gabriel is the kind of rock star who seems to come up with ridiculous ideas on regular basis; last year he announced he was setting up an organisation that would enable apes to communicate using the internet. The internet encourages self-indulgence in the most unassuming people, as proven by the vast number of weblogs and homepages featuring gripping pictures of pets. When rock stars get involved with it, all sense of quality control goes out the window. (Petridis 2004)

What could cause this kind of reaction to basically harmless and benign practices of the eccentric rock star? Gabriel's public image has always oscillated between unassuming geniality and reluctance to play the rock star, and the theatrically performing minstrel who can also publicly unmask his passions and private life. His preferred 'weekend stardom' to superstardom (Jackson 1987: 28), his seriousness and family-man image conflict with the image of the boffin, outraged at global injustices and seeking to apply his imagination and enthusiasms to the messianic goal of making the world a better place.

The photograph on *So* (1986) represented the final casting off of Gabriel's mask (Bright 1989: 208) and finding a way back to 'normality', with hints of moodiness and an almost saintly aura. His brief spell as a superstar in the late 1980s did not affect his world-view significantly. His experience of stardom was encapsulated in his wry comment on the subject: 'I've always said that celebrity is a great place to visit but a lousy place to live' (Williamson 2006: 20).

This nonchalant critique of celebrity-led consumerist society marks him as an 'old-fashioned elder statesman of rock', who is rather difficult to idolize in terms of contemporary star culture. Exploration of themes of deviance and normality have now become a part of the mainstream culture, especially through reality television. The freaks of 'The Barry Williams Show' – daddy's girl selling sex, the dominatrix, the child molester and the sex-change girlfriend – perform macabre versions of frankness, and at the same time make the 'original eccentric spirit' look like a quaintly embarrassing reminder of the playfulness of bygone times.

Chapter 4
How Peter Gabriel Got His Mozo Working

Kevin Holm-Hudson

In July 1986, Peter Gabriel's 'Sledgehammer' beat his former band Genesis's 'Invisible Touch' to the top of the US pop charts, having hit No. 4 in the UK charts two months before. After the dark, ominous and sometimes paranoid tone of his first four solo albums, 'Sledgehammer' seemed to resemble nothing else Gabriel had recorded, with its playful excursion into soul and surreal sexual double-entendre. The song's success brought attention to Gabriel's latent soul tendencies; after *So*'s release an inordinate amount of interview column space was devoted to explicating this apparent stylistic detour, critics invariably bringing up the 'Motown lite' of Gabriel's former band mate Phil Collins, as well as Paul Simon's collaborations with (some said exploitations of) South African musicians. In response, Gabriel would contend that 'the flow is always going in all directions. The idea that musical culture is pure is absurd to me. All artists, all peoples, gravitate and grab the things that excite them' (Healey and Guccione 1991: 72). Furthermore, Gabriel usually pointed out his own long-standing indebtedness to American R&B and soul music, as he told *Musician* writer John Hutchinson:

> I knew that by using any brass at all I would invite comparison with Phil [Collins], but ever since I was at school, Atlantic soul and Stax have been a pivotal influence on me, and I've always wanted to emulate them … . On 'Sledgehammer' I had the opportunity to work like that. I consider my approach to be very similar to 60s soul, whereas I think Phil's style is more contemporary. In any case, I was definitely trying [to] borrow the style of that period, and it is no coincidence that the man leading the brass section is Wayne Jackson, who is one of the Memphis Horns. (Hutchinson 1986: 70)

Indeed, 'Sledgehammer' can be seen as a return to his musical roots, dating back to his earliest formative musical experiences while still a student at Charterhouse, the tradition-bound 'public' boarding school where he spent his teenage years. For Gabriel and his schoolmate Tony Banks, with whom he would form Genesis, the music of black American soul artists was a cathartic antidote to the repressive atmosphere of Charterhouse; they found Stax and Motown records to be 'very free and open and liberating', a 'pivotal' experience (Bowler and Dray 1992: 9).

Gabriel remembers that Charterhouse had a 'really beaten-up, old Dansette record player in a wooden cabinet … . I used to take my Otis Redding records in there and turn them up full volume and dance until I was in a frenzied sweat. This ritual gave me an immense feeling of relief' (Bright 1988: 25). Gabriel also vividly recalls seeing Otis Redding perform live at the Ram Jam Club in Brixton on 18 September 1966 (Bright 1988: 24). 'It is still my favourite gig of all time ... . He was my hero as a singer, definitely, and a lot of that music was part of what drove me to consider music for myself. I was a teenager, very impressionable and very ready to be impressed' (Bright 1988: 25).

Therefore, although 'Sledgehammer' still seems like something of an anomaly in his output up to that point, especially as his world-music activities came to dominate his public persona, there was always a latent 'soul' element to Gabriel's performances that sometimes appeared to be at odds with, or sublimated by, the music of his band mates. Such stylistic eclecticism was, of course, part of the progressive aesthetic: as a member of Genesis, Gabriel remembers 'trying to break down barriers with style ... . We would put in influences from hymns, soul music, and pop music. It was a big mixing thing' (Healey and Guccione 1991: 72).

Edward Macan (1997: 39) notes that the prevalent vocal style in progressive rock featured 'a strong preference for tempered singing, with relatively little sliding to and from pitches'; the 'straight, pure head tone' of the progressive rock vocal style arguably had its origins in the influence of Anglican church music. Singers such as Jon Anderson of Yes and Greg Lake of King Crimson and later Emerson, Lake and Palmer, as well as Pye Hastings and Richard Sinclair of Caravan and Andy Latimer of Camel, readily come to mind. Gabriel's voice, on the other hand, was more rough-hewn and world-weary than any of these, sounding ages older than his 20-some years, causing many critics to describe his singing as something like the voice of an ancient mariner or otherworldly sage. Among the 'classic' progressive-era singers of the 1970s, only Charisma label-mate Van der Graaf Generator's Peter Hammill comes close to Gabriel's timbre, but Hammill's voice is more 'bipolar' in its flexibility, shifting rapidly from straight-tone Anglican choirboy to harsh declamatory rasp. Gabriel's vocal timbre, on the other hand, is more generally consistent, influenced, at least in part, by 60s soul singers such as Otis Redding and Nina Simone, still named by Gabriel as his favourites.

Some of Gabriel's earliest vocals with Genesis betray an awkward but earnest soul influence that seems to have been downplayed as Genesis honed their 'surreal-Victorian' image. For some examples of how American soul and R&B influenced Gabriel's performance style early on, one can turn to Genesis's first and often ignored album, *From Genesis to Revelation* (*FGTR*). The album, produced by fellow Charterhouse alumnus Jonathan King, is widely regarded by the band and fans alike as a 'pop' experiment, a nod to the then-popular melodic pop of the Bee Gees, with little relation to their later musical direction. However, some songs on the album, as well as other tracks since included on later pressings of *FGTR*, have a decidedly harder edge. One such example is 'One-Eyed Hound', apparently a lyric cousin of Robert Johnson's 'Hellhound On My Trail' that begins (0:00–0:07) with an electric guitar break reminiscent of the Rolling Stones' 'On With the Show'. 'One-Eyed Hound' shows Gabriel's soul-inflected 'belting' style to good effect in its choruses (2:08–2:15, for example), and it shows how Gabriel's approach to

R&B differed from the other British 'beat' groups that he recalls listening to as a teenager, such as the Stones and the Yardbirds. Gabriel wisely avoided adapting an affected 'black' tone or southern-American accent as did, for example, Mick Jagger, perhaps knowing that the results might come closer to the watered-down 'white-Brit-soul' of the Yardbirds' Keith Relf. Instead, Gabriel would employ the melismas and blues-inflected 'sliding' notes of American R&B while retaining the distinctive 'grain' of his own voice. He still sounds British, and white, but he does come across as far older and more authoritative than 19 years old. The downward glissando on the word 'hound' (for example, 2:11–2:15) though unfortunately over-saturated with pseudo-psychedelic reverb, seems to imply the impending doom of anyone who should go 'chasing the one-eyed hound'. The overall menace, however, is diluted by the song's predominantly acoustic guitar and piano-driven arrangement, as well as the pastoral-sounding background vocals (0:11–0:16 and elsewhere). Other songs on the album with somewhat timid soul and R&B inflections include 'In The Beginning', 'The Serpent', 'That's Me' and 'When the Sour Turns to Sweet'.

Genesis's emerging style, shown on the transitional album *Trespass* (1971), moved more toward pastoral soundscapes and melodrama, and Gabriel seems to have put aside his soul inclinations. Nevertheless, on the opener 'Looking for Someone', Gabriel's vocal – unusually exposed as the album begins – still retains its soulful vestiges. In the first two seconds of the song, note the near-crack on the high note concluding the opening 'someone' (a Gabriel trademark which is still heard on later solo tracks like 'Digging in the Dirt'), as well as the wavering melisma at the end of the line 'I guess I'm doing that' (0:06–0:11). Quickly, however, this initial 'soul' character is contradicted by the more 'classical' textures of the ensemble arrangement and dynamic contrasts within the song. Another example is 'Going Out to Get You', a staple of the group's early live shows until 1972. 'Going Out to Get You' is indicative of the band's rather schizoid style at the time; while the introduction features a melodic figure (on Banks's organ) that would not be out of place in a Stax number, and the chorus is characterized by a syncopated riff reminiscent of the Doors' 'Touch Me', the instrumental break is dominated by triplet arpeggios that evoke a Bach toccata.[1] Significantly, the song

---

[1]   Because this song was never officially released, specific timings vary according to the recording consulted. Two different performances of 'Going Out to Get You' – on the bootlegs *Besides the Silent Mirror* (recorded 7 March 1971 in La Ferme, Belgium) and *Rare Tapes* (various venues; the performance of 'Going Out to Get You' is from the Piper Club, Rome, 18 April 1972) – were consulted for this analysis. The first 2:26 of the *Besides the Silent Mirror* version consist of tuning sounds, Gabriel's introduction of the song, and audience noises; the intro Stax figure can be heard at 2:26–2:45; the 'Touch Me' rhythm pattern occurs at, for example, 3:05–3:22 and elsewhere; and the toccata-like arpeggio break is found at 3:55–4:28. On the *Rare Tapes* performance of the song, after 47 seconds of tuning and introduction, the intro Stax figure can be heard at 0:47–1:06; the 'Touch Me'

never made it to *Trespass*, being passed over in favour of 'The Knife', a decision that nudged the band onward in its more 'classical' stylistic direction.

Another, more overlooked, aspect of Gabriel's early-Genesis persona that may have been influenced (indirectly) by American R&B is his tambourine playing in live performance. Gabriel would often hit the tambourine and then raise it aloft in an arcing windmill motion as he shook it, a stance recalling The Who's Roger Daltrey, who also used a tambourine as more than a simple timekeeper. Daltrey, of course, was heavily influenced by American Motown and R&B groups, so Gabriel's use of the tambourine early on may be regarded as a second-degree soul influence. This is clearly seen in an early television appearance on Belgian TV (20–21 March 1972), particularly during the instrumental 'rave-up' that concludes 'Twilight Alehouse' (significantly one of Genesis's most 'blues' influenced numbers and a live staple throughout 1971–73, but never released on album until the *Genesis Archive Vol. 1* box set). The first 'heavy' instrumental section of 'The Musical Box' was another opportunity for tambourine flourishes,[2] but on later performances of the song ('Midnight Special', ABC-TV US, 20 December 1973 and ORTF-TV 'Melody' programme, France, 12 February 1974) Gabriel's tambourine playing is much more restrained. Thus, as Genesis's group persona came to be seen as more 'artsy' and theatrical, Gabriel's own performance style took in other influences, including Kabuki, pantomime and Victorian music hall.

One final – and striking – lapse into soul mannerisms can be seen in a 1974 French TV performance of 'Supper's Ready'. For a moment in the song's conclusion Gabriel seems to change character completely; as if in acknowledgment of the bizarre star-studded studio visuals given the broadcast by the producers, he begins to sing with a swaggering Daltrey-esque machismo, pumping out his bare chest from under his jacket.[3] This is a very different, almost mocking, performance, especially when compared to the more mystical and rapturous renditions that can be seen in the 1973 Bataclan (France, 10 January) and Shepperton Studios

---

rhythm pattern occurs at 1:23–1:37 and elsewhere; and the toccata-like arpeggio break is found at 2:08–2:39.

[2]   The Belgian TV clip of 'Twilight Alehouse' can be viewed at www.youtube. com/watch?v=0NetKCTVFEA (accessed on 14 August 2008); the instrumental 'rave-up' begins at 4:37 into the clip. 'The Musical Box' can be viewed at www.youtube.com/ watch?v=UQh4_5Csh40 (accessed on 14 August 2008); see especially 3:26–4:32. Note: Although the author and editors have made every effort to confirm accuracy of these citations, YouTube citations for this and other video clips cited in this chapter are especially subject to change as they are discovered by those who control copyright of and access to the clips. Nevertheless, the site is easily searchable.

[3]   An extract of the ORTF-TV 'Melody' performance of 'Supper's Ready' can be viewed at www.youtube.com/watch?v=upi6wpANBh4 (accessed on 22 August 2008). The final section begins at 4:10 into the clip. On another note, Gabriel's stage make-up for this performance prefigures (or foreshadows) the 'monkey mask' of the *Security* tour, as seen on the cover of *Plays Live*. I thank Sarah Hill for bringing this connection to my attention.

(30–31 October) performances.[4] It is also about the last that we see of Gabriel the Soul Man during his time with Genesis, with perhaps the exception of the fleeting melisma concluding 'Counting Out Time' on *The Lamb Lies Down on Broadway*.

Gabriel's first solo album, released in 1977, was a stylistic hodge-podge, with moody, vaguely apocalyptic proggish epics ('Here Comes the Flood') alongside nimble folk-rock ('Solsbury Hill'), big-guitar arena rock ('Modern Love'), and even barbershop-quartet stylings ('Excuse Me'). Subsequent albums found him exploring even quirkier directions, from new wave to African drumming. Gabriel may have sought to put the image of a theatrically inclined front man for an epic prog band behind him once and for all; for the critics, however, it seemed that there was no new identity to replace the old. *New York Times* critic Jon Pareles also saw this fluidity of identity in Gabriel's songwriting:

> Since he left the group Genesis in 1975 for a solo career, Mr Gabriel has written about amnesia, about faith healing, about psychosis, about revelations, about torture, about transcendence – all moments when the 'self' disappears. And at a moment in rock when marketing wisdom decrees that a successful musician needs to stick to a recognizable image, or identity, Mr Gabriel avoided one, letting listeners conjure him for themselves. His first four solo albums didn't even have their own titles, just his name. (Pareles 1986)

Given Gabriel's ongoing reassessment of his musical direction, it is interesting to note that when he at last began titling his albums again, reportedly at the insistence of his record label, he chose the title of a 1964 Otis Redding song. In his song 'Security', Redding expresses ambivalence toward fame and money (a sentiment Gabriel himself expressed in such early songs as 'Solsbury Hill' and 'D.I.Y.'); in lieu of money or fame, the singer has 'all of these things' by possessing security.

Certainly, Gabriel was deeply ambivalent about his own fame and the rapidly bloating 'star-making machinery' that he saw all around him in the music business: 'You don't become a performer unless you want attention. It took me awhile to sort of accept that' (Healey and Guccione 1991: 72). During his self-imposed sabbatical from the public eye, Gabriel sought security in the comfort of family, especially his wife Jill. In the second verse, Redding similarly finds security with the love of a woman; this was also to become a theme of later Gabriel songs such as 'In Your Eyes'.

At the same time, Gabriel's early solo work appeared to be a very peculiar way of 'finding oneself', manifesting itself in the deconstruction of identity noted by Pareles. When Gabriel remarked in his famous press release after

---

4   An edited clip of the Bataclan performance of 'Supper's Ready' can be viewed at www.youtube.com/watch?v=IedPm_EvSpI (accessed on 22 August 2008); the final section begins at 5:54. An excerpt from the Shepperton performance of 'Supper's Ready' – which includes the concluding 'Eggs is Eggs' section, beginning at 6:02 – can be viewed at www.youtube.com/watch?v=PN1IWmQ6A_I (accessed on 22 August 2008).

leaving Genesis that he was not 'pulling a Bowie' – referring to David Bowie's announced 'retirement' onstage at his final Ziggy Stardust concert in 1973 – he was in fact 'pulling a Bowie' by his ever-shifting, chameleon-like persona. The first four albums can be seen (especially in their cover art) as successive self-effacements and identity reconstructions. 'Mozo' was one of Gabriel's first 'identity reconstructions' during this period – a mercurial, shapeshifting figure who 'came from nowhere, disrupting people's lives and causing changes and then disappearing' (Bright 1988: 126). Certain aspects of Mozo resemble Coyote in Native American stories, a trickster character whose pranks and exploits are often sexual in nature (see for example Rothenberg 1972). This aspect of Mozo, at least, seems to have persisted, as Gabriel playfully explored sexuality in ways that were never brought to the fore during his career with Genesis. As *Village Voice* writer Barry Walters observed, 'it's hard to imagine the sweet, chirpy Gabriel really meaning the subtext of "Sledgehammer," which is something like "Lay down and let me pummel you with my big heavy dick"' (Walters 1986: 67). Against the playful – if bizarre – sexual metaphor of 'Sledgehammer', Gabriel arguably *becomes* Mozo in the video, his jittery stop-motion face continually morphing into various computer-generated distortions.[5] Through Mozo, it can be said, Gabriel got in touch with his mojo; unshackled from the progressive–pomp–storytelling image of his persona with Genesis, Gabriel was free to explore the soul roots of his adolescence (part of a more general 'return to childhood' trend in Gabriel's music, seen in songs such as 'Solsbury Hill' and the child-like cover art for the 'Growing Up Live' tour).

The set list for Gabriel's return to live performances in 1977–78 frequently included Marvin Gaye's 1965 hit 'Ain't That Peculiar', a song choice that seemed rather bizarre alongside songs like 'Here Comes the Flood' and 'Moribund the Burgermeister'. In retrospect, Gabriel's choice of 'Ain't That Peculiar', like his choice of *Security* for an album title, reveals more about him on closer inspection of the song itself. As Bill Friskics-Warren (2005: 52) remarks, Gaye's early records 'might have been marketed as the "Sound of *Young* America," but to this day they convey adult concerns that are more sexual and that carry more philosophical-existential freight than aw-shucks titles like "I'll be Doggone" and "Stubborn Kind of Fellow" suggest'. Miracles member Bobby Rogers, who co-wrote 'Ain't That Peculiar', remembers: 'A few of the songs we wrote with Smokey were about Marvin and [Motown mogul Berry Gordy's sister] Anna … . One of them was "Ain't That Peculiar" which we wrote about them' (Dyson 2004: 28). The song is unusually psychological and self-scrutinizing for a 'love' song, which evidently attracted Gabriel. Clearly, Gaye sings from the perspective of being trapped in a dysfunctional relationship, one in which he is continually hurt and lied to – nevertheless, he confides, 'each hurt makes my love stronger than before'. He then takes a more objective perspective in the chorus: 'Ain't that peculiar / a

---

5   For detailed analyses of the 'Sledgehammer' video, see the contributions by John Richardson (Chapter 14) and Brenda Schmahmann (Chapter 5) in this volume.

peculiarity'. Gabriel's choice of the song at this stage of his career may have been a subconscious identification with his own marriage at the time; one of the reasons for his departure from Genesis, and the nearly two-year retirement from the music business that followed, was the need to regroup with his wife Jill and their infant daughter. Jill had had a brief affair with Genesis's road manager during the *Selling England* tour, which she later called 'my pathetic bid for attention' (Bright 1988: 75); some of the solo songs of the *So–Us* period ('That Voice Again', 'Come Talk to Me') seem to indicate another rough patch in their relationship. 'The work part of my life – I feel quite good about it ... . It's much harder work for me sorting out my personal life, I think' (Healey and Guccione 1991: 72).

Comparing the two versions of 'Ain't That Peculiar' is instructive. Gaye's version, characterized by prominent offbeat handclaps, certainly sounds as though it could have been a hit for Smokey Robinson and the Miracles. Although Gabriel performs the song in the same key and nearly the same tempo, the rhythmic feel is totally different. Gabriel opts for a sinuous half-time funk feel, already anticipating the style of 'Sledgehammer' and 'Digging in the Dirt'. The introduction of the song introduces elements of the band gradually – piano, a 'rattlesnake'-like closed hi-hat roll, a subtle glissando on a rubbed conga head – much like the gradual introduction of instruments in the introduction to Gaye's anthem of betrayal 'I Heard it Through the Grapevine'. The arrangement makes Gabriel's version seem angrier and more suspicious; unlike Gaye, Gabriel is not courting sympathy but is instead accusatory. This threatening mood is enhanced by the band 'rave-up' toward the end of the song, where the overall dynamic and rhythmic intensity build to a climax before a sudden release, leaving the piano riff exposed.[6]

'Ain't That Peculiar' was dropped from Gabriel's live set lists by the time he released his third album in 1980; thus, it does not appear on his first live recording *Plays Live* (recorded during the *Security* tour) and can only be heard on bootlegs. Gabriel occasionally performed other Motown material during these early solo years, notably 'I Heard It Through the Grapevine' (a live version of 'Grapevine' is included on the bootleg *Book of Memories* [Heartland ZP 234878, German release]). Nevertheless, with the exception of a bootlegged performance of the Four Tops classic 'Reach Out (I'll Be There)' at a 1983 performance at the Guildford Civic Hall in the UK (included on the Genesis bootleg *The Lamb Woke Up Again* [Stonehenge STCD2008/2009]), he seems to have moved from performing soul

---

[6]   This description is based on two widely bootlegged performances: one in Cleveland on 15 March 1977 and one at the Roxy in Los Angeles on 10 April 1977. In the Cleveland performance, the intro build-up occurs at 0:00–0:36 and the band 'rave-up' occurs at 3:34–4:02. In the Roxy performance, the intro build-up occurs at 0:00–0:32 and the band 'rave-up' occurs at 3:25–4:18. It is interesting to note that in comparing the two introductions the order of instrument entries – and even which instrument (for example, guitar or piano) plays certain parts in the texture – differs in the two performances, not quite a month apart, indicating that specifics of arrangement took a back seat to an interest in spontaneity and groove.

covers altogether by the time of his third album. By now, soul music had worked its way deeper into his own personal style, as Gabriel also traced its roots to, and found inspiration in, African music itself. In programming the Linn drum computer for the *Security* album's rhythm tracks, for example, Gabriel replaced the machine's factory presets with 'recordings of non-European music and old Tamla/Motown hits' (Fricke 1983: 22). More specifically, Gabriel's first MTV-era success, 'Shock the Monkey', was 'Gabriel's idea of a Tamla/Motown rhythm' (Fricke 1983: 22) – 'I tried to get a Tamla-Motown feel and … a stretch of the song was supposed to be in Tamla style', Gabriel confided on a *Warner Brothers Music Show* radio programme in 1982.

Security's follow-up, *So*, at last brought the hitherto latent soul influences to the fore. The album's breakthrough single, 'Sledgehammer', is Gabriel's 'Motownesque' number, its vocal stylings and arrangement particularly evocative of Marvin Gaye. Interestingly, the allusions that critics used in describing 'Sledgehammer' are far from uniform: John Dilberto, writing for *Down Beat*, described it as 'a rollicking dance groove that borrows heavily from Martha and the Vandellas' "Dancin' In The Streets"' (1986: 30), while Jon Young in *Musician* described the song as 'a blend of [David Bowie's song] "Fame" and "In the Midnight Hour" that initially seems simply a goofy salute to Stax/Volt' (1986: 96, 98), and the *Village Voice*'s Barry Walters similarly heard it as a 'Stax-y hit single' (1986: 67). Perhaps this 'on-the-tip-of-the-ear' play of genres is a musical manifestation of Gabriel's Mozo mojo. Comparing the song with Phil Collins' more bland appropriation of soul (as in his cover of the Supremes' 'You Can't Hurry Love', for example), Dilberto wrote, 'Gabriel is saying a lot more with this ['Sledgehammer'] groove than Phil Collins [would]. It's a maturing Gabriel taking an infectious fling through our lingering adolescent fantasies' (Dilberto 1986: 30). With the *So* album, Gabriel kicked the habit and shed his skin; Coyote would approve.

What factors, then, contribute to the 'almost recognizable' specific soul elements in Gabriel's two most successful (and 'soulful') songs, 'Sledgehammer' and 'Steam'? It will be useful to examine several elements at this point: tempo, arrangement and instrumentation. Since Gabriel often remarked around the time of the release of *Security* that he tended to compose songs from the rhythm up, we will begin with tempo and rhythm.

According to popular-music theorist and historian Walter Everett, the favoured 1960s-soul dance-based tempo was crotchet = 128 beats per minute (bpm), heard in a number of songs including (but certainly not limited to) 'Baby I Need Your Lovin'', 'Back in My Arms Again', 'Going to a Go-Go', 'It's the Same Old Song', 'Out of Sight', 'Papa's Got a Brand New Bag', 'Rescue Me' and 'Ride Your Pony' (Everett 2002: 32). Gabriel's models for 'Sledgehammer' and 'Steam' are all slightly slower, but the parallels are still compelling. One of the clear forebears of 'Sledgehammer', for example, is Stevie Wonder's 'Superstition' (note, for example, the identical horn lines coming out of the chorus at [1:18–1:23] and elsewhere in 'Superstition' and coming out of the second chorus in 'Sledgehammer', at [3:08–

3:18]). 'Superstition' clocks in at a tempo of 100 bpm, very close to the 96 bpm for 'Sledgehammer'. Marvin Gaye's 'I Heard it Through the Grapevine', one of the likely models for 'Steam', has a tempo of 116 bpm, again very close to the 'Steam' tempo of 112 bpm (identical, incidentally, to Wilson Pickett's 'In the Midnight Hour', as well as Otis Redding's 'Security'). Gabriel probably did not consciously match tempos to the songs' stylistic antecedents; it is, however, an uncanny – if unintentional – similarity. (Interestingly, 'Shock the Monkey', an earlier attempt at a Tamla-Motown groove, clocks in at 148 bpm, considerably faster than the 128 bpm template. If anything, his sense of stylistic acuity with regards to nuances of tempo seems to have sharpened.)

A key element of the 'Motown sound' was its strong backbeat, 'created with anything from wood blocks to tambourines to tire chains' (Smith 1999: 155). 'Ain't That Peculiar' provides a vivid example; the backbeat is isolated to one stereo channel, calling attention to itself by its sonic placement as well as the larger-than-life reverb. Gillett notes that beginning around 1963, the musical arrangements – which now included tambourines, handclaps, an insistent 'four-even-beats-to-the-bar rhythm', and call-and-response vocal patterns – 'were closer to the accompaniments that commonly backed up gospel singing' (Gillett 1972: 226).

The Stax Records 'Memphis Sound' was also rooted in gospel traditions, although vocally its overall sound was a good deal earthier, lacking 'smooth' interpreters comparable to Motown's Supremes or Miracles. Co-founder Jim Stewart told a *Billboard* writer, 'that beat – a hard rhythm section – is an integral part of our sound. The combination of horns, instead of a smooth sound, produces a rough, growly, rasping sound, which carries into the melody. To add flavor and color there is topping with the piano and fills with the guitar or vocal group' (Bowman 1997: 60). Like Motown productions, Stax engineers brought the backbeat to the fore in the mix.

There were certainly localized differences as well, of course – James Jamerson's superb bass lines were a defining feature of Motown's sound, as the Memphis Horn section left its mark on Stax productions. There was another element to Stax's rhythmic groove, however, which certainly made its imprint on 'Sledgehammer' – the delayed backbeat, an innovation that came about during the recording sessions for Wilson Pickett's 'In the Midnight Hour' in May 1965. Rob Bowman writes that the distinctive Stax rhythm, a 'minutely delayed beat two and four', was inspired by producer Jerry Wexler's dancing of the then-new northern fad, the Jerk (Bowman 1997: 61–2). Guitarist Steve Cropper explained to Bowman how the delayed backbeat innovation came about:

> I credit it to the fact that we didn't play with headphones and we were in a big room … . There was a lot of delay between the singer and us. When you put headphones on, everybody just sort of tightens up. We learned to overcome [not wearing headphones]. I had to learn basically to play watching Al [Jackson]'s left hand rather than by going by what I heard in my head. I started anticipating
> …

The Jerk was a delayed backbeat thing … . When Jerry Wexler was down there helping to produce 'Midnight Hour,' he made a whole thing about this move, this delayed backbeat thing. We started being more conscious of putting the kick drumbeat dead on and delaying the 'two, four,' which became an actual physical thing, not room delay at that point. We worked on that … . So, we started overemphasizing that and made it a whole way of life because it seemed to work all the time. (Bowman 1997: 62)

Another notable feature of Stax's rhythm patterns – which distinguished Stax's drummer Al Jackson from Motown's Benny Benjamin – is that Jackson generally avoided embellishments to his playing; even his fills were spare and 'part of an interlocked pattern worked out with bass, guitar, and keyboards' (Bowman 1997: 129). Gabriel's drummer on the *So* and *Us* albums, Manu Katché, works from a similarly minimalist groove-oriented aesthetic: 'I'm not a technical drummer concerned with speed, nor am I interested in technique. I'm more interested in grooves and fills' (Saccone 1991: 22).

Cymbals, interestingly, were also purposefully de-emphasized in the Stax sound. Steve Cropper remembers: 'We used to basically try to keep cymbals out of most of the songs … . We thought cymbals were offensive. Demographically we were told that research [showed] that girls bought probably seventy to eighty percent of the records and, if a guy bought one, it was usually because he was buying it for his girlfriend. We thought that women's ears were a little more sensitive and they didn't like cymbals so much, so we tried to keep them way down in the mix almost all the time' (Bowman 1997: 128). This makes for an interesting, if probably unintentional, sonic connection with Gabriel's third (the 'Melt' cover) and fourth (*Security*) albums, as the drum tracks for those were famously recorded without cymbals; *Village Voice* writer Barry Walters opined that the third album's 'lack of cymbals muffle [sic] release: there's lots of rumble but no ride' (1986: 67).

Gabriel conceives of his songs in recording-based terms from the start. As Zak (2001: 30) puts it, Gabriel 'deals with recorded sound from the earliest sketch stages and is guided throughout the compositional process by his responses to aural images'. Gabriel himself has succinctly put it: 'if a sound is a great one it almost has a song within it' (Zak 2001: 30). The 'writing process' for the *Us* album overlapped with the recording process; according to engineer David Bottrill, 'We run DATs [digital audio tape] all the time as we're recording just for a reference, so that if a great performance happened about 15 minutes ago, we'll just spin the DAT back' (Zak 2001: 30–31). The studio process is thus seamless between composition and recording, an aesthetic similar to Stax's groove-oriented recording method where instrumental beds were often recorded live all in the same room. An audible consequence of this process can be found in 'Sledgehammer'; after the 'shakuhachi solo' at 3:17–3:35, the verse–chorus pattern that had been established is jettisoned in favour of a lengthy improvisational vamp dominated by gospel-influenced call-and-response vocal patterns.

'Sledgehammer' also borrows from mid-1960s soul its distinctive, brassy horn opening, coming in after a deceptively quiet shakuhachi prelude that encourages the listener to turn up the stereo (0:00–0:16). According to Walter Everett, such 'opening horn mottos' (if not shakuhachis) are found in a number of mid-1960s soul hits, including Martha and the Vandellas' 'Dancing in the Street', Wilson Pickett's 'In the Midnight Hour' and Stevie Wonder's 'Uptight (Everything's Alright)'. Of the three, Everett writes, 'Pickett's Stax-built example … was the most influential globally', notable for 'its cascading tones of the minor-pentatonic scale' that later turned up in soul-derived rock songs of the late 1960s such as Credence Clearwater Revival's 'Proud Mary' (Everett 2002: 32). 'Sledgehammer' similarly begins with a cascading minor-pentatonic hook (0:17–0:20), which then builds in a dramatic, ascending line up to the vocal entrance (0:27–0:38). Horn-ensemble hooks were especially essential to the Memphis Sound. As Wayne Jackson of the Memphis Horns (who also played on 'Sledgehammer') remembers, the idea initially came from working with Otis Redding 'and we just carried it over to other artists because it worked so well and it involved all of us. We enjoyed doing it' (Bowman 1997: 89).

Greg Kot (1992: 63), in his *Rolling Stone* review of *Us*, dismissed 'Steam' as 'the least satisfying' of the radio-friendly tracks on the album – labelling it 'essentially Son of "Sledgehammer"'; there are, however, crucial differences between 'Steam' and the earlier 'Sledgehammer'. 'Steam' lacks the 'opening horn motto' that so distinctively opens 'Sledgehammer', but at the same time the horn ensemble sound is much more integral to the overall arrangement, being used throughout the song rather than for occasional emphasis. If 'Sledgehammer' – with its tambourine-heavy backbeat and athletically agile bass line – is Gabriel's tribute to the 'northern' soul of Motown, 'Steam' is where Gabriel steeps himself in the sound of 'southern' soul; the thick horn texture and prominence of horns throughout the song evokes the Stax/Volt 'Memphis sound'. Thick and churning, the song's image of 'steam' is both industrial and sultry, its exuded heat seemingly distantly related to James Brown's 'Cold Sweat'. Indeed, the thick, brassy neighbour-note seventh chords that accompany the recurrent 'Stand back' groove, beginning at 0:20, strongly recall the horn riff in James Brown's 'I Got You (I Feel Good)' (1965).

Bowman writes that Stax's horn players 'were interested in a simple but fat sound. To achieve this goal they often played unison lines' (Bowman 1997: 130) – very much like the solid octaves that accompany the choruses of 'Steam'. Another set of Stax references can be found in the guitar work, the work of Gabriel's longtime collaborator David Rhodes, and Leo Nocentelli of the New Orleans band The Meters. Nocentelli's guitar fills, 'sliding sixths' figures that discreetly appear in the 'Give me steam' chorus sections, such as beginning at 0:54, directly evoke Steve Cropper's famous guitar solo in the introduction to Sam & Dave's 'Soul Man', which topped the R&B charts in 1967 and reached No. 2 on the pop charts. Cropper's 'sliding sixths' fills are a distinctive feature of his style; they can also be heard to good effect on Otis Redding's '(Sittin' On) The Dock of the

Bay', especially the second verse. The 'sliding sixths' in 'Steam', then, are as directly referential to 'Soul Man' as the horn line just before the shakuhachi solo in 'Sledgehammer' is to 'Superstition'. Cropper also contributed the slide guitar part in the 'Soul Man' chorus, a feature which David Rhodes evokes in his slide lines on the 'stand back' sections of 'Steam', such as beginning at 2:06. As directly as the brass and guitar in 'Steam' refer to the Memphis sound, however, Gabriel's choice of collaborating musicians reveal that there may be a broader 'pan-Southern' soul style at work; guitarist Nocentelli and baritone sax player Reggie Houston are from New Orleans, and the horn riff draws upon Georgia native James Brown's 'I Got You (I Feel Good)' as much as Stax.

Kot's (1992: 63) description of 'Steam' as 'essentially Son of "Sledgehammer"' highlights the musical similarities between the two songs; along with the features already discussed, both songs are in the key of E♭ (which is also the key of 'I Heard It Through the Grapevine' and 'Superstition'). The staging of 'Steam' and 'Sledgehammer', seen in a 1994 performance documented on the *Secret World Live* DVD, makes the conceptual link between the two songs even more explicit. Most of the performances on the DVD begin with a small-screen animation, inset in the centre of a black background. In contrast to the bright computer animation that introduces other songs, however, both 'Sledgehammer' and 'Steam' employ loops of grainy black-and-white film that invoke the aesthetics of Soviet Socialist Realism. 'Sledgehammer' focuses on a muscular worker repeatedly swinging a sledgehammer, while 'Steam' alternates between a close-up of churning steam engine wheels and a railway signalman holding a flag aloft; Gabriel emphasizes the 'industrial' connotations of 'Steam' by pumping his arm forward rhythmically at the end of each verse ('but I know you'), a gesture that is suggestive of movement of the train wheels' connecting rods shown in the video. The choreography of Gabriel with David Rhodes and Tony Levin in both DVD performances of 'Sledgehammer', which may be described as a lumbering, aggressive swagger, suggests a strange filtering of Motown routines through a robotic industrial aesthetic – Kraftwerk covering the Temptations.

Gabriel's in-performance transformation of the second verse of 'Sledgehammer' into a duet with his female background singer (Paula Cole on *Secret World Live*, and his daughter Melanie on *Growing Up Live*) re-interprets the verse as a romantic duet, recalling the great Motown duets of Marvin Gaye with Tammi Terrell or Diana Ross. Even Gabriel's bizarre jacket in the *Growing Up Live* 'Sledgehammer' performance, a blazer festooned with lights, suggests a comically exaggerated, futuristic version of the shiny sequins that often adorned the lamé jackets of the Motown groups. The staging of 'Sledgehammer' and 'Steam', then, draws upon established musical and visual tropes of Motown, especially, often inserting them into distorted 'fun-house' contexts.

The critical respect accorded to Gabriel's solo work is an extension of what Macan (2006) has called the general 'blues orthodoxy' of rock criticism from the mid-1970s to the present, and the lasting effect that ideology has had on rock historiography since 1970. As Allan F. Moore (2001: 74) asserts, 'the biggest single point of condemnation leveled at much progressive rock was its lack of black influence'. Macan and Moore have both critiqued the prevailing critical opinion of progressive rock for its implicit essentialism; such an ideology, they point out, brands progressive rock as 'artificial' and 'contrived' *because*, conversely, it equates African-American musical genres with 'authenticity' and 'unmediated' emotional expression. As this chapter has pointed out, however, Gabriel's vocal style has always drawn more from soul models than from 'classical' or Anglican performance traditions, although those influences are admittedly in the mix as well. Also, the directness of soul influence has fluctuated at various times in Gabriel's career, from an early transparency as Genesis were writing their first songs to a much more muted presence for most of his tenure with the group, then surfacing again with his solo career and reaching a peak of prominence with the *So* and *Us* albums. With his follow-up studio album *Up* (2002), the direct soul influence appears to have again receded, but Gabriel has always shown himself to be an artist with a restless muse, for whom genre boundaries have always been artificial and permeable.

Chapter 5

Staging Masculinities: Visual Imagery in Peter Gabriel's 'Sledgehammer' Video

Brenda Schmahmann

Directed by Stephen R. Johnson, made at Aardman Animation and involving the Brothers Quay,[1] 'Sledgehammer' is undoubtedly the best known video of Peter Gabriel's music. The winner of a record-breaking nine MTV awards in September 1987, including Best Video of the Year, it remains vibrant and intriguing more than two decades after it was first broadcast.

Produced from a song on Gabriel's 1986 *So* album, 'Sledgehammer' is a reworking of soul music associated with the Stax studio in Memphis and, in particular, the love songs of Otis Redding. Indeed, trumpet on the song was played by Memphis-born Wayne Jackson who, in 1961, joined the Mar-Keys (later called the Memphis Horns) – the group that, together with Booker T and the MGs, would be the studio band at Stax who imparted its characteristic sound.[2] Using a horn introduction and a delayed backbeat distinctive to Stax,[3] the lyrics to 'Sledgehammer' seem to refer to Redding's 'That's How Strong my Love Is', albeit through erotic puns not present in the source.[4] Further, the technique in

---

[1]   The contributors are as follows: Director: Stephen R. Johnson; Producer: Adam Whitaker; Animation: Nick Park, The Brother Quay, Peter Lord, Richard Goleszowski; Lighting camera: David Sproxton; Production company: Aardman Animations.

[2]   In contrast to the Motown studios in Detroit, which carefully controlled all aspects of a performer's output, grooming its artists to effect an image palatable to white audiences and to tone down some of the seemingly 'raw' aspects of gospel as well as rhythm and blues styling that form the roots of soul, the Stax studio adopted a sound that seemed rather more gritty and 'authentic' – although it was doubtless self-consciously constructed to appear thus. A conception of Stax as offering a less refined sound is evident in, for example, the programme *Dancing in the Street: A Rock and Roll History*: 'to some, Motown had begun to polish the artists too much for white audiences with its cabaret presentation. For these dissenters, you would still find the real soul music but you had to go down south [to Memphis]' (Thomson 1993).

[3]   See Kevin Holm-Hudson, Chapter 4 of this volume.

[4]   In an ironic counterpoint to 'I'll be the ocean so deep and wide', for example, Gabriel offers 'I want to be your sledgehammer'. One can look for other kinds of inversions. Against 'you can go swimming', he sets up 'you can have a big dipper', for instance, and against 'anything that I can do / I'll be good for you', he offers 'all you do is call me / I'll be anything you need'.

much soul music of affecting a 'dialogue' between vocalist and instrumentation (Gibson, Norris and Alcock 1992: 131) is also invoked in 'Sledgehammer' prior to backing singers assuming the primary imitative role (a shift that commences at 03:36 with the lyrics 'I've kicked the habit').

Both in terms of its engagement with soul music and in terms of the style of its imagery, 'Sledgehammer' would seem to be especially comparable to Gabriel's later 'Steam', which was also directed by Johnson – a connection that is often noted.[5] But 'Sledgehammer' might also be considered in light of another video accompanying a song on the *So* album, even though it might seem initially to have no commonality with it. Matt Mahurin's 'Mercy Street', which focuses on the work and life of the confessional poet Anne Sexton (1928–1974), adheres closely to the imagery and meanings invoked by Gabriel's song. Visualizing themes and ideas which feature in Sexton's poetry such as religiosity, obsession with death, eroticism and incest, for example, it (along with the song itself) takes the distinctly unusual step of placing Gabriel, a male artist, in the subject position of a female creative figure.[6] The exuberant 'Sledgehammer' may in some sense be the counterpoint to this dark and hermetic elegy to Anne Sexton, but, as I suggest in this essay, it does nevertheless share with 'Mercy Street' a transgression of gendered norms and conventions – a seriousness belied by its ebullience and playful lyrics.

'Sledgehammer' was broadcast and achieved popularity after there had been a buyout of the controlling interest in MTV Networks by Viacom International in 1986. Reputedly the most played video on MTV, it would also be broadcast extensively on VH1, which was launched by MTV Networks in January 1985 and catered for an older audience (Goodwin 1992: 137). The network's syndicated packages outside of the United States, introduced from 1987 (Goodwin 1992: 137–8), created still further reach. The release of the video thus came at an auspicious time: changes and developments at MTV enabled it to be viewed by a larger and more diverse audience than it might have done if it had been created a couple of years earlier.

But if these factors boded well for its popular reception, so too was its departure from what Zoglin (1987) describes as the 'yawn-provoking rut' of the vast majority of other videos from the mid-1980s. Some of its impact may be attributed to its rapid visual tempo which, as Goodwin (1992: 62) observes, was a deliberate strategy adopted by its director, Johnson, to prevent the video from

---

[5]   John Richardson (Chapter 14, this volume), for example, observes: 'The legacy of the song and video ["Sledgehammer"] is impressive, not least in Gabriel's own subsequent work, including songs like "Steam", "Kiss that Frog" and "The Barry Williams Show".' See Holm-Hudson (Chapter 4 in this volume) for a comparison of Gabriel's engagement with soul music in 'Sledgehammer' and 'Steam'.

[6]   As Carol Vernallis (2004: 280) notes, men 'write few songs about women artists, and even fewer in which the male singer adopts the subject position of a woman artist'. Vernallis' discussion of 'Mercy Street' from her book on music video is republished in this volume in Chapter 6.

being grasped during a single viewing. But 'Sledgehammer', which has visuals that prompt interpretations that are not facilitated by its lyrics or instrumentation alone, also provided an exemplar of the way in which the translation of music to video might not compromise its capacity to facilitate imaginative and critical work. It is in fact the visuals in the video, more than the song itself, which have cues that encourage a viewer to consider its engagement with gender.

Performing Gender

When MTV was launched in 1981, there had already been academic work on constructions of masculinity in rock and pop music,[7] and scholars in this field would eventually turn their attention to music video as well. But early work on gender in relation to music video was undertaken primarily by film theorists such as E. Ann Kaplan (1987) and Marsha Kinder (1987) who deployed a Lacanian focus derived from Laura Mulvey's 'Visual Pleasure and Narrative Cinema' (1989), first published in 1975. Although this interpretative method would receive extensive criticism in writings on music video from the early 1990s (see in particular Goodwin 1992),[8] it needs to be acknowledged that it was important in its grasp of the potential complexity of visual representation and in ensuring that an emerging field was not dominated by a brand of criticism which assumed that images were simply transparent reflections of norms and practices in society.[9] Furthermore, this

---

[7]   In an essay first published in 1978, Simon Frith and Angela McRobbie initiated discussion about the ways in which rock music works to represent masculinity. Drawing a distinction between 'cock rock', on the one hand, and 'teenybop' on the other, they argued that the former is 'music-making in which performance is an explicit crude and often aggressive expression of male sexuality' and where boys form its core audience while the latter, 'consumed exclusively by girls', presents an image 'of the young boy next door: sad, thoughtful, pretty and puppy-like' (Frith and McRobbie 1990: 374–5). This proposition, innovative for its time but nevertheless reductive in its argument, resulted in further work which sought to complicate the terms of this dichotomy. For example, Will Straw (1990: 106–107) reveals overlaps between the masculinist iconography of heavy metal and British progressive rock (including Genesis), indicating that distinctions between their audiences began to dissipate in the late 1970s. Some examples of other interpretations that produce alternative readings of masculinity in rock music are Walser (1993), Whiteley (1997) and Palmer (1997).

[8]   Music video does not deploy the same conventions as Hollywood movies, it is proposed, and Mulvey's arguments depend in any case on a too narrow understanding of how viewers might glean pleasure from the visual realm. There is also a criticism of these writings' stress on postmodernism and a suggestion that this approach depends on reductive constructions about MTV as well as lack of focus on the material conditions of the music industry. There is also criticism of film theorists' lack of focus on music itself.

[9]   For an example of the narrow and literal interpretation that can be the outcome of a lack of focus on representational polemics, see Seidman (1992) who uses quantitative

work instigated the deployment of other psychoanalytical theories – most notably those concerned with masquerade and performativity – in popular music theory.[10]

The idea of gender being a 'masquerade' was initiated by Joan Riviere in an essay entitled 'Womanliness as a Masquerade' published in *The International Journal of Psychoanalysis* in 1929.[11] As Emily Apter (1992: 243) notes, Riviere developed 'the notion of womanliness as a feint or cover-up' and, rather than identifying any 'absolute femininity beneath the veil', suggested that there are only 'codes that normatively induct the feminine subject into the social practice of "being" woman through mimesis and parroting'. In *Gender Trouble: Feminism and the Subversion of Identity* (1999), Judith Butler questions the postulation that the masquerade might be assumed by a woman 'to hide the possession of masculinity and to avert the reprisals expected if she was found to possess it', as Riviere (1986: 38) had argued. But her own theory of 'performativity', like Riviere's notion of a 'masquerade', refutes the idea of an absolute femininity – and, in her case, also masculinity – that might underpin its corporeal presentation. For Butler (1999: 173), acts, gestures and enunciations made by an individual in his or her everyday capacity are performative of gender in the sense that 'the essence of identity that they otherwise purport to express are [in fact] *fabrications* manufactured and sustained through corporeal signs and other discursive means'. While creating 'the illusion of an interior and organizing gender core' which constitutes identity, the gendered body actually 'has no ontological status apart from the various acts which constitute its reality'. Thus, rather than 'expressing' a pre-existent inner identity, an individual's performances and gestures enacted on the surface of his or her body actually constitute the full sum of the identity they are assumed to signify (Butler 1999: 180).

For Butler (1999: 174), retaining the *illusion of* an interior core which determines gender identity not only works to regulate sexuality in such a way that heterosexuality is constructed as normative but also 'precludes an analysis of the political constitution of the gendered subject'. But to reveal that the concept of an 'interior and organizing gender core' is nothing but a fiction would be to expose and challenge the unequal relations of power that such a construction would seek to obscure. But how might one effect such a transgression?

Butler proposes drag and cross-dressing, finding a play on the distinctions between the anatomical sex and gendered enactments of the performer to be potentially transgressive and thus liberating: 'In the place of the law of heterosexual

---

analysis to ascertain the degree of sexism in music video.

[10]   Notions of performativity have been deployed in, for example, an analysis by Stan Hawkins of Annie Lennox's 'Money Can't Buy It' (Hawkins 1996: 33) where they are used to consider the musician's parodying of the role of the diva on the album cover *Totally Diva*; Stella Bruzzi's discussion of k.d. lang's use of drag (Bruzzi 1997: 197); and Marion Leonard's chapter entitled 'Strategies of Performance', where she explores negotiations of gender norms in the music industry through a focus on 'indie' rock (Leonard 2007).

[11]   See Riviere (1986), where it is republished.

coherence, we see sex and gender denaturalized by means of a performance which avows their distinctness and dramatizes the cultural mechanism of their fabricated unity' (Butler 1999: 175). A play such as this was surely effected by Gabriel when, through his wearing of the 'Foxtrot' outfit at the Dublin National Stadium on 28 September 1972 just prior to the release of the Genesis album of that name, he constructed a persona midway between fox and female (see Thompson 2005: 87). But other strategies can be equally productive – and it is these, I believe, that are at play in 'Sledgehammer'.

A performance in which there is an apparently knowing exaggeration of gestures and actions that would normally code the identity of the subject as authentically 'masculine' or 'feminine', for example, may well be as potentially disruptive as one which creates a disjuncture between the markers of gender signified by physiognomy and those inscribed through gesture or dress. Through overstatement, markers of gender become denaturalized and, as in drag, this strategy exposes the fact that the enactments being imitated are themselves already performative. Equally, in the field of music video one is at liberty to inscribe specific references to the theatre, whether through setting or technological means, thus stressing the idea that gestures assumed to be 'natural' are in fact staged; or indeed to allude to mirrors and reflections, and thus to place emphasis on mimicry and imitation. Further, a video might simply show the star gesturing or offering other corporeal self-presentations that, while not actually 'drag', are nevertheless in defiance of those assumed appropriate to his or her gender. Finally, and perhaps most crucially in a context of postmodernist inter-textuality, music video can quote not simply the discourses of the body itself but also discourses which *represent* bodies and their stylized corporeal inscriptions – in other words, texts which parody bodily gestures that, in terms of Butler's theorizing, are already imitative. These might include bodily inscriptions in well-known imagery such as paintings, films or other visual media and, rather than being empty pastiche, such quotations may in fact deploy irony to offer critical interrogations of understandings about 'masculinity' and 'femininity' that underpin those sources.

Staging the Glance

The process of making 'Sledgehammer', Gabriel indicated in an interview (Guttenberg 2005), was to 'lay out ideas as storyboard videos first'. The making of the video, which 'took about a month', included working 'through ideas with Stephen Johnson for a week', and thereafter, he notes, 'we'd spend two weeks in development with Aardman Animation and the Brothers Quay and a week filming in stop animation'. While Gabriel noted also that he 'thinks visually' and will often 'picture things' when he is writing (Guttenberg 2005), the imagery identified for the video was presumably the outcome of a collaborative process of working.

Shot on film in the first instance, 'Sledgehammer' acquired visual complexity without the aid of a computer. David Sproxton, co-founder of Aardman Animation, comments on the blossoming of the flowered wallpaper that appears about four and a half minutes into the video: 'We shot it in a student theatre and it looked extraordinary ... but the fact is, there were guys pulling and lowering backdrops' (quoted in Fitzpatrick 1997). For Gabriel, this avoidance of slick technology affected the mood and 'feel' of the video in a way that was appropriate to the music: 'Because we did not use computer-generated images, "Sledgehammer" has a funky feel to it.' He observes also: 'Technology can produce perfect stuff, and we humans are good at imperfection. I like to see the evidence of human touch' (quoted in Legrand 2004). This quality of a 'human touch', which is in the very fabric and structure of all the visuals in the video, means in fact that the singer himself might be engaged with empathetically. But there are still other ways in which this avoidance of slickness can affect viewing.

For all their focus on Mulvey's 'Visual Pleasure and Narrative Cinema', whether to deploy it or to offer a critique of it, analysts of music video habitually miss a key argument in her essay. For Mulvey, the attainment of voyeuristic pleasure depends on a blotting-out of any sense of the workings of the medium itself, on an elimination of signs of the production process that would interrupt the illusion. She points to the ways in which an effacement of the camera's presence in Hollywood cinema has the effect of dispelling a sense of the passage of time prior to the viewing moment.[12] The film is implied to emerge fully formed rather than being subject to a process of decision-making and exploration. Mulvey's point provided a precedent for arguments by Norman Bryson about viewing via the 'gaze' versus the 'glance' which, while focused on paintings and drawings rather than film or indeed video, are pertinent here. According to Bryson (1983: 94), works that obliterate signs of the production process by, for example, using pigment to erase evidence of changes that a work has undergone, invite access via the gaze – that is, a 'synchronic instant of viewing which will eclipse the body ... in an infinitely extended Gaze of the image as pure idea'. But paintings or drawings which expose transitions and shifts that have occurred during the production process, he suggests, encourage viewing via the 'glance' – a mode of looking that 'addresses vision in the durational temporality of the viewing subject' (Bryson 1983: 94). Imagery which prompts perusal via the 'glance', he comments, 'does not seek to bracket out the process of viewing, nor in its own techniques does it exclude the traces of the body in labour' (Bryson 1983: 94). In 'Sledgehammer', one might argue, the inscription of a sense of 'human touch' into the video means that a viewer is located bodily within one temporal instant and then another as

---

[12]   Mulvey (1989: 25) observes: 'There are three different looks associated with the cinema: that of the camera as it records the pro-filmic event, that of the audience as it watches the final product, and that of the characters at each other within the screen illusion. The conventions of narrative film deny the first two and subordinate them to the third, the conscious aim being always to eliminate intrusive camera presence and prevent a distancing awareness of the audience.'

the imagery unfolds, and is not so momentarily transfixed that he or she loses all consciousness of the process and fact of looking.[13]

There is a further significance to this sense of 'constructedness' in 'Sledgehammer'. The stop-frame and claymation techniques used to produce the video involved staging theatrically the elements that were filmed. In 'Sledgehammer' these techniques were not reserved simply for objects surrounding the singer but were also used on Gabriel himself. The video, Joe Gow (1992: 58) observes, involves 'a dizzying array of changes wherein inanimate objects (e.g. sledgehammers or fruit) are brought to life' and 'human beings (in particular, the singer) take on jerky, mechanistic movements'. This staging for the camera of not only objects but also the singer contributes significantly to the sense that gendered identities are being 'performed' in the video.

Imaging Masculinities

The 'Sledgehammer' video, Goodwin (1992: 67) notes, takes lyrics which 'play with a series of sexual metaphors', adapting them into 'a variety of images of reproduction, beginning with the fertilization of an egg and moving through to a concluding image of the night sky, whose multiple twinkling starts suggest nothing less than a literally universal image of creation'. Yet, despite its seeming emphasis on the cycle of nature and biological drives, 'Sledgehammer' actually focuses rather more on the rituals and enactments of culture. Indeed, after an introductory montage which shows sky, egg/sun, a primal orgasmic firmament, travelling sperm and pulsating arteries, Gabriel is introduced in such a way that he is implied to be entering not only a condition of sexual arousal but also the realms of language and discourse. The video presents a montage showing close-ups of, aside from the tap of Gabriel's finger on his temple, an eye, his mouth and his one ear twitching delightfully improbably: in addition to registering desire, this montage suggests the testing of sight, language and hearing.

The video cuts to a sequence of head-and-shoulders portrait views of the musician, originally in sophisticated white collar and black coat, then in a graduation gown and in the role of a teacher, and thereafter against a backdrop of popcorn – at one point with his head submerged in candy floss and then water. In tandem with the first hook or chorus ('I want to be your sledgehammer / why don't you call my name / oh let me be your sledgehammer'), Gabriel appears upside down, as if via a reflection. The reflection in a pool, while perhaps simply a jibe at narcissistic self-presentations by stars in music videos, may also allude to the mirror/narcissistic nexus in Lacanian theory (that is, the so-called 'mirror stage', where the ego becomes constituted) and which, for Mulvey (1989), explains the

---

[13]   Likewise Richardson (Chapter 14 this volume) emphasizes how a sense of the workings of the medium is in evidence in the video and how this elicits in viewers an alertness to 'the material foundations of visual production'.

pleasure gleaned from looking at a film. Further, it alludes to a tradition in art of producing a self-portrait by looking into a mirror, invoking ironical reference to the idea that such an image might yield hidden 'truths' about the artist's personality or state of mind. In keeping with poststructuralist discourses which question the notion that there is an essential identity within an individual subject, this reflection in the pool positions the subject as having the illusion of depth while being in fact nothing but a refraction of an image on a surface.[14]

There is then a cut to a head and shoulder view of Gabriel in which his head is frozen in ice (as if the refraction in the pool had somehow solidified into a carapace) and surrounded by flames. A sledgehammer enters the frame, shattering the ice, and he is surrounded by ivy, then flecks of starlight as well as serenading fish and other forms of sea life. If one were not familiar with the video, 'I want to be your sledgehammer' (apart from its obviously phallic connotations) might be understood to mean that the artist is looking to break through the icy-cool or rock-hard demeanour of an object of desire. Yet through visualization in the video, the lyrics suggest the artist's imperative to shatter *his own* defensive shield.[15] Furthermore, in tandem with the visual displacement of 'I will be *your* sledgehammer' to what is, in effect, 'I will be *my own* sledgehammer', playfully conceptualized phallic symbols penetrate only the star himself. In what amounts to an allusion to masturbation, there are Freudian fish which enter his ears, for example and, in the sequence accompanying the lyrics 'Show me round your fruit cage', a banana divested of its skin – a reference to a slapstick or vaudeville routine – does the same.

The idea of cracking a shield or carapace, which is introduced here, is reiterated in the course of the video, and its ultimate message is to deflect a focus away from metaphors of penetration toward the notion of peeling off layers of different selves, one beneath another, each of which also readily morphs or transmutes into something else or some additional self. While the lyrics 'I'll be anything you need' may imply the idea of *voluntarily* adapting oneself to suit the (sexual) needs of an object of desire, the video implies that the self is multivalent and ultimately unknowable – that there is in fact no essential identity beneath the many carapaces that the subject might assume.

---

[14]   See the Introduction in my study of women artists' self-representations (Schmahmann 2004: 4–9), where I explore the implications of a use of mirrors in self-portraiture and indicate how the motif of the mirror has functioned historically as a way of associating the possession of subjectivity with masculinity.

[15]   This message is reinforced in live performances of the song during which Gabriel, along with his pelvic jerks, gestures toward his head in an approximation of the idea of 'hammering' at a surrounding 'carapace'. While music video is sometimes conceptualized as a reinterpretation of music that lacks the impact of the live performance, Gabriel's live performances of 'Sledgehammer' have undoubtedly gained much from their approximation of the effects and enactments in the music video.

With a repeat of the hook 'I want to be your sledgehammer / why don't you call my name', wooden planks descend forming a barrier between the singer and viewer that is at once a quasi-face and an imperfectly constituted DIY contraption. An opening reveals the musician, who shatters this barrier. Adjustments to Gabriel's physiognomic integrity are restrained up until this point: the performer may be overlaid by fruit or other objects, and stop-frame techniques may mechanize his movements, but he is figured with some degree of naturalism. In the next sequence, initiated by the lyrics 'I'm your sledgehammer / there can be no doubt about it' (02: 54), however, his body is systematically broken down and divested of stable boundaries. Transformed into a claymation version of himself, Gabriel bangs two clay bricks into either cheek; his head morphs into a full figure which flies upwards and off screen, and is substituted by a yin-yang moon-shaped head and splits into two fishes which spin and fall into a blue clay pool. A blue longitudinal but vaguely anthropomorphic head emerges from the clay sludge, with two arabesque females serenading and moving through it, and the scene transmutes into an approximation of Gabriel's head, which slices open at the skull to absorb these two strange sylphs. There is a cut to a Cubist-inspired collaged head, then to a field of red which becomes overlaid with Jackson Pollock-like spatters of pigment, and thereafter to a blue anthropomorphic clay obelisk which in turn morphs into another image of the head of the artist, who wields a sledgehammer.

In *Purity and Danger*, first published in 1966, anthropologist Mary Douglas (2002: 150) argued that 'all margins are dangerous', but most especially matter issuing from the orifices of the body, such as blood, milk, urine or faeces. Taboos on such matter, she suggested, are not because they are 'dirty' but rather because they are intricately linked to endeavours to maintain social boundaries and stable terms of categorization. Julia Kristeva (1982: 4), in an adaptation of Douglas's ideas, defined bodily marginal matter as 'abjection', arguing that the abject 'is that which disturbs identity, system, order. What does not respect borders, positions, rules. The in-between, the ambiguous, the composite.' The claymation sequence in 'Sledgehammer', which constructs Gabriel as just so much untempered bodily matter which might approximate one identity briefly only to dissolve into another, positions him in just such a space of transgression – one where appropriate masculinities as well as the structures for ordering social behaviour are exposed as provisional and malleable rather than absolutes or essences.

The representation of marginal substances is not, however, effected iconically (that is, in terms of approximating the appearance of the substances invoked): one does not see blood or bodily matter in their direct form, but is instead presented with representations of clay, paint and other materials associated with visual representation. Notable here is the playful and subversive reworking of an aesthetic of abstraction. The Cubist-inspired head becomes the 'self-portrait' of the performer himself. Invoking generic reference to a pre-First World War emphasis on the avant-garde male artist as both sexually and creatively virile that was especially manifest in self-portraiture (see Duncan 1982), it alludes more specifically to Pablo Picasso – the artist who perhaps enacted most famously the notion of a synthesis between the tempestuous male genius and the tempestuous male lover. This message is reinforced through a reference to Jackson Pollock,[16] whose process of 'drip painting' – immortalized in movie footage shot by Hans Namuth in 1950 – was frequently explained in such a way that it naturalized the idea of pigment as semen and the canvas as a receptive female. In 'Sledgehammer', however, such male posturing is rendered ridiculous by its interpretation as cartoon-like. Equally, by being invoked through signifiers that no longer work indexically (that is, through physical trace or imprint), the materials of masculinist aesthetic prowess lose their supposed 'authenticity'. In other words, one is not presented with actual paint, as in Pollock's work, but its approximation in clay, which is in turn transmuted into film and then video. These spatterings of 'pigment' consequently become *symbols* for a virile creativity rather than a convincing *testament* to its presence or embodiment.

A sense that gender is being 'performed' is reinforced through the introduction of an image of the theatrical stage immediately after the claymation sequence. In tandem with an interlude in the lyrics, the sledgehammer sets in motion a performing egg which twirls and transmutes first into one and then two chickens that enact their dance of love before an audience comprised of a row of army helmets. Alluding humorously to the dance called 'The Chicken', this sequence may also refer more specifically to James Brown's funky 'Hot Pants (Part 1)' which includes the following lyrics: 'The girl over there with the funky pants on / She can do the chicken all night long / The girl over there with the hot pants on / She can do the Funky Broadway all night long'.[17] But what is the significance of the army helmets?

Margaret Iversen (1997: 80–82) observes that Lacan viewed 'display' as the masculine parallel to a feminine 'masquerade', finding that it involves two strategies – camouflage and intimidation – to defend a body that is highly vulnerable. Camouflage 'means becoming invisible, like putting on a uniform', and 'the sacrifice of visibility is compensated by authority and rank within a total hierarchy' – an idea manifest here through the lining up of the row of alike army helmets to witness the performance. Intimidation, the complementary strategy, finds its source 'in the natural world where, Lacan observes, the male animal swells up and gives himself "something like a mask, a double, an envelope, a thrown-off skin, thrown off in order to cover the frame of a shield"'. Is the cracking of the egg and then the presentation of plucked and headless chickens before army helmets articulating an anxiety of being divested of psychic 'armour'?

---

[16]   Indeed, the yin-yang moon shape alludes to imagery in which Pollock combined appropriations from Native American art with Jungian motifs – the latter seemingly in response to his encounters with Jungian psychologists. See Leja (1993) for a discussion of Pollock's use of Jungian motifs and their adaptation.

[17]   My thanks to Michael Drewett for alerting me to this sequence's probable reference to the James Brown song.

The lyrics 'I've kicked the habit / shed my skin' (03: 30) introduce a new sequence in the video. The dancing chickens leap upwards acrobatically, the video cuts to the leaping musician himself, and six female backing vocalists slide into the frame, as if on an invisible escalator. Like elsewhere in the song, the lyrics have erotic connotations (with 'I've kicked the habit' implying not a move into sobriety but instead, paradoxically, the refusal of the chaste garb of the monk). But the imagery in the video operates slightly differently to early sequences where suggestive lyrics were negotiated by a faux naïve representation of them in literal terms – the steam train, the aeroplane in the blue sky, the big dipper, the bumper cars and the fruit cage. Here, the words 'shed my skin' are not represented by a lizard or snake, for example, but instead via an image of Gabriel, holding out his arms and appearing to 'shed' a sequence of shirts. It is as if the visuals were emphasizing the idea of masculinities being performed through sartorial strategies but with each bodily adornment being no more a signifier of any 'true' identity than another.

With the lyrics 'this is the new stuff' one is once again shown the musician and the backing singers, and with 'I will show for you' a pink television on a stand enters the scene, one which reveals a close-up of singing female lips on its screen, which mime the words before this object exits the frame. Exaggeratedly fetishized, this woman/television alludes generically to surrealist representations of females where there may be visual puns between mouths and genitalia or which manifest a penchant for the anthropomorphizing of inanimate objects and the construction of improbable creatures through the game 'Exquisite Corpse'.[18] In an early interpretation of music video, Marsha Kinder (1984: 5) distinguished surrealism as an historical movement which 'used dream rhetoric as a radical strategy to undermine the power of bourgeois ideology' from music video which 'uses dream images to cultivate narcissism that promotes our submission to bourgeois consumerism'. Yet, despite her feminism (which admittedly was clearer in her 1987 article), Kinder overlooked the fact that numerous tropes in surrealism depended on the construction of woman as an allusive 'other' who is divested of subjectivity in order to manifest this rebellion against the bourgeoisie. In surrealist thought, the male subject's obsession with a female object of desire offered him the possibility of liberation from rationality and logic[19] – an idea which, though

---

[18]   In Exquisite Corpse, an image of a figure is composed by three participants. One draws the head and shoulders, the next the torso, and the third player draws the legs. On completion of their contributions, the first and second participants fold over the paper: components are thus added without each contributor seeing what others have already drawn.

[19]   This concept is clearly epitomized via Nadja, the enigmatic figure of André Breton's novel of the same name, which was first published in 1928. Toward the end of the novel, Breton writes: 'freedom, acquired here on earth ... must be enjoyed unrestrictedly as it is granted, without pragmatic considerations of any sort, and this human emancipation ... remains the only cause worth serving. Nadja was born to serve it, if only by demonstrating

its exaggeration in the cartoon-like woman/television, is not only staged as an absurdity but, through a self-referential engagement with music video as a medium, is also suggested to underpin contemporary constructions of gender in popular music broadcasting.[20]

With the last articulation of 'show for you' in the lyrics, the imagery shifts to a party scene and one is shown exuberant but awkward dancing by Gabriel's two daughters and their young friends (and subsequently various items of household furniture). If, as Vernallis (2004: 71) suggests, music video often uses images of dance to provide a lesson in 'how music is to be experienced in the body', the choreography in this sequence – with its emphasis on jerky and inelegant gestures – seems to discourage a conception of movement as 'natural' and instead invites the viewer to glean an experience of the body as performative. Further, an inclusion within this component reiterates the idea of gendered enactments that has been developed throughout the video. Twice within the sequence one is presented with a 'male' figure that is simultaneously a preposterous DIY gadget, constituted entirely from hammers, who dances into the frame and past the represented window. Illustrating the hook of the song ('I want to be your sledgehammer'), he is implied to be both a manifestation of the singer himself and the embodiment of knocked-together masculinities.

With the commencement of the lyrics 'I have been feeding the rhythm', Gabriel, who has collapsed in his armchair, stands up and proceeds towards a fantastical doorway. Automaton-like, and as if the beat of the percussion were his own heartbeat, he is absorbed by the galaxy and, after the cessation of sound, one is presented with the same image of a night sky that began the video.

Conclusion

While 'Sledgehammer' began its life as a song which gave Otis Redding's music and Stax sound a contemporary twist, the video produced from it ended up including imagery which articulates the idea of 'masculinity' as a construction without an essential core and comprised only of a series of parodic enactments. Indeed a central irony in the video is that the seemingly 'authentic' articulation of masculine desire in Stax love songs, such as those of Redding, is coupled with

---

that around himself each individual must foment a private conspiracy, which exists not only in his imagination – of which it would be best, if only from the standpoint of knowledge alone, to take account – but also – and much more dangerously – by thrusting one's head, then an arm, out of the jail – thus shattered – of logic, that is, out of the most hateful of prisons' (Breton 1960: 142–3).

[20]   My interpretation here contrasts with that offered by Richardson's 'Plasticine Music' (Chapter 14, this volume) in a number of ways. The most crucial of these resides in our different ways of interpreting the function and workings of inter-textual references in the video. 'Sledgehammer', I would argue, *parodies* rather than *deploys* surrealist tropes.

visuals which speak of such enunciations as stylized enactments that were *already* imitative prior to their reworking in 'Sledgehammer'.

Whether an ironical engagement with constructs of masculinity was due to input from Gabriel himself is not possible to say, however. Equally, it would be impossible to prove that the video's transgressions were actually deliberate, or that Gabriel, Johnson or any other member of the production team aimed to offer a comment on the machismo posturing in prior MTV hits such as the predatory 'Hungry like the Wolf' by Duran Duran or the fetishistic 'Addicted to Love' by Robert Palmer. Indeed, when Gabriel was asked whether his early videos were a reaction to what was on MTV, he replied: 'Not so much a reaction to other stuff – more a chance to play around and work with some interesting people' (Guttenberg 2005).

Was this response disingenuous? I would argue that the answer hardly matters. If one subscribes to a poststructuralist standpoint that irony 'might be activated and put into play by the reader' rather than being inscribed into a text by its author, and that it 'results from the act of construing carried out by the interpreter who works within a context of interpretative assumptions' (Hutcheon 1994: 122), speculations about whether the ironical disruptions in 'Sledgehammer' were intentional on the part of its creators are actually beside the point. The fact that the video *can be read* as subversive means that it *is* subversive.

Simon Frith and Angela McRobbie (1990) concluded their study of gender in rock music by asking: 'Can rock be nonsexist?' Arguing that the answer must necessarily be 'no', that rock can never be gender-neutral because it is 'only intelligible in its historical and discursive contexts', Robert Walser (1993: 176–7) makes the important point that it can nevertheless be anti-sexist:

> we can spot many examples of rock music that use the powerful codings of gender available in order to engage with, challenge, disrupt or transform not only rock's representation of gender, but also the beliefs and material practices with which those representations engage.

If one were to rewrite this passage in such a way that one substituted 'rock music' with 'music video', one could cite 'Sledgehammer' as an example of a text in which the viewer might discern precisely such a transgressive reworking of gender codes.

Chapter 6
Peter Gabriel's Elegy for Anne Sexton: Image and Music in 'Mercy Street'[1]

Carol Vernallis

Figure 6.1   Images from Peter Gabriel's 'Mercy Street' video

---

[1]   An earlier version of this chapter first appeared in Carol Vernallis, *Experiencing Music Video: Aesthetics and Cultural Context* (Columbia University Press, 2004). Reprinted by permission. The music and lyrics for Peter Gabriel's "Mercy St." are published by Real World Music Limited. All quotes from Anne Sexton's poetry are reprinted by permission of Sterling Lord Literistic, Inc. © Anne Sexton.

Matt Mahurin's video for Peter Gabriel's 'Mercy Street' begins with a man taking a boat out onto the water. He carries some unidentified cargo that might be a person – alive or dead. A woman, possibly institutionalized, prepares for death through the practices of Catholic faith. These strands move at different paces, and the relation between them is never clarified. At the video's end the man remains on the boat, but the woman is still unknown. The figures become more iconic as the video progresses; their appearance changes, but it's uncertain whether any transformation has taken place.

Screened only a handful of times on MTV, the 'Mercy Street' video was not tied to a hit single or Gabriel's appearance. Moreover, it deals with serious themes, contains frequent temporal disjunctions, and makes an unusually broad range of music–image connections. The video's obscurity and complexity notwithstanding, 'Mercy Street' is one of the most handsome and forceful in the canon, and makes a good choice for close analysis. Many of the devices that structure 'Mercy Street' illuminate the genre, and hint at what music video has the potential to become.

The song's subject is the poet Anne Sexton, and the video can be described as, in roughly equal parts, homage, elegy, pastiche and biography. Sexton was an untutored housewife and mother who, under her psychiatrist's advice, began to write poetry at 28, and quickly achieved renown. Her books of poems (one for which she won a Pulitzer Prize) are most admired for their powerful and surprising metaphors. In 1974, at the age of 46, she committed suicide.

Reading 'Mercy Street'

This chapter analyses the ways the audiovisual codes of 'Mercy Street' operate in a temporal flow. A sequential reading, following the song's form, is interspersed with fuller descriptions of music–image relations, as well as fragments from Sexton's poetry. Such an approach aims to suggest a viewer's experience of music video. Watching often encourages multitasking: following a narrative or processual trajectory, piecing together music–image relations, and placing lyrics, we make sense of the whole. The individual descriptions of musical parameters can be used as a tool for reading music video in general. The excerpts of Sexton's poems may encourage the reader to find out more about her life and work.[2]

---

[2]   Neither Sexton's poems nor her life provides great insight into 'Mercy Street' as song or video. One or two lines from the song 'Mercy Street' may borrow from Sexton's poem '45 Mercy Street': 'searching for a street sign' becomes 'swear they moved that sign' and 'in order not to see my inside out' becomes 'wear your inside out'. The more outrageous moments of the poem have been left out, however. Later in the poem, Sexton starts pulling fish out of her pocketbook and chucking them at street signs. Her poems are predicated on showing greater aggression. Because the song functions more as elegy than as biography, this analysis takes the video as its primary text. Sexton herself might have sanctioned such an approach, being quite loose about borders between life experience and art. She often

The multivalency of 'Mercy Street' makes any streamlined approach difficult. The video narrates a woman's experiences as she struggles with mental institutions, the memory of incest, and the threat of suicide or being drowned; the story is told out of sequence and in fragments, and the viewer must struggle to learn the piece. The song itself is unpredictable, based on a drone that allows for various materials to be brought in and out of the mix, and containing irregular section-lengths. In addition, Mahurin's imagery and Gabriel's music share an affinity of tone and affect, allowing space for any individual element or image to depart from the norm. The sporadic appearance of a boat going out on the water provides one thread of continuity. Without much to serve as a guide, however, the viewer must crawl from one shot to the next: each shot must be interpreted in light of musical and visual cues, as moment by moment, relations among music, image and lyrics shift. Instances of Eisensteinian montage disrupt the audiovisual flow (viewers forge new meaning through the collision of independent shots). Alternately left out and given clues, pushed away and drawn in, the viewer's subject position becomes unstable. Two-thirds into the video, direction changes course: after an allusion to annihilation, the image and music drive forward, to either a light at the end of a tunnel or death. In the final analysis, the video may concern itself less with revealing anything for the viewer than with its own 'blanking out' or withdrawal. The tension between six storylines and one philosophical perspective (the last grounded in nothingness, and told graphically rather than narratively) contributes to the video's prismatic opacity.[3]

Introduction

The opening of 'Mercy Street' quickly establishes itself as 'other' to Anglo-American pop through its modal harmonic materials and Brazilian percussion. (Hushed, solemn and vaguely religious are good descriptors for its affect.) The video's first shot contains a thin man or woman in half light, with a flowing garment and bare feet, walking on sand. Taken with the introduction's music, this image suggests a mystical figure in a desert setting. Upon closer examination, however, other elements block any idealized reading. The figure, for instance, wears two sticking-plasters – what type of wounds along the edge of the feet might need

---

read her poems live to musical accompaniment (with a musical ensemble called Her Kind). Excerpts from Sexton's poetry are taken from Sexton 1999.

[3]   Because this description differs from most close analyses of film, it will be worth explaining quickly how it is organized. Close analyses of film usually use the shot or the scene as the fundamental unit of analysis, and close readings of music video have tended to do the same. Here, the method of detailed description is similar, but the fundamental unit is the musical section, rather than the scene or the shot. The use of the musical section as the fundamental unit places an emphasis upon varied repetition of materials over linear development of plot. Treating the form of the song as the analytical ground for the video better reflects its semantic and formal structure.

covering? Are they stigmata, or do they suggest ritual or aestheticism? Are they a reference to Oedipus?[4] Subsequent viewings suggest that the sticking-plasters serve both graphic and narrative functions. The director's manipulations of shape will suggest a concern less with people and events than with a form that empties out.[5]

In the second shot, we see the lower half of someone's legs. As the legs rise in the frame, they stop moving, perhaps suggesting a loss of consciousness. When the motion ceases, however, the surdo enters, sounding almost like a heartbeat. This seeming contradiction in affect – the music asserting vitality as the image shows death – raises several questions: is it the image or the music that provides the video's impetus? Which figures are animate, and which inanimate? The heartbeat alongside the dead body may suggest the spirit's release from the body, allowing it to wander across the landscape of the video. A ghostly cinematic point of view is reinforced in shots 13, 23 and 33. Do these shots belong to a ghost, a youthful or older Anne Sexton, Peter Gabriel, the spiritual guide, the boat rower, a father, the viewer or some combination of these figures?

Contour

By tracing the contours of movements of objects within the frame across several edits, one can gain an even greater appreciation for the song's melodic materials and their affective characteristics.[6] The song's introduction presents a four-note 'cambiata' motif several times in different registers,[7] and the movement of the objects in the frame traces that of the cambiata: the rise and fall of the shadow in the first image of the foot follows the contour of this motif, sometimes appearing a bit before or behind the melody, but still responsive to it. A second synthesizer part enters, playing the same cambiata figure in a lower register. Similarly, the line of the shadow crosses the foot and repeats its rise and fall. The low bass note

---

[4]   In Greek mythology, Laertes damaged his son Oedipus's feet and left him to die to avoid the fulfilment of the prophecy that the King's son would kill the father and marry the mother. One of the themes of 'Mercy Street' is incest.

[5]   In 'Mercy Street', shapes such as circles, crosses and lines continually reappear, change and then thin out. We can trace the gap of the sticking-plasters in shots 3, 4, 16 and 17, and the parallel lines in shots 2, 8, 18, 19, 25, 35, 36 and 40–46.

[6]   The musical lines in a piece of music – the melody, the bass, the inner voices – have contours; composers often talk about these musical lines as visual shapes. In music video, the shape of the musical line can correlate to the shape of the visual image.

[7]   The cambiata is a musical figure that usually begins with a downward second to an unaccented note, then a downward third followed by an upward second to another unaccented note, so that it ends a third away from its beginning. Both the second and third notes can be dissonant. It may be inverted.

is matched by the feet hitting the sand. Just as the foot's next step launches the following image, the bass 'pushes off' into the body of the song.

A related example lies at the point in the verse when Gabriel sings 'with no leak at the seam'. This melody begins with a rising skip of a third, and is repeated three times with an overall contour that emphasizes downward motion. The image draws our attention to the melody's gradual descent by presenting three shots of objects falling slowly through the frame.

> my real dream,
> I'm walking up and down Beacon Hill
> searching for a street sign –
> namely MERCY STREET.
> Not there.[8]

Verse 1: Shots 1, 2

Verse 1 begins by establishing a fragile connection between music and image. The vocal line is doubled at the octave. Similarly, images of houses have a pale border both above and below, and these parallel lines slowly fall through the frame. Aspects of the ghostly houses serve more than musical functions: the houses are shot through a mirror or puddle, and this mirror image raises questions of both the identity and the position of the viewer. The lyrics ('Looking down on empty streets, all she can see') also lead one to imagine a subject and the town or city that surrounds her. Because the second falling house is older and less distinct than the first, it may suggest the memory of an earlier house, perhaps evocative of childhood.

Verse 1: Shots 5, 6

Shot 5, of a woman's head low in the frame, plays on the video's opening. In the first shot, the foot creates a hole in the sand, and its corresponding sound – the bass's initial attack – a kind of sonic pothole. In shot 5, conversely, the sound seems to flood over the woman's head, suggesting the inverse shape, a dome. Following shot 5 is one of a woman praying as she falls through the frame, yet we do not know if she is the same one who traversed the sand, died in the water, or looked onto the city streets. We may be reluctant to consider her as the video's protagonist.

---

[8] *45 Mercy Street* by Anne Sexton.

Bridge Fragment

The verse's B section (composed of images of feet stepping in sand and hands pushing the boat, shots 7 and 8) exists as a fragment inserted between repetitions of the verse and can be heard as the kernel from which the more substantial bridge grows. Because Gabriel's hushed, semi-spoken singing sounds tender and conspiratorial,[9] one might guess that Sexton remembers a moment from her childhood or a secret wish: she and her brother steal away to take a boat out to sea. Since this small section will grow over the course of the song, something illicit yet beloved develops in the video. Perhaps this is one reason why the video does not have a completely dark tone, despite its focus on suicide. A woman's half-lit face (shot 9) closes the section. The face is shown in three-quarter shadow – a shocking effect. The image, here, seems to run ahead of the song.

The image–music connections also become more like puns. The whistling sound might fit the wind blowing across the woman's face. The strong attack and nasal vowel of the word 'comes' recall the feet stepping on sand and the surdo's 'heartbeat', respectively.

> We are fishermen in a flat scene.
> All day long we are in love with water.
> The fish are naked.
> The fish are always awake.
> They are the color of old spoons
> and caramels.
> The sun reached down
> but the floor is not in sight.
> Only the rocks are white and green.
> Who knows what goes on in the halls below?[10]

Continuity

In 'Mercy Street', repeated or varied visual patterns create a subtle mode of continuity that compensates for the video's narrative lacunae and more drastic visual transformations: it does not rely on character or plot to create stability. The video establishes continuity from shot to shot using a variety of techniques – graphic matches, repetition of visual patterns and schemes, and preservation of tonal values. Continuity is first established in the video's opening through an

---

[9]   See Serge Lacasse's 'The Introspectionist' (Chapter 15, this volume), which analyses Gabriel's expressive uses of processed voice (through techniques like overdubbing, reverb, timbral nuance, filtering and spatialization), and the ways these vocal sounds influence form and affect.

[10]   *Water* by Anne Sexton

unbroken line across edited images; the verse's middle through number and light; and the chorus through matching shape.[11]

At a near-subliminal level the many images of crosses (ten in total) provide continuity.[12] At first, the imagery is so submerged in the tape that these crosses seem purely coincidental. Later, however, it becomes clear that Christian imagery is central to the video. Images of passage also carry us forward: figures always appear in the middle of some activity – swimming, rowing, pushing, pulling, waving, falling, stepping, pacing, reaching, dropping, murmuring, carrying, towing, passing, kneeling, tapping, circling, gliding.

Whereas many videos derive their strength from a tension between musician and video-maker, 'Mercy Street' benefits from the affinities between Mahurin's

---

[11]   Three techniques structure the video's beginning. A pattern of continuity – an establishment of an unbroken visual line – begins at the video's opening with a foot stepping on sand. Toward the end of this shot, the foot and its shadow fill the lower right-hand corner of the frame. Next, a shot of feet drifting in water begins in the lower right of the frame and moves toward, and exits from, the upper left. Next, comes a series of shots contains objects dropping from the upper left-hand corner, each object starting a little lower than the previous one. The last image, of the crown of the woman's head, is planted at the bottom of the frame. In traditional Hollywood narrative, the editing techniques work to suggest the viewer's mastery of the space (through shot/reverse shot, 180-degree rule, eyeline match and point of view). According to David Bordwell, 'once graphic continuity is achieved, the editing can concentrate upon orienting us to scenographic space. Crosscutting creates a fictive space built out of several locales ... classical crosscutting presupposes that shifts in the locale are motivated by the story action. More often, editing fulfils the narrational function of orienting us to a single locale (a room, a stretch of sidewalk, the cab of a truck) or to physically adjacent locales (a room and a hallway, the rear of the truck). Thus the principles and devices of continuity editing function to represent space for the sake of the story' (Bordwell 1985: 56). Music videos forego such mastery in order to create the sense of a continuous line. The editing usually attempts to keep the eye moving fluently through the space in a way that supports the directionality of the song. In the middle of verse 1, a sense of continuity is preserved no longer through an unbroken line that leads the eye, but through number and light. Two falling spheres – which turn out to be a head and clasped hands – are followed by two shins and then two arms (shots 6–8). Shadows pass over and cover these images until the sequence ends with a woman's head in three-quarter shadow. The chorus is structured around matching shapes: the lace on the girl's hat blends into the crest of a wave. The final images all contain a vertical band of light in the centre of the frame. One striking (if subtle) kind of continuity comes in the second instrumental: continuity is preserved through shape – here, a circle and a cross (shots 33–7). The priest's cross, with its circular movement, reappears as the cross formed by the lines cut into the cement below the dogs. The dogs are echoed in the following image by a circle of sand with two feet and a hand.

[12]   The video's images of crosses include an antenna on a falling house, a pattern on the lace that covers a woman's head, a design on a kitchen floor, a misshapen cross, the lines in cement under two circling dogs, the sidewalk from a bird's-eye view, the crossbars in a lit window at the end of a hallway, and a shot of the father in the boat that resembles the top part of a cross.

and Gabriel's work. Mahurin's dark imagery complements Gabriel's hermetic style; this basic similarity provides continuity when elements diverge from the mix. While the 'Mercy Street' song is brooding and grim, constructed without clear outlines, Mahurin's charcoal drawings frequently contain a rounded representation of an isolated figure standing stiff-limbed against a richly textured background (an overcast, sooty sky). Dim but luminous light breaks through the background.[13]

Verse 1: Shot 10

For the first time, the lyrics come to the fore, yet just as suddenly they recede into the mix. The image responds to the line 'Nowhere in the corridors'. During the emphasized word 'nowhere', a hand searches upward against a black background with lace streaming from the fingertips, before image and text fade away. As the second hand takes the lead, a counter-melody in the synthesizer comes to the fore. The phrase 'There in the midst of it' follows the image of the boat going out, and the word 'there' and the boat's bow seem to pierce the darkness. The coming forward and fading away of the text 'nowhere in the corridors of pale green and grey', and 'nowhere in the' suggest a treacherous journey or an unreliable guide. The boat holds what appears to be a severed head. Gabriel's lyrics 'like bone', though barely audible, reflect this image.

> In north light, my smile is held in place,
> the shadow marks my bone.
> What could I have been dreaming as I sat there,
> all of me waiting in the eyes, the zone
> of the smile[14]

Lyrics

The lyrics fragment into chunks ranging from two to six words each. Even adjacent words drift away from one another, while other more distant words, linked by some tangential feature in the image or the music – a repeat of a hand tapping another, or the return of a riff – are eerily bound together. Although the lyric's sense fades, the words change into sensual objects, the harsh word 'bone' and the softly labial 'Mercy Street', wrapped in sound and linked to individual images, become talismanic. The hook line, 'looking for Mercy Street', exhorts us to remain patient while the murky image and music unfold, because we are seeking something, possibly a street, possibly redemption.

---

[13]   Mahurin has served as a graphic artist for *Time*, *Newsweek* magazine and the *Los Angeles Times*.

[14]   *The Double Image* by Anne Sexton

Verse 1: Shot 12; Chorus 1: Shots 13–17

The face of a woman who may represent Sexton becomes an unyielding mask, a dead end. The close-up of the ocean provides a surprising moment of renewal, suggesting the fullness and breadth of the self, the bounty of nature. Half a bar later, the synthesizer plays a four-note flourish that suggests running water. The flourish confirms the sense that this pure image of water provides a respite from the video's largely ominous tone. The video soon returns to its former tone, however. The shot of the mysterious man in a large black coat throwing a rope into the boat gives a sense of foreboding: his return to the boat seems to discourage any hope of a positive outcome. An earlier shot reveals a human figure in the back of the boat, but does not adequately explain the severed head in the boat's bottom and the corpse tethered to the board. Additionally, the chorus is livelier and fuller than the verse, the movements just described – of the father and the boat – serve to bracket a segment of the melody. Here, effort is needed to keep the melodic line moving upward, and the weariness of the voice reflects this difficulty. This audiovisual 'snapshot' points to other moments of weariness and labour in the verses.

Chorus 1: Shots 13–17

The chorus' music is lilting and soothing, yet the image leaves us to our own devices, as the instances of close synchronization between music and image become more sporadic. Despite the lack of direct music–image pairings, a more subtle kind of connection derives from the repetition of simple shapes. Three breaking waves correspond to the fully orchestrated chorus while isolated pairs – two houses, two hands, two feet, balled head and hand – match the thinly textured verse. As in many music videos, this repetition of small numbers of objects in successive images helps us to chart the flow of the song's form.

Chorus 1 closes with a long shot of the father pushing the boat with his daughter in it. Because this cut is so abrupt, we may feel set adrift. Within the rhetoric of narrative film, a long shot at the end of a section typically suggests that the viewer possesses some insight and is prepared to move on to the next sequence; here, however, we have no idea what the man is doing or why. The image might show a pastoral scene with a father spending an afternoon with his child just as easily as a suicide or murder. Perhaps the man is the spiritual guide in shot 1, or the rower who carries a drowned body tethered to the bow in shot 2. The viewer must watch, without knowing the meaning of the scene and yet sensing that the song's chorus is drawing to a close. This produces a sense of anxiety, even impotence.

And what of the dead? They lie without shoes in their stone boats. They are more like stone than the sea would be if it stopped. They refuse to be blessed, throat, eye and knucklebone.[15]

Sectional Divisions

Repeated viewings of 'Mercy Street' show that its verses are oriented toward the individual, the intimate, the secret and the illicit; those in the chorus explore personal relations and provide the narrative; and the music and image of the instrumental sections are objective and resolute. This represents an unusual rhetorical structure for a music video. In most videos, the verse traces the plot and the chorus presents a more general observation. In this video, the chorus carries the burden of the narrative. In the first chorus, the father takes the girl out to sea. They acknowledge and confront each other in the second chorus. The third chorus shows the father abandoning the daughter or assisting in her death. Though the verse shows the effects of Sexton's grief – her prayers, her writing, as well as her shock treatments – these images tell of a general truth more than a particular story. We know that the heroine is doomed, in part, because the placement of the imagery against the song departs so far from most pop songs.

Individual sections of the song grow and diminish. The verse becomes shorter each time it appears. By contrast, the chorus seems to grow out of the B section of the verse. The chorus also contributes to the song's transitory nature: ten bars long, instead of the expected eight, it creates a subtle hesitation and keeps the song slightly off-balance. In response to the stretching and shrinking and general unpredictability of sectional lengths, the video plays with the length of time occupied by sequences of images. Most shots last about five seconds, but a few last much longer. In verse 2, the shot of the hand fills the frame for twelve seconds – the total amount of time taken by three shots from the previous verse. This shot suggests that the video's materials can be stripped bare.

Each kind of section – chorus, verse and instrumental – can be understood to have its own affect. The final chorus gains strength through greater expressivity and grain while the verses gradually seem to wane. By contrast, the instrumentals hold fast. They maintain a consistent length and seem isolated from other sections. The final instrumental's performerly touches – the Andean flute melody becomes more emphatic and the percussion more prominent – function simply as a means of enhancing the instrumentals' resoluteness. The instrumentals hint that a sense of extreme distance, of being 'beyond' things, is a state one must experience. Both final sections feature high-angle shots that observe rote activities.

The beginnings of musical sections are marked by threshold imagery (a hand pulling out a drawer) and the ends of sections are matched with images of closure (the father leaving). Formal shaping within sections is partly determined by the

---

[15]   *The Truth the Dead Know* by Anne Sexton.

image of the woman's head. Partial views – the crown of her head or her half-seen face – occur mid-section. The ends of sections are announced by her face filling the frame. Her head position cues us to the level of musical continuity: when it faces the camera, there is a sharp break between verse and chorus. A less frontal head signals a smoother transition.

> I was forced backward.
> I was forced forward.
> I was passed hand to hand
> like a bowl of fruit.[16]

Instrumental 1

One hand passes a piece of cloth to another, but the image and music seem disconnected. On the one hand, the visual activity may tempt us to anticipate an approaching event, perhaps a funeral or wedding. On the other hand, the melancholic flute draws our attention to the past, perhaps by way of an allusion to the panpipe solo in Simon and Garfunkel's 'El Cóndor Pasa', a version of a traditional Peruvian tune.[17] In addition, the plaintiveness of the Andean flute melody suggests subjectivity and, more strongly, a sense of loss, encouraging us to review what we have seen thus far. Because the image's and music's temporal cues conflict, the viewer's attention is drawn in two directions.

> Suddenly
> a wave that we go under.
> Under. Under. Under.
> We are daring the sea.
> We have parted it.
> We are scissors.
> Here in the green room
> the dead are very close.
> Here in the pitiless green

---

[16]   *Briar Rose (Sleeping Beauty)* by Anne Sexton.

[17]   Through tone, material has also carried from image to music (from the man in the boat to the panpipe solo). 'El Cóndor Pasa' is a song from the *zarzuela* 'El Cóndor Pasa' by the Peruvian composer Daniel Alomía Robles. (Written in 1913, it was based on traditional Andean folk tunes.) A cover version by Simon and Garfunkel (together with Urubamba, a group of musicians from various South-American countries, who introduced Paul Simon to Andean music in the early 1970s and then toured and recorded with him) appeared on their *Bridge Over Troubled Water* album (1970). Perhaps Gabriel's echo of 'El Cóndor Pasa' functions as an acknowledgement of European borrowings from third-world cultures.

where there are no keepsakes
or cathedrals[18]

Arrangement

By reflecting the sense of fullness or emptiness in the musical texture, the image
hews to the music. At the opening of the chorus, the song becomes more densely
orchestrated, while the instrumentals are more sparsely textured. This reduction in
sound does not work as it might in disco, for example, in which the listener can
find pleasure in the sparser texture of the break by inhabiting the song's underlying
groove. Rather, in 'Mercy Street', the more thinly orchestrated sections constitute
moments of abandonment. As the synthesizer pad is removed, the bottom drops
out. Additionally, the voice cracks and threatens to break apart, becoming almost
inaudible. The video responds to these moments of fullness and emptiness. As
previously mentioned, in the beginning of the choruses, the image becomes
more dense (the shots of water), and in more thinly textured sections, it seems
to wane (a searching hand or a murky cross). The image plays with the music's
threat of absence by itself threatening to blink out. The edits shift from patches
of slow dissolves, to quick fades to black, to firm cuts to black. The video's most
frightening moment may occur when an image of the father and the boat dissolves
into a long stretch of pure black.

The image's content reflects that of the melody. As the video unfolds, things
lose their specific characters, becoming simply undefined shapes. First we see
a house, then the shadow of a house, next a rounded head, and finally a hand
and a head. This last image, however, is more like two abstract circles of light
than a human body. By the time we see the head, it seems like a raised surface
with indented areas. Because the video begins with a small cluster of images, the
moments when the material flattens out are even more disturbing.

Similarly the vocal line, because it eschews either teleology or embellishment,
comes to resemble the video's simple forms. The singing at times is only murmured;
the melodic line falls or wanders. The chorus' vocal line, on the other hand, is
distinctly hymnlike, composed of several simple lines, with clear voice-leading
and without ornamentation. The voice moves impassively through the musical
texture toward its own destination: it reminds one of Lutheran hymnody in its
steadfastness and purity. Its refusal to be altered begins to seem recalcitrant.

The image not only simplifies, it becomes indistinct. Though the image relies
upon simple forms, photographic techniques render them as vague contours and
fields. It can be hard, at first, to make out the figures, both those that are high key
against a black background and those shot in very low light and a middle grey.
Similarly, the arrangement is deliberately indistinct at times, despite the clarity of
its registral scheme. In the song's highest register, the arpeggiating synthesizer part

---

[18]   *The Boat* by Anne Sexton

blends with the triangle sounds, the parts fading in and out of the mix rather than entering discretely. Gabriel's baritone is often recorded with a lot of reverb, doubled at the octave, and multitracked. In addition, three different analogue synthesizer patches overlap in the mid-register, all of which project long reverberations. A heavily processed sound that seems like backward distorted guitar – but may in fact be a saxophone – helps to close sections. The conga, surdo and fretless bass form a murky rhythmic stratum in the lowest register.[19]

> For months my hand had been sealed off
> in a tin box. Nothing was there but subway railings.
> Perhaps it is bruised, I thought,
> and that is why they have locked it up.
> But when I looked in it lay there quietly.[20]

Verse 2

Verse 2 is immediately preceded by an image of textured black along with the 'backward guitar' sound. The opening of this verse pulls the viewer over a threshold: its music contains more reverb, additional vocal samples and an extra synthesizer pad. Objects and figures fall more aggressively from the top of the frame. The hollow space of the drawer and the blurry images of the hand and paper complement two features of the reverb – its distorting effect as well as its sense of space. Not only the music (the isolated words, like 'nowhere', overdubbed on separate tracks), and the lyrics ('word upon word'), but also the images point to distant memories.

Verse 2's audiovisuals may evoke moments when dream images seem to take control of the body. The open drawer suggests an abyss. The hand loses control and drops the drawer and the knees give way and land on soft grass. The flickering light on the sheet of paper resembles water, and the creeping shadow dimly recalls the shadow of the foot in the opening shot. Because the paper's text, which potentially contains secrets, is illegible, one becomes a voyeur hungry for more information.[21]

---

[19]   In a general way, music–video image can adopt the experiential qualities of sound – the objects depicted can become more processual than concrete: they can have soft rather than firm boundaries and can be seen to ebb and flow. 'Mercy Street' provides good examples of this phenomenon.

[20]   *The Touch* by Anne Sexton.

[21]   'Mercy Street' invites the viewer to read characters, but strongly asks that he or she not do so. (More than in most videos, its progress is fragmentary, and events are revealed incompletely.) To do so is an act of trespass. However, while constructing scenarios may be an invasion of the director's and possibly Anne Sexton's privacy, to do nothing but simply watch the video is also transgressive. Already implicated for seeing something that should not be shown, viewers are kept witness to a number of primal scenes, yet neither can they

As in verse 1, verse 2's lyrics 'like bone', 'handle the shocks', and 'father' seem to pierce through the texture. The image of feet, wrapped in cloth and stretched out on the linoleum floor, as well as the fragmentation of the text, suggests a woman who is institutionalized and attempting to escape her past, as well as the anointing of feet as part of a funeral rite.

The section closes with three staggered entrances across media: image, lyrics, music. A woman prays, the text 'Mary's lips' comes to the fore, and the synthesizer's arpeggiated figure returns, matching the repetitive motion of the lips.

> I feel the earth like a nurse,
> curing me of winter.
> I feel the earth,
> its worms oiling upward,
> the ants ticking,
> the oak leaf rotting like feces
> and the oats rising like angels.[22]

Local Transformation of Material

Gabriel is an avowed tinkerer. He sifts through hours of recorded improvisations, listening for 'magical' gestures and then piecing them together against a backdrop provided by pre-recorded rhythm tracks.[23] 'Mercy Street' contains many idiosyncratic details and a mix that changes frequently: notice the raspy sound that appears briefly at the ends of instrumentals and in the chorus; the shifts in the timbres of the synthesizer in each verse; the sudden entrances and exits of the high-pitched synthesizer and the triangle; the changing amounts of reverberation on the vocal tracks; the moments when the conga and surdo are brought up and down in the mix. Like the song, the image seems the result of a careful sifting through much material, and it, too, draws upon a limited set of themes. The shadow of the cloak in the first shot anticipates the cloth imagery. Dark pits in the sand suggest the hollow sockets of the woman's eyes. Certain elements of the song become associated with visual features: the arpeggiated figure in the synthesizer matches the images of transient phenomena, like rippling water, dappled light, the twirling rosary, the motion of lace and cloth. The long decay of the synthesizer pad reflects slower processes, like the sun setting on still water in the closing shot.[24]

---

interfere with the unfolding events nor piece together who the victims are in relation to the perpetrators.

[22]   *Letters to Dr Y* by Anne Sexton.

[23]   See Milano 1989.

[24]   For more about one-to-one connections among music, image and lyrics, see Michel Chion's work on synchresis, what he calls 'the spontaneous and irresistible weld produced

In a video that leaves the motivations of its characters – and even the nature of their actions – vague, the relations between the song and the image help to reveal what the figures are doing and thinking. As we see shots of a foot striking sand and an oar pulling through the water, the bass slides up from the seventh scale-degree to the tonic; the finality of the tonic lends authority to a gesture that would otherwise seem more perfunctory. In verse 2, the guitar suggests the rough surface of the wooden drawer, and the upper partials of the synthesizer reflect the softness of the grass. When verse 2 presents images of isolated body parts, the exaggerated, shifting postproduction effects on the voice remind us that these images depict the trials of a complex subject.

Sometimes the video grants agency to objects and body parts that seem almost autonomous.[25] Because each body part is often depicted separately – hands reaching for unseen objects, feet suspended motionless with soles up, heads drooping toward the bottom of the frame – each, eerily, possesses its own thematic function: the hands function as a vulnerable first line of defence; the feet are cleansed through a series of trials; heads seem to become inert matter. The video links these images, which are not contiguous, by responding closely to shifts in the musical arrangement: when the production of the voice is more or less flat, we see images of houses. When the multitracked voices overlap, figures meet each other. When the voice sounds tinny and distant, the father is far away, out on the water.

> There are brains that rot here
> like black bananas.
> Hearts have grown as flat as dinner plates.
> Anne, Anne,
> flee on your donkey,
> flee this sad hotel[26]

Chorus 2

The girl of chorus 2 confronts several male figures. Perhaps this is the only moment that functions in the classical Hollywood narrative mode. The exchange of sightlines between father and daughter grants the viewer's position a momentary

---

between a particular auditory phenomenon and visual phenomenon when they occur at the same time' (Chion 1990: 63).

[25] The sand in the first shot can be understood to brush across the woman's face at the close of the first verse. It dissolves the cloth and hand imagery into nothingness as the final instrumental ends. In the B section of verse 1, we see an assertive hand; in the subsequent A section of that verse, a more tentative hand; in verse 3, an emaciated hand. The video almost suggests that the world is animated, not by people, but by cold, platonic forms – spheres and boxes, circles and lines.

[26] *Flee on Your Donkey* by Anne Sexton.

stability. For once the figures' relationship becomes clear. Because the image looks like it is projected onto a screen, viewers are reminded of its unreality, and may even become conscious of its proximity to Hollywood film.

Though music and image seem closely related at this point in the video, they are actually far removed from one another in terms of affect. The second chorus becomes warmer and fuller than the first through a vocal arrangement that incorporates countermelodies and heterophony. The image, by contrast, is cold and a bit frightening. Music and image are linked, however, through an association with water. The synthesizer parts, particularly, serve to connote the sea in which the figures float.[27]

On subsequent viewings we may want to assign characters to the figures. The figures who look at one another are similar to those who appear in Freud's 'A child is being beaten'. In 'Mercy Street' a priest/father may leave a girl to drown, while a sibling or the child's other self watches on. The latter case would be the most disturbing, as it would mean the obliteration of one part of Sexton's self.[28]

This section begins and ends with an image of the boat, but it is dominated by shots of heads against dark or watery backgrounds. Toward the end of the section, most of these images are situated high in the frame. Because it occurs gradually and without apparent design, this process achieves a feeling of suspension. There

---

[27]   In *Analysing Musical Multimedia*, Nicholas Cook provides a description of relations among music, image and text based on a scale of conformance, complementation and contrast. How would this section be interpreted through Cook's model of conformance to contest? Because the warm, soothing elements of the music seem distant from the element of terror embedded in visual track, the relation might be considered one of contest. (Because slumber and nightmare are intimately linked, these relations may seem less adversarial than, say, a couple fighting against romantic music, however.) Within the large-scale form of the video, we might say that this moment creates a snug fit, a relation we might ultimately want to call complement. ('Mercy Street' plays a Freudian game of *fort/da* in which image, lyrics and music are repeatedly brought into close relation and then pushed apart, while the viewer, at the same time, is brought into confidence and then left outside. The moments of gap and then sync seem to grow more extreme as the video progresses; the example above appears at a node of relatively close connection, so this is a relation we might ultimately want to call a complement). In addition a shape shared by music and image – the rising contour in the melodic lines and the gradual progression of the boat on the water from the bottom to the top of the frame – suggests a relation of iconicity and therefore congruence. This moment contains relations based on contest, complement and congruence (Cook 1998: 98–106).

[28]   This moment of a person watching a projection of another (potentially some aspect of the self) echoes a moment in Peter Gabriel's video for 'Digging in the Dirt'. This mirroring moment could be said to reflect Gabriel's second stage of musical and personal development. See Sarah Hill's Chapter 2 in this volume, which describes the trajectory of Gabriel's work from progressive rock to a more inward, questing mode, to cross-cultural engagement.

are parallels in the music: the chorus introduces an additional vocal line in the upper register and contains a prominent upward leap in the main melody.

> but my father
> drunkenly bent over my bed,
> circling the abyss like a shark,
> my father thick upon me
> like some sleeping jellyfish.
> Those times I smelled the Vitalis on his pajamas.
> Those times I mussed his curly black hair
> and touched his ten tar-fingers
> and swallowed down his whiskey breath.
> Red. Red. Father, you are blood red.
> Father,
> we are two birds on fire.
> In the mind there is a thin alley called death
> and I move through it as
> through water.
> My body is useless.[29]

Harmony

With its constant Latin percussion tracks and tonic-heavy fretless bass part, 'Mercy Street' would seem to emphasize unity of affect over internal differentiation. The song's harmony, however, tells a different story. The verse can be described in terms of functional harmony, but it clearly sounds more modal than tonal. Thus, it follows the 'exotic' tendencies of the song's texture. The chorus, however, presents a chord progression that recalls Protestant hymnody. This section contains a full, multitracked vocal arrangement that works according to eighteenth- and nineteenth-century rules for voice-leading and chord-spacing. The word 'mercy' falls on the first convincing major tonic as well. It therefore works against the South American and Asian elements of the song. This may be why the imagery gradually becomes more Christian toward the middle of the song: with shots of a confessional and a priest, the chorus is able to assert its harmonic weight, particularly as the verse progressively diminishes in length. By contrast, imagery that might seem to support the song's exotic elements comes at the beginning and the very end of the song. Here, we see shots of swaddled feet and boats that might look Arabic or Indian.[30] By positing England as the sheltered interior of the song

---

[29]   *Begat* by Anne Sexton.

[30]   The surdo, congas and triangles suggest the samba; the bass's slide up to the tonic from the seventh sounds like Indian classical music; a flute sound may echo Andean music.

and by reflecting the music's ethnic elements in only the vaguest ways, the video raises questions about the song's use of its musical materials.[31]

> Perhaps the earth is floating,
> I do not know.
> Perhaps the stars are little paper cutups
> made by some giant scissors,
> I do not know.
> perhaps the moon is a frozen tear,
> I do not know.
> Perhaps God is only a deep voice
> heard by the deaf,
> I do not know.[32]

Bridge 2: Shots 33–7

A shot from the window of a sanatorium, and subsequent shots, might suggest a cleansing – a taking leave of the world – and the field of muddled grey might point to cremation, where the spirit leaves the body, rises and surveys the world, and then disperses among the elements. 'Mercy Street' offers six depictions of death (or blanking out), frequently followed by a sense of rebirth:

1. The video winds down and exhausts its small set of materials. Before instrumental 2 begins, the frame fills with a blur of grey and white, and the soundtrack turns into a buzz of white noise. As the boat drifts out of our view, the video seems to come to an end. This is true for the soundtrack as well, for the noise functions like a fade at the end of an outchorus. It comes as a surprise that the video continues past this sense of an ending, through a recycling of exhausted material.
2. The autonomy of individual body parts suggests a preternatural animation that extends beyond death. In the video's opening, feet drift away and affect lifelessness, but a musical heartbeat (the surdo) continues. Most of the physical contact between figures or parts of the body in 'Mercy Street' is minimal: one hand lightly taps another, or is moved in front of a face. The video's closing shots contain a woman's hand moving back and forth before her face; this last image, along with the hand brushing off sand, suggests a sort of character development.[33]

---

[31]   The chorus could be heard as Protestant hymnody filtered through folk revivalism. This still places the chorus in common harmony practice. See Bohlman 1988: 39.

[32]   *The Poet of Ignorance* by Anne Sexton.

[33]   The fact that the hand that passes in front of the woman's face may not belong to her also suggests a Catholic ritual associated with death. Sexton believed that her parents

3. A person's death is depicted six times. Like a cat with nine lives, the character lives on.[34]

4. The reconfiguration of past and future also suggests some freedom from time's arrow. The shot of a hand brushing sand off feet marks the video's true beginning. The character readies herself to begin the journey out to sea. After brushing the sand from her feet she then steps into the first shot of 'Mercy Street' where, swaddled in cloth and veiled in half light, she leans forward and pushes the boat out onto the water. The video's first image functions as a flash forward; the feet on the floor in the second verse suggest the recovered drowned body in the morgue.

5. The video grants an adult woman, understood as Anne Sexton, her ambiguous wish to live the present as a return to childhood.[35]

6. By the video's end, the father's story acquires greater prominence and viewer identification than the woman's. His story might be reconstructed as follows: his role in Sexton's suicide – both as facilitator and as ultimate cause – draws him into her emotional world and sends him into a deep depression. Through a collection of fleeting images, the video shows the father's breakdown, presenting his body as a collection of fragments and his life as the senseless repetition of empty forms.[36] The video's ending

---

molested her, and she, in turn, molested her daughter. More frightening than the witnessing of a primal scene is the video's suggestion of incest. Anxiety about this scene could be said to be displaced onto adjacent imagery in the video – the isolated hands that seem to flutter guiltily throughout the video.

[34]   The video alludes to several drownings as well as cremation, electrocution and decapitation.

[35]   The video complicates the simple structure of real present versus remembered or imagined past. The woman's experiences occupy, not the present, but the recent past. They work as a collection of images from a painful adulthood. Without attempting to maintain a temporal sequence, the video presents the woman's medical treatment, institutionalization, confessions and obsessive prayer. Because these scenes have an inky or murky look, they seem as much like flashbacks as do the scenes of childhood – perhaps more so, judged in purely cinematic terms. By contrast, the scenes that depict the father's taking the daughter out in the boat are more fleshed out, with clearer backgrounds and a higher level of detail. They seem also to possess a linearity and contiguity that the adult scenes do not. It is important to note as well that the scenes of childhood obtain greater weight through their association with the song's chorus. The immediacy of the childhood scenes reverses the logic of the flashback, making the past more real than the scenes of adulthood. This is so despite a viewer's sense that the video's distant past may constitute an imagined childhood while the events depicted in the adult scenes have actually taken place. Such a childhood would thereby occupy the video's present, just as the final stanza of the lyrics ('Anne, with her father is out in the boat') might be understood as recording this transformation from the perspective of the song's present.

[36]   The song's male voice encourages the viewer to seek out a male perspective. This male voice, both frequently sung in the first person, and alternately addressing the listener

echoes that of Hitchcock's *Vertigo*; the viewer feels bereft because the man has failed to save the woman, but triumphant because he survives.

Rhythm and Articulation

The downbeat often possesses the authority of the bar; this is true in 'Mercy Street', especially because the surdo articulates it. The images in the first half of the video emphasize the downbeat through either editing or movement within the frame. After the second verse (and the video's main themes have been brought into relation),[37] the video avoids drawing attention to the downbeat, shifting to an emphasis on beats two and four. This shift gives the image a more relaxed feel and, more importantly, helps to explain why the first half of the video is hard to bear in mind while one views the second.

The arrangement exhibits a considerable amount of rhythmic variety. The triangle and conga articulate the offbeats. Images of dappled light on water and patterned stucco seem to reflect these rhythmic features, but since these images are merely textural, they push the percussion's offbeats into the background. The rhythmic vitality of the song is thereby muted in the video. The image focuses instead upon the trajectory of the voice. This careful tracing of the voice provides continuity across the video.

Although this close tracking of the voice might threaten to become monotonous, the video establishes variety through staggered phrasing among the voice, the synthesizer and the image. The synthesizer pad tends to move in similar motion with the voice, but it lags a bit behind. The figure in the frame is often revealed through flooding light, and this light appears after the pad enters, creating even greater rhythmic play. Conversely, the revelation of a figure sometimes presages moments of greater activity in the music, as at the end of verse 1, when light fills a face just before the chorus begins.

The surdo was most probably recorded first, along with the other percussion instruments, while the other parts, including the voice, were added later. Although this sequence conforms to conventional recording practice, it takes on a special role in the context of the song's division between white male subjectivity and 'ethnic' percussion. As a result of this division, the percussion seems to inhabit

---

and Sexton, expresses a kind of vulnerability through its narrow ambitus, falling motifs and feminine endings; this feminine quality derives from voice-breaks and intimate whispering at certain moments. One section, the chorus, might represent the narrator's own desires ('mercy, mercy, looking for mercy'). While the sections addressed to the listener refer to the father in the third person, those written in the second person ('let's take the boat out'; 'wear your inside out'; 'swear they moved that sign'; 'in your daddy's arms again') seem to adopt his perspective.

[37]   The main themes comprise the power of religion to control as well as comfort, death, and the family romance.

its own conceptual realm, outside of the subject matter of the song. It sounds almost like the percussionist does not know that the song is an elegy for a female European American poet who committed suicide.[38]

The rhythm of exertion and relaxation governs the phrase-structure of the image as well as that of the song. The image follows this rhythm: a person stepping forward, then legs floating passively; the boat going out and then a motionless head. This visual rhythm responds to the mostly symmetrical phrase-structure of the vocal line. Finally, the images of figures murmuring out of sync with the music provides an extra rhythmic layer, perhaps outside of the music's grasp.

> Let's face it, I have been momentary,
> A luxury. A bright red loop in the harbor.
> My hair rising like smoke from the car window.
> Littleneck clams out of season.[39]

Structural Overview / Formal Unity

At almost every hierarchical level in 'Mercy Street' processes work to obscure its form, even as a few illuminate it. Earlier I described the ambiguity linked to the

---

[38]   A listener may also be tempted to hear the voice as white male subjectivity trying desperately to hold its own against the unyielding percussion. Gabriel justifies his musical choices by arguing that musical cultures need new influences to remain vibrant. He speaks about how much the musicians from other cultures that he has met hunger to play rock and roll, and how much he gains from playing with these musicians. He acknowledges that the system of exchange is not equal, and, as an act of respect and appreciation, he has released their music on Real World Records (see Schapiro 1997). To stop here, however, would fail to raise the question of how the borrowed elements work within 'Mercy Street'. It may be important to point out that Sexton's imagery of other cultures seems naïve and limited by today's standards. Gabriel's strategies for supporting the distribution of world music suggest possibilities for music video. Currently, world music is most often recorded in such a fashion that the timbral and performerly nuances of particular musics are erased in favour of a sound that is amenable to Western ears. (A comparison of Ry Cooder's recording of the Buena Vista Social Club with more traditional Cuban music recordings is a good case in point.) The distribution of music videos made by people from the communities where the music originated would be positive; however, western viewers would need to become engaged with not only indigenous musical but also visual codes – dress, movement, ways of moving the camera, editing and the like. Both Black Uhuru and Herbie Hancock have released versions of 'Mercy Street': Black Uhuru, *Mystical Truth Dub* (Mesa Records 1993), and Herbie Hancock, *The New Standard* (Verve Records 1996). It has become unusual for African-American musicians (reggae and jazz) to cover a recent British pop song. These questions of representation, and the recording of the surdo – a drum which in the context of the song suggests a mute, wild voice – are not present on these covers.

[39]   *For My Lover, Returning to his Wife* by Anne Sexton.

length and function of sectional divisions, and the role of visual details. Let me take a moment to describe two more: large-scale divisions and the relations among shots.

Large-scale Divisions

Perhaps the video's difficult path, the fact that it's hard to follow or recall, derives from the presence of a number of visual strands in place of a single, overarching line. It moves unpredictably among four sites: the shore; houses and a hospital; intimate interiors; and above and below the surface of the water. Nevertheless the prominent thread of a boat's going out onto the water provides some direction.[40]

The video's opening also works on the subtle structural device of colotomy (a musical practice common in gamelan); here, the relative speed of the various musical parts is determined by register. The image, too, moves at different rates based on the weight and momentum of each object.[41] A subtle change then occurs as the song gradually shifts registral emphasis from low to high, as does the image.[42] Because 'Mercy Street' is dominated by round shapes and soft edges, three rectangular forms function as guide posts: the windows of the building

---

[40]   A music video analysis that loosely borrows from a Schenkerian approach and that takes into account the medium's radically different material might look quite unusual. For example, a visual background might feature a stripped-down narrative – in 'Mercy Street', the head in the boat might fall into the water and sink, to rest finally against the base of a cross planted at the bottom of the ocean. (Does the cross's tip extend past the ocean's surface?) The hook line 'looking for Mercy Street' would reduce to 'mer-street', echoing the Latin root 'mar' for ocean, or 'ocean street'. In order to leave space for image and text, the song's musical *urlinie* might be patchier than *urlinies* common to music alone. The opening C♯ and the final root of C♯ four octaves below at the video's close might serve as the two fundamental pitches. (While the video's imagery gradually rises in the frame and the song reaches a higher tessitura, the video's concern is with falling.) Layers within the middle ground might shift emphasis completely. (To reflect music video's need for a basic temporal–spatial spine, the middle ground might contain rising and falling shapes that possess similarity regardless of whether they appear in music, image or lyrics.) The foreground might contain very fine instantiations in timbre, texture and shade.

[41]   The highest register (triangle, arpeggiating synthesizer) moves the most quickly, the mid-range (voice, synthesizer pad) moves moderately, and the lowest register (bass) moves at the slowest rate. As the boat goes out onto the water, it gradually increases in speed; unidentified arms move at a moderate pace; the image of a falling head seems to slow down as the light darkens around it.

[42]   The video encourages one to hear the song as gradually shifting registral emphasis from low to high. The opening is low, grounded in the bass and surdo. Two-thirds of the way into the song, the congas become thinner, the bass disappears, and the high-pitched synthesizer sequence becomes more insistent. Similarly, the image shifts from an emphasis on the lower part of the frame to an emphasis on the higher part: the hand reaching upward and the boat's setting out from the bottom of the frame in verse 1 gives way to the dogs circling on cement high in the frame in the second instrumental.

at the beginning of the piece; the drawer in the middle; and the windows and hallway at the end. The video also contains some structural features suggestive of a palindrome.[43]

The Relations among Shots, both Contiguous and Non-contiguous

The function of many of the visual features in 'Mercy Street' tends to be unclear as they work to blur the song's sectional divisions. The seemingly neutral shots found in each section – water, sky, trees and grass – might be expected to perform as establishing shots, but they are always photographed with a particularity that renders them unfit to serve such a function. They are viewed from an extreme high or low angle, or from too close or too far, which implies a specific point of view. These shots, perhaps linked to a spirit's release from the body, appear without regard for the song's sectional divisions.[44]

The relations between adjacent shots are also frequently difficult to ascertain. The principle of Eisensteinian montage – a new concept emerges uncontained in either of the original images – often joins adjacent shots. Yet this new concept is often 'stained' by surrounding images, either those near at hand and those that 'rhyme' at a distance. In 'Mercy Street', a shot of dogs circling on cement, followed by a shot of hands brushing off sand, might signify an acceptance of the mundane. The shot of a drawer holding an illegible sheet of paper, followed by a shot of knees dropping toward the bottom of the frame suggests the imprisonment of a woman by the church. Additional images suggest the first example deals with a scatological profanity, and, the second, an even greater sense of shame.[45]

Yet the image also does not require words to show us where we are and where we will go. A shot of feet guiding us toward a boat that is then launched clearly seems introductory. When a drawer is opened we sense that a secret will be revealed. When figures gaze at one another through sightlines established across

---

[43] 'Mercy Street' suggests a teleology. The video is structured as the search for an altar. It opens with a shot of feet stepping in sand and ends with a cross in a window. Along the way, the doubling of particular images – houses plus hospitals; hands passing cloth paired with circling dogs – forms a symmetrical structure. If we consider the video played backward, it also might suggest a birth. The figure in the boat might suggest an ovum; the woman, the mother; the hall, the birth canal; and the figure in the water, a newborn child. The opening shot of 'Mercy Street' with the foot stepping into the sand would therefore suggest a desire to return to one's origins.

[44] The placement of these images works against the creation of a unified tone within each section; it also prevents these images themselves from being seen as related. It is only later in the tape, in fact, that a viewer can group these images together as a meaningful collection (shots 3, 13, 17, 23, 27, 32, 34, 35, 36, 37, 39, 48 and 50).

[45] The correlation between the shapes of the spot and prongs underneath the image of a circling cross, and the anuses, penises and tails of the dogs will make the religious elements seem profane. The light that slinks along the unreadable sheet of paper will connect with earlier images of water and hunched bodies to suggest a much greater sense of shame.

shots we expect a confrontation. The image of a cross slowly moving in circles draws us under the video's spell. When we move down a hallway toward a source of light – the light at the end of the tunnel – we know that the video is drawing toward closure (shots 1, 20, 33 and 43).

Chorus 3: Shots 39–46

At the beginning of the third chorus, the electric guitar plays an ascending phrase that reaches past the tonic, while the surdo and bass get louder, the triangle playing becomes more deliberate, and the voice breaks into plaintive moans. The accumulated momentum of the percussion now begins to determine the course of the video. Without representing the will of a particular character or suggesting a specific course of events, the percussion becomes, for a moment, the video's principal voice. As in the previous choruses we follow the boat's course. At first, since the image is in long shot, the viewer possesses little information about unfolding events. A fragile connection between music and image remains, however: the guitar ascends as a bird flies along the top of the frame.[46] Perhaps because the video has worked so hard to keep viewers adrift, the next series of shots is strangely affective. Not only are the images of hands in these shots evocative in themselves, but the music also carefully tracks their course: hands reach forward in the water, and the boat oars row forward and pull back. A descending vocal line accompanies these shots: the music seems to follow the contours of the figures' arms as the father strokes the oars and the other figure swims. For the first time, the video depicts ongoing, directed activity. (The surdo's increase in volume may also suggest forward motion.) Even though the video may be allowing a woman to drown in the water, it is refreshing finally to be moving somewhere, to be leaving behind the disturbing, static images. We can sense that something lies ahead of us, and the woman's losses produce a guilty pleasure.

The use of montage culminates in the juxtaposition of two shots: one of the father in the boat and another of a long hallway with a lighted window at the end. The shadow of the window's crossbars forms a cross on the floor. The path down the hallway, with the 'light at the end of the tunnel', suggests that the father is on a quest. The prominent cross, in the context of the video's Christian imagery, lends a religious overtone to his journey. These shots are more balanced than most in the video, and thereby provide a ground: unlike the earlier, spinning cross on a rosary, the cross on the floor gives momentary stability, turning the hallway into an altar.

---

[46]   The juxtaposition of a bird and a high note may seem hackneyed. If taken seriously, however, it can serve a structural function: it completes a gradual ascent to the top of the frame that starts at the beginning of the video. After this shot, the video winds down toward closure.

That this is clichéd imagery – rowing toward God and finding the light at the end of the tunnel[47] – only adds to its stabilizing effect.

For a moment, when the image of a wave appears, the singer's call of 'mercy' is buried in the musical arrangement. It is as if the call concerns not only the woman but also the father or even the singer himself. At this moment the emphatic articulations of the triangle, the synthesizer's crescendo, and the steady bass and surdo energize the image of a wave, and our contact breaks with whomever we assume is assigned to the surdo, lost in the rush of the oncoming wave. The woman passes her hand before her face as the surdo and triangle drop out: the end of the self. The video concludes with a shot of the father in the boat as the song articulates the tonic.[48]

'Mercy Street' focuses our attention on a woman and her trials. Suddenly, in the video's last shot, we are confronted with a man who seems alone, and who may have assisted in the drowning of his daughter. What role did he play in this drama? Is he grieving? We may wish to understand his predicament, but when we watch the video again the woman's story takes over. Music videos frequently end in a way that tells us we have missed crucial details and need to watch once more.

> I come like the blind feeling for shelves,
> feeling for wood as hard as an apple,
> fingering the pen lightly, my blade.
> With this pen I take in hand my selves
> and with these dead disciples I will grapple.
> Though rain curses the window
> let the poem be made.
> The woods are underwater, their weeds are shaking
> in the tide; birches like zebra fish
> flash by in a pack.
> Child, I cannot promise that you will get your wish.[49]

When the viewer takes up the video's story about the life of a young Sexton, 'Mercy Street' loses its radical edge – its drive toward a blanking out, absence and negation. Yet a focus on purely formal devices seems to neglect the claims of a protagonist. To the extent that 'Mercy Street' is a mood piece, it derives some of its power from the seamlessness of its music/image relations, many of which elude

---

[47]   This imagery also echoes the title of Sexton's posthumous volume *The Awful Rowing Toward God* (1975).

[48]   One might wonder why the song ends on such a strongly emphasized tonic chord since it is pointedly a modal song. Perhaps Gabriel felt a need to contain the song and prevent it from seeping into other tracks on the album. As it stands, the degree of closure that the final chord provides seems excessive, as the song has been brought to completion by other means.

[49]   *Mother and Jack and the Rain* by Anne Sexton.

our grasp. 'Mercy Street' shimmers: lullaby and nightmare, sociable and closeted, life-affirming and inert. It denies closure.

Perhaps 'Mercy Street' might equally be understood as the site of a conversation among three very different artistic sensibilities. Men write few songs about women artists, and even fewer in which the male singer adopts the woman's position.[50] Sexton herself was haunted by other artists, both contemporary, like Sylvia Plath and Robert Lowell, and earlier, like Yeats. Mahurin's encounter with the song reflects yet another subject position. One might wonder whether the sphinxlike aspect of the piece derives from Mahurin's imagining himself as Gabriel, who imagines himself as Sexton, who has her sights set elsewhere.[51]

---

[50]   Elton John's 'Candle in the Wind' is one such example, but it is a rather one-dimensional homage to Marilyn Monroe (and as a cultural icon, not as an artist).

[51]   To judge from the numerous websites and books devoted to Plath (including Rose 1996), this line of enquiry might be interesting in itself, especially inasmuch as 'Mercy Street' involves tracking another poet who left complex traces.

PART II
Politics and Power

Chapter 7

The Eyes of the World Are Watching Now: The Political Effectiveness of 'Biko' by Peter Gabriel[1]

Michael Drewett

Introduction

In September 1977 leading South African anti-apartheid activist Stephen Biko was killed in detention. Biko's death received international news coverage and prompted Peter Gabriel to research his life and the context of his death, and he subsequently wrote the song 'Biko', released on Gabriel's third solo album in 1980. The initial meaning of the song was therefore one of political sentiment, a reflection of Gabriel's outrage at the death of Biko. As an increasingly widespread audience heard the song it became regarded as a source of encouragement to opponents of apartheid and also a call for mobilization against the South African government. The political nature of the song and its growing influence shifted it into the arena of contest where its meaning, at least in part, became shaped by the confrontation between Gabriel's message and the discourses of apartheid and human rights abuses which the song opposed. In South Africa the contest was clear. Soon after Gabriel released the song the apartheid state's official censor, the Directorate of Publications, banned it. When Gabriel took the song to audiences around the world he used it as a challenge, ending his shows with the song and challenging the audience: 'I've done all I can do. The rest is up to you.'

The concern of this chapter is in the political impact of the song. I wish to explore various readings and people's experiences of the song, in the hope of providing an insight into how it has worked as a political song, and in John Street's (2001: 249) words, how it has engaged with the particular political moments and issues Gabriel attempted to encapsulate. More specifically, I wish to explore the way in which 'Biko' by Peter Gabriel has worked as a protest song which successfully conveys not just a slogan (as argued by Simon Frith [1996: 165]) but ideas about Biko's death. Through the song people have been challenged to react to the death of Stephen Biko; an investigation of how this has been achieved is the purpose of this chapter.

---

[1]   This article is reprinted from Drewett 2007 with minor edits.

Biko's Death: An Historical Context

Stephen Biko was a leading anti-apartheid activist within South Africa during the 1970s. He was central to the mobilization of black resistance despite severe government repression. As a founding member of the Black People's Convention in 1972 he travelled the country espousing the empowering philosophy of black consciousness (Bernstein 1978: 8). As part of his commitment to black consciousness Biko joined the Black Community Programmes (BCP) as a programme officer in 1972. The BCP initiated skills development within the black community, and Biko's brief was to coordinate black youth leadership training (Wilson 1991: 34). He tackled this task successfully and rose to prominence. As a result the South African government 'banned' him in 1973. This meant that he was banned from speaking in public, from meeting with more than one person at a time and from publishing his work, and was restricted to his hometown, King William's Town. Despite these restrictions Biko continued his activities in a clandestine manner, meeting with people and spreading his ideas. He befriended Donald Woods, the editor of the East London *Daily Dispatch* newspaper, and met with a wide variety of influential people (including United States senators and embassy officials, and local and international journalists). As a result of these contacts his political philosophy and programme received periodic coverage in the international press (Brown 1980).

In the aftermath of the Soweto uprisings in 1976, the government severely clamped down on anti-apartheid organizations, and during this period Biko was detained three more times before finally being arrested in August 1977 for breaking his banning order. Biko and a colleague were returning from a clandestine trip to Cape Town when they were apprehended at a roadblock on the outskirts on Grahamstown. After being detained overnight in the Grahamstown police cell Biko was sent to police headquarters in Port Elizabeth. He died on 9 September as a result of severe injuries sustained from beatings received during a period of detention without trial (Bernstein 1978: 10). The fact that Biko was a prominent and respected leader who had never been found guilty of a crime in a court of law meant that his death was widely reported, leading to local and international outrage. This was especially based on the foreign press's perception of Biko 'as a moderate, responsible voice for change' (Brown 1980: 47). As a result he was venerated in the international press. The *New York Times* described Biko as 'the country's most influential black leader' (Brown 1980: 31), while in a front page article the *Washington Post* referred to him as 'one of the leading figures of black protest in South Africa' (Brown 1980: 32). The effect of such widespread and powerful reporting was to establish Biko as the first truly international anti-apartheid martyr, personifying the struggle against apartheid through his name, face and life. It was by way of the BBC's coverage that Peter Gabriel heard about Biko's death and eventually responded with his song. It was not the first song about Biko,[2] but it proved to be the most powerful. This chapter now focuses on the song itself, exploring the music, lyrics and context in an attempt to uncover its importance as a means of political expression.

'Biko' by Peter Gabriel as a Political Message in the Mix

A number of theorists including Robin Balliger (1995), Simon Frith (1996) and John Street (2001) have argued that songs need to be analysed as fuller texts than just the lyrics. Songs are an interwoven combination of lyrics, voice, music, style and other factors too, such as social and political context and perhaps dynamics of stage performance where this is relevant. This is most certainly true of 'Biko' by Peter Gabriel. This chapter begins with a brief consideration of how the song itself works.

One of the most immediately evident features of the song is the presence of a fairly hypnotic African drumbeat. The drumbeat as it accompanies the first verse and first singing of the chorus is particularly stark, the only other instrument to feature at this stage being an electric guitar (see discussion on page 102). Gabriel was introduced to African drumbeats through the soundtrack LP *Dingaka*, which 'inspired the direction for the music of the song "Biko"'[3] (Gabriel, sleeve notes to the 7-inch single version of 'Biko', 1980). The resulting sound, however, was a simplistic attempt by Gabriel to capture what he imagined to be an exotic African drumbeat without really approximating the sound he imitated. The effect is a pseudo-African drumbeat, seemingly commodified for a Western audience. Indeed, it seems that Gabriel's use of a generic drumbeat is an indication of an imperial imagination, connecting Biko 'the African' with a simplistic, duple timing 'African drumbeat' – almost the equivalent of a kick drum and snare in a rock concert. Indeed, it is within the rock concert arena that the song is performed most powerfully, when Gabriel discards the pretense of the African drumbeat for a fuller rock-music sound.

A similar pseudo-impression is created at the end of the first singing of the chorus when a bagpipe effect (played on a synthesizer) is introduced, providing a quasi-militaristic backdrop to the rest of the song, evocative of a call to struggle. The incorporation of bagpipes might seem out of place, but is an early indication of Gabriel's experimentation with layering sounds of different origins on top of one another, what William P. Malm (in Taylor (1997: 41) refers to as 'polystylistic

---

[2]   In 1978 Tapper Zukie released 'Tribute to Steve Biko' and Tom Paxton 'The Death of Steve Biko', and in 1979 Steel Pulse released 'Biko's kindred lament' and Roger Lucey referred to Biko's death in 'Thabane', also released in 1979.

[3]   The soundtrack to *Dingaka* can therefore also be seen to signal Gabriel's interest in 'non-western music' more generally, which ultimately led to the founding of WOMAD (World of Music and Dance – a festival exploring collaborations between western and non-western music) and the establishment of Gabriel's Real World record label.

polyphony'. The fact that Gabriel evokes the sound of bagpipes (along with a reference to African drumming), to create a stirring emotional effect would seem to be a matter of Gabriel (unfamiliar with African instruments which might evoke the desired effect) borrowing from his own culture, his sense of Britishness, to create the effect he wants to evoke for a predominantly British audience. Perhaps in imitating sounds which sound like, but are not, the instruments they mimic, Gabriel adds to the global aesthetic of the song, forging a space which is everywhere yet in a sense nowhere in particular. In defending the use of the bagpipes, Gabriel later (in 1989) noted:

> I've always found that this instrument has something very African about it. I checked up with some musicologists and ... (discovered) that the instrument in fact had an oriental origin and not at all northern. Which gave more reason to my un-Scottish conception of the pipes. (Cited in St Michael 1994: 43)[4]

The specific effect of the bagpipes, however, is to introduce an anthem-like sentiment to the song, heightening the effect of the lyrical message. Despite misgivings about the appropriateness of the instrumentation used (and performance thereof), the drum and bagpipe effects undoubtedly heighten the emotional impact of the song. The significance of the song is further evoked through the dramatic effect of a blaring, heavily distorted electric guitar,[5] the most prominent instrument in the song.

Throughout the song Gabriel's vocal delivery is clear and powerful, underlining the magnitude of the lyrical message, which documents the death in detention of Steve Biko and includes an emotive warning that Biko's death has not silenced resistance to apartheid. The political nature of the lyrics is fairly straightforward, moving from what Peter Hammill (cited in Bright 1988: 133) described as 'the mundane to the absolutely global'. Certainly, an important part of the effectiveness of the lyrics is the way in which they capture the listener's interest through the description of an everyday scene and then gradually move into a general (global) call for action. Gabriel successfully uses this powerful storytelling technique to convey an important message. He draws the listener into the song by beginning with a matter-of-fact account of the day Biko was killed: the time and place, a

---

[4]   In an interesting coincidence, St Andrew's College in Grahamstown has a pipe band, part of the school's Scottish heritage. When the band practices, the sounds of bagpipes become part of the Grahamstown soundscape. Unknowingly, by using the bagpipes, Peter Gabriel stumbled across a musical connection between his song and the city outside of which Biko was arrested and in which he was imprisoned for one night before being sent to neighbouring Port Elizabeth, where he was famously detained in Room 619.

[5]   Although Robert Fripp, Paul Weller and Dave Gregory are also listed as guitarists on the album, in all likelihood the guitar player here is Gabriel's longstanding guitarist, David Rhodes. The album sleeve notes do not specify who plays which instruments on each individual song.

comment on the weather and how it was just a usual day at the office for Biko's interrogators. But the last line seemingly holds a twist: detailing the precise room number. 'Police Room 619' sounds sinister, reminiscent of Room 101 in Orwell's *1984*.

Out of the verse rises the chorus, which reveals the significance of Room 619: Biko has been killed there. The brutality of his death is never openly spelt out, but is implied. The first version of the chorus seems to mourn Biko's death, laments what happened to him. And also explains it. He was killed, because he was Biko – an anti-apartheid activist who stood up to the apartheid state. In Xhosa 'Yihla moja' means 'descending spirit', indicating that although Biko is dead, his spirit is still with the people, and will give them strength in the struggle against apartheid.

There is an interesting shift in the music at this point (the introduction of the bagpipe effect), contributing toward a defiant reading of the second verse onwards. The second verse provides a context for Biko's death, referring to the bloodshed of the repressive regime, in maintaining the supremacy of white South Africa. Biko's death was a consequence of the government's attempt to maintain the hegemony of whiteness. Partly because of the words that preceded it, and although the words remain the same, the chorus which follows seems to move from lament to defiance. Biko has died for a reason, opposing the unjust apartheid state. The third verse shifts the song into a global context and is a clear call for action, indicating that Biko's death is not in vain, given that it is part of a broader movement toward change. Gabriel says it is possible to blow out a candle but not to blow out a fire because 'once the flame begins to catch the wind will blow it higher'. The statement doubles as a truism and also a direct statement directed at the apartheid regime, reminding them that, in the long run, their attempts to smother opposition is futile.

The final chorus, with the same words as before, is clearly defiant, rising out of the symbolic flames of the third verse. It is followed by a break from the verse–chorus–verse–chorus structure. Gabriel offers words of encouragement to anti-apartheid activists and the oppressed in South Africa, which in turn act as an open warning to the apartheid state, that the eyes of the world are now focused on South Africa. The song reaches a climax with the onset of a rousing chorus of male voices, the effect of which is clearly heightened by the drone of bagpipes and the drumming, rather reminiscent of 'Mull of Kintyre' – a group sing-a-long folksong.

Apart from the music itself, Gabriel employs what Roland Barthes (1977: 23) refers to as 'signifying units': recorded effects connoting additional meaning. Barthes uses the term to describe elements within photographs, but in 'Biko' Gabriel incorporates various sounds which can be seen to provide a soundscape, or sonic landscape. For example, the singing of 'Senzenina' ('What have we done?') by mourners at Biko's funeral at the beginning and end of the album version of the song (the 7-and 12-inch single versions of the song begin and end with a recording of the ANC's defiant national anthem, 'Nkosi Sikeleli' ['God Bless Africa']), the primitive-sounding war-cry type voices at the beginning of the song, the voice shouting '*A Luta Continua*, the struggle continues' at the end, and the double drumbeat (which sounds distinctly like gunshots) in the final moment of the song. The gunshots signify repression more generally: they do not relate directly to Biko's death (he was not shot), but they give a strong feeling of the finality, suddenness, aggression and violence of his death. They also sharply cut off the singing of the funeral mourners, indicating the relentlessness of the repressive government. These signifying units are given their meaning by the lyrical framework, yet are intrinsically part of the musical make-up of the song. The lyrics have not merely been added to the music, but once combined with music they have enabled the meaningful use of certain signifying units which otherwise would not have been included.

Individual Experiences of 'Biko' by Peter Gabriel

Having given brief consideration to some aspects of the song and how its different components work together, the focus briefly shifts to three instances in which individuals have been affected by the song. This is useful because it provides an idea as to how the song works on audiences, and is more than simply a reflection of Gabriel's sentiments. Direct quotes are used as 'a powerful way to express experiences, … ideas and emotions' (Coetzee 2003: 7) of subjects. The three quotes below capture the way individuals experienced and reacted to the song in varying contexts. The first account is my own, a reflection on my experience of the song as a white teenage South African male:

> I was a scholar at a well-to-do government high school in the northern suburbs of white Johannesburg in the early 1980s. A friend and I were closely bonded in our obsession with popular music. One of our many schemes for increasing the size of our music collections was to order music from Cob Records in Porthmadog, Wales. We took a catalogue to school and hassled our friends and teachers into ordering imports at lower prices than in the local shops. We placed our orders without regard for import regulations, waiting in anticipation for the albums to arrive in the post …
>
> A turning point came when a university friend asked us to order Peter Gabriel's 3rd album (1980) for him, because it was banned in South Africa and he could not get it in the local shops. I ordered two copies, so as to add one to my collection. I was keen to get a copy for myself as it included 'Games without frontiers' (1980), a song with which I was familiar because it had been played on Capital Radio earlier that year.
>
> The album was banned because of the song 'Biko'. My friend and I knew nothing about Steve Biko, so when the album arrived with our consignment we hurriedly listened to it, wanting to know what the fuss was about. While our

precise reactions are difficult to recall, we were outraged at the banning of what seemed to be a perfectly reasonable song. When given the task of presenting speeches in our English class we decided to jointly present a speech questioning the South African government's approach to the censorship of music. To do so we needed to find out more about Steve Biko. On the advice of our History teacher we searched microfiche records at the *Rand Daily Mail* archives. What we discovered was for me, a challenging revelation: the emotive coverage of the death, by torture, of an innocent man because of his political convictions. Biko had never been found guilty of a crime in a court of law. It suddenly became clear what censorship was about: a government trying to hide things from the public, not for the supposed public good, but for its own manipulative reasons (Drewett 2004: 1–2).

It was at that point that I first became aware of apartheid as a struggle, and it was the first time I articulated my own position within that struggle.

The second account is remarkably similar to my own experience of the song, but comes from the United States. It is a message submitted to the 'What Peter Gabriel's songs mean to us' website. Keith Hartford wrote:

I was only 5 when Steve Biko was murdered. Against the backdrop of more 'famous' killings (John Lennon, Kennedy etc.), I might never have heard of Steven [*sic*] Biko. I remember hearing the song and wondering who this person was. I went to the library, but I couldn't find him in any books. So I asked the librarian who Biko was. She looked at me and saw a 16 year old who should have been out talking to girls and creating a ruckus. Instead I was in strange place asking about a man I never knew from halfway around the world. 'A hero from Africa,' she said. Well, I was entranced. And I was also aware. This is what the song 'Biko' did for me. It helped to open my eyes to something new.

The third account is a well-known case also from the United States, and which is again surprisingly similar in the way the song affected an individual. It is the story of (Little) Steven Van Zandt's experience of the song. In 1980 he was sitting in a cinema waiting for a film to begin when he noticed the music that was playing. This is his account:

The projectionist put this tape in, and it was the most extraordinary thing. I had no idea who it was or what he was singing about, but it was very, very moving. I went upstairs and said to the projectionist, 'What is that?' It turned out to be Peter Gabriel singing 'Biko' and I went out and got it. I got such an emotion from that song I had to find out what it was all about. That's the ultimate musical accomplishment, I guess, to move you to do something. (In Bright 1988: 173)

In a well-documented account, Van Zandt's experience of the song moved him to research the South African situation. He even visited South Africa to find out more.

His political journey was the impetus for the Artists United Against Apartheid Sun City project, which galvanized widespread support for the cultural boycott against South Africa. The Sun City Project, which included a record, video and book, itself was a mobilizing exercise aimed at educating people about apartheid and the cultural boycott. On the album cover Van Zandt said: 'I would like to especially thank Peter Gabriel for the profound inspiration of his song "Biko" which is where my journey to Africa began' (*Sun City* sleeve notes).

The interesting aspect of these accounts is the manner in which the song, simply by being heard, moved individuals to find out more about who Biko was. The combined effect of the music and lyrics as considered earlier was significant in achieving this interest in Biko, yet the lyrics were not so obvious as to make the overall impact of the song immediate. The emotive nature of the song created an interest in Biko which led individuals to explore the song further. In this way the song can be seen to have provided pointers to be explored in order for Gabriel's audience to realize deeper political challenges hidden within the lyrics of the song.

The Apartheid State Censors' Reading of the Song

There is another reading of the song which is important, and which it would be useful to consider, given the contestation of which the song was a part. In September 1980, South African Customs and Excise seized a copy of the 7-inch single and submitted it to the Directorate of Publications, the official apartheid state censor, which banned the single and the album because of the song 'Biko'. The banning was indicative of the way state censors launched attacks on controversial material, policing the boundaries of the dominant discourse. Director of the Publications Appeal Board, Van Rooyen (1987: 3) admitted this much when he suggested that the role of the state censors was to provide 'for a framework within which the arts may be performed'. This constituted the state's duty to maintain 'order in society' (Van Rooyen 1987: 3). Although Van Rooyen's appointment in 1980 signified a more liberal approach to government censorship,[6] 'Biko' by Peter Gabriel was regarded as a severe attack on the apartheid state which could not be allowed into the homes of South Africans. In particular it was to be kept out of the homes of black South Africans, who were regarded as the likely audience of the song.[7] The

---

[6]   By Van Rooyen's own admission (interview with author 1998) in the first year or two in his new position he was too afraid to seriously rock the boat, and only later did he begin to stamp his more 'liberal' authority onto his decision-making.

[7]   Van Rooyen's era included a change in the Publications Act which shifted the focus from the general interests of the public to those of the likely audience of the material in question (for more detailed discussion of this issue, see Van Rooyen 1987; Merrett 1994, Coetzee (1996: 163–84). For a detailed analysis of the process of apartheid music censorship see Drewett (2004: 78–136).

state censors' reading of the song usefully outlines the reasons for perceiving the song as a threat to the apartheid order:

> The song 'Biko' is harmful to the security of the State. The Committee's finding rests on the following considerations: The song is presented – especially concerning the beginning and the end – as typical African music and as a song that will have considerable emotional impact on the average black listener. This song, with high emotional impact, is about Biko, and the following facts regarding him are important: Biko is known throughout South Africa. Biko was the President of the banned Black People's Convention. Biko died in jail and till this day rumours are spread that he was tortured and then killed in jail by the police. Since Biko's death in 1977, people, both overseas and locally, try to celebrate his death as a martyr. Looking at the previous facts, it is obvious that the subject of Biko is a very sensitive issue with great symbolic power for the black people. It is the fire that Biko started that cannot be put out. It is his spirit that has to descend (Yihla Moja), that according to the black man's belief, has to come and help the black man and has to create a condition, for which the eyes of the world are watching. The Committee therefore decided that the record will contribute to a condition that will be harmful to the security of the State.

Clearly the Directorate of Publications was worried about the effect of the song on a black audience, but in addition, as Coetzee (1996: 188) suggests, in such cases it was the censors themselves who were offended, and thus declared publications 'undesirable'. The censors were particularly offended by the information included in the song lyrics and on the sleeve of the 7-inch single release (see page 108). The song was regarded as a threat to the state, and, as composer and singer of the song, Gabriel was perceived as one of those on the outside agitating for insurrection, an agent of change whose song needed to be counteracted in the interest of state security.

There is an interesting convergence between the individual experiences of the song discussed earlier and the apartheid state censors' reading. In all cases the song is regarded as an inspirational protest song, but there is disagreement on the ideological sentiments, indicative of the political contestation of which the song was a part. Significantly, the banning of the song 'restricted' the song to the international arena, where it was performed repeatedly and remained a powerful protest song, but for that reason it was never adopted by the populace as a grassroots-level freedom song, as happened with 'Nkosi Sikeleli'. Consequently, 'Biko' remained an international protest song without a strong presence in South Africa, from which it was prohibited.

Gabriel's Intervention as an Instance of Counter-hegemony

Van Zandt's experience (described on pages 105–6) gives an indication as to the song's journey outwards, to an increasingly large and widespread audience. For whatever reason the song also moved a number of musicians to record covers of it, thereby increasing its coverage, albeit in different forms. Some of the artists to record versions of the song are Robert Wyatt (1984), Patti and The Dep Band (1986), Joan Baez (1987), Simple Minds (1989), Manu Dibango (1994), Ray Wilson (2002) and Paul Simon (2010). Dibango's version features Alex Brown, Peter Gabriel, Ladysmith Black Mambazo, Geoffrey Oryema and Sinéad O'Connor.

The political contestation over the song and what it represented played a central role in how the song worked the way it did, becoming arguably the most significant non-South African anti-apartheid protest song. Indeed, Keyan Tomaselli and Bob Boster (1993: 3) suggest that: 'The roots of incorporation of anti-apartheid messages into pop music can be traced to Peter Gabriel's *Biko* … and the Special AKA's *Free Nelson Mandela*. Both became "cult classics" in America [*sic*],[8] especially *Biko*, which was used by the Amnesty International tours and records, and during Freedomfest[9] itself'. Certainly, a crucial variable in this respect came from the way in which Gabriel framed the song: the political context (explaining who Biko was and how he died, with accompanying photographs) which he provided on the sleeve of the 7-inch and 12-inch single releases of the song,[10] his decision to donate all proceeds from the sale of the single versions (which in the end amounted to over £50,000) to the Black Consciousness Movement (Bright 1988: 174), his challenge to audiences in live performance, his performance of the song at the two Mandela concerts (in 1988 and 1990), and the way Gabriel positioned himself as an advocate of Amnesty's cause. At one stage Gabriel also handed out Amnesty leaflets challenging his audiences to get involved. In the leaflet (cited in Bright 1988: 180–81) he stated that:

> The work I have done with Amnesty is very important to me. I was very moved to meet some of the people that had been rescued from torture and unjust imprisonment, for whom Amnesty had been the only line of hope.

---

[8]   Indicative of the effect of the United States of America's global domination, the authors conflate one country (the USA) with two continents.

[9]   'Freedomfest' was the name the Fox Television Network gave to its five-hour edited televised version of the first Nelson Mandela tribute concert. The concert involved a variety of musicians and was held at London's Wembley Stadium on 11 June 1988 (Tomaselli and Boster 1993: 8).

[10]   Gabriel specifically released the song as a single because he '[w]anted the song to be available to anyone who did not want to spend the money for an album' (Gabriel, 7-inch single sleeve notes 1980).

Although there is still so much that needs changing, there is no doubt that Amnesty, in its twenty-five years, has changed the attitudes of governments on human rights all around the world. Through the simple tools of letter writing and the embarrassment of publicity, Amnesty has been surprisingly effective.

It is part of a process that is making ordinary people aware of the power and responsibility they have in improving our world.

I ask you to get involved.

In this way Gabriel forged a clear link between his music and the politics he believed in, and between himself and the political movements he supported. In a further expression of his political beliefs, Gabriel, together with the Lawyers Committee for Human Rights and the Reebok Human Rights Foundation, also founded the human rights organization *Witness*. Thousands of people around the world were introduced to Biko and the problem of apartheid and political detention and torture through the song and these related activities, and the song moved many South Africans (especially those in exile), reassured by the support it represented.

Certainly Gabriel's decision to reposition himself differently (Hall in Grossberg 1996: 138) is very significant. By drawing on the context of political organization Gabriel fostered a different way of conceiving cultural practice, as a means to taking forward a particular political position. Ron Eyerman and Andrew Jamison (1998: 164) have usefully conceived this repositioning as musicians taking up the role of Antonio Gramsci's (1971) organic intellectuals. As such musicians – whether working in close collaboration with a social movement or not – develop a political awareness which they voice through their music, in the performance of their music.

Eyerman and Jamison (1998: 164–5) correctly note that social movements are the contexts of social change. They argue that musicians acting as 'activist-performers' creatively combine culture and politics to facilitate social change. They argue that within movement space musicians are able to uncover a new dimension to their work and a new identity for themselves and their music. Ultimately, these activist-performers assist in constituting the 'cognitive praxis of social movements' by giving voice to the movement, creating the possibility of transforming the hegemonic culture. Social movements offer musicians opportunities within which to explore counter-hegemonic ideals. Within this context the musician 'can become a political as well as a cultural agent, and thus help shape an emergent cultural formation' (Eyerman and Jamison 1998: 165). Importantly in terms of 'Biko' by Gabriel, the movement context was a means to promote the song, providing a ready audience for the musician's efforts. In return, Gabriel can be seen to have become an ambassador for the anti-apartheid cause, championed by the anti-apartheid movement who used 'Biko' to publicize and promote its struggle against apartheid.

However, it is argued here that Eyerman and Jamison place greater emphasis on musicians' positions within social movements than is often warranted. A freer conceptualization of the musician as agent is needed, one which posits a more flexible understanding of the relationship between musicians and social movements. Importantly, Gabriel's act of repositioning himself to identify with anti-apartheid sentiments was temporary. From the outset Gabriel expressed doubts as to his motives in writing the song. He was not sure whether the song simply reflected his own concerns or was also partly an attempt to establish credibility. Tom Robinson (in Bright 1988: 181) reassured Gabriel, saying that: 'If what is achieved is that attention and money get directed in the right direction, you can be as much a hypocrite as you like, it doesn't matter'. What is clear is that Gabriel was aware that a repositioning had taken place. The song, in other words, was reflective of a particular moment in his life (whatever the intentions), one that was far less typical than the many songs he has written about his own personal issues, for example. It follows, therefore, that the different instances in which Gabriel aligned himself with the anti-apartheid struggle did not constitute membership of or strict allegiance to the anti-apartheid movement. To view Gabriel in this way would romanticize, essentialize or exalt the part he played in anti-apartheid struggle. Gabriel's political songs and his involvement in political campaigns do not reduce him to one-dimensional political being, acting as an organic movement intellectual or artist. Rather, his political actions are moments in which his aesthetic reflections combine with political and social convictions to create instances of counter-hegemony. In this moment, the hegemonic status of the values of the apartheid state was being challenged.

The strength of a social movement is in drawing together various strands of resistance which otherwise would remain isolated. Gabriel's alignment with the anti-apartheid and Amnesty movements in this way played an important part in the widespread impact of the song as a global freedom song. In addition, the live version of the song was re-released as a single to promote Richard Attenborough's film *Cry Freedom*. Although the song was not part of the official soundtrack, the video for the single included excerpts from the film. Significantly, the song indeed became a sort of soundtrack to Biko's life, informing people's collective memory. Nick Hornby (2003: 131), for example, relates how Biko became an integral part of Britain's liberal-left political landscape of the early 1980s because of Gabriel's song. Likewise, in South Africa, more than 30 years after Biko's death, the song was looped in the background to an exhibition on the life and death of Steve Biko at the Apartheid Museum in Johannesburg. As reporter Lucille Davie (2008) noted, 'the constant refrain of Peter Gabriel's song, simply entitled Biko, first released in 1980, echoes hauntingly around the museum'. A similar example is found in one of the chapters in the most comprehensive book yet published on the legacy of Steve Biko, edited by Barney Pityana and others (*Bounds of Possibility* 1991). In a chapter on Biko's life Lindy Wilson (1991: 15) begins with the opening verse of Gabriel's song, and uses it to introduce the chapter. In this way the song indeed forms a soundtrack to Biko's life and what he stood for. It would seem that it is the ordinary and personal nature of the song which allows people to relate to it in such a powerful manner. Although the lyrics mobilize they do not so through the use of straightforward slogans. Certainly, audiences are able to relate to the lyrics because they are simple and direct, but the song also challenges individuals on a personal level, pointing toward a political commitment to the injustices it encapsulates. In this sense the song is able to intersect with the political consciences of individual audience members in a way which, while on some levels similar, is nevertheless distinct from 'collective identity formation' (Eyerman and Jamison 1998). The latter term refers to an identity formation developed in a collective context, such as at a concert or political rally. It is quite likely that Gabriel's live performances of 'Biko' have this effect on some audience members, yet, as has been documented in this chapter, the song is also clearly able to communicate with individual audience members whatever their listening context. This makes the song a powerful political conduit.

Conclusion

This chapter has involved an attempt to make sense of the challenge of 'Biko' by Peter Gabriel. The song has achieved more than simply reflect Gabriel's thoughts or feelings: it has brought about an awareness of Biko's life, the South African situation and the plight of prisoners of conscience the world over, and it has challenged people and ultimately changed their lives. The simultaneously anthem-like and penetrating nature of the song, particularly as sung by Gabriel, was crucial to the song's impact. The effects were heightened by the context of extreme injustice and oppression related in the song's lyrics, yet with a strong sense of defiance and promise in the future. The fact that the song was written and performed within a political terrain of fierce contest strengthened its impact even further. It is argued that 'Biko' by Peter Gabriel is not simply a political rally song with an ability to facilitate 'collective identity formation' (Eyerman and Jamison 1998) but a protest song able to intersect with the political consciences of individual audience members, emotionally and intellectually challenging individuals' understandings of the world.

Chapter 8

Musical Markers as Catalysts in Social Revolutions: The Case of Gabriel's 'Biko'

Ingrid Bianca Byerly

Introduction

The South African transition from apartheid to democracy stands as an unprecedented example of relentless and ingenious strategies toward a peaceful resolution in the face of political crisis and social upheaval. From the initially thwarted attempts at armed struggle to rectify the injustices of an oppressive political system, to the gradual yet concerted shift toward peaceful negotiations between dissenting parties within that system, the process of resistance and protest moved increasingly creatively toward artistic endeavours of protest, to result in the democratic elections that heralded the end of apartheid. The transformation has since been widely documented from innumerable perspectives, both theoretical and practical, and, gradually, increasing recognition has been given to the seminal role that music and musicians played in the struggle (Kivnick 1990; Smit 1992; Byerly 1998; Tenaille 2002; Ansell 2004; Grundlingh 2004; Laubscher 2005; Hopkins 2006). This case study builds on two previous analyses[1] of the ingenious musical strategies that served as catalysts in the struggle toward conflict resolution. The first (Byerly 1998) introduced the concept of the *music indaba*, presenting the idea of the *indaba*[2] – an event or meeting place where consensus is met – as the approach musicians took, through both negotiation and confrontation, toward forging an increasingly polyphonic soundscape out of historically detached musical genres. This approach was both mimetic and prophetic of developments in the wider social and political landscape. The second (Byerly 2008) presents a model of the 'anatomy of a music revolution' as a theoretical template exploring the structure of musical movements that turn the tide of history. The structure revealed the primary waves of resistance and protest which each contain secondary currents of

---

[1]   This work serves as a focused case study within a wider analysis of the music revolution in South Africa: building on two previous publications: 'Mirror, Mediator and Prophet' in *Ethnomusicology* (Byerly 1998), and 'Decomposing Apartheid' in *Composing Apartheid* (Byerly 2008).

[2]   The word *indaba* can be found in the Nguni languages, which include Zulu and Xhosa. It alludes to both a tangible 'conference' event, and a more metaphorical space within which agreement is forged.

contention and conciliation, from a revolution to its intended resolution. Within this theoretical framework, the persistent contributions of musicians and their musical ingenuity reveal the appearance, and importance, of musical markers as catalysts in both reflecting and furthering the cause of a revolutionary movement. Musical markers, being songs or musical pieces that either observe or influence turning points in social histories, expose the depth and complexity of conflict, and define seminal moments in political transitions. In the anti-apartheid struggle, diverse social arenas produced musical catalysts that could inform and unite dissidents in the movement, while transforming visions of the future.

In this analysis we attempt to explore how a song written by a foreigner to South Africa managed to become a seminal musical marker in the anti-apartheid movement, and elevate the composer to the status of a primary anti-apartheid dissident within the struggle. We explore how the song was situated (in terms of both reflection and causality) within the grander scheme of musical protest and social politics, to what extent it both revealed and mobilized the resistance movement within the country, how it achieved its goals musically, lyrically and aesthetically, and what the interplays and differences were between its success both internally (nationally) and externally (internationally).

In 1980, a song by the British rock musician Peter Gabriel simply entitled 'Biko' appeared, controversially, on the South African music scene. The details surrounding Steve Biko's death, and the political significance of the event, have been discussed by the South African sociologist Michael Drewett in the previous chapter. Importantly, Drewett reveals two seminal points: first, the process by which Biko became 'the first truly international anti-apartheid martyr', and, second, the route the song took to bring attention to the martyr, serving a function that extended far beyond the boundaries of South African dissent. Many South Africans, and most foreigners, had never heard of Stephen Biko until his death, and if there had been any ignorance or apathy on the part of the international community toward apartheid until then, it could be argued that the song 'Biko' both heralded and ensured that 'the eyes of the world are watching now'. The song itself was hauntingly powerful, with a hypnotic drumbeat thundering beneath commanding guitar, lyrical bagpipe dirges and the intense eulogy of Gabriel's voice. It triggered a political awakening and turning point that caused many to listen to music with different ears: scrutinizing both the sound and sentiment of song. Drewett himself described his first encounter with the song as a 'challenging revelation', not unlike the description he gives of Steven van Zandt's reaction: that the ultimate accomplishment in music is 'to move one to do something' (Bright 1988: 173). It moved many not only to find out more about the man behind the song, but also to search for more music that spoke to the political and social realities of apartheid South Africa.[3]

---

[3]   Examples of this can be found in the impact of the song on the author (a South African student at the University of Pretoria at the time) and an American student attending Duke University at the time. For the South African student, it was the first protest song that

To those unfamiliar with Biko the political activist, the lyrical content of the song was at the time both cryptic and revealing, alluding to an intellectual freedom fighter[4] who died suspiciously in detention for his cause. Biko achieved his status as a martyr when a Johannesburg journalist[5] exposed the facts surrounding his death. While the story became prominent news to politically involved South Africans (primarily the disenfranchised who considered Biko their leader),[6] and to the select segment of the international community who read publications such as the *New York Times* and the *Washington Post* (Drewett 2007: 40), the wider populace, both within and outside South Africa, were largely unaware of Biko's struggle and death. But Gabriel's offering in song soon moved from a heartfelt tribute to an international 'fanfare for the common man', and introduced Biko to a far more general public than may have been envisioned. Gabriel had managed, through song, to convey what Biko himself, as a banned individual,[7] had not been allowed to express in speech:[8] it was time to end apartheid.

---

caused her to be 'moved to do something' – in this case learn more about the politics behind the music. For the American student, the song offered a compelling message to foreigners that the anti-apartheid movement in South Africa 'was gaining unstoppable momentum', especially through the provocative lyrics 'you can blow out a candle, but you can't blow out a fire'. It is notable that it would be Gabriel, a musician on a third continent, who would bring both the native (as insider) and the foreigner (as outsider) to pay closer attention to the meaning behind the music.

[4]   Biko was trained in medicine, and followed the teachings of Fanon and Aimé.

[5]   Helen Zille of the *Rand Daily Mail* was the first to uncover the truth regarding Biko's death, and journalist Donald Woods was to heighten awareness of the brutality of his murder during his exile abroad in Britain, a process later documented in the motion picture *Cry Freedom*.

[6]   Mandela had long been imprisoned, and Biko had in 1972 been elected honorary president of the Black People's Convention, the flagship of the Black Consciousness Movement in South Africa.

[7]   'Banning' individuals was initially authorized in the Suppression of Communism Act of 1950. 'Banned' individuals were confined to their homes, and could not speak to more than one person (besides family) at a time, were not to be quoted in any publication, were prevented from speaking publicly, and essentially became social 'non-entities'.

[8]   Biko had had two attempts to silence him. The first was when he was banned in March 1973 in an attempt to suppress his ideas and influence. The second was following his arrest in August 1977, after which he was tortured in detention, his injuries leading to his death on 12 September.

Bi-directional Causality: The Place of 'Biko' in the Music *Indaba*

The song 'Biko' became a musical marker that both revealed the tireless political struggles of some (in the wake of government intrigue), and punctuated the political awakening of others (at the mercy of censorship). Within the confines of a segregated South African society, the banned song soon found a receptive and captivated audience among those that were able to hear it, or to own a copy of it. This was the case not only in the black community (as feared by the censor board), but also in the white community (as achieved by Gabriel himself). The success of the song was not merely because of the provocative subject and musical aesthetic, but, more ironically, because its status as a banned song initiated a wave of extensive bootlegging[9] that possibly ensured far more widespread distribution than if it had merely been another track on an open, uncensored music market. The influence and impact of 'Biko' in receptive circles was immediate and profound, and the reasons for this are salient and important to understanding the interplay between music and society in revolutionary contexts in general, and between protest and censorship in South Africa at the time of the anti-apartheid struggle in particular.

The all-important question of causality is central to this analysis. What exactly is the role of music in any struggle, and how powerful is it within any given political context? Does is reflect change, or does it cause change? Can a piece of music fundamentally redirect the course of history, or does music merely echo its complex influences? David Coplan rightly claims, in an earlier reference to the history of South African musical innovation, that 'new forms arose from processes within the total field of relations of power and production within the South African social formation' (Coplan 1982: 358). To what extent could one claim, in reverse, that new processes also arose from music within the total field of relations between power and production? Could one conceive that processes of mobilization cause artistic innovation while innovation simultaneously causes social change? It cannot be otherwise. The recognition of bi-directional interplays between seminal social events and innovative musical markers is essential for an understanding of music in relation to society, as such an acknowledgement of dual causality reveals both the complexity and the depth of underlying socio-cultural realities. While semiotic mediations in mental processes have an effect on individual understandings, so too does music function as a semiotic mediator in both the expression and development of social structures. The cultural and symbolic implications of the appropriation of language as power in political struggles have been undeniable, particularly in the colonial experience (Comaroff and Comaroff 1991). Similarly, the implications of

---

[9]   Banned music, once in possession, was often 'bootlegged' (copied privately and illegally) so that individuals could share their recordings through the re-taping and pirating of numerous copies for personal distribution. Those in the anti-apartheid struggle viewed bootlegging as an added act of defiance against the official machinations of the government, and a subcultural contribution to the struggle.

the appropriation of belief systems and resistance through art forms shed further light on the use of such cultural weapons in political struggles (Fanon 1968). Music manages to express dynamic social processes through ever-changing forms, while seminal musical markers constantly influence political ideologies. The subtle and intricate processes that produce both discord and harmony profoundly affect both the individual within society and the society of individuals; just as the fragile and complex processes that define a culture profoundly affect the artistic creations of that culture. The relationships between society and art, history and sound, then, must be recognized as one of mutual agency. Of course all societies lack eternal coherency and stability, and transformation is inevitably brought on by what Durkheim would present as the 'deviants' within a seemingly stable society (the 'superorganic'), to unsettle the equilibrium and mobilize change (Durkheim 1984). It is within this constant flux between harmony and discord, constancy and innovation, that the active environment containing enterprising individuals operates bi-directionally with the mediums they have at their disposal; the one feeding off the other as the ever-spiraling consequences of the individual creative mind affects the resourceful society, and that creative society produces the innovative works of art. In turn, these further influence the individual creative mind. And so the circle is unbroken, with no ever-reigning, primary agent, but rather an eternal spiral: Schleiermacher's proverbial 'hermeneutic circle', where both context and interpretation are key to comprehension, and institutions make way for innovation, while innovation creates new institutions (Bowie 1998).

Music further expects a series of interpretive moves on the part of the listener, each interpretation being the result of a unique set of accumulated sociopolitical and cultural experiences, as described in Bourdieu's (1977) notion of 'habitus'. Musicians (both performers and their audience) attach a unique meaning to every phrase of music, and in so doing become mediators of the music. Between variation in performances, and distinctions between receptions, there lies personal mediation which, in fact, prevents acts of playing or listening from being identical. The importance of the influence of music in South Africa lies in the fact that it is representative of people's individual and shared experiences. As such, it can strike similar chords with people from vastly different backgrounds, while also striking different chords with people from very similar backgrounds. Just as it is not necessary to be an Austrian prodigy to understand Mozart, or an eccentric Catalonian to value Dalí, so too it is not necessary to be an exiled Cape Townian to appreciate Dollar Brand, or a persecuted rocker to identify with Roger Lucey. People often, however, affectively react to certain music in extremely different ways. Theresa falls in love to the accompaniment of Beethoven in *The Unbearable Lightness of Being*, while Alex is driven to commit mayhem while listening to Beethoven in Burgess's *Clockwork Orange*. Hitler and Lévi-Strauss both considered Wagner their favourite composer, and they came to this preference through very different lives. This notion is further explored in the suggestion that 'music is a medium through which individuals' brains are coupled together in shared activity' (Benzon 2001: 23), even if those individuals are not coupled in the same social history.

Music is not a static entity, but can be transformed to constantly reflect its social milieus. In all its forms (as Ballantine has pointed out in relation to the jazzing subculture), music 'has a history of openness to change and to creative engagement with other styles but also of fierce battles around such issues; *it has a history shaped by, but also shaping itself in resistance to, the fundamental social and political stakes of a deeply repressive and exploitive social order*' (Ballantine 1993: 45).[10] Music itself, however, can probably not be considered a sole agent of change. A uni-directional proposition of this nature would substantiate Kingsbury's (1988) critique of lending it almost anthropomorphic characteristics, as though it can inherently be imbued with 'intention' and 'character' through the complex configuration of its attributes, rather than the explicit or implicit motive of the composer or the performer. Music, rather, causes both effects and affect, while simultaneously allowing individuals and societies to express issues of effect and affect. Frith says it best when he suggests that 'Music constructs our sense of identity through the experiences it offers of the body, time, and sociability, experiences which enable us to place ourselves in imaginative cultural narratives. Such a fusion of imaginative fantasy and bodily practice marks as well the integration of aesthetics and ethics' (Frith 1996: 275). It is this fusion of 'imaginative fantasy' with aesthetics and ethics that drives the music of social revolutions, none more so than the songs of the music *indaba* in the anti-apartheid movement, and few examples are more idiosyncratic and influential in both origin and style than Gabriel's 'Biko'.

Components of a Social Revolution

With the bi-directional nature of agency in mind, we move to the issue of social movements, which has become a prominent field of research, especially with a view to finding models of effective resistance movements resulting in successful dissent (Snow and Oliver 1994; Tarrow 1994; Balliger 1995; Meyer and Staggenborg 1996). The intricacy of the music *indaba* in the anti-apartheid struggle revealed six salient components of a successful revolutionary movement toward democracy. First, resistance and protest happen in waves, and every time 'official' forces suppress a wave of resistance, a counter-movement in the form of a stronger wave of 'unofficial' subcultures rises up to repress the contestation. Initially, as Hebdige (1979) suggests, these subcultures are simultaneously disregarded (as innocuous), feared (as sinister) and ridiculed (as meaningless), until their power and significance are recognized. Second, dissent does not come only from a single sector of the community, such as the disenfranchised (in which case the result would merely be an overthrow of government). Rather, it adheres to the same rules of social diffusion

---

[10]   Emphasis added.

as any social movement, as described by Strang and Soule (1998) and Myers (2000), and experiences eventual contestation from both the powerless and the powerful (in which case the result is consensual, and thereby democratic, political transition). Third, as protest spreads, dissenting voices become reliant on each other's efforts, existing not as insular 'pockets' of dissent, but rather as increasingly connected, interdependent parts or 'dynamic interactions' (Koopmans 2004: 21) within an expanding revolutionary whole. Fourth, as a result of the vying players in the field of protest, the process of a transition inevitably contains constant interplays between contentious or conciliatory commentary leading to either maintenance of the *status quo* or a move away from it, until the balance hangs in favour of the latter. To that end, the fifth component is that a 'tipping point' (a transformational influence which thaws frozen ideologies, inspires moments of truth, or instills changes of heart) must be reached. At this moment, individuals previously loyal or connected to the governing power, whether in service or principles, break rank and join the protest movement themselves, essentially strengthening the contestation against their former ideological partners.[11] Finally, perseverance reveals dissenting parties' awareness of a constantly changing political arena through the duration of a revolution, so that incidences of breakdown, or the loss of momentum toward the shared goal, serve not as harbingers of failure, but as lessons toward a revision of tactics that would lead to eventual victory.

The music *indaba* of the anti-apartheid movement adhered to all six components of a successful democratic revolution. It consisted of two primary waves: the first of resistance and the second of protest. Each wave further contained secondary currents of contention. The former contained an initial current consisting almost entirely of the disenfranchised community, followed by one that was joined by the empowered elite who already disagreed with apartheid. The latter contained not only those in the earlier wave, but, following the crucial 'tipping point', also the critical defection of those previously affiliated with the governing party to the 'opposite' side. It is, of course, subject to opinion which musical markers most profoundly punctuated the basins and crests of the protest waves, but there is strong consensus on a few songs that served as catalysts – either for separate groups, or for more inclusive sectors of the society. Strikes Vilakazi's 'Meadowlands' (1956), and Basil Coetzee and Dollar Brand's 'Mannenburg'[12] (1974) both lamented the hardships and forced removals between the 1950s and 1960s, and the latter piece enjoyed a solid revival, of near anthemic proportions, in the mid-1980s at the height of the anti-apartheid movement. By the time of the 'Mannenburg' revival, its popularity had spread from a predominantly black

---

[11]   A pertinent and extreme example of this was that of Paul Erasmus, a South African security-branch policeman assigned to end Roger Lucey's career, who eventually became an ardent fan and supporter of Lucey's music. (See the video *Stopping the Music* 2002, and Drewett 2005).

[12]   Dollar Brand (Abdullah Ibrahim) co-wrote 'Mannenburg' with saxophonist Basil Coetzee.

audience to a more inclusive one, reflective of a growing trend in both music and society at the time. The unanticipated appearance of Gabriel's 'Biko' from outside the country's borders in 1980 coincided, interestingly, with an unexpected turn in the music of the Afrikaans community. Koos du Plessis' 'Kinders van die Wind' (1979) led the way to a new direction in Afrikaans music, springboarding the introspective songs of the *Musiek en Liriek* era. While not politically revolutionary, the songs of the era provided the first challenge for Afrikaners to re-evaluate their history and identity: a crucial step toward also reassessing their role in the future of apartheid. With 'Biko' appearing from beyond the borders, and 'Kinders' from within the stronghold of the empowered Afrikaans community, the die was cast, and introspections and challenges were no longer the lone domain of the disenfranchised or the small anti-apartheid group of white 'liberals'. Reflective confrontations and political protest had diffused effectively to gradually include an increasing number of previously stalwart apartheid ideologues and the international community. 'Biko', in particular, had burst open the seams of insular protest by coming from a respected foreign source, leading the way to include an international outcry that assisted in bringing the resistance movement of the music *indaba* to its peak, and leading to seminal turning points in the revolution. It could be argued that Johnny Clegg and Sipho Mchunu's trailblazing collaboration in Juluka (1976–86), or the appearance of Ladysmith Black Mambazo on Paul Simon's *Graceland* album (1986) and concert (1987) were seminal turning points, each bringing heightened attention to a political crisis and social inequities, while issuing in new awareness of the potential of musical and social fusions. But the final tipping point, or the 'doodskoot' (death-shot) for apartheid was in the markers that finally turned the tide, and caused the majority of young Afrikaners to break rank and join the resistance movement: musical catalysts such as the critical revue *Piekniek by Dingaan* (1988), the contentious *Voëlvry* tour across campuses (1989), and the controversial Kerkorrel album *Eet Kreef* (1989).

The trend at the time of these dramatic 'theatre-pieces' was more to ridicule the status quo (including their own history and identity) than to consciously mobilize political revolution. As a result, the transformational effects of their art on society came as an unexpected surprise to the maverick leaders in the *beweging* (movement). Kerkorrel himself claimed:

> We never really set out to end apartheid through music. We were arrogant, but not that arrogant. We were mostly just angry. But also having a lot of fun. Really, we were trying to expose the craziness of the world our parents had created for us, and somehow it had this enormous effect. People took us far more seriously than we took ourselves.[13]

---

[13]   Author's interview with Ralph Rabie, also known as Johannes Kerkorrel. (Personal communication with author: Hard Rock Café, Cape Town, 4 January 1996.)

Each of these musical ventures, however, was responsible not only for breaking the seal between the powerful and the powerless, but especially for eroding the cohesion of the elite, and in so doing weakening the stronghold of the ruling party. By the time the elections took place, and the suppressed[14] anthem 'Nkosi Sikele iAfrika' (God Bless Africa) became the new national anthem in a new South Africa of 1994, the music *indaba* had reached its goal (Figure 8.1). Consensus had finally ushered in a new democracy, with Nelson Mandela at the helm.

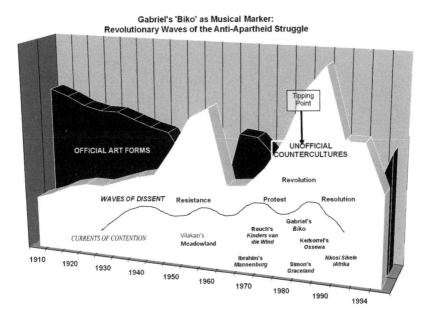

Figure 8.1   Diagrammatical representation of the music *Indaba*. Adapted from an earlier version of the diagrammatical representation of revolutionary waves in Byerly (2008)

---

14   Unlike other music considered potentially dangerous to the State during the resistance, 'Nkosi Sikele iAfrika' was not banned, but rather restricted in performance. It was not illegal to sing it, own a copy of it or to sell a copy of it. According to the SABC censor, Cecile Pracher, it was permissible to play it, as a hymn, on the black radio stations of the SABC, but it was forbidden to be broadcast on English and Afrikaans radio. (Unpublished interview with Michael Drewett, September 2000. See also *Rand Daily Mail*, 5 February 1985).

Gabriel the Outsider Becomes Gabriel the Insider

'Biko' is an example of the right song written at the right time by the right person: the coming together of a prolific, socially conscious musician and a fertile, socially distressed circumstance that resulted in an outcome far surpassing even the loftiest goals of those involved. Within the waves of dissent in South Africa, 'Biko' was the song that met a shallow shore – and caused both the breaking of a wave, but also the momentum to create another. While indigenous protest was largely restricted to local audiences,[15] 'Biko' was seen as the single most influential 'global' representative of anti-apartheid musical initiatives in the resistance movement, and it heralded not only a new fervour in international involvement in the struggle, but also the beginning of Gabriel's deep involvement in issues of worldwide human rights. Gabriel expressed outrage 'that people could not only suffer, but that their stories could be really effectively denied, buried and forgotten'[16] and wrote 'Biko' to illuminate a single hidden case of torture as representative of more numerous incidents globally. His interest in both visual and auditory expressions and revelations of injustices were to become expanded, and well documented, and just as the song 'Biko' inspired South Africans to 'hear it, fight it, change it', Gabriel's later project *Witness* encouraged people to video-document cases of human rights abuses through the motto 'see it, film it, change it'. Gabriel's deep commitment to global human-rights issues through political activism, especially through the arts, have since resulted in political awakenings far wider than the initial intentions of his writing of 'Biko'.

The extent of Gabriel's success with the song, and his appeal as a figure in the struggle, could be attributed to numerous factors, mostly related to his unique persona as an already-established, respected and eccentric musician. It was not, after all, as if the murder of Biko had not been dealt with in song before.[17] But in South Africa, being recorded was easier than being heard.[18]

---

[15]   Although exiles such as Miriam Makeba and Hugh Masekela reached many audiences abroad, it is argued, controversially, that their influence was not as substantial within the confines of South Africa itself during apartheid itself. This contentious stance was discussed between Senegalese host Bouna Ndiaye and Masekela himself on Ndiaye's radio show *Bonjour Afrika* on WNCU 90.7 in the United States on 16 April 2006.

[16]   Recorded in the American PBS (Public Broadcasting Service) newsletter NOW, referring to David Brancaccio's interview on the radio show 'In Your Eyes', 21 April 2006, Washington, DC.

[17]   In 1978 and 1979, two songs had focused on the tragedy: Zukie's 'Tribute to Steve Biko' and Steel Pulse's 'Biko's Kindred Lament'. When the ever-persecuted Roger Lucey wrote 'Thabane' (1979) with allusion to Biko, the song was as stillborn as the rest of his banned work.

[18]   3rd Ear Music (which recorded Lucey's albums) and Shifty Records (which recorded artists such as James Phillips and many of the artists in the *Afrikaans Alternatiewe Beweging*) were two of the most maverick small independent record companies that specialized in recording and releasing protest music of the era, much of which was refused

Peter Gabriel was different for two reasons. First, he held the rank of the foreign 'untouchable', a unique position not lost on his audience. In the wake of ruthless suppression of dissent within the country, as well as South Africans' fascination with the outside world, Gabriel became the outsider speaking for the insider, an informed voice that, when it came to international exposure, was beyond the reach of the South African government, but who had the power to be heard by millions globally. By the same token, he quickly became seen as an insider speaking for the outsider too, maximizing his credibility and influence. Through this unusual double role, he could transfer his privileged status to expose injustices, and speak for the disenfranchised. Interestingly, this role reversal reflected on the South African society he was targeting too: the manner in which the lyrics both supported and chastised various sectors of the community intentionally forced breaches and alienations, and, in doing so, insiders (those being rebuked) became outsiders (by being disaffected), and outsiders (the disenfranchised) became insiders (by being embraced in their cause). This shift in voice is in keeping with Gabriel's fascination with belonging, identity and representation – of seeing the shifting self engage with the dynamic 'other', trying to identify the small within the large, attempting to situate the local in relation to the global. He attempted to find a balance, and recognize interplay between self-analysis on the one hand and social analysis on the other. The tactic is further substantiated when Gabriel the outsider becomes a bona fide insider the moment his song does, in fact, get banned. Its outlawed status only strengthened its appeal and influence through the very cultural capital it gained in the criminalizing process. And when Gabriel sang 'The eyes of the world are watching now', he meant just that. The song became both initiator, and proof, of pledged vigilance. It both offered and revealed international support. It was, in fact, both a threat (to those in power) and a promise (to the disempowered), reassuring some South Africans that they were being watched critically, and others that they were being watched over. The double meanings and bi-directional movement that the song brought to the *indaba* were significant because protest had reached the critical point of simultaneously not only rising up from inside, but also bearing down from outside. Those in favour of apartheid were not only having to ward off contestation from within – they were being surrounded. The strength of this groundswell meeting external forces in the middle was destined to result in optimal impact, and provide the momentum that, together with a growing groundswell of protest music within the confines of the country, spurred the final wave of dissent in the demise of apartheid.

Gabriel was different for a second reason: his credibility was enhanced by an intriguing move from renowned eccentric, both theatrically and musically (in his earlier stage work with Genesis), to serious spokesperson, both lyrically and artistically (when he embarked on his solo career). Having earlier ensured a fascination for his persona, and a respect for his creativity, his status allowed him

---

airplay by the South African Broadcasting Corporation (SABC), and some of which was banned by the Directorate of Publications.

an interesting freedom, not only in who he could be as a solo musician but also in what he could express as an independent writer. His reputation as both an exuberant individual of a certain 'calculated madness' in the past, and a sensitive man on a 'concerted mission' in the present was solidly cemented with the commencement of his more pensive solo works. From the autobiographical 'Solsbury Hill' (1977) and reflective 'Excuse Me' on his first solo album (*Peter Gabriel 1*), to the darker introspections on fear in 'Mother of Violence' or 'Here Comes the Flood' on the second (*Peter Gabriel 2*), Gabriel had established his place as both respected entertainer and thoughtful realist. The move to compassionate activist, in writing 'Biko' on the third solo album (*Peter Gabriel 3*) was, then, not so much a giant leap, as a fitting stride.

He found himself, in fact, in good company as the archetypal character who moved from playing the 'calculated clown' to the 'compassionate critic' in order to be heard. Many dissenting musicians, both powerful and disenfranchised, have played what Volkov (1979) calls the 'yurodivy', or the proverbial 'holy fool'.[19] Volkov stated that:

> The yurodivy has the gift to see and hear what others know nothing about. But he tells the world about his insights in an intentionally paradoxical way, in code. He plays the fool, while actually being a persistent exposer of evil and injustice. The yurodivy is an anarchist and individualist, who in his public role breaks the commonly held 'moral' laws of behavior and flouts conventions. But he sets strict limitations, rules, and taboos for himself. (Volkov 1979: 36)

Through the ingenious employment of art and intellect, the holy fool manages not only to expose, but also to outwit the authorities in a censored environment.[20] He

---

[19]   In his controversial work *Testimony*, Volkov names the Russian composer Shostakovitch a 'yurodivy', or 'holy fool', as his music was claimed to intentionally reveal knowledge, insights and strategic creativity to outwit Stalinist critique. Although *Testimony* has widely been critiqued as a fraudulent document (and not, as Volkov's claims, the result of extensive interviews with the composer over a period of nine years), the archetypal model of the *yurodivy* is a valid, useful and relevant one in the description of certain idiosyncratic dissenting individuals in revolutionary movements. While the controversy surrounding the legitimacy of Volkov's testimony persists, his definition of the holy fool remains useful, as it encapsulates the attributes of both the 'foolish' literary figures (whose observations in sober moment offer insights often more moving and revelatory than their 'serious' social counterparts), as well as many of the eccentric dissidents of the music *indaba* (whose music in lucid times offers revelations often more touching and topical than their 'solemn' musical colleagues). Gabriel is a sobering example of such a figure, as his earlier eccentricity allowed him to risk things other musicians could not, moving from the early guise of the astute yet unconventional 'holy fool' to a darker, more socially conscious commentator who has insights that few others have.

[20]   In the apartheid era, singers like Dolly Rathebe and Thandi Klaasen, for example, managed numerous performance antics, and avoided many a scrape with the law through

becomes an integral part of the subculture that is often misjudged as containing merely outrageous (and therefore ostensibly innocuous) dissent, as Hebdige (1979) suggests, yet this seemingly harmless 'lunatic fringe'[21] achieves a great deal in its quests. This cunning role has long been regarded with respect, since the clowns, tricksters and court jesters in literature often presented the voice of reason and insight within social commentary while counterfeiting folly in times of turmoil. Shakespearean characters like Yorick in *Hamlet*, Feste in *Twelfth Night* and Touchstone in *As You Like It* all made observations that were perceptive and revealing, while camouflaged in the character of the village idiot. Many sombre soliloquies by such characters – most memorably that of Falstaff in *Henry IV* – turned out to be heartbreakingly serious in the face of their early folly. This trend could be seen as reminiscent of the almost-absurd seriousness with which a desperate or angst-ridden ballad or love song is taken when sung by a proverbial 'bad boy' in rock. Under the circumstances within which Gabriel wrote 'Biko', then, his appearance moved from the unconventional player to insightful commentator, and when he turned up in sober, conventional (some would say conservative) guise to reveal critical social truths, his history as a notorious eccentric lent a certain type of cultural capital within the framework of this artistic convention.

Biko: The Music Behind the Man

The innumerable components fashioning any musical piece make it, in sheer volume and variability, the consummate site to express defiance and protest. The intricacy of melodic configurations, harmonic textures, rhythmic variation, instrumental interplays and lyrical options (especially access to code-switching between languages and musical styles) allows a musician to dare, and dodge, within the treacherous confines of a revolution within a suppressed society. Music could echo social tensions and suggest conflict resolutions in song, while the critical presentations of irony and humour could further expand the boundaries of meaning. And while ingenious musical techniques were increasingly used to outwit censors, it became further known that banned songs possessed a unique value, and as such became sought-after commodities.

Musically, and lyrically, Gabriel's 'Biko' operated influentially on a number of levels. The opening beats are reminiscent of a conventional drumcall where, as Meki Nzewi describes it, 'a particular drum that a people identify by sound or location, is used to summon members of a community to a particular form

---

deliberately foolish or comical play-acting, and light-hearted (pretence at) subservience or deference to authorities. See also Drewett 2002.

[21]   'The Lunatic Fringe' was the term given by Des Lindberg, an anti-apartheid folk musician, to those who managed to outwit the censors through their consciously foolish antics during the 1960s and 70s in apartheid South Africa. (Personal communication with author, July 1994.)

Example 8.1   Syncopated opening drumbeat: the call to arms

of important gathering or event'.[22] The hypnotic throb of a syncopated opening rhythmic pattern (Example 8.1), created through the heavily gated reverb of the tom drum, is mimetic of the traditional African 'speaking drum', which relates messages between individuals and groups (Nzewi 2001). The slow syncopation and increasing volume creates a tension, powerfully suggestive of things to come.

It was this aesthetic that was to alarm the censors, who quickly identified the song as an attempt to connect with the disenfranchised black community, and so potentially be a call to arms, and a cause of uprising.[23] What they did not anticipate was the extent to which the members of the white community who did manage to gain access to it (whether through determined bootlegs or more serendipitous events[24]) would embrace it as well, especially once it had been endowed with the mystique of being banned. But the genius of Gabriel's composition lay in the very nature of its inclusive music aesthetic. From the lone drum, the beat is gradually layered in texture by the addition of a powerfully sustained electric guitar pedaltone drone, first on the tonic, and then distorting around the tonic chord.

Lyrically, the song moves from a sinister narrative, in third-person retrospective, recalling to a vivid, symbolic first-person lament describing the hauntingly disturbing consequences of Biko's death on both personal and national levels. The finality of the fate of Biko (the man) is stressed in the distraught calling out of his name in the chorus. Gabriel makes a semantically and musically interesting move at this point, repeating the call on a syncopated beat, to slide the unexpected intonation of his name (caused by a shift in the accent to the first syllable) to a fluid repeat morphing into the word 'because' … because Biko *the man is dead* (Example 8.2).

---

[22]   Nzewi adds that 'For some types of events or gatherings cognitive members of a community track the beginning and progress of the event that is transpiring by interpreting the event-music messages or sections. Drum themes intended and communicated as signs or formulaic language denote different events or purposes'. (Personal communication with author, March 2008.)

[23]   This trend was a common pattern of action taken by censors, according to Ilse Assman, archivist with the South African Broadcasting Corporation (SABC). (Interview with author, SABC archives, Aukland Park SABC Studio, 17 January 1995.)

[24]   An example of this was when 'Biko', although banned at the time, was featured on the television show *Miami Vice* during a car-chase scene (in the episode entitled 'Evan'). The event serendipitously ensured its receiving prime-time exposure, undetected by the SABC censors at the time of the airing. This incident was reported in the liberal South African press at the time.   See www.wildhorse.com/MiamiVice/music/musicA-g.html (accessed on 28 September 2010).

Example 8.2 Shift of rhythms and semantics

As the song progresses, a bagpipe dirge enters to skirl around the tonic chord in a mournful minor eulogy, and below the bagpipes Gabriel punctuates rhythmic, primordial-sounding vocal utterances ('huh huh'). With this combination of Gaelic and African overlays (Example 8.3), the dense and unusual instrumentation, structured to reflect the global inclusiveness of the sentiment, is complete. The effect is mesmerizing, both aesthetically and symbolically, as the instrumentation presents an unexpected, yet surprisingly harmonious cognitive dissonance. This stylistically fitting contradiction serves as a striking harbinger of the polycultural polyphony that would define future collaborative protest music in crossover styles between artists from differing genre backgrounds.

Example 8.3 Cross-cultural overlays of style

As the listener is swept into the meaning behind the narrative and the splendour of the music, Biko's spirit is invoked with the Xhosa entreaty 'Yila Moja' ('come spirit'), to implore his spirit to descend and rejoin the resistance movement. While Biko the man may be dead, Biko's spirit is not, as Biko was more than a man. He was, in the eyes of his followers, a visionary who became a hero, and who died a martyr. Once again Gabriel manages to cement the authenticity of his mission by using an indigenous tongue not even all South Africans, and few outside the country (besides political exiles) would know. The words tempt curious listeners, compelling them to find out more: to become, like Gabriel, insiders to the struggle. Through summoning Biko's spirit, Gabriel both pleads, and thereby ensures, that Biko remains part of the revolution. His presence, through the invocation, continues as a guiding force. His death may have made him a martyr, but Gabriel's song ensured his status as a revolutionary who played a seminal part in the anti-apartheid movement both at home and abroad – known even to those who would not otherwise have heard of him.

The focus of the song turns to a message – both a warning, and an assurance. Gabriel introduces a metaphoric allusion to the revolution itself. Through the images of candles, flames and fire, he warns that attempts (on the part of the apartheid regime) to suppress dissent may be temporarily effective, but will be ultimately unsuccessful given the extent to which protest will rise and spread. His image is, in fact, not dissimilar to the more common depiction of revolutions happening in waves that cannot be contained once momentum sets in. Just as small currents make up the larger waves of dissent, so too the igniting of single candles can cause larger fires, and 'the wind' (forces which strengthen, like tides on currents, or participants in a revolution) will augment it until it annihilates what it has set out to destroy.[25]

Example 8.4 Vocal audience participation in finale: the taking up of arms

The final warning turns the lens from Orwellian-like observation in a small brutal place described at the start of the song (in the Port Elizabeth police headquarters) to an assurance of human-rights-like global vigilance (ensured by the world population). The past (September '77) is overpowered by the present (now), and the warning becomes both a threat and a promise: 'And the eyes of the world are watching now'. 'Watching now' is repeated twice more, accentuating the warning. In live concerts where the song is performed, such as the 1986 Amnesty International event,[26] Gabriel repeats the final phrase (Example 8.4) numerous times, and then holds the microphone out to the public, to be joined by thousands of audience members in the repeated three-note close.

The mass vocals grow fittingly into a united chant over the circular skirl of the bagpipe, and a passive audience become active participants – symbolically not only in song, but also in sentiment. Gabriel has passed the symbolic flame on to those previously ignorant of, or uninvolved in, the anti-apartheid movement: in his words, 'The rest is up to you'.

---

[25]   One is reminded in this wind-image of the historical speech by the British Prime Minister Harold Macmillan, presented initially in the Gold Coast (Ghana) and later to the South African Parliament in Cape Town (1960), where he declared that 'The wind of change is blowing through this continent. Whether we like it or not, this growth of national consciousness is a political fact.' The phrase was later adopted by Robert Wyatt in his single 'The Wind of Change' when he became involved in the liberation struggle in Namibia. Wyatt was also, incidentally, to record Gabriel's 'Biko' in 1985.

[26]   The video of the 1986 Amnesty International Concert can be viewed on the YouTube link www.youtube.com/watch?v=iLg-8Jxi5aE (accessed on 28 September 2010).

Conclusion

Calls of the South African disenfranchised may have been important in expressing grievances, defining allegiances and drawing attention to the struggle and the atrocities of apartheid through music. But those calls alone did not end apartheid. What mobilized final actions, catalysed consensual changes and ensured historical transitions was a complex contrapuntal revolution in polyphonic harmony – an essentially inclusive and polyphonic music *indaba* between the powerful and the powerless, the local and the global, the audience and the activist. And, as in many war situations, the activists were essentially also the pacifists, working in non-violent ways toward peaceful resolutions to a conflict – in this case calling to arts rather than calling to arms.

This analysis attempted to situate the arena within which 'Biko' managed to play a seminal role in eroding previously tight strongholds in apartheid South Africa. These strongholds had persisted through the perpetuation of insular ideologies and ethnocentric belief systems, causing profound and prolonged cultural dissolutions and social disintegrations. Official strategies, employed to 'compose apartheid', exploited art forms, whether blatant 'divide and rule' strategies to segregate music (and simultaneously, society), or subtler monitoring and censoring of art forms to suppress dissent (and, consequently, revolution). Remarkably, it was these very art forms, especially music genres, which issued in new styles of polycultural polyphony, mimetic of the complex social affiliations being forged: syncretic music genres that eventually managed to reverse the process, and succeeded in 'decomposing apartheid'.

'Biko' is a song capable of reinforcing the undeniable power of certain musical markers as catalysts in social histories – markers that at times yield more influence than any politicians, political policies or military ploys. 'Biko' is also a song capable of unsettling the most hardened cynic, and with good reason. The issues raised by Biko's death under Terrorism Act 83 remain so compelling because the issues are timeless. They raise questions and explore considerations that affect every individual, in every country, every day. When resistance to autocratic regimes is suppressed, and administrations suspend *habeas corpus* and other crucial liberties, whether in Sierra Leone or Northern Ireland, whether at the command of P.W. Botha in South Africa or of Rafael Trujillo in the Dominican Republic, whether on Robben Island or at Guantánamo Bay, this song serves as an admonitory lament. When law is suspended to allow authorities whatever tools it needs, legal or not, to 'maintain law and order' through the brutal silencing of dissidents, this song stands as a cautionary cry. The warning stands all the clearer as essential liberties are exchanged for illusions of temporary safety, whether through Act 83, just another number for a political smokescreen in twentieth-century South Africa, or the Patriot Act, just another name for a political smokescreen in the twenty-first-century United States. The cynical social commentator H.L. Mencken wrote: 'The whole aim of practical politics is to keep the populace alarmed (and hence clamorous to be led to safety) by menacing it with an endless series of hobgoblins, all of them imaginary' (Mencken 1922: 53). All of them may not be imaginary, but a disturbing many of them reside in the very Terrorism Acts that are constructed under the guise of protecting citizens from danger; albeit themselves or others. Both 'Biko' the song and Biko the man demanded that outrage and action continually question and condemn inhumane acts of suppression and torture, so that protest is not restricted to lone dispute, or silenced in the face of political destabilization, but that it rises to heights where dissenting individuals ignite enough opposition to ascend above the fray, and create a united society that decides its own fate.

Chapter 9
'Nothin' but the Same old Story': Old Hegemonies, New Musics[1]

Timothy D. Taylor

There are no bands anymore ... There are projects ... – (Michael Whitaker, Director of Marketing, A&M Records, quoted by Angel 1994: 43)

Introduction

The title of this chapter comes from a song by Paul Brady, a singer/songwriter/ guitarist from Northern Ireland, who sings in this song of a fictitious Northern Ireland man who travels to live in England, finding himself constantly angered by English assumptions that because he's from Northern Ireland he is a pre-modern bigot.[2] Peter Gabriel, too, makes assumptions about the subalterns with whom he works, or whose music he appropriates, assumptions that are deeply rooted in metropolitan and colonial ideologies, so deeply rooted that these musicians are unaware of them most of the time. At the same time, Gabriel attempts to make empowering statements about the preservation of world musics, and the empowerment of peoples from around the world. But his positionality as a westerner and as a male star in the music industry means that his musics are always appropriative in some ways.

Much of the theoretical foundation of this chapter relies on Antonio Gramsci's concept of hegemony, which has proved extremely important since the early 1990s. Gramsci derived his theory of hegemony from Marx and Engels, who posited two kinds of dominance: for them the class that was the ruling material force was at the same time the ruling intellectual force. Gramsci borrowed from this idea and theorized two superstructural levels of society, which he termed 'civil society' or, he writes, 'the ensemble of organisms commonly called "private"'; he labelled the other level 'political society' – that is, the State (Gramsci 1971: 12). The tensions I am going to outline in this chapter in the music of Peter Gabriel help point out that hegemonies of the intellect and hegemonies of the material are intertwined and interdependent, even in the practices of a single musician or band, and even if those musicians try to work around them.

---

[1] This article is reprinted from Taylor 1997 with minor edits.
[2] The song appears on the collection *Bringing It All Back Home* (1991).

Another one of the most lively and provocative bodies of theory to emerge since the 1980s is the study of postcolonialism, and it, too, will be important in this chapter. One feature of postcolonial theorizing is that its practitioners appear to be more interested in the colonialized nations and subjects than the colonializing powers and subject positions of the colonializers.[3] Part of the reason for this is that much of this theory is written by the former colonialized, principally South Asians and Africans. Rather than focusing on colonialism as historical fact, I will here attempt to tease out the threads of colonialist ideologies that are still with us in cultural practices as Gramscian hegemonies in a more globalized world. These colonialist ideologies inform the ways in which formerly and currently colonialized peoples and/or nations attempt to reform their culture and identities. Fernando Coronil makes a similar claim about the historicity implied by the term 'postcolonial', writing that 'postcoloniality appears as something of a euphemism, one that at once reveals and disguises contemporary forms of imperialism' (Coronil 1992: 102). When western musicians appropriate music from somewhere else and use it in their music, or even work with other musicians, the old subordinating structures of colonialism are usually reproduced in the new music, though in complex ways that need to be analysed carefully.

For appropriation is rarely just appropriation. As Steven Feld reminds us, any sort of cross-cultural musical interaction is an appropriation with multiple implications. 'Musical appropriation', he writes, 'sings a double line with one voice'. One of those lines, he says, is admiration, respect, homage; the other is appropriation (Feld 1994: 238). This observation leads us to ask how such appropriations are enacted, and in what kind of political framework they occur. Stuart Hall's two globalizations – the older corporate model that attempts to distance and contain difference, and the more recent one that evinces a more ambivalent attitude toward difference – are both exemplified in the following example by Peter Gabriel. He speaks openly of his attraction to musics from other cultures and attempts to treat those other musics and musicians with equanimity and respect, at the same time benefiting from his positionality as a westerner.

Some writers on 'world beat' have noticed that most discussions of this music tend to be polarized around issues of authenticity and appropriation, or tend to be excessively focused on the personal politics of the western musicians (see Goodwin and Gore 1990; Mitchell 1993; Feld 1994). While I would agree with these criticisms, at the same time it is necessary to point out that authenticity, appropriation and positionality *are* some of the key issues: fans care about these themes, as do the musicians from whom the appropriated musics are taken. Writing around these concepts without oversimplifying or mistaking a particular

---

[3]   I use the word 'colonialize' and its related forms rather than 'colonize', for the former term implies not only physical colonization, but ideological as well. The first anti-colonialist writers well understood this. See, for example, Césaire 1972 [1955]; and Fanon 1968. See Ringer and Lawless (1989) for useful discussions of this and its related terms.

musician's subject position for the more general positionality of stars in the music industry is the tack I hope to maintain in what follows.

Peter Gabriel: *Us*

In an interview on National Public Radio, Daniel Lanois, Peter Gabriel's' producer on his album *Us* of 1992, indicated that one of the ways Gabriel treats borrowed music is to record over it (Gabriel 1992). 'Come Talk to Me', the first track on *Us*, features Gabriel's improvisations over an African drumming field tape of the Babacar Faye Drummers he recorded in the field in the early 1980s.[4] The pre-recorded material is prominent throughout the song but subservient to Gabriel's music. Gabriel at the same time treads new aesthetic/technical ground, for the resulting texture is extremely thick: musical lines piled on lines on lines on lines. Rather than some sort of hierarchical structure as found in most western music,[5] Gabriel instead makes a kind of deep sandwich without the bread: it is all one good thing on top of another. But Gabriel's music constitutes the top layer. William P. Malm used to employ the term 'polystylistic polyphony' to describe a polyphonic texture that wasn't any other kind (not homophony, heterophony or contrapuntal)[6] but the word seems to me to be a bit of a misnomer, since most western music until fairly recently did not use noticeably different styles within one work. The term 'polystylistic polyphony' would work well, however, to describe the texture used by Gabriel, and other musicians who layer sounds of different origins on top of one another. And Gabriel himself says that he is interested in hybrids, not entering a particular style or genre entirely. 'In my own work, I've tried to take elements and integrate them into a sort of no-man's land that isn't England or Africa' (quoted by Brooman 1993: 12).

Gabriel also made use of borrowed music in this way for his soundtrack to *The Last Temptation of Christ*, the controversial film directed by Martin Scorcese. The first track from *Passion* (the soundtrack album), 'The Feeling Begins', is based on Armenian *doudouk* music, a sound that Gabriel has said in several places he finds enormously moving.[7] This music – unmetred – begins the track. But after about

---

[4]   Paul Simon reports that his album following *Graceland*, *The Rhythm of the Saints*, was made in much the same way: he recorded the percussion ensemble Olodum in the town square, then took the tapes back to New York where he improvised music and words over them, and added other layers of music (Simon 1990).

[5]   For discussions of hierarchies in western music, see Shepherd 1991 and Small 1980.

[6]   Malm used this term in his lectures to freshman music majors in an introductory course he taught for years at the University of Michigan, and for which I was a teaching assistant for four years. I would like to thank him for that time, and this term.

[7]   A *doudouk* (also spelled 'duduk') is a large double-reed instrument of Armenia and Georgia. Gabriel says of the *doudouk* that, 'If played properly, it can make you cry' (Colbert

22 bars, a percussion track begins, and from that point on the presence of the western drums regularizes the metrically free quality of the Armenian music into an unchanging 4/4 metre. This repackaging of time marks one of the most salient impositions of western concepts on the musics of other cultures.[8]

Us, though, is more eclectic than *Passion* (which, incidentally, was a favourite among listeners of 'ambient' music, showing again the overlap of music categories).[9] The list of additional musicians provided after the lyrics in the album shows a remarkable array of musics and instruments from around the world: Drums: Manu Katche Sabar drums: The Babacar Faye Drummers, Drum loop: Doudou N'Diaye Rose; Programming: David Bottrill; Bass [chorus]: Tony Levin; Guitar: David Rhodes; Shaker, guitar [telecaster] and additional vocals: Daniel Lanois; Additional verse keyboards: Richard Blair; Bagpipes: Chris Ormston; Doudouk: Levon Minassian; Vocals: Sinéad O'Connor, Dmitri Pokrovsky Ensemble; Programming, triangle, keyboard bass, keys: PG. All these musicians – from Russia, Ireland, Senegal, England, Armenia, France, Canada – contribute to the audible ethnoscape that is 'Come Talk to Me', and the entire *Us* album. But the resulting sound is Gabriel's: he sings over everybody, and he owns the copyrights. And his notes accompanying the album *Plus from Us* make his proprietary stance clear. 'I have an extraordinary band who provide the foundation of my records and at the same time I am very lucky to be able to work with musicians from all over the world. They make an enormous contribution to the sound of my work' (Gabriel 1993). And they do.

While the sounds in 'Come Talk to Me' come from many different peoples and places, this and other songs like it should not be thought of as pastiche or postmodern; the polystylistic lines are indeed polystylistic *in toto*, but because of metre, harmony, rhythm and Gabriel's orchestrations, all the parts come together to form a unified whole, one that Gabriel uses to promote the messages of the song's lyrics.

1992: 23). Gabriel used a doudouk on *Us* and recounts the story of trying to find a player (since the doudouk playing on *Passion* was pre-recorded). '[T]rying to find a *doudouk* player is a little more difficult than I thought – you try Yellow Pages and the *doudouk* column is very empty. So we then tried for any Armenian contacts we could find; in other words, people selling carpets or jewelry or whatever it is. We had a lot of interesting avenues trying to find someone, and eventually got hold of Levon [Minassian], who actually works as a jeweler in Marseilles. He's a wonderful player. He was quite suspicious of us, and rock and roll at the beginning, but then I think really had a great time and jumps at the chance to do anything ever since' (Gabriel n.d.)

[8]   Max Weber wrote about the rationalization of pitch organization in western music in *The Rational and Social Foundations of Music* (Weber 1958), and his argument – that musical tone organization was rationalized into something calculable, known – could easily be extended to time organization. See also Shepherd 1991 and Small 1980.

[9]   For example, *Passion* appeared on the Ambient Mailing list online as the sixth most recommended ambient albums in a call for the top ten nominations.

The lyrics showcase Gabriel's artsy sensibility, producing lines such as 'The earthly power sucks shadowed milk from sleepy tears undone / From nippled skin as smooth as silk the bugles blown as one'. These words and the song as a whole raise problems of communication, the assumption of guilt rather than innocence. Gabriel sings the words with his famous intense vocal style, so the song takes on the feeling of an estranged lover pleading with his ex. This may well be the case. Rumours had been circulating about the break-up of Gabriel's 20-year marriage and a new relationship, and Elysa Gardner of *Rolling Stone* asked Gabriel about this. 'This record follows the breakup of a marriage and the breakup of another quite intense relationship. I had a five-year period of going to therapy, first as part of a couples' group, then with a singles' group. I think it was a period when I was trying to understand what was going wrong and, in doing so, recognized bits in me that I didn't want to look at, that I didn't like' (quoted in Gardner 1992: 27).[10]

The album's cover, which depicts Gabriel straining, alone, against unknown forces, contributes to such an interpretation of estrangement, as does Gabriel's interactions with the other singers on the album. Sinéad O'Connor's backing vocals are mixed so far into the background that the distance Gabriel sings about isn't overcome.[11] And the one time Gabriel's plea does seem to be answered – by the Dmitri Pokrovsky Ensemble singing in the background after the second chorus – it is sung in Russian, and mixed so far into the background it is more of an instrumental line than a texted one. Further, the instrumental parts grow increasingly longer throughout the song – from 4 bars to 8 to 16 – as if these growing parts without words stand for the growing chasm between Gabriel and whomever he addresses.

If we get a little more musically technical we can discover other ways that 'Come Talk to Me' works affectively, for the song's use of harmony further adds to the estrangement theme.[12] Gabriel makes frequent use of the subdominant, which for centuries has carried connotations of the church (as the first of the two chords in the plagal cadence, the 'Amen'), as if, in this case, Gabriel is attempting to bring in the sounds of an elemental spiritual dilemma. Also, the chorus line that gives its title to the song is often harmonized with a deceptive cadence (on f♯ minor) – you may think you know where the music is going, but it doesn't go there. This cadence, which serves to signify the futility of ever achieving any kind of communication, is only part of a larger tonal structure in which the dominant, usually the harbinger of a cadence (or a momentary cadence itself called a half-cadence) is bypassed in favour of a ii–♭VII–I progression (b to G to A in verses 1–3). Such harmonic motion, rather than giving a sense of tonal closure, sounds more like a modal cadence (since many of the ancient church modes conclude

---

[10]   For more interpretations of Gabriel's personal life and *Us*, see Pareles 1992 and Infusino 1993.

[11]   For this observation I am indebted to one of my students, Jeff Rhode.

[12]   Thanks are due to one of my students, Bennett Brecht, for pointing out the significance of Gabriel's use of harmonies here.

with a flattened seventh rather than the raised seventh as in the major and minor modes), as if Gabriel, along with the instruments such as the bagpipes and drums, is attempting to make his cry seem primordial.

Lyrics, harmonies and eclectic instrumentation all contribute to a sense that 'Come Talk to Me' grows out of Gabriel's life; at the same time, however, Gabriel has ensured that the meanings of the lyrics are universalized: he may as well be talking about classes, races, ethnicities, genders or nations that aren't communicating. This more general theme of estrangement bears an important relationship to the appropriated musical materials. The uses of musics and musicians from around the world on this album provide a kind of remedy for this distancing, perhaps illustrated by the album's title *Us* – not, say, *Us and Them*. Gabriel himself says, in answer to an email question from a fan, that

> the title means 'us' as in two people, a relationship, and 'us' as in all of us. I read somewhere that the measure of man's civilization is where he places the line between them and us. When you put people in the box marked them, you can kick them around a lot more easily than you can when they're in a box marked us. So I think it's useful to try and empty the box marked them and fill up the box marked us.[13]

Gabriel's political activism bears out this position. But the music of 'Come Talk to Me', instead, builds and builds and builds, clearly indicating that there has been no rapprochement, or that there can never be one. Even though the song fades out at the end, 'Come Talk to Me' seems to build toward crisis, not communication. The video, included on *All about Us*, reinforces this interpretation. Seemingly drawing on the famous 'morphing sequence' from Michael Jackson's *Black or White* video of 1991, Gabriel's disembodied face undergoes numerous alterations, through make-up, lighting and probably other kinds of technology. Interspersed with these shots are views of Gabriel performing with a band in a powerful blue light. The video is all about Gabriel, cut off from the rest of the world as his face is cut off from his body.

Gabriel's practice of distancing the original drummers – described by Steven Feld as 'schizophonia' – a practice becoming increasingly widespread as 'world beat' music increases in popularity, is the way in which traditional music can be used, appropriated and modified, all without the permission or collaboration of those who originally made the music (Feld 1994). Rather than problematizing this split, Gabriel dramatizes it nearly to the point of irony.

Gabriel is sensitive to issues of appropriation, clearly having thought about what is at stake.

> I know all the arguments concerning appropriation, but at the end of the day, providing you try and balance the exchange and allow for the promotion of

---

13   http://realworld.on.net.pg/tina/pgfaq4.html (accessed in June 1997).

the collaborating artist and their own music, rather than just taking, I feel very comfortable with this idea of dialogue ... . So, given these parameters, more is gained than is lost ... it is possible now for artists from different cultures and countries to reach a limited audience worldwide, making a living from it, and there is much more focus now than there was ten years ago. (quoted by Brooman 1993: 14)

Even though Gabriel speaks intelligently and sensitively about the issues at stake, better, perhaps, than any other rock star, at the same time he employs an aesthetic discourse that threatens to override the political: he likes the tunes; he was looking for rejuvenation. For example, *Us* 'has a wonderful selection of players and colors. Once you get to know the musics, it's almost impossible not to incorporate them. I got interested in world music as a failed drummer; I was able to look for fresher rhythms. It just seemed fresh, wonderful, more live and spiritual than most pop' (quoted by Watrous 1992: 14). Aesthetics – and I do mean 'high'-culture aesthetics – and the economic underpinnings such as copyright make possible the incorporation of all sounds under the name of a single creator, just as colonialism itself made peoples from around the world subjects of this or that western European empire.

Gabriel probably doesn't intend some sort of appropriation that could be considered as colonialist. His interest in world music appears to be deep, and he records and promotes much of it with the organization he helped found in 1982, WOMAD,[14] and the record company that records many musics by musicians from around the world, Real World.[15] He is also a well-known activist for Amnesty International. WOMAD and Real World Records will ensure that the musicians with whom Gabriel works (and more) will be heard on their own; 'it is a vehicle', Gabriel says. 'An artist can come from another country and get onto a circuit that they will find very hard to achieve anywhere else – and get visibility, get heard, and hopefully find an audience that will allow them the following year to come back and tour under their own steam' (Coburn n.d.). Elsewhere, Gabriel discussed the loftier goals of WOMAD, employing a kind of 'natural culture' view of non-western peoples that is very common. 'There are two jobs to be done', he says. 'One is to protect and preserve the seed stock of as wide and varied a base as you can keep alive. The other is to try out as many hybrid possibilities as you can that will give you the most vibrant, pulsating new life forms. Hopefully, the WOMAD festivals in America will reflect this mixture of ancient and modern' (quoted by Sinclair 1993: 85).

Bringing Gabriel's intentionality into the picture isn't a mistake or theoretical lapse; even though contemporary theoretical discourse privileges interpretation as the primary site of the creation of meaning, not creation, or the creators' utterances,

---

[14]   For more on WOMAD, see Cosgrove 1988; Sinclair 1992; Jowers 1993; Lambert 1993; Pride 1993; Sexton 1994; Blumenfeld 1995.

[15]   For more on Real World, see Bridger and Nunziata 1991.

it is nevertheless the case that members of the 'rock aristocracy' (as Simon Frith [1983] calls it[16]) – musicians who enjoy particularly privileged positions in the music industry and thus the culture at large – need to be scrutinized, for they have some power to shape how their works are received.[17] I want to conclude this chapter by theorizing the idea of intentionality with relation to Gabriel's music.

In discussing what happens in collaborations as represented in albums such as *Us*, Michel Foucault's notion of the 'author-function' would work well; he writes that 'we could say that in a civilization like our own there are a certain number of discourses that are endowed with the 'author function' while others are deprived of it' (Foucault 1984: 107). And certain people, such as the members of the rock aristocracy, are endowed with the author-function, or author-authority, as we have seen in the production of *Us*.

Useful as this concept is, Foucault goes too far in denying authors any authority or agency. So I am less willing to give up the author as person or, perhaps better, persona who is capable of shaping interpretation of his or her own work. I would argue that, in some cases, the makers of cultural texts do matter, particularly when they are stars, or when they occupy strategic points in the web of late capitalist relations. Partly this is because these makers of contemporary texts are still around, able to inflect, even direct to some extent, interpretations of their texts. In this short space of contemporary cultural production, many of the deconstructionist/ poststructuralist ideas about the role of the author must be limited.[18] Edward Said wrote that 'it is probably correct to say that it does not finally matter *who* wrote what, but rather *how* a work is written and *how* it is read' (Said 1991: 31, emphasis in original). The key word is *finally*. But in the contemporary world – which, after all, is the only world we have – it *does* matter, for a time, who wrote it, and what they said about it. When authors are still around, when they go on talk

---

[16]   Keith Negus also discusses the power afforded to stars: 'They can use their considerable material assets to directly influence the production and consumption of popular music; through their ownership of companies, labels, song catalogues and studio recording facilities; by directly or indirectly admitting or excluding lesser known performers from certain prestigious events and tours; and by using their commercial clout to influence record company acquisition policies' (Negus 1992: 139). Celebrity, as a kind of powerful currency in late capitalist cultures plays a role here, too, though I don't have the space to explore it in this chapter; but see Gamson 1994.

[17]   Susan McClary (1991) also makes the important point that it is important to examine intentionality when the music is popularly perceived to have no ideas or control over their own work; in her example, Madonna.

[18]   See Roland Barthes, 'The Death of the Author' (1977). Barthes's argument is widely influential in poststructuralist and deconstructionist thought, and holds that since we can never know *exactly* what the author intended, meanings are made in interpretation, not creation. So readers and the texts themselves became the primary forces behind making meaning. In Barthes's words, 'The birth of the reader must be at the cost of the death of the Author' (Barthes 1977: 148). For a typically shrewd analysis of the situation, see Rushdie 1996.

shows, or give interviews to internationally distributed magazines, newspapers and broadcasts, their utterances on their works inevitably shape the way those works are received, even though they cannot shape reception totally. After all, most people who listen to popular music still believe in authors as people, and in the authority afforded those who produce these widely consumed cultural forms.

Thus, it is necessary to think in terms of a field of cultural production in which cultural producers take positions, aesthetic and otherwise, and, using their visibility as figures in popular culture, endorse and explain those position-takings (Bourdieu 1993). For a time, what they say about their works can be influential on their interpretation. But ultimately, listeners, governed by their habitus and life experiences, will hear what they are in a position to hear.

Chapter 10

'Hand-made, Hi-tech, Worldwide': Peter Gabriel and World Music

Dave Laing

In 1991, Peter Gabriel contributed a short introductory article to the North and West Africa section of Philip Sweeney's *Virgin Directory of World Music*, a pioneering volume that predated the *Rough Guide to World Music* by several years. Gabriel's piece began:

> Around 1976/ 77, a number of things began to build up my interest in African music. Some were pure chance – about that time, for instance, BBC Radio 4, which was my regular morning diet, moved frequency and one day while I was trying in a zombielike state to find it on the dial, I ended up on a Dutch station which was playing some fascinating music. It was from the soundtrack of a Stanley Baker film[1] – it wasn't a particularly great piece of music but it had some really nice elements. There was a traditional African choral piece called 'Sho Sholoza' – a beautiful song, sung straight from the heart. It took me about a month to track it down at the specialist movie soundtrack shop in Soho. That started me listening to other things. (Gabriel 1991: 1)

As that extract indicates, the article is an autobiographical account of Gabriel's early encounters with music from Africa. It goes on to describe his renewed interest in drumming whose 'main impetus was the invention of the programmable drum machine', his early enthusiasm for black music from South Africa and Zimbabwe, and visits in the early 1980s to Senegal to meet Youssou N'Dour and to record the master drummer Doudou N'Diaye Rose. Both musicians subsequently performed and/or recorded with Gabriel.

By 1991, also, Gabriel was recognized as a key figure in the WOMAD festival, whose first three-day outdoor festival took place in Somerset in 1982. Several albums of recordings made at WOMAD were issued in the 1980s, and in 1989 the Real World record label was launched.

---

[1]   In an interview with Lou Reed, Gabriel identified the film as *Dingaka*, directed by Jamie Uys in South Africa in 1965. The interview was published in 1999 in *Real World Notes 8*, a newsletter published by the Real World organization. Subsequent references to this periodical are in the form RWN 8: 1999.

Taken together, these various experiences and events situate Peter Gabriel (with his WOMAD and Real World associates) as one of the architects of 'world music' as a popular music form and as a sector of the popular music industry. Although there have been many other contributors to the formation of the world music phenomenon, he was unusual, if not unique, in his three-fold involvement in the world music process. The three roles taken by Gabriel have been as a creator/ performer, as an autodidactic ideologue and as a music-business entrepreneur. This chapter will describe and analyse those three roles after a brief discussion of the contested meanings of world music itself, as an aesthetic and commercial category.

What Is World Music?

The moment at which the world music genre was named has been dated precisely to a 1987 meeting of British independent music company executives, planning a combined marketing campaign for their specialist areas of music. This story has been told by several authors, most cogently by Jan Fairley who quotes from an article about the event written in 2000 by *fRoots* magazine editor Ian Anderson:

> This was the first bunch [of people] who you can blame for 'World Music' as the genre that now exists ... The logic ... was that an established, unified generic name would give retailers a place where they could confidently rack otherwise unstockable releases, and where customers might both search out items they'd heard on the radio (not knowing how to spell a mis-pronounced or mis-remembered name or title) and browse through a wider catalogue. Various titles were discussed including 'Worldbeat' (left out anything without drums), 'Tropical' (bye bye Bulgarians), 'Ethnic' (boring and academic), 'International Pop' (the death-by-Johnny-and-Nana syndrome). 'World music' seemed to include the most and omit the least, and got it by a show of hands. Nobody thought of defining it or pretending there was such a beast; it was just to be a box, like jazz, classical or rock (Fairley 2001: 278)

And, like jazz, classical or rock, there has been a constant lack of consensus about what should be in that 'box'. The ethnomusicologist Philip Bohlman and the US journalist Richard Nidel have attempted to define 'world music'. In the preface to his book *World Music: A Very Short Introduction*, Bohlman wrote that 'there's ample justification to call just about anything world music' (Bohlman 2002: xi), while Nidel's introduction to *World Music: The Basics* states that 'in some respects it is easier to state what is not world music' [than what is], and goes on to list 18 genres that he considers not to be world music, from 'rock'n'roll' through 'Broadway', 'classical', 'heavy metal' and 'new age' to 'pure pop'. Nidel does, however, make an exception for 'hip-hop' by adding in parentheses 'with some exceptions' (Nidel 2004: 2).

A more useful starting-point for this discussion of the role of Peter Gabriel, the WOMAD festivals and Real World and its associated labels is a description from *Western Music and Its Others* published in 2000 and edited by Georgina Born and David Hesmondhalgh. These editors argue that:

> World music' is generally used to mean:
>
> a. the music of Western stars who have shown an interest in non-Western pop
> b. non-Western and/or non-rock popular musics distributed in the West, especially commercial, hybrid forms such as salsa, zydeco, rai, soca, highlife, juju
> c. supposedly 'traditional' musical forms such as Balkan *a capella* choirs.
>
> (Born and Hesmondhalgh 2000: 53)

Each of these categories illuminates the Peter Gabriel connection with, and contribution to, world music. He has probably been the most consistent of the 'Western stars' in pursuing an interest in the music, and WOMAD and Real World have been strongly involved for over 20 years in both (b) and (c).

The World Music Creator

Peter Gabriel's 'interest in non-Western pop' has manifested itself in his own music-making through collaborations with 'non-Western' musicians in recordings and performances and the occasional recording trip to West Africa or the Amazon river. The range of musicians involved has been considerable. As his autobiographical article indicated, the first links were to African musicians. But later came the connection to the Indian subcontinent through the drummers of the London-based Dhol Foundation and vocalists such as Sheila Chandra and Nusrat Fateh Ali Khan, and to Eastern Europe via the duduk players Djivan Gasparian and Levon Minassian, and the Russian chorus led by Dmitry Pokrovsky. Many of these musicians performed on Gabriel's solo albums after 1986. And he reciprocated in some cases, singing backing vocals for African singers Maryam Mursal from Somalia (on her 1998 Real World album *The Journey*) and the Senegalese Youssou N'Dour (on *Joko. From Village to Town*, 2000), among others.

Away from the recording studio, Gabriel has regularly taken world music musicians on tour as the opening acts of his concerts. This is a ubiquitous pop music industry practice, where 'bill-topping' artists often choose a band or soloist whose work they like to fill this role. In Gabriel's case, the support act has frequently been signed to Real World. Among the support acts have been Youssou N'Dour, the British-based Indian singer Sheila Chandra, Hukwe and Charles Zawose from Tanzania, and the American gospel quintet the Blind Boys of Alabama.

Additionally, Gabriel has combined music from diverse sources on several film soundtracks, setting the pattern with Martin Scorsese's *The Last Temptation of Christ* in 1989 and *Rabbit Proof Fence*, whose music, released on CD as *The Long*

Walk Home in 2002, included tracks featuring Nusrat Fateh Ali Khan and the Blind Boys of Alabama. Some of these musicians also contributed to the soundtrack of Scorsese's 2002 film *Gangs of New York*.

The manner in which Gabriel worked with musicians from other cultures in creating his solo albums is examined by Timothy D. Taylor in his 1997 book *Global Pop*, of which the section on Peter Gabriel appears as the previous chapter in this volume. Taylor points out that 'Come Talk to Me', the opening track of Peter Gabriel's 1992 album *Us*, included contributions from seven nations: Russia, Ireland, Senegal, England, Armenia, France and Canada. In his detailed analysis and critique of this track, Taylor asserts that 'while the sounds in "Come Talk to Me" come from many different peoples and places … [a]ll the parts come together to form a stylistic unified whole, one that Gabriel uses to promote the messages of the song's lyrics' (Taylor 1997: 44).

Taylor notes that the 'stylistic unified whole' is composed of a studio mix that creates 'musical lines piled on lines on lines on lines' but adds disapprovingly that Gabriel 'sings over everybody, and he owns the copyrights' (Taylor 1997: 41, 43). Taylor's impressively concrete critique is illustrated with notated examples of drum patterns and chord sequences, but it is followed by a dubious leap in the argument that posits a homology between Gabriel's studio techniques and the horrors of European colonialism. Having quoted from an interview in which Gabriel spoke of world music as 'fresh, wonderful, more live and spiritual than most pop' Taylor writes that 'Aesthetics – and I do mean 'high' culture aesthetics – and the economic underpinnings such as copyright make possible the incorporation of all sounds under the name of a single creator, just as colonialism itself made people from around the world subjects of this or than western European empire' (Taylor 1997: 50).

Taylor's argument has both ethical and aesthetic aspects. Ethically, the first point to be made about Peter Gabriel's attitude toward his co-workers on the track is that he is behaving in exactly the same way as hundreds, if not thousands, of singer-songwriters, be they American, European or even African. However much they may contribute ideas at a session, collaborating musicians on such albums are necessarily subordinate to the featured artist and his or her producer. This has been a generally accepted practice since the early 1960s. 'Economic underpinnings such as copyright' are part of this practice, as the featured artist claims copyright over the whole work and the collaborating musicians receive session fees for their contribution.

In principle, this practice is colour-blind as to the origin of the musicians involved. A singer-songwriter will invite people to play on a session because of the particular skill they can bring to it – be that a special way of playing a familiar instrument or their ability to play an instrument from a different culture from that of the featured musician. In this instance, both the *doudouk* player Levon Minassian and the electric guitarist David Rhodes are in a similar relationship to Gabriel, although one is from a world music context and the other from a conventional English rock background.[2]

This is not to say that Taylor's misgivings about 'Come Talk to Me' are wholly misplaced. It appears that the contribution of at least one of those credited as collaborators with Gabriel was sampled or adapted from a pre-existing recording rather than specifically created for this track. Taylor says that the track 'features Gabriel's improvisations over an African drumming field tape of the Babacar Faye Drummers he recorded in the early 1980s' (Taylor 1997: 41). What is unknown is how these drummers were rewarded for their participation in 'Come Talk to Me' or whether their permission was sought before their music was included. Taylor, perhaps with some justification based on cases such as that of Deep Forest and the music of Central African pygmies (Feld 2000a, 2000b), assumes that there was no reward or permission. He writes that 'Gabriel's practice of distancing the original drummers ... is the way in which traditional music can be wholly appropriated or modified, without the permission or collaboration of those who originally made the music' (Taylor 1997: 50). The argument has some force, but there is no evidence to support it, or indeed to contradict it.

The aesthetic issues that arise from the process of combining elements of different genres in a single track are linked to these ethical questions, but should be regarded separately from the ethical issues. They might be simplified to this: is the purpose of the singer-songwriter to enhance his or her own musical vision by adding new sounds, or is this to be a piece of fusion music or hybrid music, where sounds from different sources are separately audible as well as heard in combination in a relationship of equality?[3] While Timothy D. Taylor's analysis clearly points to the former, if Peter Gabriel were to answer the question, he would probably claim to be trying to achieve both the clarity of vision of the singer-songwriter and the hybridity resulting from an encounter between music from different cultures.[4]

---

[2]   Theodore Gracyk has attacked Taylor's argument against 'Come Talk to Me' from a different perspective. He claims that even when 'texts and styles are appropriated ... their originating culture is not ... the text's cultural dimension is left behind, untouched and undiminished' (Gracyk 2001: 131).

[3]   A valuable and precise definition of hybridity is that of Marwan M. Kraidy, who states that it 'involves the fusion of two hitherto relatively distinct forms, styles or identities ... Cross-cultural contact ... is a requisite for hybridity' (Kraidy 2005: 5).

[4]   A similar question could be asked of the musical practice of the Afro Celt Sound System (ACSS), a much more problematic member of the Real World *équipe*. The ACSS is a collective of African, Irish and South Asian musicians led by English programmer and producer Simon Emmerson. In an interview published in RWN 7: 1998, Emmerson described the production of a song: '(W)e had a session where Moussa Sissokho on the talking drums, N'Faly Kouyate on balafon, kora and vocals, James McNally on bodhran, Johnny Kalsi (of the Dhol Foundation) who's a dholak player – those Indian drums you can hear tanking away – and myself got together. I put some basic beats on the computer and they played over the top and you get a kind of rhythmic template'. 'Basic beats on the

Probably the only conclusion to be drawn definitively from that discussion is that each musical instance should be examined in and of itself before a general verdict is made. It is also important to recognize that while the use of world music elements on his solo recordings is undoubtedly an important part of Gabriel's creative engagement with the genre in the studio, it is only one aspect of that engagement. It should be counter-balanced by an understanding of his musical relationships with a number of individual musicians, most notably Youssou N'Dour and Nusrat Fateh Ali Khan.

The Senegalese singer and composer Youssou N'Dour first played in London in 1984. This led to Gabriel visiting his club in Dakar, to N'Dour's collaboration on the track 'In Your Eyes' on *So*, and to his appearing as support act on two world tours by Gabriel in 1986–87. Both singers later took part in the 1988 Amnesty International Human rights tour and recorded together on tracks that appeared on two of Youssou N'Dour's albums recorded for European record companies.

Gabriel's initial influence on N'Dour was described by Lucy Duran in 1989: 'Working with Peter Gabriel has had an immeasurable impact on Youssou. This is most obvious in his new style of stage presentation. Most excitingly, Youssou has proved that the old rumours that he "can't dance" are far from true – in fact, he dances exceptionally well, with great charm and impeccable sense of timing' (Duran 1989: 282).

In 1989 Gabriel and N'Dour co-wrote and duetted on 'Shakin' the Tree', a densely layered track on the latter's album *The Lion* for Virgin. The song had a pop-style verse–chorus structure, its lyrics were sung partly in Wolof and partly in English, the theme was the lack of female emancipation in Senegal, and the title was taken from Gabriel's mispronunciation of a Senegalese name. This was a collaboration of equals, where even the composer credits were equally shared between the two musicians, while the production is credited to both Peter Gabriel and the Senegalese-born producer George Acogny.[5]

A second example of how these musicians worked together is 'This Dream' from *Joko: From Village to Town* recorded by N'Dour for Sony Music Entertainment France. The track is listed as 'featuring Peter Gabriel'. In a kind of role reversal, Gabriel is in the same 'subordinate' situation (in Taylor's terms) as the African and European backing musicians on 'Come Talk to Me'. He intones the song title as a chorus with N'Dour's thrilling tenor soaring above him. Real World and N'Dour's own Xippi were among the three studios where the track was recorded.

---

computer': this reads, and some of the ACSS recordings sound (like many DJ-led hybrids of world music and dance beats), as if the polyrhythms of the diverse percussionists are being delimited and reduced in order to conform to the regularity of computer-generated rhythms.

[5]   Incidentally, Taylor states erroneously that this song – which he calls 'Shaking the Tree' was 'by Peter Gabriel' rather than a joint effort. This error possibly came from a critical article about the Gabriel–N'Dour collaboration by US journalist Brooke Wentz from which Taylor quotes (Taylor 1997: 135).

In contrast to his relationship of equals with Youssou N'Dour, Gabriel has proclaimed the *qawwali* singer Nusrat Fateh Ali Khan as a major influence. In his tribute to Nusrat Fateh Ali Khan following the latter's death in 1997, Gabriel wrote 'My two main singing inspirations, Nusrat and Otis Redding, have been supreme examples of how far and deep a voice can go in finding, touching and moving the soul' (RWN 5: 1997).

Peter Gabriel first heard Khan in 1981, when a cassette of his music was sent to the WOMAD organizers by a Mr Ayub of Oriental Star Recordings in Pakistan. Nusrat Fateh Ali Khan subsequently appeared at the WOMAD event in Mersea, Essex in 1985, and Real World records issued eight of his albums before his death.

Coming from one of the two great families of Pakistani *qawwali* performers, Nusrat Fateh Ali Khan was one of the leading figures in the genre, which is a devotional music of Sufi Muslims. The texts of all Khan's performances and recordings have a religious basis and, as such, it was surprising that he was able to adjust to the secular contexts in which he made his world music festival appearances and recordings, as well as the film soundtracks into which his music was incorporated.

Interviewed by David Toop in Lahore in 1996, Khan took an almost ecumenical view of his role: 'The message of *quawwali* is not only for Muslims. There have been very great people in all religions. Christians, Hindus, Sikhs, they all had good Sufis. The message of the Sufis is the same – how to reach to God – but they all have different ways' (Toop 1999: 211). Another explanation for this flexibility can be found in Regula Burkhardt Qureshi's study of a leading *qawwali* musician in India, where she analyses the 'context sensitive grammar' of the music through which the context of performance shapes the course of the music (Qureshi 1986).

The unlikely incorporation of his music into films was also used as a tribute to Khan at a concert in Pakistan witnessed by Toop. 'the MC bawled his introduction: "Last Temptation of Christ, Dead Man Walking, Bandit Queen, Natural Born Killers "' (Toop 1999: 209). The track used in *Natural Born Killers* was 'Taboo', a collaboration between Khan and Gabriel, which Ashwani Sharma says has a double effect, both as a 'management of Otherness ... within a centred hegemonic discourse' and an undermining of 'a misanthropic whiteness' through its 'uncontrollable "alien" presence within the anarchic play of the film' (Sharma 1996: 29). Film music was the site of most of the collaborations between the two, although a track featuring Khan's voice was included posthumously on Gabriel's 2002 solo album *Up*.

The most radical recontextualization of Khan's devotional music occurred in his studio collaborations with Canadian-born producer Michael Brook. There, the Khan voice was placed in a musical context wholly separate from his group of *qawwali* singers and instrumentalists, and placed in front of synthesizer and guitar sounds, as on the albums *Mustt Mustt* (1990) and *Night Song* (1996). The booklet notes to *Mustt Mustt* describe how some of the tape edits 'were not acceptable to Nusrat, because we'd cut a phrase in half – sometimes there were lyrics that we made nonsense of ... A compromise was achieved – important lyrical phrases were restored without losing the musical structure Michael had developed. So a halfway point was reached between East and West in songwriting, in performance and in attitude'. The description of this collaboration as one of compromise to reach a halfway point indicates that hybrid music can be as much a result of negotiation as of spontaneous fusion. It supports Marwan M. Kraidy's assertion that 'Rather than a single idea or a unitary concept, hybridity is an association of ideas, concepts, and themes that at once reinforce and contradict each other' (Kraidy 2005: vi).

The Autodidact of World Music

The *Oxford English Dictionary* defines an 'autodidact' as 'one who is self-taught'. In the period to the middle of the twentieth century, autodidacts were drawn from the proletarian or plebeian classes, a process described for Britain in Jonathan Rose's *The Intellectual Life of the British Working Classes* (2001). The autodidact was normally someone excluded by social or political circumstances from secondary and tertiary education; with the extension of educational provision in the second half of the twentieth century the pool of potential autodidacts had shrunk.

The characteristics of the autodidact include an eclecticism of intellectual interests that often ignore the categories and divisions of the formal education system, enabling the individual to make unusual or even absurd connections and discoveries. Peter Gabriel's career has exhibited a number of these autodidactic qualities, even though he should be classified as a bourgeois autodidact, the child of middle-class parents who attended a fee-paying school but did not follow the same path as almost all his contemporaries to Oxford or Cambridge University: he was offered a place at a London film school, which was not taken up. It is significant that his father Ralph Gabriel was an electrical engineer and inventor who had taken out patents on 'farming and cable TV inventions' (Bright 1988: 15).

Evidence of this autodidactic intellectualism is found in profusion in Spencer Bright's 1989 authorized biography. The book mentions Gabriel's deep interest in a range of ideas and philosophies. These included Buddhism, Taoism, Jungian psychoanalysis, Werner Erhard's EST psychotherapy and Stanley Milgram's notorious experiments on obedience and torture. The interest in Milgram led to a plan for a film that was never made and a track on *So*, 'We Do What We're Told – Milgram's 37', while the track 'The Rhythm of the Heat' (1982) had been originally called 'Jung in Africa'. A more self-reflexive impulse was evident in Gabriel's membership of the British branch of the International Association for the Study of Popular Music (IASPM) for a brief period during the 1980s.

Over a decade later, the press pack issued in 2002 with the album *Up* noted that 'in the past seven years Peter has been working on over 130 different ideas and after *Ovo* and *The Long Walk Home* this is the third project to be developed from this batch of material' (Gabriel 2002: 1). Among the ideas mentioned in this document (which declares itself to be written by Gabriel himself) were an involvement with Witness, a human rights organization 'that uses video and computers to deliver powerful images', and a music-making experiment with Bonobo great apes:

> He encouraged them to play the keyboard and try to respond to their phrases in much the same way that jazz musicians jam together or the multicultural interactions that happen so often at WOMAD and Real World Studios. Peter was blown away by the results and by their abilities and has suggested the creation of an organization to enable Great Apes around the world to communicate and take advantage of the potential of the internet, as a communication medium and educational resource. (Gabriel 2002: 1)

While the Great Apes project may seem somewhat eccentric, it displays one of the key motifs underlying the Gabriel world music ethos. A combination between vernacular music and new technologies is a constant feature of Gabriel's approach to music-making and of the spontaneous ideology he has propounded in various pronouncements. For instance, a 2000 comment in his newsletter *Peter Gabriel News* that 'the invention of the rhythm box ... encouraged me to start listening to the rhythms of other countries' was a restatement of something mentioned in the introduction to Sweeney's book a decade earlier. This motif was expressed most succinctly in his first idea for a slogan for Real World: 'hand-made, hi-tech, worldwide' (cited in RWN 12: 2001).

A second, and less unusual, motif found in statements and interviews is a familiar trope of the world music discourse that finds authenticity and freshness in musical forms and traditions outside those of mainstream European and North American popular music. While the disc jockey Charlie Gillett, a key British intermediary in world music, was 'converted' by the sound of guitar playing from Central Africa, voice and rhythm formed the basis of Gabriel's attachment to 'non-Western' musics, expressed in the contribution to the *Virgin Directory of World Music*:

> Although Senegalese music is very rich – the griots' role in transmitting history and so on – it doesn't matter to me that I don't understand all the words of a song. The voice is such a powerful means of communication, and it's so direct, it can transmit a feeling without having recourse to words. (Gabriel 1991: 2)

Hybridity and multiculturalism, two additional motifs associated with the world music ethos, are also features of Gabriel's pronouncements. For him, hybridity is not only an aesthetic, but an ethical principle. In 1998, he gave a speech at the annual conference of the Piomanzu International Research Centre in Rimini, Italy. His title was 'Making peace for the planet and rediscovering mankind'. This included some very high claims for hybridity:

> The most vibrant examples of plant, animal and human life appear when different genetic stocks are mixed. I believe the same applies in culture. It was Picasso's adoption of African masks in his painting Les Demoiselles d'Avignon that was acknowledged to be one of the foundations of the modern art movement. (RWN 7: 1998)

The 'multicultural' is to some degree a contrast with hybridity – where the latter is intended to exhibit a mixing of cultures, in multiculturalism the separate elements are encouraged to emerge side by side. Gabriel used the idea of multiculturalism in describing the musical show he co-created to be presented at the controversial Millennium Dome, a structure built by the British government to celebrate the year 2000.[6] He wished 'to present two views of Britain. One is the British sensibility, with references from history and folk music. Against that we wanted to set a more contemporary Britain, which would be more multicultural and would include Asian elements, African, Australian, a sort of broader mixture of influences' (RWN 10/4 2000). Even though the interview was edited before publication, this seems a naïvely expressed dichotomy between old and new, between a historic Britishness (i.e. white, rural) and contemporary cultures of immigration.

Hybridity and multiculturalism are structural features of both WOMAD and Real World. WOMAD USA included a workshop 'African kora meets Celtic harp' in 2001, while the Real World catalogue has numerous examples of hybrid recordings made jointly by world music artists and musicians from Western Europe or North America. Some examples are Brook and Khan, English guitarist Sam Mills and South Indian musician Paban Das Baul, and Bhutan monk Lama Gyurme with French musician Jean-Philippe Rykiel. But the festival programmes and the Real World list of releases equally include sequences of juxtaposed monocultural music. The 2000 WOMAD event in Britain featured 52 acts, of which only a handful were cross-cultural hybrids. Of the remainder, 11 were Asian, 10 from Africa and 5 from Asia. There were also 11 UK-based performers and groups, 5 from Australia and 4 from North America.

The World Music Entrepreneur

World music is not only a set of production practices and a discursive field but it is a subset of the cultural economy, in the form of a 'genre-market', a term used by Keith Negus in the most substantial study to date of such markets in the context of the transnational recorded music companies, with case studies on rap, salsa and country music (Negus 1999). Other genre-markets include classical music, jazz, folk, heavy metal, Christian and gospel music and, of course, world music.

As a keynote to his study, Negus quotes from Simon Frith's book *Performing Rites* on the formation of such genre-markets. Frith writes:

---

6   For a critical account of the Dome project, see McGuigan and Gilmore 2002.

> A new genre world … is first constructed and then articulated through a complex interplay of musicians, listeners, and mediating ideologues, and this process is much more confused than the marketing process that follows, as the wider industry begins to make sense of the new sounds and markets and to exploit both genre worlds and genre discourses in the orderly routines of mass marketing. (Frith 1996: 88)

Frith's metaphorical term 'genre-world', with its interactionist and sociological emphasis, incorporates many features of the world music genre-market, of which three will be discussed here.

Firstly, the world music genre-market vertically segments the macro-economy of music as opposed to the horizontal segmentation that splits that macro-economy into geo-political regions. Like jazz and European classical music, world music replicates its genre-market across national boundaries. The genre's musicians can expect to find similarly acculturated promoters and audiences in Tokyo, Vienna, San Francisco and Manchester. But this vertical segmentation is not found uniformly across the globe. World music genre-markets exist most strongly in countries where the music did not originate, but these markets are non-existent or barely existent in world music's countries of origin. In the terminology of the United Nations and its associated agencies, the split is almost equivalent to that between developed nations and developing ones.

The second feature of world music, and of all genre-markets, is that it is recognizable through, and recognizes itself in, representative institutions such as sales charts, radio formats, specialist written media, festivals, specialist record companies, trade associations and fairs and audience demographics. The relative weight of each type of institution varies between genre-markets in what Frith calls the 'confused' process of the construction of the genre-world. A significant contribution to the consolidation of the genre-market was the decision of the influential United States industry publication *Billboard* to introduce a world music top-ten list in May 1990 (compiled from sales in 40 stores), followed by the first Grammy award for world music the following year (Taylor 1997: 10–11).

In Europe, the genre-market took shape through such institutions as the European Broadcasting Union's monthly list of the most played albums by European specialist radio programmers (Fairley 2001); the proliferation of independent record companies such as Piranha (Germany), World Circuit and Real World (Britain) and Mélodie (France); touring circuits and annual festivals, of which WOMAD was an important prototype; and WOMEX, an annual trade fair for the world music industry inaugurated in 1990.

The third distinctive feature is 'audience demographics', one of the institutional features listed earlier. A strong argument can be made that the genre-market of world music is primarily defined by the character of its audience, especially in the metropoles of North America, Europe and parts of the Asia Pacific region. At those sites, world music events are typically attended by varying combinations of 'internationalist' or cosmopolitan natives and members of diasporic communities linked to the countries of origin of the music.

The importance of diasporic communities and their construction through migration is a vital factor in what has sometimes been called 'globalisation from below'. This point is emphasized by Martin Stokes: 'The global movement of migrant underclasses is as vital to the creation and transmission of "global" cultures as is the movement of commodities. This is as true in a musical context as anywhere else' (Stokes 2003: 303).

Among the cosmopolitan native followers of the genre, a commitment to world music is aligned with support for globally oriented charities like Oxfam, Amnesty International or Medecins sans Frontières, and radical tourism organizations such as Lonely Planet or the *Rough Guides*. This alignment is made explicitly in, for example, the extension of the *Rough Guide* series to CD compilations of varieties of world music and to encyclopaedic books about the genre, and the branding of such CDs as fundraisers for the charities. Real World itself released a CD to raise funds for Greenpeace in 1996 and the *Spirit of Africa* CD in 2001, a joint initiative of the label and the Mercury Phoenix Trust to raise awareness of AIDS in Africa.

Writing in 1995 of this component of the world music audience, a British commentator, Mark Hudson, rather dismissively defined this demographic as a 'mature audience, nurtured on Sixties idealism, disillusioned with the vacuity of contemporary pop, and all ready to be awed by billowing robes and frenetic drumming' (Hudson 1995: 28). On the other hand, the ethnomusicologist Andy Nercessian offers a more positive and less generation-specific definition of world music fans as possessing 'the capacity of audiences from one culture to experience under suitable circumstances, perhaps as fully as audiences in the home culture, the music of a culture with which it is unfamiliar' (Nercessian 2002: 8).

In some ways, Peter Gabriel is a typical member of the world music demographic, combining a fascination for musical features of other cultures and a commitment to humanitarian and human rights causes. In this respect, it is instructive to note that he was highly critical of the organization of the Live 8 extravaganza in 2005, principally because this attempt to raise awareness of poverty in Africa failed to include African artists amongst its participants. Gabriel enhanced this critique by organizing with Youssou N'Dour the Africa Calling concert at the Eden Project in south-west England.

But as well as a fan and devotee, Gabriel is a businessman. He has been something of a serial entrepreneur, in the fields of technology and world music. In 1980, he set up Syco Systems as British agent for the synclavier and Fairlight synthesizer, and much later became the main shareholder of the Internet music download companies OD2 (2000), we7.com and Music Club (2008). In the music industry sphere, the various companies operating the festivals, record company, music publishing, recording studio and online sales employ about 80 people and are subsidiaries of Real World Holdings Ltd, whose 'Ultimate Parent' is listed in its accounts as Peter Gabriel Ltd (Dane 2001: 332). This company, which also receives royalties and fees from Gabriel's solo recordings and tours, is therefore the apex of Gabriel's small business empire.

The first WOMAD event was held at the Bath & West Showground at Shepton Mallet in Somerset in 1982 with the stated aim 'to focus wider UK public attention on the traditional and contemporary arts of non-western cultures' (RWN 14: 2002). It had been conceived by a group of community arts enthusiasts in Bristol, with the enthusiastic support of Peter Gabriel (Jowers 1993). Referring to his enthusiasm for the WOMAD concept, Gabriel said in 1987 'I was getting very excited by some of the things I was coming across. So I thought, if they were exciting me, I'm sure they will be interesting to a lot of other people too. So I was sitting on a train one evening and I thought, wouldn't it be great to have an event which could bring in a large audience with a few rock and roll groups, and have that audience exposed to a lot of this stuff' (St Michael 1994: 61–2).

This pioneering event made heavy losses, however, and Gabriel took part in a Genesis reunion concert to raise funds for WOMAD, following which his company became the effective owner of the event (Bright 1989: 141–6). WOMAD eventually became a global brand with events in North America, continental Europe, South Africa, Asia and Australasia as well as the annual UK three-day festival.[7] A charitable arm, the WOMAD Foundation, was set up in 2003.

Starting with the 1982 live compilation *Music & Rhythm*, a few albums had been issued on a WOMAD record label before the Real World record company was set up in 1989. Real World has issued over 150 titles since its inception and its associated Real World studios has been the site of many recordings of world music, not least in the series of 'recording weeks' that involved participants in the WOMAD festivals. The *Big Blue Ball* album, released in 2008, contained remixed tracks that originated in mid-1990s recording weeks.

The first five releases in 1989 were individual artist works by Tabu Ley (Africa), Nusrat Fateh Ali Khan (Asia) and Orquesta Revé (Latin America/Caribbean) plus *Passion*, Gabriel's collage-like soundtrack for the film *The Last Temptation of Christ* and *Passion Sources*, a various-artists collection compiled by Gabriel with tracks from African and Asian artists whose work had been incorporated into the film music. After ten years, the label had sold three million albums; the biggest-selling releases were by UK Indian experimental singer Sheila Chandra, Ugandan musician Geoffrey Oryema, Nusrat Fateh Ali Khan with Michael Brook, and the Afro Celt Sound System (RWN 8: 1999). Although an independently owned company, Real World has close links with Virgin Records, a subsidiary of the major record company EMI. Virgin/EMI handles the manufacture and distribution of CDs for Real World.

In 2008, the label's website listed 99 artists or groups that were signed to Real World. Of these, half were from Africa (28) and Asia (22) combined. There were 15 acts from continental Europe (Finland to Russia) but only 2 from Latin America and 5 from North America. Of the remainder, 15 were British acts and 13 were

---

[7]   For an analysis of the Australian festival Womadelaide see Bloustein 2004.

hybrid bands or projects including members from more than one country and/or continent. This range is broadly comparable to other leading independent world music companies in Europe, although the commitment of Real World to Asian music is greater than that of most of its competitors, such as the German company Piranha and the French label Mélodie.

In its marketing practices, Real World is also broadly typical of the world music industry as a whole. This is the text of an advertisement for *Yol Bolsin*, an album by Severa Nazarkhan issued in 2003:

> A new, searingly beautiful voice from one of the most ancient cultures in the world. Imbued with the warmth and spice of the Silk Route, this modern recording of traditional songs from Uzbekhistan is the first international release from the local pop star, Severa. In her country, the traditional and the modern exist side by side, together creating a society where their biggest pop star can sing these amazing songs of life and love, devotion and hope. Fortunately we can share in the benefit

Aside from the adjectival superlatives, the promotional strategy is to demonstrate that this music comes from a culture that achieves something absent from our own – combining tradition and modernity through the pop star who sings songs of profundity.

As well as selling CD albums and downloaded tracks, Real World has licensed many of its productions for use in films and commercials. For example, 'Taboo' by Gabriel and Nusrat Fateh Ali Khan was used in a Citroën automobile advertisement as well as *Natural Born Killers*. Every track on the first two Afro Celt Sound System albums was licensed for soundtracks of television programmes, film, advertising or computer games. The group was also sponsored by Taylor Made Golf Clubs (RWN 12: 2002).

The Real World organization also includes a music publishing division that has signed many Real World recording artists as well as other musicians active in the world music sphere. Real World publishing is active in licensing compositions for use in television and film. It registers songs with the Performing Right Society in Britain, through which airplay royalties flow back to composers signed to the publishing company.

Conclusion: Anxiety and Celebration

Steven Feld's essay 'A Sweet Lullaby for World Music' uses the contrasting emotions of anxiety and celebration in order to summarize many of the dilemmas, fault-lines and paradoxes of the contemporary genre-world and genre-market. Feld characterizes 'Anxious narratives' as those that 'start from the suspicion that capitalist concentration and competition in the recording industry is always productive of a lesser artistry, a more commercial, diluted and sellable version of a world once more "pure", "real" or less commodified'. In response, celebratory narratives 'often focus on the production of hybrid musics. They place a positive emphasis on fluid identities, sometimes edging toward romantic equations of hybridity with overt resistance' (Feld 2000b: 152). In interviews, Gabriel himself has shown his awareness of this double-sided aspect of world music. In 1993 he said: 'You do get this two-way exchange now – people quite often see it just as these white colonialists coming along and ripping off these Third World artists, but it's actually quite a real exchange, I think. But there's some responsibility on those of us who do take ideas from elsewhere to help try to promote the sources of the music' (St Michael 1994: 65).

The contrasting views of the reception of world music presented by Hudson and Nercessian exemplify Feld's categories of anxiety and celebration. Mark Hudson's position asserts that the white European or North American fan is a jaded seeker after the exotic, the kind of cultural tourist familiar in the history of orientalism as much as among composers such as Ravel and Mozart (Jonathan Bellman's edited collection *The Exotic in Western Music* [1998] discusses an impressive array of such works) as among consumers. Nercessian sees the world music fan in a more positive light, as a carrier of cosmopolitan idealism, having the potential to overcome the split between 'West' and 'Other' upon which so much postcolonial cultural debate is based.

One significant aspect of the world music audience that has relevance to this debate is the relationship between listeners and language. This is a genre where, in general, most listeners (but not, of course, members of the relevant diaspora) cannot understand the semantic content of songs. In this situation, how far is it possible to realize Nercessian's claim that a non-native audience might experience world music 'perhaps as fully as audiences in the home culture'? Is the non-intelligibility of lyrics a barrier to such fullness of experience, or is it transcended by what Gabriel referred to as Senegalese music's ability to 'transmit a feeling without having recourse to words'.

Since writing his 1997 book with its critique of Gabriel, Timothy D. Taylor seems to have become even more anxious about the institution of world music. His 2007 work *Beyond Exoticism* redescribes 'hybridity' as 'joining authenticity as a marketing handle for musics by Others and as a criterion that shapes the ways musics by Others are heard by critics, fans and listeners' (Taylor 2007: 141). This assertion that the idea of hybridity has lost its efficacy because of its appropriation by the music industry contrasts with the recognition in parts of the earlier book of at least a partial dialectic between globalization from above and from below.

The idea of a globalization from below was applied to the analysis of world music by Simon Frith in his contribution to the Born and Hesmondhalgh volume. He wrote that 'the concept of globalization, with its intimations of the inexorable forces of history and/or capital, should be replaced in the discussion of world music by an understanding of networks – globalization from below, as it were' (Frith 2000: 319).

In this article, Frith concretizes the issue by introducing a rarely heard musicians' perspective, quoting from the autobiography of the Cameroonian bandleader Manu Dibango: 'Stick to African music! How many times have I heard this *diktat* ... I have found myself stuck, labelled, locked in behind prison bars ... talent has no race; there simply exists a race of musicians. Musicians – and composers even more so – perceive pleasant sounds around them and digest them' (Dibango 1994: 125–6).

An echo of Dibango's perspective can be heard in Iain Chambers' broadly celebratory account of the sounds of world music which 'offer a space for musical and cultural differences to emerge in such a manner that any obvious identification with the hegemonic order, assumed monolithic market logic, is weakened and disrupted by the shifting, contingent contacts of musical and cultural encounters' (Chambers 1994: 79). The 'shifting, contingent contacts' are those that produce Dibango's perception of 'pleasant sounds', and those that necessarily occurred at WOMAD or the recording weeks at Real World studios.

Steven Feld summed up the development of the world music genre-market in the 1990s, by stating that:

> If the 1990s created a world of consumers increasingly familiar with musical groups ... diverse in history, region and style ... it was due to a major reconfiguration of how the musical globe was being curated, recorded, marketed, advertised and promoted. World music was no longer dominated by academic documentation and promotion of traditions. (Feld 2000b: 151)

If Peter Gabriel would undoubtedly recognize himself in Dibango's portrait of the 'race of musicians', he has also played a not inconsiderable role in the reconfiguration described by Feld. As creative artist, ideologue and entrepreneur, he has embodied many of the contradictions of world music as an aesthetic and cultural industry phenomenon, although his standpoint is clearly that of celebration rather than anxiety.

PART III
Production and Performance

Chapter 11

Nursery Crymes and Sirens' Cries: Peter Gabriel's Use of the Flute

Rebecca Guy

Just before a wild and frantic climax, there came a quiet passage where Gabriel's flute playing established a sense of order and beauty, before the chaos of war reigned once more. (Welch 1998: 41)

Introduction

Peter Gabriel is unlikely to go down in history as one of rock's most prominent and prolific flute players; that accolade must undoubtedly be reserved for Ian Anderson of Jethro Tull, followed perhaps by characters such as Thijs van Leer of Focus and Andy Latimer of Camel. However, he can surely be credited alongside these players for having incorporated the flute into some of the most infamously 'progressive' soundscapes of the period; the output of Gabriel-era Genesis, a group considered by some to epitomize the progressive rock genre,[1] is peppered with brief but significant appearances of the instrument, and it frequently features on available video footage of live performances. The quotation above, from Chris Welch's biography of the singer, refers to what is perhaps one of the instrument's most atmospheric and effective contributions to the group's repertoire; the central episode of 'The Knife' from *Trespass* (1970). Following a swift, driving opening section led by keyboard and guitar, this 'quiet passage' is heralded by a shift in tonality and the adoption of a slower pace, established primarily by a pulsating, monotone bass guitar line and other-worldly, sustained keyboard sounds (Track 6, 3:08). Into these textures the flute enters with a low-pitched, haunting modal melody, clear-toned and controlled, the focal point of this brief, calm respite before samples of riot noises lead into further fast-paced, rock-oriented material. Significantly, this atmospheric episode is chosen to open the DVD documentary

---

[1]   Some examples from progressive rock literature: Macan (1997: 86) includes 'Firth of Fifth' from *Selling England by the Pound* (1973) as one of his case studies that are 'particularly representative of the progressive rock era'; Borthwick and Moy (2004: 73–4) do the same with 'Anyway' from *The Lamb Lies Down On Broadway* in their chapter about the genre; Stump devotes several pages to a description of a development of the progressive nature of their music across the first few albums (1997: 173–9).

Inside Genesis – The Gabriel Years 1970–1975; in eerie black-and-white footage originally broadcast on French music programme Pop Deux in 1973, the first thing to be seen is Gabriel wielding a flute, slowly raising it in front of him like some sort of Excalibur.

This chapter explores the use and effect of the flute in the music of Genesis, focusing mainly on the albums from *Trespass* (1970) to *The Lamb Lies Down on Broadway* (1974). There is necessarily some description of musical examples, with which I can of course only hope to supplement the listening experience and not replace it. However, through discussion of performance technique and musical material I aim to contextualize Gabriel's flute-playing both within the music of the band and in relation to wider progressive rock practices and various musical traditions within which the flute is involved.

Background

The flute has had an interesting relationship with progressive rock; in a genre in which creative processes are dominated by ideals of eclecticism, experimentation and borrowing of elements from other musical styles, the flute appears to have multiple routes into the repertoire. Perhaps most easily associated with Western classical music, it has also become established in various forms of jazz, and can easily provide musical reminiscences of either genre if required. The sonic similarities between the mechanized Boehm flute[2] familiar within most western musical contexts and its siblings found in folk musics across the world – a universality to be expected of an instrument with such a simple acoustic provenance, basically a hollow pipe in which the air passes across some form of sharp edge, producing pressure oscillations and allowing a standing wave to be created – lends it the ability to insert 'folk' and 'world' music connotations into other musical contexts, if only in the broadest generic sense. Many examples of flute-based genre-blending can be found in progressive rock, at least for listeners with the necessary codal competences – namely, with sufficient familiarity with the other relevant musical genres to be able to perceive similarities and make links.[3] The flute's role within progressive rock has been small, relatively speaking, in terms of the number of rock bands using the instrument compared to the scope of the genre as a whole; however, its multiple other-musical associations has given it far more prominence than, for example, fellow orchestral wind instruments such as the oboe and bassoon.

---

[2]   The most common form of flute within Western classical music, jazz and quite possibly rock is the transverse, keyed concert flute, usually made of silver or similar metal, based upon the model developed by German goldsmith Theobald Boehm in the middle of the nineteenth century. For more details see, for example, Toff 1996: 50–61.

[3]   See Guy 2007 for further discussion of the transference of flute-based musical coding.

Genesis was formed at Charterhouse public school in Surrey in the late 1960s, and the group's music was originally very much rooted in the progressive rock ethos. Holm-Hudson (2002: 3–4) describes the band, alongside Yes and Emerson, Lake and Palmer, as one of the genre's 'most commercially successful groups', sharing 'an emphasis on virtuosity and a tendency to explore suite-like song structures'; these are the bands for whom the conception of progressive rock as an 'attempt to merge "classical" music with rock, thereby enabling rock to "progress" beyond its blues-based roots' (Holm-Hudson 2002: 3–4) best applies. Numerous Genesis songs from the early 1970s extend beyond the typical three-minute rock song standard, and incorporate frequent changes of pace, dynamic and texture– practices that can be considered reminiscent of compositional methods prevalent in classical music. In some respects, Peter Gabriel's use of the flute fits right in with these progressive rock tendencies and classical aspirations, providing colouristic contrast and – via its long association with western classical music – having the potential to assist in the processes of genre-blending. However, as I shall discuss in this chapter, the role of the flute in the music of Genesis transcends that of a mere art music signifier.

From the outset the instrumentation of the group was founded upon a line-up of drum kit, bass, guitars, keyboards and vocals, with Gabriel's flute periodically contributing to instrumental sections. The flute is thus the principle timbral intruder within a fairly typical rock ensemble, although the various electric keyboards of course provide a sizeable arsenal of tone colours, and there are occasional appearances of other distinctive 'non-rock' instruments such as the oboe (played by Gabriel on *Foxtrot* and *Selling England by the Pound*) and cello (played by bassist Mike Rutherford on *Foxtrot*). Gabriel learned the flute at school,[4] and so presumably received classical training to at least some degree; thus, unlike the self-taught Ian Anderson, the origins of his playing style can be considered to be rooted in the classical flute tradition. Genesis biographer Dave Thompson (2005: 27) suggests that the decision to use the flute within the band was 'at least partially in emulation of Crimson's Ian McDonald' – wind player for King Crimson's first album *In the Court of the Crimson King* (1969); however, the flute appears on Genesis' first album, *From Genesis to Revelation* released in March 1969, some seven months before King Crimson's first release. Jonathan King, mentor and producer for the first Genesis album, later gives his opinion of Gabriel's flute playing:

> Peter had learnt the flute very, very badly and wanted to put in a few flute passages. I thought I could bring a session musician in to do this, but he wanted to do it and he did it, and it sounded really nice, because he wasn't trying complicated things, he was working within his limitations (Dodd 2007: 45).

---

[4]   Fellow ex-Charterhouse student John Hutchinson writes 'Peter learned to play the flute and piano at school, but in his own words, he was "an unexceptional music student"' (Hutchinson 1986: 70).

Gabriel offers his own opinion of his performance abilities (Cavanagh 2007: 80): 'We were always songwriters first and musicians second. I played the flute – badly – and the oboe very badly, and the drums pretty badly, but all enthusiastically.' Chris Stewart, drummer for Genesis before they recorded their first album, recalls how whilst at Charterhouse Gabriel taught him the drums because 'he needed someone to take over the drums in his band so he was free to play flute and sing' (Dodd 2007: 46); this suggests that Gabriel had thoughts about including the flute in a rock context at a very early stage in his musical career. Early Genesis guitarist Anthony Phillips offers a fascinating anecdote concerning Gabriel's flute technique with regards to 'The Knife' discussed above:

> Pete was also quite a good, intuitive flute player, although he wasn't that versatile. 'The Knife' was in A Flat Minor and Peter couldn't really play in A Flat Minor, a tough key on a flute, but he had a solo part. So what he used to do was pull the flute out a bit so he could use the keys in A Minor, which was easier for him to play. Tony Banks would always remember, just before the start of the song, to tell him, 'Pete, flute!' and Pete would go 'Oh, yeah' and adjust his flute. But very occasionally this was omitted and so you'd hit this point where the song would go quiet for this lovely solo, and suddenly Pete's flute would come in a semitone out of tune. Fantastic. (Dodd 2007: 64)

Even if the flute had made its way into the music of Genesis before *In the Court of the Crimson King*, this album does much to illustrate the instrument's potential within a progressive rock context. That the fledgling Genesis found King Crimson's first album particularly inspirational is well documented; Thompson (2005: 26), amongst other biographers, describes how it was 'a disc destined to take up permanent residence on the turntable, just as its so-distinctive cover ... was hung on the wall of the rehearsal room to remind Genesis of the standards to which they now aspired'. On this album wind-player McDonald contributes prominent flute solos to two numbers, the second – 'I Talk to the Wind' – and the closing title track. In the former the flute provides double-tracked interludes between verses and some clear-toned, sustained counterpoint to portions of the vocal line, as well as two brief, restrained solo episodes which lend a lounge jazz feel, improvisatory in manner with extensive use of syncopation, tiny glissandos, grace-note ornamentation and rapidly repeating fragments. The central flute solo of the latter is similar in style and mood, sparsely accompanied by bass, guitar and kit interjections, and contrasting with the dramatic, dense, mellotron-led textures that pervade much of the rest of the song. The influence of classical music is as prominent in the music of King Crimson as it is for Genesis, not least in this flute solo; Crimson biographer Sid Smith (2001: 66) quotes McDonald revealing that he borrowed from the *Sheherazade* orchestral suite by Russian composer Rimsky-Korsakov. However, suggestions of jazz flute playing are also once more strong, through the improvisatory, fragmented phrase construction and spontaneous ornamentation. Clarinets and saxophones are also prominent on this album, the former primarily as colouristic devices and the latter promoting elements of jazz fusion; however, the flute is the most prominent wind instrument in providing sonic and atmospheric contrast, alongside some possible semantic connotations with regards to the pastoral references of 'I Talk to the Wind'.

This description of McDonald's flute-playing accentuates one aspect of the flute's role in progressive rock: providing suggestions of jazz. Many prominent progressive-rock flautists – including Anderson, Van Leer and Latimer, alongside McDonald and his King Crimson successor Mel Collins – frequently appear to be using the flute to provide or support jazz-fusion elements within their music. This element is much less obvious in Gabriel's playing; his predominant performance style, across the studio albums at least, is clear-toned and gentle, providing low-pitched, seemingly pre-composed melodies which rarely utilize the more forceful, aggressive possibilities of the instrument (sometimes exploited in jazz and brought to prominence by Jethro Tull's Ian Anderson). The example from 'The Knife' discussed above epitomizes the role of the flute throughout the Gabriel-era repertoire; restricted mostly to slower, gentler, atmospheric sections in which drum-kit rhythms are conspicuously absent, it is deliberately used as an 'effect', a means of creating suggestions of 'order and beauty' to contrast with more typical, energetic rock band textures.

That there is an element of improvisation in Gabriel's flute performance is demonstrated by the differences between flute lines on the studio albums and in live recordings; the above-mentioned footage of 'The Knife' presents flute material which, whilst retaining the atmosphere and modality of the studio version, is more fragmented and moves into a higher register of the instrument. However, the focus is clearly not upon the demonstration of flamboyant improvisatory skills for their own sake; for Gabriel the flute usually functions as an instrument for providing restrained, sweet-toned contrast to the surrounding, more aggressive rock-band sonorities, rather than trying to emulate them in any way.

Trespass (1970)

The flute appears in every track of *Trespass*; its contributions are generally similar in style to that of 'The Knife', although the surrounding musical contexts are quite varied. Its first entry within the opening track, 'Looking for Someone', is unusual in that it appears, three and a half minutes in, during quite a rock-oriented section; the drum kit is present, and the flute joins an aggressive lead guitar and piano line. However, the flute line contrasts rather than blends with these instruments, low-pitched and unforced with a clear tone, and with significant artificial reverb applied. This brief shared passage leads into a more typical Genesis flute-using episode – gentle and atmospheric, lacking a regular beat – via two flute trills (Track 1, 3:35), the second of which is created by over-blowing to the first and second harmonics on the fingering of the first ($F\sharp_4$–G_4 – the sound can be heard to crack and fall back to the original pitch at one point). The kit then drops out and the guitar and flute share a gentle melody; the sound is once more clear and unforced, but the obvious vibrato that would be expected in classical flute playing is noticeably absent – an issue that will be further discussed below.

In 'White Mountain' the flute's various brief solo lines and counter-melodies are to be found only in the more atmospheric, acoustic guitar-led portions of the track, which alternate with a rock-oriented refrain dominated by kit and keyboard. The sustained, controlled lines with occasional neat, turn-like ornamentation function as strong art-music signifiers. Such flute lines predominantly use the first octave of the instrument; at one point (Track 2, 5:10) the sound can be heard to split and waver between two octaves when a second-octave note, A_5, is attempted. In 'Visions of Angels' the flute doubles portions of the melodic line when the material of the restrained opening piano introduction returns halfway through the song (Track 3, 3:43). 'Stagnation', after a gentle opening, builds to a kit-driven climax that is suddenly halted (Track 4, 3:57); the flute is the first instrument to break the brief silence, providing a few notes to herald the next vocal entry. The flute also initiates the final sequence of this multisectioned track, introducing a simple repeating melody (6:56) to which other instruments are subsequently added in unison, creating a procession-like accompaniment to the closing chorus-like vocals.

The penultimate track, 'Dusk', exhibits a slightly more forceful manner of playing; following the first two stanzas there is a short instrumental (Track 5, 2:06) to which the flute contributes repetitions of a brief, syncopated motif incorporating a rapid, downwards flourish, preceding a low-pitched, sustained melody (2:51), chromatically sliding around the lowest notes of the instrument, to which obvious artificial reverb is applied. The 1969 demo version of this track made available on the *Genesis Archive 1967–1975* release (1998) has an additional flute solo at the end (Disc 3, Track 6, 4:26); this mostly consists of a simple, repeated melodic fragment, with some hints of variation and improvisation creeping in as it progresses. Air noise is clearly audible and some unstable notes are once more in evidence.

Flute technique and style

Although the *Archive* recording is of an early demo and therefore the sound quality is understandably reduced, this latter point highlights an important issue; whilst Gabriel's flute-playing is generally sweet-toned and restrained in nature, he is not striving for technical or tonal perfection in the manner that would usually be expected in art music performance. The occasional cracks and wavering harmonics – which would be regarded as faults within most classical music training – are evidence of the fact that rather than trying to conform to the norms of a pre-existing playing tradition, he is bringing the flute into a new musical context, namely rock – a repertoire in which personal expression and sonic experimentation tend to override adherence to established instrumental techniques. As discussed above, the influences of classical music in the output of Genesis are obvious and varied, forming an important aspect of their 'progressiveness'; folk elements sometimes appear, in the form of an emphasis upon acoustic guitar reminiscent of the singer-songwriter tradition, but suggestions of jazz are rare. However, Gabriel's flute-using practices cannot simply be interpreted as the inclusion of a classically trained player in order to promote genre-blending. The quest for sonic clarity and harmonic richness dominates much classical flute training (notwithstanding avant-garde influenced exploration of 'extended techniques' and noise elements that increasingly feature, at least at conservatoire level). Such issues are less important in rock flute performance; this fits with the typical rock aesthetic, which freely permits adaptations of existing instruments and techniques, forceful, aggressive playing styles and prominent use of distorted sounds.

Whilst not setting out to develop a firmly rock-based style of playing, as seems to be the case for Jethro Tull's Ian Anderson – who frequently employs a forceful, distorted sound, sharing riffs with the electric guitar and emulating its tone colours – Gabriel seems to at least some extent to be aligning his flute performance with approaches more typical to jazz or rock practices, in which players sometimes appear to be deliberately seeking to differentiate their playing styles from more established (namely art music) instrumental traditions. This notion can be related to the issue of Gabriel's vibrato technique mentioned above. The use of vibrato – regular, slight variations in pitch and/or intensity of instrumental or vocal sound – in western art music appears to date back to at least the Middle Ages; Moens-Haenen (2001: 523–5) writes that its use has been documented since this time, but that it was originally applied mainly as a form of ornamentation, and only in the early twentieth century did its continuous application become the norm. For woodwind instruments there are two main techniques for producing vibrato, 'finger vibrato' created by rapid movement of the fingers near to an open hole in the tube whilst playing sustained notes, and 'breath vibrato' controlled by the muscles of the respiratory system; the former persists in various forms of folk and historic flute performance, but it is the latter which is usually employed on the Boehm flute in classical technique. Vibrato can be a problematic aspect of flute training; it generally begins to appear naturally as a student progresses on the instrument, but often less experienced players initially produce rapid, uncontrolled, fluttery oscillations, created in the throat instead of by the abdominal muscles – the latter more usually being considered 'correct' technique. In jazz and rock flute playing vibrato is one of the parameters which can provide an opportunity for experimentation and differentiation from typical art music practice, and can be exaggerated or suppressed for sonic effect.

Vibrato is frequently conspicuously absent from Gabriel's flute playing, as in the example from 'Looking for Someone' discussed above, but sometimes he employs a prominent, rapid, almost forced wobble; one such example is from 'Supper's Ready' on *Foxtrot* (1972), which is nearly 23 minutes long and contains seven titled subsections. Toward the end of the first of these ('Lovers' Leap'), the flute enters with a brief counter-melody (Track 6, 3:19), low-pitched and sweet-toned but with a very rapid, quivering vibrato which gives the impression of being applied as a special effect. The next flute entry (5:44) links the second and third subsections with a gentle paraphrase of the opening 'Lovers' Leap' vocal line; the sound has an occasional quiver but not the forced, rapid vibrato of the previous entry. The flute subsequently appears within a gentle musical episode preceding the sixth subsection of the track (14:19), the heavy-rock 'Apocalypse in 9/8'; many notes lack vibrato, but in places the sound adopts a rapid wobble which seems unpredictable and less deliberate in comparison to that of the 'Lovers' Leap' section.

Later Albums

Trespass forms the most extensive outing for the flute in the Genesis repertoire; the instrument is not used quite so frequently on later albums, but does make some significant appearances – most of which, as on *Trespass*, are restricted to gentler, less rock-oriented episodes. 'The Return of the Giant Hogweed' (*Nursery Cryme*, 1971) opens at a lively pace with typical rock band instrumentation, and – unusually for Genesis – maintains these textures through much of the song; the flute enters halfway through (Track 3, 4:15), first in unison and then in harmony with the electric guitar. The tone is fairly clear-toned and gentle, contrasting with rather than attempting to emulate the electronic distortions of the guitar sound, and some intricate quaver figuration is introduced toward the end of the episode (4:46), which promotes suggestions of classical music. 'I Know what I Like (in Your Wardrobe)', from *Selling England by the Pound* (1973) was the group's first hit single, reaching number 21 in the charts. This song retains a gentle rock beat and a periodic harmonic structure throughout; near the end (Track 2, 3:09) some flute flourishes are heard, interspersed between repetitions of an ascending figure on a bizarre, keyboard-generated voice. The flute material here is some of the most florid and jazz-tinged to be heard in the Genesis repertoire.

Semantics

As well as playing a colouristic role in the music of Genesis, on several occasions the flute's semantic associations are called upon. In programmatic art music repertoire the flute is repeatedly used to support depictions of themes such as the pastoral, the feminine, seduction, exoticism and mythology – and sometimes combinations of all five. Examples include its prominent role in 'Dance of the Seven Veils' from the biblical opera *Salome* by Richard Strauss (1905); *Prélude à 'L'Après-midi d'un faune* (1895) and *Syrinx – La Flûte de Pan* (1913) by Debussy, linking the flute to the pastoral, mythological characters and, in the latter, a tale of (failed) seduction; the love story *Daphnis and Chlöe* (1912) by Ravel – in which the prominent Act III flute solo significantly falls at the point in the ballet at which the characters re-enact the story of Pan and Syrinx.

All of these semantic themes feature in lyrics of Genesis, often in close proximity with flute material. The instrument contributes to the central instrumental section (Track 7, 3:49) of 'The Fountain of Salmacis' (*Nursery Cryme*, 1971), which re-tells the Greek myth of Hermaphroditus, son of Hermes and Aphrodite, who was seduced by the nymph Salmacis as he bathed in her fountain in the woods, and fused with her into one body which thus had characteristics of both sexes (see Howatson 1997: 273). However, this example could be regarded as a strange choice of instrumentation as the flute is alongside, and almost obliterated by, first electric guitar and then a prominent keyboard line. The flute appears to play a dramatic role in 'Firth of Fifth' (*Selling England by the Pound*, 1973), the text of which fuses historical, mythical and rural references. Following the lyrics 'Undinal songs / Urge the sailors on / Till lured by the sirens' cry' (Track 3, 2:54) there is an instrumental interlude commencing with a forceful line on piano, which then provides accompanying broken-chord patterns – alongside bass guitar – beneath a modal flute melody which is easily interpreted as a manifestation of this 'sirens' cry'. The vibrato is inconsistent and in places quite rapid, but the lyrical nature of the tune seems to be intended to exploit the instrument's relatively sweet tone qualities, and by extension its connotative links with femininity and seduction, with hints of the pastoral thrown in. The line involves some quasi-Baroque oscillating figuration (3:56), played in unison with the piano; this musical idea also forms the basis of much of the following material, which is led first by piano then by electronic keyboard. On some later recordings of this song, following Gabriel's departure from the band and drummer Phil Collins' adoption of the role of lead vocalist, this prominent melody is intriguingly provided by an other-worldly keyboard voice.[5]

'The Musical Box' (*Nursery Cryme*, 1971) cleverly exploits the flute's timbral qualities and semantic associations, lending musical irony to the twisted, ghostly interpretation of what should be an idyllic childhood nursery scene. The album sleeve notes provide the setting for the song, explaining the story of nine-year-old Cynthia Jane De Blaise-William who, having beheaded her eight-year-old companion Henry Hamilton-Smythe during a game of croquet, finds his musical box in the nursery; this, when opened, causes Henry's ghost to appear and try to seduce her. The track continues the progressive trend of contrasting musical textures within a song, juxtaposing slower, quieter sections in which the gently pulsating rhythms and intricate finger-picked guitar patterns are clearly suggestive of the sounds produced by a mechanical toy music box, with rock-oriented episodes based on lead guitar, electric keyboards and thundering drum kit. The flute only participates in the early sections of the song, before any heavier material appears, its first entry being a brief solo line following the lyrics 'Play me my song / here it comes again' (Track 1, 1:30). The non-diatonic pitch-set (F♯ Aeolian) lends hints

---

[5]   See for example the version on the live release *Seconds Out* (1977).

of exoticism, which perhaps can be considered to convey the other-worldliness of Henry's current supernatural situation. Following the next brief vocal stanza, the flute enters again in harmony with a gently plucked electric guitar, playing a diatonic, almost playful duet idea (2:09). It then continues to add some melodic fragments, low in the mix within the guitar-based texture, before the reiteration of the 'play me my song' lyrics heralds a shift to more rock-oriented, kit-led material. The flute's sweet, ethereal timbre contributes effectively to the gentle but mysterious atmosphere of the first part of this track, the musical setting for lyrics that fuse themes of childhood, the supernatural and seduction.

'The Cinema Show' (*Selling England by the Pound*, 1973) contains an episode in which the flute and oboe interact quite closely. The oboe enters with a brief, simple melody over a shimmering guitar and keyboard accompaniment constructed around repeated broken-chord patterns (Track 7, 3:09); Gabriel demonstrates some proficiency on the instrument, incorporating some rapid ornamental mordent figures. The flute then enters with a contrasting, fragmented middle-octave melody, ending with a flourish in which the notes are forced and can be heard to split. The oboe and flute then briefly interact as the former plays a phrase which is immediately developed on flute. As the music leads into the next vocal section the flute continues to provide some improvisatory melodic fragments (3:40), although mostly at a lower pitch and with a gentler tone colour than its initial entry; some spatial manipulation is introduced, as some fragments seem more distant than others within the acoustic space. Flourishes on both instruments also appear as part of the atmospheric instrumental that closes 'Dancing with the Moonlit Knight' on the same album.

The Lamb Lies Down on Broadway (1974)

The group's final studio album before Gabriel left Genesis was the epic *The Lamb Lies Down on Broadway*, a concept album telling the surreal story of Rael and his underground adventures following the descent of a mysterious black cloud upon Time Square. This immense project epitomizes many typical practices of progressive rock, abounding in frequent shifts of mood and texture, and utilizing a vast and colourful soundscape that is dominated by electronically generated and keyboard-based sonorities. The surrealist nature of the story that the album tells clearly promotes the use of unusual, other-worldly tone colours, which relies predominantly upon electronic technology rather than familiar acoustic instruments. Thus whilst the complex, quasi-symphonic textures continue to suggest the influence of art music, it seems that there is less need for timbral art music suggestions. The piano is used frequently, but Gabriel's flute makes a significant appearance in only one track, 'Cuckoo Cocoon' – a short, gentle song (less than three minutes long) based on pulsating, chord-outlining patterns on guitar and piano. The flute has a solo line following the second vocal stanza (Track 4, 1:02), a low-pitched melody that approximates D Aeolian, but is modally ambiguous as it alternates between F and F$\sharp$. The flute sound is thinner with fewer harmonics than would usually be expected in art music performance, and it has an almost non-existent vibrato and a slightly breathy edge. Another flute solo concludes the track (1:50), which further increases the modal ambiguity as it uses both B$\natural$ and B$\flat$. In this second solo the flute ascends into the second octave, and at one point (the final G$_5$ of the sixth bar) the sound can be heard to crack. In this context the thinner, breathier tone colour that Gabriel uses could be interpreted as a strand of the musical depiction of the 'other-worldly' scene; a more familiar, 'classical', rich tone with regular vibrato would be inappropriate to the track and the soundscape of the album as a whole. In the live version of the album that appears on *Genesis Archive 1967–1975* the two flute solos utilize the same pitch-set as the studio recording and develop similar melodic ideas, but in places diverge quite considerably from the originals, once more indicating the improvisatory nature of such flute contributions.

Beyond Genesis

The flute makes only minute appearances in Peter Gabriel's solo material released after his departure from Genesis. It features in the credits of his first self-titled album (1977), on which it participates, alongside recorders (also credited to Gabriel) in the brief, atmospheric woodwind collage which links the tracks 'Down the Dolce Vita' and 'Here Comes the Flood'. On *Passion* (1989), based on his soundtrack for Martin Scorsese's *The Last Temptation of Christ* (1988), he includes flute and 'flute samples' in the blend of electronically manipulated sounds which makes up the short track 'Gethsemane', and a 'flute whistle' adds occasional sustained counterpoint to the pounding, percussive rhythms of 'Of These, Hope' and its reprise.[6] An ambiguously named 'Mexican flute' is also credited to Gabriel on 'Secret World', the final track of *Us* (1992). None of these contributions have the prominence of his flute solos for Genesis; as Gabriel's interest in technology and world music developed, it seems his use of the flute (and related members of the woodwind family) became restricted to barely discernible splashes of exotic colour.[7]

Although the first portion of Gabriel's musical career was virtually entirely focused upon Genesis, one rare early excursion into the world of a session flautist is noted by biographers as a less than comfortable occasion. Producer Paul Samwell-Smith, who worked with Genesis on some BBC sessions in January 1970, invited Gabriel to add flute to the song 'Katmandu' on Cat Stevens' album

---

[6]   Guest woodwind players on this album include Kudsi Erguner playing ney flute ('Before Night Falls', 'Wall of Breath'), Robin Canter on oboe and cor anglais ('With this Love') and Richard Evans on tin whistle ('Bread and Wine').

[7]   The song 'Sledgehammer' (*So*, 1986) provides a further connection with 'exotic' flutes, opening with sampled *shakuhachi* sounds.

Mona Bona Jakon (see Thompson 2005: 33). Thompson records Samwell-Smith describing how Gabriel 'came into the studio, very young and very, very nervous. He almost couldn't play the flute because his lip was shaking, and his hands were shaking. I had to go out and tell him, "Don't worry, it'll be alright"'. In Gabriel's own words:

> I was so nervous ... a session man, you know ... I thought, wow! And they taped my breaths while I was nervously preparing for my little line, and made it a joke track which they all laughed at afterwards, when I'd gone. (St Michael 1994: 75)

Despite the nervousness, Gabriel's flute contributions – consisting of a tiny flourish within each vocal stanza and a brief recurring melody between verses, the second of which is developed into a more extended solo – add effective colour to a track otherwise dominated by acoustic guitar and vocals; situated at some distance within the acoustic space, in contrast to the close recordings of the voice and guitar, the ethereal, slightly airy sound aids in the promotion of suggestions of exoticism – one of the flute's established semantic associations as discussed above.

Conclusion

As the above analysis shows, there is so much more to the role of the flute in the music of Genesis than merely being something for the lead singer to do in instrumental sections, as an alternative to manic tambourine-waving (as can be witnessed on numerous extracts of video footage). The flute is clearly an important instrument in the sonic toolkit, exploited for its gentle, unabrasive acoustic tone colours, principally in the creation of atmospheric instrumental sections which contrast with more rock-oriented, pulse-driven material, and as such play a dramatic role in the musical settings of Genesis' intricate lyrical themes. As discussed above, the presence of the flute and the manner in which it is generally used fit in with the group's ethos as a committed progressive rock band, unashamedly drawing upon classical influences – not least timbral ones. Macan relates the classical preferences of progressive rock bands to sociological and geographical issues, suggesting that 'the continuous references progressive rock musicians make to classical music are ... emblematic of the musicians' middle- and upper-middle-class backgrounds' (1997: 13), and making the following generalizations:

> Progressive rock has been a phenomenon mainly of southern England. Most of the major progressive rock bands of the 1970s formed here ... many major progressive rock musicians were born in this region, and even those who were born in other regions of the United Kingdom were often raised here. ...

> There is no doubt that the educational backgrounds of English progressive rock musicians as a group go a long way in explaining their familiarity with the European classical repertoire, without which progressive rock would not have developed. They would have become acquainted with the music both by virtue of their class background … and because of the considerable training in classical music they often received. (Macan 1997: 145, 148)

Although this model does not neatly fit all groups that received the progressive rock moniker (for example, Jethro Tull originated in Blackpool, and the Moody Blues in Birmingham, as Macan [1997: 145] points out), it appears to be epitomized by a group such as Genesis, originating in an exclusive public school in south-east England, at which art music would have featured prominently in the curriculum and there would have been easy access to private instrumental tuition. That Gabriel is drawing on some classical training is evident from his generally restrained, sweet-toned playing style; that this formal training did not progress as far as it could have done is suggested by the fact that, in studio recordings, his playing is restricted mainly to the first two octaves of the instrument and is sometimes unstable in the second, the erratic vibrato, and Phillips' admission that Gabriel was not fluent in the key of A♭ minor.

Gabriel appears to be 'working within his limitations', as Jonathan King noted; given the musical context – intricately constructed, expressive, often programmatic soundscapes – the result is all the more successful for this. He so successfully and effectively integrates the flute into the progressive rock soundscape that such 'limitations' become irrelevant; his performance style takes its place as one of the defining elements of the unique Genesis idiolect. Peter Gabriel's flute-playing plays a small but enriching role in the early output of Genesis, both sonically and semantically; the intriguing and diverse world of rock flute performance is also so much richer for his contribution.

Chapter 12
'I'd Like my Record to Sound Like This': Peter Gabriel and Audio Technology

Franco Fabbri

Pointing at the Sound

Piero Milesi, composer, arranger, producer of Fabrizio De André's last album (*Anime salve*, 1996), revealed that at some point during the production the artist came to his recording studio with a copy of one of Peter Gabriel's albums, suggesting it as a reference for the recording's overall sound. 'I was a bit disturbed, because we were not just at the beginning: I felt like he did not trust me' (personal communication, October 2007).

Fabrizio De André (1940–99) had been one of the best known Italian *cantautori* (singer-songwriters), since the mid-1960s, and *Anime salve* was praised as one of his best albums: for many, the best sounding anyway. There are no specific reasons why it should be compared to any of Peter Gabriel's recordings, though there are contacts between the artists' biographies and attitudes: De André had been linked – since the end of the 1960s – with the Italian progressive rock scene (where Genesis were successful even earlier than in their own country), toured with PFM (Italy's best-known progressive rock band), and released an album in 1984 (*Creuza de mä*), co-written with former PFM member Mauro Pagani, which was full of the sounds of 'Mediterranean' instruments (most probably influenced by pieces in Eno and Byrne's seminal *My Life in the Bush of Ghosts*, as well as by Italian folk-revival groups and Gabriel's third album: see Plastino 2003). De André was (and still is, years after his death) a charismatic leader in Italian popular music, a defendant of the poor and marginalized, if possible a figure (not only generationally) in between Georges Brassens and John Lennon, or Peter Gabriel.

The episode revealed by Milesi is significant because the status of De André in Italian popular music is that of a leader, a poet, a creator, an innovator, someone who would not base his own work on such evident external models. Which is not exactly true, as – on the contrary – De André's main strength was his ability to put together various materials, making them his own, like he did with his exemplary translations from Brassens, or with the mixture of Algerian, Turkish and Greek musical styles assembled by Mauro Pagani for *Creuza de mä*. As a matter of fact, De André's widow Dori Ghezzi, guardian of his memory as a creator, rebuts the episode as unlikely, though she did not actually attend that recording session. Milesi does not remember which of Gabriel's albums was involved ('I think it had Gabriel's face on the cover', which is not very revealing, but – as we shall see – is enough to circumscribe our guesses), and Dori Ghezzi was not able to say if Fabrizio had any in his record collection. Quite tellingly, while all books, sketchbooks, notebooks and press cuts owned by De André were delivered after his death to the University of Siena, where they are being studied in great detail, the artist's record collection remains at home, and nobody (except for his wife, son and daughter) knows anything about it.

It is likely that when, in 1995–96, Fabrizio De André told his producer 'I'd like my record to sound like this', he had in his hands (and in his mind) a copy of Gabriel's third (1980) or fourth (1982) album, immensely popular amongst record producers (in Italy and elsewhere) in the early 1980s, or *So* (1986) or *Us* (1992). According to Milesi it was not 'particularly new, it was something we knew already'. This also explains his reaction. What was abnormal and disturbing, then, was that the artist had not come with his request at the beginning of the production, but later on, and the example he had brought was not 'new'; by 'we' Milesi meant producers, musicians. Milesi's remark does not exclude the (then) most recent albums, as it can be argued that the innovative potential of the earlier albums was higher; from the detail about the cover, however, it can be guessed that the reference album for De André was Gabriel's third, fourth, or *So*. In fact, De André's and Milesi's episode is just a demonstration that even in Italy in the mid-1990s, and with two of the most highly esteemed singer-songwriters and producers on the national scene, Peter Gabriel's innovation in production from the 1980s was still as influential as it had been during the whole decade the world over. One can guess on how many other occasions since 1980 an artist had come to his producer bearing a copy of one of Gabriel's albums, and formulating that particular request.

The process of suggesting a desired effect or overall sound by actually playing a record in the studio is not at all uncommon in popular music, and in the recording industry in general. Verbalizing aspects of sound (timbre, reverberation, stereo effects, etc.) implies the usage or creation of linguistic codes whose competence may not be widespread, and often it is easier to 'point at' the specific sound than to suggest it metaphorically or procedurally. This is obviously more necessary when new artistic partnerships are established (in De André's case, Milesi had worked for him previously as an orchestral arranger, but for *Anime salve* Milesi was going to be producer and, for most of the production time, sound engineer), and is more likely to happen when the reference comes from another country or genre. When one cannot expect to share a code for exchanging information about music, it is easier is to go for the music itself: this is quite common in briefings for film music or commercial jingles, by directors or advertising managers. When Sergio Leone asked Ennio Morricone to compose the soundtrack for *A Fistful of Dollars* (1964), he put on the record player a disc with the 'De Guello' by Dimitri Tiomkin (from *Rio Bravo*, 1959). Morricone commented:

At that time, already, I did not like to imitate, so I told him to find another composer. My friend, however, was not someone who would easily let it go, so diplomatically he said: 'I am not telling you to imitate. I am telling you to make something similar'. I felt the dignity that every composer must have and I did not even like to 'make something similar' passively. But I did not want to disappoint him, and just then a theme that I had written for the television came to my mind. (Minà 2004)

Listening to Morricone's title theme for *A Fistful of Dollars* and to Tiomkin's 'De Guello' is revealing with regard to concepts like inter-textuality, imitation, 'making something similar', passively or not. As with De André and Milesi, the composer's dignity is out of question; the two episodes also have in common that the examples brought had in their respective times – to use Morricone's words – 'hit the audience's sensitivity'.

Technology's Champion Speaks Out

'De Guello' was actually a big hit all over the world, both in the singles charts and in the movie's soundtrack. Peter Gabriel's third and fourth albums were hits in the commercial sense (though much less than the following two albums), but definitely hit the sensitivity of a special audience: that of amateur and professional musicians, record producers and sound engineers. British magazines *Electronics & Music Maker* (*EM&M*) and *Sound On Sound*, aimed at that specific target market, covering the release of Gabriel's fifth album *So* with long interviews (Goldstein 1986; Hammond 1987), respectively in June 1986 and January 1987, have the artist's photograph on the front cover (both in a studio environment: one near an Emulator II sampler, the other sitting at a keyboard, with a background of multitrack recorders and outboard equipment). 'Peter Gabriel' appears on top of the headlines; on *EM&M* the name is followed by 'Technology's Champion Speaks Out'. An intermediate (and important) step on the way to becoming 'Technology Champion' was a documentary made by London Weekend Television (for *The South Bank Show*, broadcast by ITV on 31 October 1982) during the making of the fourth album, where Gabriel was offered the opportunity – amongst many other things – to show his usage of a Linn programmable rhythm box, and especially of a Fairlight Computer Musical Instrument (CMI). At that time, however, Gabriel was already a leading figure in the usage of audio technology in popular music, thanks to the sound of his third album and the much rumoured inventions of 'no cymbals' and 'gated reverb' sounds.[1]

---

[1]   I have no bibliographic evidence about those rumours; however, in those years I was a professional recording musician, and learnt those techniques from sound engineers. The usage of the noise gate to create peculiar drum sounds is referred to in Fabbri 1984a, which was written in 1983.

These inventions are paradigmatic of how innovation processes work in a recording studio. According to one version (Bright 1989: 98–101), it was Peter Gabriel who 'suddenly announced that he did not like cymbals and hi-hat because they were too normal'. Hugh Padgham, the sound engineer, reported: 'We [Padgham and producer Steve Lillywhite] said this is great news because now we can get a really big ambient sound putting the mikes further away.' Phil Collins (hired as a drummer) was disoriented, as his arms moved automatically to hit a cymbal at the end of a fill: so the drum kit was modified, adding toms in the positions where the drummer's automatic gestures would look for a cymbal. While Collins was rehearsing, he became aware of a new sound effect he could hear in his headphones, while the talkback system was open: the new Solid State Logic console had a noise gate incorporated in the talkback system, with the purpose of closing it down when no sound was made. As the drum kit had no cymbals (whose prolonged decay would have kept the noise gate open), any time a drum was hit it would resonate shortly with a 'big ambient sound', and then would be closed 'unnaturally' by the gate. Gabriel was amazed; Padgham and Lillywhite too. Collins (who first noticed the effect) was asked to play the same pattern ('boom-boom tshh'; he is credited on the album's inner sleeve: 'drum pattern by Phil') for some minutes in order to adjust the sound and make a recording, then Gabriel took the tape home to write a new song, 'Intruder'.

The 'gated reverb' effect (the reverb usually being the result of a sound processor, rather than the natural reverb of the studio like in that session, and the noise gate being applied to the reverb processor's return signal) is nowadays available as a standard plug-in on all recording software applications. It became famous almost immediately, thanks to Phil Collins' greatly successful 'In the Air Tonight' (recorded in the same studio with Hugh Padgham as engineer and co-producer), and to Gabriel's third album. There was some controversy and mixed feelings, as all participants in that session claimed their own role in the invention. Gabriel said: 'It's silly really. At the time I was pissed off because Phil's album was an enormous seller, and then people would say to me, "Oh, you are copying the Phil Collins sound"' (Bright 1989: 100). But it is clear that those effects were a collective invention: Gabriel, Collins, Padgham and Lillywhite are all involved, as is the anonymous designer of the mixing desk's talkback system.

Layering Sound

Gabriel's third album's appeal as audio technology reference for the 1980s is not just based on the drum kit's sound, though that was one of the most imitated features. Another aspect is sound layering. Popular music, as a product of recording technology and processes, can be understood as the result of various sound layers, codified in many genres' conventions and ideologies: the idea of a 'basic track' with drums, bass and accompaniment guitar (and/or piano, or organ) onto which solos, backing voices and lead singing are overdubbed, definitely has been part of the common sense of composers, musicians and producers since the 1950s, and became a kind of 'classical style' by the mid-1960s. But it can be argued that in the 1970s and 1980s the idea of layering became more generalized, and its meaning was extended to the superimposition of any kind of material with different timbres, speed or tempos, under the influence of European art music, non-European music (gamelan, African polyrhythms) and American experimental ('minimalist') composers. Examples can be found in pieces by various progressive rock bands, like King Crimson's 'Fracture' (1974). Albums from the same group's reincarnation in the 1980s (*Discipline*, 1981; *Beat*, 1982; *Three of a Perfect Pair*, 1984) are paradigmatic for an almost systematic usage of layering in the newer sense (see Conti 2007). They are also worth mentioning here both because they are contemporary to Gabriel's third and fourth albums (1980 and 1982 respectively), and because of the collaborations between Peter Gabriel and Robert Fripp, on Gabriel's second album (1978, produced by Fripp), Fripp's *Exposure* (1979, which includes a version of Gabriel's 'Here Comes the Flood', where Frippertronics are layered onto Gabriel's accompanying piano),[2] and Gabriel's third.

A key example of layered composition/production is 'No Self Control', one of the third album's strongest pieces, which is opened by loops that sound like Fripp's, though they may have been created differently (Larry Fast is credited for 'synths & processing'). The loop on the left side of the stereo image (a three-note chromatic ascending scale) sounds as if it was played on an electric guitar, while the immediate response on the right channel (two chords) has a polysynth sound; after two stereophonic calls and responses, a guitar riff is introduced (split with short delay on the two channels, and sounding 'open centre'), and then a fuzz guitar (or bass) sound bursts out in the centre (this, or both, could be what is credited to Fripp as 'guitar burst'). Then two marimbas enter, with contrasting rhythms (*à la* Steve Reich), the guitar bursts cease, and Peter Gabriel's voice enters over the layers formed by the guitar loop on the left, the synth chords on the right, the marimbas (one with a softer timbre on the left, another with sharper attack on the centre-right), the bass drum playing a fast 'heartbeat' pattern, and voices repeating fast notes on a high pitch. All these materials have different pitch range, timbre, speed, tempo and stereophonic placing, and appear to fill the whole 'sound-box' (left to right in the stereophonic panorama, bottom to top in the frequency range: for a definition of sound-box, see Moore 1992) with a brilliant texture, in stationary balance. As all instruments have their own place in the spectrum, the overall

---

[2]   'Frippertronics is defined as that musical experience resulting at the interstice of Robert Fripp and a small, mobile and appropriate level of technology, vis. his guitar, Frippelboard and two Revoxes. The system of recording by which two Revoxes form a signal loop and layer sound was introduced to me by Brian Eno in July 1972 … My own work with it began during June 1977 while in New York and was first used on record for Daryl Hall's *Sacred Songs* album which I was producing between August and October of that year.' Robert Fripp, inner sleeve of album *God Save The Queen/Under Heavy Manners*, Polydor 2311005 (sleeve notes dated 4 January 1980).

perceived loudness is larger than real, as it becomes apparent during and after the very loud drum fill (by Phil Collins) that opens the intermediate section leading to the refrain, and again with the amazing fill that ends the same section. The refrain itself is based on a layered structure, though different and to some respect more 'traditional' than in the verses; what makes it unique, however, is the drumming, because the fast patterns performed by Collins on the toms and the absence of hi-hat and cymbals leave a lot of 'air' in the sound-box. So, layering and 'no cymbals' are linked, as the latter allows a better construction and perception of the former.

Electronic Skiffle

'Biko', probably the most famous song on the third album (and of Gabriel's solo career, before 'Sledgehammer'), is less radical in its layering structure, compared to 'No Self Control'. Though it can clearly be perceived that the idea of layered meaningful materials (the initial recording of a South African mourning chant, and particularly Larry Fast's synthetic 'bagpipes' on the left channel, probably a Fairlight preset) is behind the concept of this piece as well, yet the song sounds more like a 'traditional' 1970s slow rock ballad, with a soloist's voice over a basic track (sustained fuzz guitar, piano, drums). However, the unusual drum pattern (credited to Gabriel himself, see below) and the 'African' shouts make it 'exotic'. In *The South Bank Show*'s documentary on the making of the fourth album (this being one of the few references to earlier work), Gabriel explains that the drum pattern is actually the foundation of the whole piece. He says that 'traditional rock rhythms were very limiting', and that rhythm is 'like the spine' of a song, whose final shape depends on and is adjusted to the structure of this rhythmic skeleton. In a following scene in the documentary Gabriel shows how he 'stole' a drum pattern from a Ghanaian cassette, listening to it and performing it at the same time on a programmable rhythm machine (a Linn). After the actual basic skeleton of the pattern is recorded, Gabriel adds other percussive sounds (handclaps, hi-hat, etc.), to create the groove on which one of the pieces for the new album is based. Gabriel himself speaks of the rhythmic spine of a piece as something that can be 'conceived' or 'stolen', indifferently. A further example of the process is offered with a recording of Ethiopian folk music, which is actually sampled and presented at the beginning of a piece ('The Family and the Fishing Net'): Gabriel says that the song is based on the intervals of the Ethiopian piece.

A description of the origin of these procedures, and their relation to world music, is given in a 1987 interview:

> I found this Dutch radio station and I heard a soundtrack from a Stanley Baker movie called *Dingahka* – I've heard it since and it doesn't impress me that much, but at the time it made a big impression on me. I thought 'there's an atmosphere here that is very strong'. It coincided with the arrival of my first rhythm box which was a $50 or $100 electronic kit, from a company called PAIA ... That

preceded Linn and so on, and that was a wonderful thing because for the first time I found I could start putting in my own rhythms and the frustrated drummer in me was able to come out. I could get back to rhythm, which was where I started really. Then I started using those sounds. I think 'Biko' was the first written with that technique and then 'Lead A Normal Life' and 'No Self Control' on the third album. Then I think there was a growing African influence with the Eno records and with Can. I think that, too, showed me another way of integrating things and I was influenced by their work. My interest hasn't faded because I find that a lot of rock rhythms don't make me want to dance any more. (Gabriel, quoted in Hammond 1987: 42)

Commenting on these procedures in *The South Bank Show* documentary, Gabriel speaks of a 'new age of electronic skiffle', an idea that the publishers of magazines like *E&MM* or *Sound On Sound* would gratefully subscribe to.[3] In fact, the whole *South Bank Show* documentary seems to focus mainly on this aspect, rather than on the fourth album's songs, as confirmed by the final words of Melvyn Bragg, the presenter, before the start: 'We wanted to see how he would combine these two elements: new technology and the Third World's rhythms'.

The newest representative of audio technology (and best tool of the trade of both 'stealing' and 'conceiving') in the production of Gabriel's fourth album was the Fairlight Computer Musical Instrument (CMI: simply called Computer Musical Instrument on the third album's inner sleeve, where no direct reference in the notes to individual songs can actually be found).[4] It was a very complex and expensive computer system, not exactly compatible with Gabriel's idea of 'electronic skiffle': but if that was a vision for the future, definitely samplers (and sampling software in PCs and Macs) are today's washboards and tea boxes. The way Gabriel uses the CMI, however, is no different from his approach to cassette players or rhythm boxes: the Fairlight is seen as an instrument to play with, sometimes with irony (like when Gabriel refers to its light pen as a 'phallic symbol'), and its sounds are used as suggestions for grooves and song structures. In the documentary Gabriel

---

[3]   It must be noted that in the early 1980s the term New Age was used (especially by journalists in the UK) to indicate a larger assembly of styles and practices than it came to indicate later on, as a genre label. At that time, the expression was used to refer not only to acoustic 'atmospheric' productions, in the styles supported by record labels like Windham Hill, but also to the music of artists like Brian Eno, Laurie Anderson and Peter Gabriel.

[4]   Bright (1988: 103) writes that on the third album the Fairlight 'can be heard in the fade out to "I Don't Remember", a pulsating drone drowning out the incomprehensible whisper of the amnesiac's memory'. Other Fairlight sounds could be the bagpipes in 'Biko', the orchestral strings in 'Start', some synthetic sounds heard in the centre of the stereo panorama in 'Intruder', others heard in the left channel during the verse of 'And Through The Wire', and so on. But all of these (except perhaps for the bagpipes) could also be generated at that time by analogue polyphonic synths. Bright (1988: 103) writes that 'though it did not change the album drastically it did give it additional colour'.

shows how the main rhythmic backbone of 'The Rhythm of the Heat' derived from a repetitive pattern included in one of the CMI's library sounds.

Gradus ad Parnassum in the 1980s

Gabriel's involvement with the Fairlight goes beyond that of an advanced user or even an endorser. After one of the instrument's inventors, Peter Vogel, came to visit him during the production of the third album (he stayed for a week and helped using the CMI here and there in the pieces),[5] Gabriel decided to set up a company to distribute high-end digital synthesizers in Britain and Europe. Actually the idea came to Gabriel's cousin Stephen Paine, who already worked as a synthesizer sales manager in a London shop (London Synthesizer Centre), and attended the sessions with Vogel. Obviously Gabriel's popularity and accountability made the deal possible, and Syco Systems was founded and started operating; it distributed exclusively also Fairlight's main competitor, the Synclavier (Bright 1989: 103). Gabriel's business relationship with audio technology would continue with the establishment of his Real World Studios at Box, near Bath, in 1986. Syco and Real World were at some point operating as different firms in the same group: in the January 1989 issue of *Studio Sound* (an authoritative magazine for professionals in the recording and broadcasting industry in Britain) there is a review of the Audio Tablet hard disk stereo editing system from Real World Research; a final note explains that the system was developed initially at Sycologic, an R&D branch of Syco Systems, and the project was subsequently transferred to Real World Research. 'Real World Research, Sycologic and Syco are related companies and Syco have sole worldwide distribution' (Hashmi 1989). It could be argued that Gabriel's extensive demonstration of the CMI's features and advantages in the 1982 *South Bank Show* documentary was also an advertisement for Syco Systems, and the suggestion that most of these business activities actually drained money from album royalties, rather than being an additional source of income, may not avert some perplexity about the interactions amongst Gabriel's layered activities as an artist, businessman, world music activist and so forth. But the very image of interacting layers (which appears so often in Gabriel's speech and practice that it can be thought of as a kind of guiding metaphor for him) dispels that of the shrewd rock tycoon acting with different faces (and, possibly, ethics) on different stages. Rather, it reminds us of another kind of entrepreneur, the multifaceted

---

[5]   'Well, I'd always dreamed of a machine that allowed you to sample sounds and then play them from a keyboard, long before the Fairlight had even appeared. I can remember Larry Fast telling me about this Australian guy who was working on a Carly Simon session and trying to sell this strange box. That guy was Peter Vogel, and he was having a really hard time because no-one was interested in the concept of sampling then. But Larry picked up on it, and for me it was a sort of fantasy come true.' Gabriel quoted in Goldstein 1986: 55.

figure of composer, performer, publisher and teacher that was common between the 1780s and 1810s, such as Muzio Clementi (1752–1832), who composed for the piano (when it was as new an instrument as the sampler was in the early 1980s), performed and conducted, and was a teacher and author of didactic works (*Gradus ad Parnassum*), a music publisher and the owner of a piano factory (Rattalino 1982: 31–8). One could say, then, that Peter Gabriel in the 1980s was a kind of survivor from the late Age of Enlightenment. Or (from another perspective), that the quick development of new technology applied to music in the 1980s, and the lack of an institutionalized division of labour in the related industry (including the newly born microcomputer industry), made figures like Clementi appealing and fashionable. Neo-capitalistic 'rationality' would later make those 'dreamers' old-fashioned again.

We encounter layers again in one of the interviews (Goldstein 1986 and Hammond 1987) Gabriel gave after the release of *So*, his fifth album. They are full of critical remarks on the growing difficulty of using samplers and related electronic equipment. But Gabriel envisions possible solutions:

> There's one thing in particular that's concerned with samplers. Now I think that, particularly if you listen to a lot of tacky records, there's not enough *performance* being put into samples. That's partly the fault of the machines themselves, and partly the fault of the people using them. What I would like to see developed is the idea of a layered performance. It starts from the theory that when you're playing a piece of music in real time, you respond differently because of your adrenalin and because you're functioning in a different way than you would if you were analysing a sequence on Page R or whatever. When player pianos were really popular, there were great pianola players who were able to express a piano roll very well. They had certain parameters – volume, sustain, speed and so on – that they would influence. With the sort of system I'm talking about, the first pass would let you sort out the basic composition and correction work, while the second pass would let you use a keyboard simply as an interface for performance: instead of giving you normal keyboard information, it could give you, say, vibrato. Or you could have two sounds or 16 sounds, so that the melody is switching between voices, and the internal composition is continually changing. If these parameters were built up layer by layer and in real time, it would be like doing a dub mix; you'd have an idea and then just go for it. That kind of smash 'n' grab energy could give sound sampling personality, and help to define character through performance. (Gabriel, quoted in Goldstein 1986: 55)

A similar description is given in the 1987 interview (Hammond 1987: 43), where Gabriel adds: 'I've been talking for a while to some of the designers at Fairlight about the concept of the "layered performance"', which sheds some light on the interaction between Gabriel's professional layers as an artist and businessman. However, while he was involved in these projects, he was already becoming less radical in his approach to audio technology: 'what I wanted to do on the album

[*So*] was more solid songs – perhaps sparser, and I think that it is more feel-based than sound-based. In a way there's *less* technology used than before' (Peter Gabriel in Hammond 1987: 43). A sign that some of the most radical choices from the two preceding albums have given way to a 'more subtle' (in Gabriel's words) approach can be seen – as it was noticed by many – on the album's cover, with a 'nice guy' photograph and (for the first time outside the USA) a title; but even more significant is the fact that the very first sound audible in the record is that of a hi-hat (see Fabbri 1986). While many producers were still copying the 'no cymbals' sound, the drum kit in *So* reverts to its traditional set-up, and in some of the best pieces on the album cymbals are amongst the most prominent instruments (like Stewart Copeland's hi-hat in 'Red Rain' or Manu Katché's ride in 'In Your Eyes'). But *So* was recorded partially on digital multitrack, and mixed to digital for a CD market that was growing fast, while the fourth album was released before the CD was launched (and never sounded as good, or as radical, on CD as it sounded on analogue vinyl): it can be argued that, in fact, Gabriel's success as 'Technology Champion' in the early 1980s was also due to his (and his producers' and collaborators', with a special note for Larry Fast) ability to get the most out of the old LP, before it started disappearing as a format. Similar aspects can be found in other recordings of that period, like Yes' 'Owner of a Lonely Heart' (1983, produced by Trevor Horn), where a very clever handling of filtering and presence effects creates a perceived loudness which is strikingly higher than one could expect on vinyl (see Fabbri 1984b). This is not to say that Gabriel's later albums are less convincing and influential aurally, but it can be argued that the original context for his innovative approach (a combination of limits imposed by older technology and resources offered by new devices and processes) was lost in the 1990s. As Clementi's (and Mozart's, and Beethoven's) example demonstrates, you don't have the benefit of the invention of the pianoforte twice in the history of music.

Gabriel's idiolect, resulting from the multidimensional qualities of his voice, layering processes, rhythm-based compositional techniques (he is responsible, with others, for the transition from the riff/turnaround to the groove as the fundamental principle of rock composing), can be clearly detected in later albums, like *Us* (1992) or *Up* (2002). But others, at that point, were able to use audio technology as convincingly and as influentially as Gabriel. They probably started by saying: 'I'd like my record to sound like this.'

Chapter 13

'I Need Contact' – Rock'n'Roll and Ritual: Peter Gabriel's *Security* Tour 1982–83

Jeffrey Callen

From the back of the concert hall, the five-person ensemble, four dressed in simple black clothing and one in simple white, proceeds through the crowd, playing drums. As they reach the stage, the synthesizer takes up the same rhythm and the band members pick up their instruments and don headsets. The singer, dressed in white, re-appears from the back of the stage, his face, now clear in the stage lights, in stark black and blue make-up that recalls, to some, a shaman from some non-specified culture and, to others, the image from his latest video.

Peter Gabriel's *Security* tour in 1982–83 (also known as *Playtime* 1988)[1] crystallized a moment in rock performance. The visual and auditory images that created the particular aesthetic of Gabriel's performances drew heavily upon his experience in the British progressive rock group Genesis, and also incorporated the minimalism of performance art, the immediacy of punk rock, and a frequently disorienting use of auditory and visual elements from African, Asian and Native American sources. As the leader of Genesis in the early 1970s, Peter Gabriel had helped move rock performance to new levels of theatricality; after leaving the group in 1975, his work was increasingly characterized by socially conscious lyrics and atmospheric, rhythm-driven music. Gabriel explored this new territory through an increasing employment of computer technology and non-Western musical sources. The intertwining of these elements reached its peak in 1982, with the album *Security*,[2] whose sound was highly 'technological' while remaining viscerally human, and eclectic in its musical sources without crossing the line into exoticism or stereotype. In his early post-Genesis performances, Gabriel had moved away from the extravagant showmanship of his later years with the group in favour of a minimalist stage presentation. Now, with the *Security* tour, Gabriel

---

[1]   The *Playtime 1988* tour included 23 performances in 1982. Following the release of *Peter Gabriel Plays Live* (1983), Gabriel initiated a second more extensive tour that included 56 performances. The 'show' for the second tour was essentially the same as that for *Playtime 1988*, maintaining the same repertoire and performance elements. The itinerary of the two tours is listed at the end of the chapter.

[2]   The album was released untitled in the UK but released as *Security* in the US market as a concession to Gabriel's new record company. Of the 23 performances on the *Playtime 1988* tour in support of the album release, 22 took place in the USA or Canada.

sought to move back toward a theatrical presentation built around the minimalist aesthetic that had characterized his previous solo performances. The album and the tour of Europe and the United States that supported it thus marked a turning point in Gabriel's career and sealed his impact on rock performance.

At the end of the scene offered as the prelude to this chapter, the insistent rhythm of the drums becomes the song 'The Rhythm of the Heat', the high-intensity opening of an album that is itself structured as a progression of songs of higher and lower musical intensity. The persistently slow rhythm of the album tracks (even the faster songs seem to be 'dragging', as if in self-parody) and frequent use of rhythmic displacement create a visceral response that simultaneously involves and disorients the listener. In the same way, the *Security* concerts (which included some additional material from Gabriel's earlier solo albums) are also structured around moments of higher and lower musical energy. However, in concert, the immediacy of the performance, which adds a visual element to the aural elements of the songs, acts to bring a sense of completion, as an experience of *re*-orientation is added to the initial *dis*-orientation of the listener.

The fusion of visual and aural images had been a focus of Gabriel's performances since his later years with Genesis. In fact, as one of the most commercially successful of the British 'progressive/art rock' groups of the early and mid-1970s, Genesis had increasingly emphasized the 'spectacle' of their music, both on albums and in concert. The epic storytelling that began with their second album *Trespass* (1970) culminated in the 'rock opera' *The Lamb Lies Down on Broadway* (1974). Their albums were conceived and constructed as 'concept albums' in which the individual songs were linked together thematically to create a unified work. The 'concept album' tradition in rock'n'roll had been initiated in the mid-1960s with the release of three seminal works: the Beach Boys' *Pet Sounds* (1966), Frank Zappa and the Mothers Of Invention's *Freak Out* (1966) and the Beatles' *Sgt Pepper's Lonely Hearts Club Band* (1967). The format had subsequently been extended into more narrative-driven trajectories by albums such as The Who's *Tommy* (1969) and Pink Floyd's *The Wall* (1979), both of which related a single story through a progression of songs within a mythic presentation. This tradition, which can loosely be labelled 'rock opera', brought a frankly theatrical element to the concept album which inevitably changed the concert performances of the works. These live rock operas melded elements from a variety of traditions, including rock'n'roll, opera, British music hall and Broadway theatre, to create a unique and innovative genre of musical performance.

From *Trespass* onwards, the stories and characters of Genesis' songs increasingly took on mythic proportions, and Gabriel's performance in his role of lead singer became increasingly dramatic. He had begun to emphasize the use of costumes, masks, make-up and props to create on-stage characters that were 'part comic-strip horror cartoon, part Peter Pan, part faerie' (Kamin and Goddard 1984: 50). *The Lamb Lies Down on Broadway* told the story of a young New York City street hustler Rael and his journey of self-discovery and confrontation with mortality, presented in romantic proportions via the narrative structure of a quest.

After the tour to promote the album, Gabriel announced his intention to leave Genesis in order to redefine the direction of his career. In particular, he wished to reject the role of rock star he felt was being thrust upon him, and to escape from the constrictions imposed by the group's style of music.

His first solo album was released in 1977; entitled *Peter Gabriel*, it is also known as 'Car'.[3] He has explained that his intention at the time was to jettison most of his previous stylistic associations, arguing that although the strong visual sensibility of 'art rock' was an asset, the genre had a tendency to take itself too seriously (Hutchinson 1986: 71). Expressing nervousness about facing audiences in his home country, he chose to begin his solo touring career in the United States. Unlike the extravagant performances for which he had become known with Genesis, he favoured a restrained, unostentatious style, often dressing in a plain boiler suit. While some of his early concerts received glowing reviews in British music magazines such as *Sounds* and *New Musical Express*, his appearance on the BBC-TV show *Top Of The Pops* (singing 'No Self Control') showed him looking and sounding very much like a member of any other contemporary synthesizer-based new-wave band.

Established as a solo artist, Gabriel did begin to rebuild the lyrical subjects he addressed and the musical styles he utilized. His first two albums ('Car' and 'Scratch' [1978]) both included songs that dealt with substantially darker issues than he had addressed before – experiences of isolation and estrangement. Although 'Car' contained some Genesis-like tracks, the cabaret-styled 'Excuse Me' and the lounge jazz 'Waiting for the Big One' displayed his growing idiosyncrasies, and 'Moribund the Burgermeister' and 'Humdrum' were early clues to the darker atmosphere that would pervade much of his later work. These songs were the first to exhibit the 'hard simplicity' (Kamin and Goddard 1984: 75) for which he was searching. Among the contributing musicians were bassist Tony Levin (also a member of the influential progressive rock band King Crimson) and keyboardist Larry Fast, both of whom would become key members of Gabriel's band during the 1980s.

Gabriel's second solo album 'Scratch' (produced by King Crimson guitarist Robert Fripp) featured a sound that was more experimental, but stylistically disjointed, and which lacked the cohesion his later albums would show. 'On the Air' and 'D.I.Y.' clearly demonstrated the transformations in his musical ambitions. The layers of synthesizers, driving rhythms and highly processed guitar sounds sat comfortably within the sound of late 1970s new wave rock, but were also prototypes of the evocative and rhythmic music he would perfect with *Security*.

His third solo album 'Melt' (1980) displayed a stylistic unity that the previous two had lacked. The aural picture it created skilfully matched the lyrical subjects with a sound that was more ominous and driven than anything Gabriel had

---

[3]   Gabriel's first three solo albums are all entitled *Peter Gabriel* but are probably better known by short descriptions of their cover art, as 'Car' (1977), 'Scratch' (1978) and 'Melt' (1980).

produced before, and which clearly distanced his work from his progressive rock roots and new wave preoccupations. It effectively established a distinct identity for Gabriel and, in fact, many of the album's songs were a central part of his live repertoire for the next decade (in contrast, he would only regularly perform three songs from the first two albums). 'Melt' also introduced some new components that would become increasingly significant in his later work: the reference to political subjects, a consistent use of electronic tones, the incorporation of non-Western musical elements (particularly rhythms), and a fresh approach to songwriting. In general, the political subjects Gabriel addressed were rarely explicitly stated, but 'Biko' was the definitive exception. A passionate homage to the South African anti-apartheid activist Steve Biko, who was murdered by the country's security forces in 1977, the song signalled the beginning of Gabriel's exploration of non-Western musical sources. The track opened and closed with field recordings of South African funeral music, whose rhythms provided the foundation from which Gabriel created the song.[4] Although 'Biko' was the only overtly political song on the album, other songs dealt with similar subjects more elliptically ('Not One of Us' and 'Games without Frontiers') or on a personal/psychological level ('Intruder' and 'Family Snapshot').

On 'Melt', Gabriel began to make extensive use of studio technology, including sound processing and synthesizers. It was the first album on which he employed the Fairlight Computer Musical Instrument (CMI),[5] which allowed him to achieve the sound that would come to dominate his solo work by colouring synthesized sounds with the 'human element' through extensive filtering. A vision of a 'primitive electric music' began to develop in which the application of technology would not only individualize sounds, but also break down barriers between performer and audience – objectives which reached their public climax with the *Security* tour. In the live performances following 'Melt', Gabriel began the practice of entering the concert hall from the back of the audience that he would use to dramatic effect during the *Security* tour, in order to challenge the typical concert experience that 'you can get close but you can never touch':

> I always find that walking through the audience, you see people and their surprise … and I find that the eye-contact on a one-to-one level as you pass people is much better for perspective, than if you walk from the dank pit of the dressing room into that huge bath of floodlights. (*Bristol Recorder* 1981)[6]

---

[4]   The song was later to be featured in director Richard Attenborough's *Cry Freedom* (1988) with rhythmic accompaniment provided by the Ekome Dance Company, an African drumming ensemble based in the UK. The song became an anthem for the South African anti-apartheid movement. Gabriel's work with African artists on this project was also an inspiration for his founding of WOMAD (World of Music, Arts and Dance) in 1980.

[5]   The Fairlight CMI was also central to the work of singer-songwriter Kate Bush.

[6]   The *Bristol Recorder* (also referred to as the *Bristol Recorder, Talking Book*) was a combination magazine and record album, based in Bristol, UK, that published three issues

Believing that too many concerts were 'safe, predictable rituals in which the audience sits passively to be spoon-fed this supposed nectar from the stage' (*Bristol Recorder* 1981), Gabriel wanted to transform the concert experience into an event in which the audience was actively involved – an objective that was to become an increasingly important element in his work and which would serve as the implicit framing device for the *Security* tour two years later.

At the same time, Gabriel also made a decision to change his approach to the process of songwriting that led to significant changes in both his recorded work and his live performances. Speaking of his prior songwriting, Gabriel explained:

> Usually I approached the music from the aspect of melodies and harmonies and filled out the rest later. But [keyboardist and band member] Larry Fast suggested I work from a particular rhythm, that it was the backbone of the music that could be fleshed out later. (Kamin and Goddard 1984: 75)

He decided to build on a rhythm, to experiment, and to invite the other musicians to experiment with him. On 'Biko', he began with an African rhythm; on 'Lead A Normal Life', a Bo Diddley beat. To leave space in the high range for the electronic sounds he used, and in order to match the 'primitive feel' of the rhythmically based sound he wanted, Gabriel asked his drummers not to use cymbals. He was increasingly placing his work on what he regarded as 'the fringe of rock' (alongside such musicians as John Lydon, who had left the Sex Pistols to form Public Image Limited). His need to experiment led Gabriel to incorporate influences from a variety of sources outside mainstream popular music; this included the work of avant-garde composers such as Steve Reich, whose approach incorporated musical 'grooves', borrowings from non-western musics, and an application of *musique concrète* techniques.[7] Gabriel also admitted that an increasing concern with 'the world out there' (Kamin and Goddard 1984: 78) had persuaded him to address a broader range of subjects (personal and political) in his lyrics and to introduce new elements in his music. He suspected that 'conventional rock rhythms would lead

---

in 1979–981. In its written work, the *Bristol Recorder* addressed issues of community, politics and culture; the accompanying recordings presented work from local bands. It also included a few works by more established artists, such as the Thompson Twins and Robert Fripp. For their January 1981 issue, Gabriel donated concert performances of three songs: 'Not One of Us' (from 1980), 'Humdrum' (1980), and 'Ain't That Peculiar' (1977).

[7]　*Musique concrète* is a compositional technique, developed in the 1940s by classical composers such as Karlheinz Stockhausen, in which musical tones (sometimes electronically generated) or environmental sounds are transformed electronically, recorded on tape, then re-combined to create an aural collage. This technique was subsequently applied to popular music, most notably by Beatles producer George Martin. Martin's use of *musique concrète* on *Sgt Pepper's Lonely Hearts Club Band* in 1967 influenced many other popular musicians to make use of the technique.

to conventional rock writing' (Hutchinson 1986: 72) and wished to move into less familiar territory.

From this point, his songs started to move away from traditional rock'n'roll structures toward longer formats well suited to the slow build-up that would become an integral part of the songs on *Security* and of the performances during the *Security* tour. Characterized by themes of social isolation, often from the perspective of the 'outsider', they allowed him to continue his exploration of role-playing. Frequently, he made use of masks to create an experience through which audiences could explore alternative sides of their personalities, something he felt had an important social value:

> If people have something in their culture, or entertainment, that allows them to experience harmlessly this part of their personality ... they're humans. (*Bristol Recorder* 1981)

The device of the mask is used effectively on 'Melt' in a number of songs that address different situations but which all revolve around forms of estrangement: the protagonist of 'Family Snapshot' is an adult preparing to assassinate a prominent person or, alternatively, a neglected child watching his parents move toward a divorce; 'I Don't Remember' reveals the singer as a victim of amnesia or as someone who simply no longer cares. The use of the mask in performance would be a central part of Gabriel's performances during the *Security* tour, in which he would use one visual image to portray many approaches to the theme of isolation and the need for contact and social integration.

When Gabriel began work on his fourth album (entitled *Security* for the US market as a concession to his new record company), he thus had a clear idea of the sound he intended to create – one constructed around rhythm, percussion (but not a typical drum kit) and synthesizers. The new compositions continued the device of building tracks up from initial rhythms: African rhythms provided the basis for 'I Have the Touch' and 'The Rhythm of the Heat'; 'Shock the Monkey' (the album's hit single) was inspired by dance club rhythms. While the songs' foundations remained percussion and synthesizers, other instruments (guitar, bass, trap set and keyboards) were used to emphasize transitions or other highlighted sections.

However, the album's inclusion of rhythmic and melodic elements from Africa, Asia and the Americas were referenced less to their geographic origin (as 'Biko' had been) than they were to their sonic elements. Gabriel explained that he was not trying to create pastiches of African musics, but rather to use their influences to go 'somewhere else within his own music' (Hutchinson 1986: 72).[8] Non-western

---

[8]   The first performance of material from *Security* was at the first WOMAD festival in 1981. It was also the first occasion on which Gabriel performed publicly with non-western artists, supplementing his four-person band with the African percussion ensemble Ekome and South Indian violinist Shankar. When the *Security* tour began in 1982, Gabriel

musical elements, electronic tones and environmental sounds (such as the sound of dragging concrete in the opening section of 'Lay your Hands On Me') were integrated into the songs via the Fairlight CMI to achieve a heavily textured sonic construction, and their rhythmic intensity was additionally heightened by an often slow tempo that accentuated the layering of the synthesized tracks. Lyrically, the predominant focus continued his investigations of the psychological impact of isolation and the need to dismantle barriers, both personal and political, without the patina of appropriation and exploitation that marked the 'world music' efforts of other western musicians, such as Paul Simon, Brian Eno, David Byrne and Sting.

The recording of *Security* began in early 1981 in the studio at Gabriel's Bath home; subsequently, Gabriel, recording engineer David Lord and keyboardist Larry Fast edited more than seven hours of recorded material. When the album was finally released in 1982, around 18 months of work had gone into its creation and it was distinguished by a coherence missing from his previous solo albums. The atmospheric sound, powerful rhythms and longer 'conceptual' songs gave it an immediate and noticeable intensity that reflected the length of time that went into its creation and production (Bright 1999: 201–3).

The release of *Security* coincided with the popular music industry's early recognition of the significance of music video and the appearance of MTV. The video of 'Shock the Monkey' (directed by Brian Grant) was a watershed moment in Gabriel's career, not only promoting interest in *Security*, but also firmly establishing a distinctive and innovative image for the performer. Presenting him in stark facial make-up, it mixed the iconography of the businessman with that of a shaman – a 'modern primitive' image which perfectly complemented the darkly atmospheric tone of the song, and provided the visual and ideological motifs that were to be essential components of the tour that followed.[9]

Gabriel's performances during the *Security* tour synthesized the theatricality of his work with Genesis (minus its props and elaborate staging) and the minimalism of his prior tours as a solo artist. Gabriel no longer had any interest in re-visiting the 'mythology' that had characterized his work with Genesis, and chose to emphasize instead the use of 'ritual' as an element of his work (Hutchinson 1986: 71). Indeed, the tour was not just marked but, in many ways, *defined* by his emphasis on ritual elements – repetitive rhythms, growing intensity, physical enactment and emotional/ dramatic climax (or catharsis). He continued to open concerts by entering with his band from the back of the concert hall. The band members would appear onstage

---

was backed only by his four-person band: Tony Levin (bass), Jerry Marotta (drums and percussion), Larry Fast (keyboards) and David Rhodes (guitar).

    [9]   Prior to the beginning of filming the 'Shock the Monkey' video in September 1982, Gabriel had investigated recent developments in video technology during his tour of the USA. He had also viewed video works of performance artist Laurie Anderson, avant-garde rockers The Residents and experimental video artists in the video section of the Museum of Modern Art in New York City (Bright 1999: 251–2).

to continue the rhythm they had begun at the back of the hall, which would then resolve into the beginning of the first song, usually 'Across the River' or 'The Rhythm of the Heat'. As the first song began, Gabriel would re-appear, in view of the entire audience, to the insistent drumming that commences both songs. The hymn-like 'Across the River' introduced 'I Have the Touch', whose metronomic 4/4 pattern on the traps set became part of a polyrhythmic accompaniment as additional layers of rhythm were added and increasingly complex textures were introduced by the melodic instruments. Gabriel would walk the stage, acting out the lyrics and emphasizing the attempts made by the protagonist, who lives in a world of rush hours, to break his sense of isolation: 'Pull my chin, stroke my hair, scratch my nose, hug my knees. Try drink, food, cigarette, tension will not ease. I tap my fingers, fold my arms, breathe in deep, cross my legs. Shrug my shoulders, stretch my back but nothing seems to please.'

He returns repeatedly to the phrase 'shake those hands'. He approaches the guitarist and attempts to shake hands, but is rebuffed and stretches his hand out to the audience. When he later (successfully) shakes hands with the bassist, they leap up and down together. At the climax of the song, he attempts to recreate the experience (at a distance) with the audience, by alternately offering his right and left hands, while repeatedly singing the closing line: 'I need contact'.

Songs performed during the tour came from all of his four solo albums, although those from the first three – narratives such as 'Intruder' and 'I Don't Remember' or evocative pieces such as 'Solsbury Hill' and 'Humdrum' – were generally more subdued than those from *Security*, which created the effective rationale for the performances, and which also relied on a strong visual component. Some songs, especially narrative-driven pieces without a strong lyrical or melodic hook (e.g. 'The Family and the Fishing Net'), seemed incomplete without the mix of the visual and aural elements that occurred in live performance. Progressions to moments of high dramatic intensity culminated in Gabriel's performances of 'I Have the Touch', 'The Rhythm of the Heat' and 'Lay Your Hands on Me'.

'The Rhythm of the Heat' (originally titled 'Jung In Africa') relates the story of an incident reported by psychologist Carl Jung in which he became overwhelmed by the power of the ritual drumming and dancing at an event he attended during a visit to the Sudan in 1925. At the height of the ritual, Jung, fearing that his 'shadow' was beginning to appear and that he would lose control, ran around the ritual circle to all the drummers in an attempt to prevent their playing. The song's dramatic trajectory is matched by Gabriel's increased physical involvement in telling the story as the 'rhythm takes control'. The performance builds until Gabriel falls to the ground, singing the words 'I submit to trust', only to rise again to dance to – or fight against – the powerful drumming that closes the song.

The climax of each concert on the tour was 'Lay Your Hands on Me'. The song reveals the internal conflict faced by the singer as he contrasts the emptiness of his daily life with the 'warmth' that nevertheless flows through him. At its peak, he calls out to some unidentified other (or others): 'I am willing – lay your hands on me. I am ready – lay your hands on me. I believe – lay your hands on me, over me.'

After beginning the song by pacing the stage in a subdued manner, Gabriel's performance parallels the musical accompaniment to a striking level of interaction with the audience. At the start of the tour, he would leave the stage to walk through the audience, touching and being touched by them. In later concerts, he would stand at the edge of the stage and fall backward onto the outstretched arms of the audience, who would carry him around the concert arena while he continued to sing. Criticized by some in the music press for indulging in messianic delusions, Gabriel responded that he was simply attempting to dramatically serve the moment in the performance of the song.

Musical moments (songs, performances, styles) occur, like any 'act of meaning production', in a discourse with other moments (both past and present) within a 'stylistic intertextuality' (Middleton 2000: 11–13). Musical performances cannot be experienced or interpreted outside the context in which they take place – they are a part of the tenor of their times. The times of Peter Gabriel's *Security* tour were an unsettled moment in the history of rock'n'roll. Punk, new wave/modern rock, corporate/stadium rock, and disco had faded or were nearing the end of their commercial success and influence. Musical tastes and directions were in a state of flux, without a set of ready clichés in place to (re)define genres and commercial slots. In this state of flux, the adoption and/or adaptation of musics from the margins of popular culture received an unexpected attention.

Peter Gabriel was not an isolated figure in the stylistic decisions he undertook in order to create and perform music during the early years of the 1980s. His use of ritual and the starkness of his performing style echoed the minimalism of those performance artists (most notably Laurie Anderson) who were enjoying a relatively wide exposure and influencing others' performance styles, not just in rock'n'roll, but also in theatre and film. Gabriel and David Byrne (of Talking Heads) may have been among the most prominent musicians to bring elements from performance art into their concert appearances, but numerous, less celebrated musicians, such as Indoor Life and Gang Of Four, also explored those options. Others, including Jon Hassell, Kate Bush, Holgar Czukay and Brian Eno, borrowed compositional techniques from *avant garde* classical composers such as Karl Stockhausen, Terry Riley and Steve Reich.

In particular, Brian Eno was a key figure in bringing new approaches and perspectives into the popular music of the early 1980s. Through his work as a producer and a musician – for example, Talking Heads' *Remain In Light* (1980) and David Bowie's *Lodger* (1979) – Eno helped to introduce new sensibilities regarding what could be included within the canon of popular music. They included ambient music, as demonstrated on *Ambient 1: Music For Airports* (1978) and *musique concrète* collages (built from combining synthesized music with tape samples) such as *My Life in the Bush of Ghosts* (1981). The release of *Security* came before the 'world music' phenomenon reached its greatest public exposure via the participation of mainstream pop stars like Paul Simon and Sting, but at a time when a wide variety of popular musicians were beginning to look outside western Europe and North America for musical influences and resources. Indeed, Talking Heads' *Remain in Light*, produced by Brian Eno, was probably the first commercial recording to combine African polyrhythms and rock'n'roll.

The lyrical themes of isolation and separation that Peter Gabriel visited repeatedly during the late 1970s and early 1980s were also frequently explored by other contemporary musicians, including Anderson, Byrne and Bowie. In this respect, Gabriel's success was to straddle the line between performance and pop, between mainstream and fringe categories. However, by the late 1980s, themes and styles had shifted. Gabriel's album *So* (1986) included only a few songs, such as 'Red Rain', that recalled the sound of *Security*. Its two most memorable tracks were the tongue-in-cheek dance song 'Sledgehammer' and the epic political ballad 'Don't Give Up'. In an interview in 1986, Gabriel confessed that with the completion of the soundtrack for the movie *Birdy* (Alan Parker, 1985) and *So*, he had driven the desire to create music based on rhythm and texture out of his system, and wanted to get back to writing 'songs' (Hutchinson 1986). In live performance, while he continued to seek interaction with the crowd, he now did so as a 'pop star', without the ambiguity of his *Security* performances. The spectacle and showmanship of the concerts increased, re-integrating some of the theatricality of his work with Genesis, but the emphasis on the ritual of performance faded. Peter Gabriel had moved on. It was also a signal that a window for experimentation in mainstream popular music that had opened in the early 1980s had closed.

Playtime 1988

16 and 18 July 1982 Bath, UK (Shepton Mallet)
28 October 1982 Boston, MA, USA (Orpheum Theater)
1 November 1982 Poughkeepsie, NY, USA (Civic Center)
2 November 1982 Utica, NY, USA (Performing Arts Center)
5 November 1982 Montreal, QC, Canada (Forum)
6 November 1982 Ottawa, ON, Canada (Civic Center)
8 November 1982 Toronto, ON, Canada (Maple Leaf Gardens)
9 November 1982 Buffalo, NY, USA (Shea's Theater)
13 November 1982 Passaic, NY, USA (Capitol Theater)
14 November 1982 Washington, DC, USA (Warner Theater)
16 November 1982 Philadelphia, PA, USA (Spectrum)
20 November 1982 Ann Arbor, MI, USA (Hill Auditorium)
26 and 27 November 1982 New York, NY, USA (Palladium)
1 December 1982 Milwaukee, WI, USA (Performing Arts Center)
2 December 1982 Chicago, IL, USA (UIC Pavilion)
6 December 1982 Kansas City, MO, USA (Kemper Arena)
7 December 1982 Carbondale, IL, USA (S.I.V. Arena)
12 December 1982 Houston, TX, USA (Music Hall)

14 December 1982 San Diego, CA, USA (Civic Auditorium)
18 December 1982 San Francisco, CA, USA (Civic Auditorium)
19 December 1982 San Jose, CA, USA (Civic Center)

Plays Live **Tour**

30 June 1983 Rouen, France
1 July 1983 Paris, France (Palais des Sports – two shows)
2 July 1983 Torhout, France (music festival)
3 July 1982 Werchter, Belgium (music festival – two shows)
5 July 1983 Ferrara, Italy (Stadio Comunale – two shows)
6 July 1983 Prate, Italy (Stadio Comunale)
9 July 1983 London, UK (Selhurst Park)
18 July 1983 Toronto, ON, Canada (Maple Leaf Gardens)
20 July 1983 Montreal, QC, Canada (Place des Nations)
23 July 1983 Philadelphia, PA, USA (Mann Music Center)
24 July 1983 Saratoga Springs, NY, USA (Saratoga Performing Arts Center)
27 July 1983 Worcester, MA, USA (E.M. Loew's Theater)
29 July 1983 New York, NY, USA (Forest Hills)
2 August 1983 Chicago, IL, USA (Poplar Creek)
8 August 1983 Vancouver, BC, Canada (PNE)
10 August 1983 Seattle, WA, USA (Paramount Theater)
12 and 13 August 1983 Berkeley, CA, USA (Greek Theater)
15 August 1983 San Diego, CA, USA (Open Air Theater)
16 August 1983 Los Angeles, CA, USA (Greek Theater)
5 September 1983 Southampton, UK (Gaumont Theatre)
7–9 September 1983 London, UK (Hammersmith Odeon)
10 September 1983 Birmingham, UK (NEC)
12 September 1983 Glasgow, UK (Apollo)
14 September 1983 Edinburgh, UK (Playhouse)
15 September 1983 Newcastle, UK (City Hall)
17 September 1983 Manchester, UK (Apollo)
18 September 1983 Liverpool, UK (Empire Theatre)
26 September 1983 Brussels, Belgium (Forest National)
27 September 1983 Den Haag, Holland (Congressgobow – two shows)
29 September 1983 Oslo, Norway (Ekebergshalle)
30 September 1983 Stockholm, Sweden (Isstadion)
1 October 1983 Copenhagen, Denmark (Falkoner Theatre)
2 October 1983 Hamburg, Germany (CCH)
4 October 1983 Dusseldorf, Germany (Philipshalle)
5 October 1983 Frankfurt, Germany (Alte Oper)
6 October 1983 Munich, Germany (Cirsus Crone)

8 October 1983 Vienna, Austria (Stadthalle)
10 October 1983 Hanover, Germany (Niedersachsenhalle)
11 October 1983 Berlin, Germany (Eissporthalle)
12 October 1983 Böblingen, Germany (Sporthalle)
15 October 1983 Clermont Ferrand, France (Maison des Sports)
19 October 1983 Avignon, France (Parc des Expositions)
20 October 1983 Grenoble, France (Palais des Sports)
21 October 1983 Dijon, France (Le Chapiteau)
22 October 1983 Strasbourg, France (Le Chapiteau)
24 October 1983 Lille, France (Parc des Expositions)
25 October 1983 Paris, France (Espace Ballard)
27 October 1983 Nantes, France (Parc de la Beaujoire)
28 October 1983 Brest, France (Salle de Penfeld)

Chapter 14

Plasticine Music: Surrealism in Peter Gabriel's 'Sledgehammer'

John Richardson

After a decade of relative obscurity, erstwhile Genesis frontman Peter Gabriel was effectively propelled into the popular mainstream by a single music video, 'Sledgehammer' (dir. Stephen R. Johnson, in collaboration with Nick Park of Aardman Animations and the Brothers Quay). To be sure, he was to consolidate his position with a string of hits from the same album (*So*, 1986), all of which would be complemented by similarly ambitious audiovisual offerings ('Big Time', 'Don't Give Up', and 'In Your Eyes'), but the significance of this video is not easily overstated. According to E. Ann Kaplan (1987: 73–4), 'Sledgehammer' is hard to classify, representing a maverick approach she considers 'arty' and 'avant-garde' within the broader category of 'socially conscious' videos. For Andrew Goodwin (1993: 60), as well, this was a video that broke the mould, primarily because of its unusually rapid presentation of images, which encourages perceivers to decode its 'messages' gradually, through repeated viewings rather than in a single sitting. This chapter will expand on issues raised in these earlier discussions through a close reading of 'Sledgehammer' grounded in the intersecting aesthetic and cultural meanings the video affords. A further aim is to ask how an ostensibly avant-garde music video ended up being such a commercial and critical success, winning nine MTV Video Music Awards in 1987, becoming the most played video in the history of the channel, and helping the single to top the charts around the world (Bright 1988: 270).[1]

If it is accepted that 'Sledgehammer' was influential, it was not entirely without precedent. Gabriel and his collaborators' work resonates with the cartoonish surrealism of many videos aired in the early years of MTV, including those of Tom Petty, David Bowie, Prince, Duran Duran, Frankie Goes to Hollywood, Michael Jackson and Eurythmics. More germanely, several landmark works of the genre had been partially animated, including Aha's 'Take On Me' (1985) and Dire Straits' 'Money for Nothing' (1985). Pink Floyd's 'Another Brick in the Wall, Part 2' is also worthy of mention, not least because it shares a common genealogy with Gabriel in British progressive rock. This video, which features animations by

---

[1]   http://petergabriel.com/features/Peter_Gabriel_Biography and www.mtv.com/ontv/vma/past-vmas/1987 (accessed 14 November 2007).

satirical cartoonist Gerald Scarfe[2] benefited from a significant amount of airplay in the early years of the channel, as did video promos featuring other visually aware pre-MTV artists, including Queen, Bowie and, famously, the Buggles. While Gabriel's video shares some of the arty earnestness of Pink Floyd's work, the 'serious' and existential aspects of 'Sledgehammer' are tempered by ironic humour and a funky beat.[3]

Figure 14.1   Image from Frank Zappa's 'City of Tiny Lites' (1979)

The grotesque and surrealist potential of working in stop animation with plasticine – a technique commonly referred to as 'claymation' (a contraction of clay animation) – comes to the fore in a handful of short films produced by Frank Zappa, including 'Inca Roads' (1975) and 'City of Tiny Lites' (1979) – both unsung landmarks of animated video art in which the visual narrative is powerfully driven by popular music. The latter of these films bears more than a passing resemblance to 'Sledgehammer', prompting the question, might it have been an influence? The two videos are bound, above all, by the combination of a driving funk rhythm and

---

[2]   The images in question are derived from the feature film *The Wall* (dir. Alan Parker 1982) and the album and stage show that preceded its release (1980–81).

[3]   Frith and Horne's (1987) detailed consideration of the British 'art school' movement remains the most probing discussions of the subject.

constantly transforming claymation figures (Figure 14.1). In the British context, it might be relevant to note that the video for the song 'City of Tiny Lites' was first broadcast on the television programme *The Old Grey Whistle Test*, a transmission that culminated in a full-screen shot of the show's 'starkicker' logo: a dot-to-dot figure made up of spots of light set against a celestial backdrop (Figure 14.2). Shots of Gabriel in the final moments of 'Sledgehammer' bear an uncanny resemblance to this image. In a similar vein to Zappa's claymation films is ZZ Top's video 'TV Dinners' (1983), a less ambitious undertaking involving only short clips of animated footage. More significantly, the technique of pixilation, another stop-motion technique in which human actors are filmed one frame at a time, was to feature prominently in the Talking Heads video 'Road to Nowhere', which like 'Sledgehammer' was directed by Stephen Johnson (see Bright 1997: 267). Knowledge of these antecedents feeds into an understanding of Gabriel's approach but it does not provide the answers to all the questions I will ask of these materials.

Figure 14.2   'Starkicker' logo from *The Old Grey Whistle Test*

In order to piece together a more connected understanding of Gabriel's animated videos, it is helpful to attend to two genealogical lines, one musical, the other visual: on the one hand, arty, punk-influenced 'avant-pop', marked as belonging to a British 'art school' lineage but significantly informed by New York's new wave scene; on the other, a visual line that encompasses experimental and mainstream

Table 14.1   Synopsis and audiovisual relations in the music video of 'Sledgehammer'

Form	Photo stills	Textual cues	Musical cues	Audiovisual relations
00:00 INTRO			Ornamental Shakuhachi flute sample with prolonged reverb.	Shot of microscopic semen resembles night sky. Close up reveals individual sperm, which wriggle in time with flute.
00:22 A1 PRE-VERSE RIFF 00:50 VERSE		*You could have a steam train…* *All you do is call me…*	Brass riff initiates beat with strong snare/tambourine backbeat. Texture thickens. Retro mood but production and performance point to contemporary sound.	Pumping of blood synched to beat. Body parts move mechanically. As riffing ceases, headshot of PG in pixilated motion. Stream of visual puns on images from the lyrics.
01:20 A2 VERSE 01:30 VERSE REPEAT		*You could have a big dipper…* *… a bumper car, bumping…*	Music dominated by elaborately configured groove, featuring funk guitar and brass call-and-response phrases. PG's voice occupies subjective 'centre stage'.	Almost every verbal/musical cue inflected in visuals. First instance spoofs back projection as PG rides sketchy rollercoaster. Claymation bumper cars collide with PG.
B1 CHORUS 01:25 CHORUS RUNOUT 02:02		*I want to be your sledgehammer…*	Song's hook repeated: four-to-floor beat and brass build to sledgehammer. PG joined in sharp vocal accents by backing singers.	Ice sculpture of PG unmelts in accelerated reverse motion; smashed by sledgehammer. 'Overproduced music' paralleled in surreal imagery.
A3 VERSE 02.10		*Show me round your fruitcage…*	Shortened version of verse. Texture added as rising/falling brass lines complement vocals.	Elaborate stop-motion sequence inspired by 'fruitcage' lyrics, suggestive of avant-garde while invoking harvest festival imagery.
B2 CHORUS 02:32		*I want to be your sledgehammer…*	Music intensifies with accents on each beat; brass attacks in parallel fifths. Gospel choir adds force to delivery of hook.	Cubist toolbox assembled on top of PG, whose face gradually covered. Head pops out of a sawed-out hole in synch with high-pitched cry.
B3 CHORUS 02:52 CHORUS RUNOUT 03:02		*I'm going to be the sledge-hammer…* *Sledge, sledge, sledgehammer…*	More texture added with each repetition of hook; cheesy vibrato synth interweaves with backing. Vocoded vocals imply mechanized agency.	PG's face morphs into claymation caricature. Plasticine sledgehammer hands smash open PG's psyche. Pastiche of Picasso's *Guernica* & Jackson Pollock's drip paintings.
C1 BREAK 03:11			Instrumental break: Shakuhachi flute sample from opening set against descending bass line.	Grotesque stop-motion dance by two headless chickens. An instance of inanimate objects rendered animate and vice-versa.
C2 CODA 03:31		*I've kicked the habit, Shed my skin …. show for me, And I will show for you ….*	Intensity of chorus maintained. Call-and-response exchange between PG and gospel choir.	Gospel invoked through PG's preacher-like persona and backing singers. Surreal parade of everyday objects and people encircles PG.
C3 FADE OUT 04:31 END 04:58			Abrupt fade out in all instruments except heavily processed drums. Eventually this instrument, too, fades to silence.	PG becomes star man, similar to 'starkicker' logo from *Old Grey Whistle Test*. Dancing PG freezes; imagery 'resolves' to opening: microcosm to macrocosm.

animated forms in Britain and farther afield. Opening to a wider discursive frame, these elements are infused with a sensibility that is best described as surrealist, although strong affiliations to the French surrealist movement, with its attendant psychoanalytical underpinnings, are hard to prove and to some extent irrelevant, despite the obvious sexual symbolism of the videos. More useful to the task at hand is Walter Benjamin's recognition of the subversive potential of surrealist forms. Specifically, textual readings of 'Sledgehammer' are interpreted through this theorist's notion of 'profane illumination' combined with writing on everyday life and audiovisual theory. By drawing together these diverse strands, I hope to shed new critical light on the video: its genealogy, construction, reception and legacy.

Verses: Unpacked Metaphors and Audiovisual Remainders

The initial moments of 'Sledgehammer' feature a reverberated wash of sound supported by equally formless visual imagery. A sampled *shakuhachi* flute animates stellar spots of light, macrocosm ceding to microcosm as closer focus reveals the microscopic forms to be human spermatozoa – a flashback for many viewers to uncomfortable or mirth-filled biology lessons. This coincides with a second sounding of the flute, the wriggling tail of the sperm providing a visual corollary to the ornamental flute pattern. In the shot that follows, animated semen rush toward daylight spurned on by an anticipated half-bar of strident brass riffing. As the beat takes hold, there is a sudden cut to shots of blood rushing through the veins of the song's human protagonist, this motion tightly synched with the emphatic kick-drum downbeat and its opposite number, a resounding snare backbeat embellished with Motown-styled tambourine hits. Sonically, these opening moments constitute a full-on frontal assault, which Gabriel's stylized pelvic thrusting in live performances complements aptly. But the video suggests a more analytical tack, in which the thrusting beat is sublimated by the use of intentionally dehumanized images. The results of this can be seen in a sequence of extreme close-ups of body parts: the pupil of an eye contracting and dilating like the shutter of a camera, a finger touching a temple, the corner of a mouth relaxed then stretched into a smile, an ear relaxed and then pulled backwards. The camera pulls back to reveal sections of a face – each of these images disembodied, abstracted from the humanizing totality of the face. The machine-like power of the beat reinforces the mechanical movements of the body parts, resulting in a marked absence of human agency. What is represented, then, is sex without romance, devoid of agency – a biological take on one of the more overtly sexed forms of popular music (See Table 14.1 for a synopsis and cue list with photograph stills).

Gabriel addresses the musical inspiration and a possible thematic rationale for his approach in the following passage:

> This is an attempt to recreate some of the spirit and style of the music that most excited me as a teenager – Sixties soul. The lyrics of many of these songs were full of playful, sexual innuendo and this is my contribution to that songwriting tradition. Part of what I was trying to say was that sometimes sex can break through barriers when other forms of communication are not working too well. (Gabriel quoted in St Michael 1994: 48)

But the songwriter does more than simply recreate the sounds of 1960s soul: he audibly transforms them. The Stax horn section of the opening moments is exactly that: a sequence performed by artists who appeared on records that had inspired Gabriel.[4] But it is heard in the context of musical production that draws attention to itself. As the final horn blast of the passage sustains and grows in intensity over two bars, it is suffused in the last half-bar with a shimmering analogue synthesizer chord voiced an octave higher. The chintziness of this part combines with other musical elements – the overproduced drum sound, Gabriel's 'yodelling' voice breaks, Tony Levin's surging 'stick bass' part – to produce a form of musical marking whereby the songwriter, the musicians and producer Daniel Lanois lay claim to the music they are performing. These significant musical differences are reflected in Stephen Johnson's directorial approach: nowhere in the video does he revert to the sort of imagery that would simply re-inscribe conventional meanings, tempting though this may be in light of obvious musical similarities to 'borrowed' forms.

This can be seen already in the first verse as the broken forms of the introduction give way to one of the more conventional forms of filmic representation: the headshot. Here, though, the disjunction of the opening phrases carries through as pixilation produces visual effects that render Gabriel's movements simultaneously comical and disturbing. In what follows, Gabriel becomes the straight man as a series of claymation comic foils steal the limelight with over-literal interpretations of the sexually suggestive lyrics. The Freudian imagery of a steam train is thus transformed into a Hornby train set, its tracks laid around the singer's head just in time for the model engine to pass around it. The antiquated Hollywood technique of back projection is then spoofed in a short sequence taking its cue from the line 'You could have a big dipper'. The line 'bumper car, bumping' finds the action verb's labial stops accented by cute anthropomorphized cars, which collide into the singer's head amidst a turbulent sea of animated popcorn and rock (candy). In the third verse, the line 'Show me round your fruit cage', and subsequent labouring of the fruit metaphor in the lyrics, is paralleled in the substitution of Gabriel's face with a stop-motion figure assembled from assorted fruit, tradition coalescing with the song's fertility theme as 'the sledgehammer bring[s] about a mini-harvest festival' (Gabriel quoted in St Michael 1994: 48). The technique in this sequence strongly resembles a scene in Jan Švankmajer's avant-garde film *Dimensions of Dialogue* (1982) where stop-animated fruit is arranged in the shape of a human head, only to be consumed by an adjacent head composed of assorted manufactured artefacts, a scenario that is overtly critical of the consumption-driven ethos of modern life (see

---

[4]   I am referring here to the presence of the Memphis Horns on the recording, the original Stax horn section known for their work with Isaac Hayes, Otis Redding, Rufus Thomas and others. This matter is discussed in greater detail in Kevin Holm-Hudson's contribution to this volume (Chapter 4).

Wells 1997: 180; Figure 14.3).[5] Although obviously influenced by animated video art, 'Sledgehammer' is for the most part rooted in the more high-spirited narrative traditions of popular expression. Here the animated fruit funnels into Gabriel's open mouth just in time for the opening line of the chorus.

Figure 14.3   Image from Jan Švankmajer's *Dimensions of Dialogue* (1982)

What is most striking about these sections is their exceptionally high level of audiovisual convergence. Music videos have often been criticized for a tendency toward intermedia redundancy (e.g., Frith and Horne 1987: 24), an extension of earlier critiques of illustrative film scoring practices that is encapsulated in Adorno and Eisler's (1994: 12) pithy phrase 'birdy sings, music sings'. Stephen Johnson's approach nevertheless drives home an important point regarding audiovisual relations that has been taken up by several theorists: namely, that the content of one medium is never directly transferable to another (see Chion 1994: 5–9; Cook

---

[5]   Renowned animators the Brothers Quay were responsible for animating this and the dancing chicken sections of the video. According to one unsubstantiated source, the brothers were dissatisfied with their work on 'Sledgehammer', which they consider overly derivative of Švankmajer: http://en.wikipedia.org/wiki/Brothers_Quay (accessed 14 November 2007).

1998: 82–6).[6] From this it follows that redundancy between media can only ever be partial; some 'third something', to borrow Eisenstein's aptly indeterminate designation, results from the co-presentation of sound, text and images. But the reality thus constituted is never complete, never entirely seamless, a question Kramer (2002: 174) sheds useful light on through his consideration of media-specific 'remainders'. Remainders are irreducible audiovisual artefacts that can function in two ways, covering their own tracks or 'mak[ing] themselves palpably felt', an effect that can be understood as 'a heterogeneous address to the perceiver [which] leaves moot the question of which medium, if any, is currently primary' (Kramer 2002: 174). Kramer regards music–image combinations that focus more on form than content, by placing an emphasis on the production of media per se, as fertile soil for the recognition of audiovisual remainders. Such forms maximize the semantic potential of music, inscribing audiovisual convergence with divergent undertones.

In 'Sledgehammer' such an interpellation is staged on several levels, not least of which is the interface between song lyrics and accompanying visual images, which refuses to conflate signifier and signified by taking metaphors at face value. In general, music videos interpret the content of metaphors in the lyrics while disregarding the metaphor's linguistic form. 'Sledgehammer', in contrast, takes for granted the song's obvious symbolic meanings, in this way teaching us new things about conventional speech patterns, by drawing attention both to their absurdity and their explanatory power.[7]

So far I have discussed how a high level of convergence between lyrics and visual images is achieved by interpreting figures of speech literally. Undoubtedly, such a close relationship is idiomatic to animated media. With animation, a megaphone can be transformed into an ear trumpet in the span of a single call and response phrase: 'All you do is call me, I'll be anything you need'. On the density of images in 'Sledgehammer', director Stephen Johnson has commented: '[i]t's all what I consider "thought beats." I try to have a greater number of thought beats than you often see' (Johnson quoted in Goodwin 1993: 62). The concept of thought beats might suggest a close correspondence of visual images to strophic structures in the music as well as their conceptual content. It might further suggest a closer focus on individual musical beats and temporal subdivisions within beats. Insights into what is going on at this level can be gleaned by paying closer attention to the surface details of the media as well as their material properties.

---

[6]   This is eloquently taken up in Cook's (1998: 83) writing on the emergent properties of multimedia.

[7]   For more on the conventional power of metaphors, see Lakoff and Johnson's seminal *Metaphors We Live By* (1980).

Verses II: Audiovisual Microrhythms and Synchretic Exchange

There can be no disputing that Gabriel himself occupies subjective centre-stage in 'Sledgehammer'. The singer's image – or his surrogate, animated image – is generally located centre shot, which is where the lead vocal is panned in the mix. But what of the musical environment that surrounds the voice and props up Gabriel's vocal forays? As the brassy wake-up call of the early moments subsides, the music is dominated by the gravitational push-me-pull-you of the groove. Modelled on Atlantic soul and funk, an intricate lattice of rhythms and counter-rhythms contribute to the instrumental fabric.[8] Gabriel's vocals interlock with Levin's bass part in a carefully balanced series of call-and-response phrases. David Rhodes' dampened semi-quaver guitar patterning syncs up with various rhythmic elements, including the hi-hat, snare breaks and bass response phrases, providing the song's main rhythmic anchor in combination with the kick drum and snare. Horn phrases generally fall on the downbeat, becoming more syncopated only later in the song. And these engage in swaggering call–and-response repartee with timbrally matched synthesizer accents located on the backbeat. This elaborate temporal tapestry is strongly indebted to African-American forms, even while aspects of the song's arrangement and production point in other directions. It gives rise to a pronounced emphasis on the unfolding 'now' of the groove, an aspect complemented in production techniques that emphasize the phenomenal and sensuous nature of the musical texture.

A corresponding emphasis on textural detail is found in the visuals through the use of the stop-motion techniques pixilation and claymation, which allowed the director to cram a considerable amount of visual information into the song's short time-span, responding to almost every musical and textual inflection. The expressive possibilities afforded animators in this respect resemble those available to contemporary musicians working with new audio technologies – including midi sequencing, sampling and digital music production. In both sonic and visual expressive spheres, textural details can be tweaked at producers' leisure as never before, allowing the emergence of a level of structural complexity hard to achieve when working in real time – in effect, producing a sense of condensed or magnified time. In music, this implies that considerable attention can be directed both to the temporal architecture of the groove *and* its timbral make-up. Visually, it allows attention to be divided equally between foreground and background – a feature that has come to define recent work in claymation, such as the popular animated series *Wallace & Gromit*, in which visual puns often rely on counterpoint between background and foreground events.

This new plasticity of means in both expressive spheres has other implications as well. Attention to rapidly presented details can give rise to an enhanced awareness of *visual microrhythms*, which work to hold the viewer's attention in the

---

8   For a consideration of how such rhythmic patterning works in James Brown's funk, see the chapter 'Rhythm and Counter-Rhythm' in Danielsen 2006: 61–72.

structures and textures of the unfolding present. Identified by Michel Chion (1994: 16) as 'rapid movements on the image's surface', visual microrhythms encompass such phenomena as 'curls of smoke, rain, snowflakes, undulations of the rippled surface of a lake, dunes, and so forth'. In the context of 'Sledgehammer', there is a constant surface 'buzz' of visual elements, be they sperm, indeterminate plasticine forms, fruit, body parts or domestic household object. Significantly, Chion extends his definition to include 'the swarming movement of photographic grain itself, when visible' (Chion 1994: 16). Throughout this video, the grain of the filmic media is unavoidably present: both forms of stop animation employed here engender a considerable amount of surface-level shake or 'boil', which is likely to encourage a simultaneous awareness both of the song's message and the message of the medium. Backtracking to Kramer's (2002: 174) idea of audiovisual remainders, it is this element more than anything that foregrounds awareness of the material bases of visual production.

Attention to microrhythmic detail in simultaneously presented media allows for a significant amount of what Chion (1994: 63–5) calls synchretic exchange (a neologism comprising the words synchonism and synthesis), in which sonic microrhythms latch onto similar patterns in the visual sphere and the tactile qualities of images migrate across the sensory divide into sound. In this way, the music may be perceived as every bit as malleable, or impressionable, as the plasticine images that accompany it – becoming, in a tangible sense, plasticine music. Correspondingly, the rhythmic complexities of the music are easily mapped onto the fluctuating visual microstratum, imparting to the images a greater sense of temporal organization and volition.[9]

Connotations are just as easily transferred as structural qualities. For mainstream British audiences in the 1980s, the tactile and sensory qualities of plasticine were just as likely to invoke fond memories of childhood as they were an avant-garde lineage that includes experimental animators like the Fleischer brothers and Jan Švankmajer. In addition to personal sensory experiences of the medium, the plasticine character Morph from the children's television series *Take Hart* (1977–84) is embedded in the consciousness of many British viewers of Gabriel's video old enough to remember, as are characters from the animated series *Wallace & Gromit* and *Creature Comforts* for later generations. The Bristol-based company Aardman Animations produced all of these films, and animator Nick Park from Aardman supervised the claymation sequences of 'Sledgehammer'. As much as childhood memories, the Aardman approach brings with it cultural connotations

---

9　　Although the music existed prior to the video and a proportion of listeners will have heard the music first, this reading assumes no prior knowledge of the music on the part of audiences. The point I am endeavouring to make is that from a perceptual standpoint the transferral of qualities in both directions (auditory to visual and vice versa) is likely. It is possible, furthermore, to extend the notion of malleability to encompass inter-textual uses of audiovisual materials: in this sense as well, the materials used in the video are malleable or plasticine-like.

imbued with a gentle sense of irony, an appreciation of the unplanned (or random) hilarity of everyday life, and the recognition of local (British) identity through characters who speak in endearing local dialects. Gabriel's equally subtle but inescapable Englishness[10] – very much in evidence during the days of Genesis but arguably as much a part of his post-*So* artistic output as his more controversial exploits in world music[11] – complements this aspect of the visual imagery in a way that is unlikely to escape domestic audiences. Everything from the singer's accent (middle class, southern English) to themes and images in the video reinforces this impression, including the harvest festival theme, Gabriel's daughters' attire and everyday objects seen in the penultimate scene. Humour in the video – slapstick, zany, impishly playful – can equally be seen as saturated with local consciousness, evoking cultural references ranging from the offbeat humour of the Goons or Monty Python to fast-motion chase sequences from Benny Hill. 'Sledgehammer', although drawing sap from an eclectic array of high and low, domestic and foreign sources is, for those who recognize the cultural markers, inescapably British. Looking beyond the question of local appeal, this mixed genealogy, including the incorporation of well-known popular forms, goes some way toward explaining how broad a demographic the video speaks to. In other words, it helps to explain why the avant-garde content of video might – like the heap of stop-motion fruit consumed by Gabriel in the second verse – have been easier to swallow.

Choruses: Surrealism as Subversion

If the verses of 'Sledgehammer' are thought of as cartoonish and humorous in a 'popular' way, more 'serious' and avant-gardist intentions enter the picture in the choruses. This aspect is anticipated already in the opening shots of the video, with close-ups of autonomous body parts invoking iconography reminiscent of the surrealists' fascination with uncannily transformed human forms. In order to appreciate the extent of the affinity, one only has to think of how Dalí visually transformed his wife Gala in numerous paintings, or the grotesque slitting of an eye with a razor in this artist's collaborative film with Buñuel, *Un Chien Andalou* (1929)

---

[10]   See contributions to this volume by Sarah Hill (Chapter 2), Kari Kallioniemi (Chapter 3) and Kimi Kärki (Chapter 16).

[11]   The use of a *shakuhachi* flute sample, expressive elements from soul and funk, and a gospel choir all raise questions about the ethics of musical incorporation that it is beyond the scope of this chapter to address. The songwriter's irony is arguably his saving grace, although questions concerning musical property and the politics of representation cannot simply be brushed aside. For further guidance, see some of the more judicious considerations of this aspect of Gabriel's work, including that of Taylor (1997: 39–52), reprinted in this volume (Chapter 9).

(see Bradley 1997: 69–72; Figure 14.4).[12] Detached body parts and automated human forms were part of the surrealist aesthetic from its early days. The phenomenon has two complementary dimensions, both of which are explored in 'Sledgehammer'. The first is the mechanization (and dehumanization) of the body through the isolation of its parts from the (organic) human whole; the second, the investment of inanimate objects (puppets, robots, claymation figures) with life. Victoria Nelson explores the latter phenomenon in her provocative study *The Secret Life of Puppets* (2001). Nelson attributes the popularity of such forms in contemporary society to an underlying although long-suppressed religious sentiment, 'the secularised supernatural', which denotes a movement of the supernatural back into consciousness by a kind of psychological sleight of hand through the omnipresence of animated inanimate forms in popular representations (Nelson 2001: vii–viii). Her interpretation is somewhat at odds with that of Walter Benjamin (1978: 179), who saw the subversive potential inherent in surrealism as a largely secular force. However, the concept of 'illumination' in the designation 'profane illumination' hints that the secular in this instance might just carry some residue of religious sentiment, primarily through experience of the noumenal, an extension of the phenomenal that this theorist was

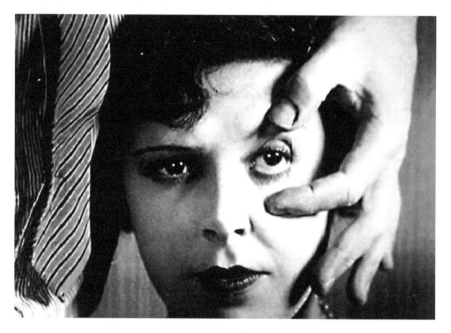

Figure 14.4   Opening scene from Salvador Dalí and Luis Buñuel's film *Un chien andalou* (1929)

---

[12]   Vernallis (2004: 251–84; reprinted in Chapter 6, this volume) discusses some of the affective implications of the use of isolated body parts in an engaging close reading of Gabriel's 'Mercy Street'.

willing to entertain – a kind of focused perception through which transcendental experience might be attained (see Eagleton 1990: 328).[13]

Benjamin's (1978) encounter with French surrealism offers perhaps the most promise when it comes to accounting for surrealist imagery in Gabriel's video. Several features in the video tally with Benjamin's understanding of a critical strain within surrealist expression. The most obvious of these is a preoccupation with past forms. Benjamin argued that by resurrecting the 'immense forces of atmosphere' in 'outmoded' forms 'to the point of explosion' (1978: 182), their revolutionary energies might be tapped. The forms in question include 'the first factory buildings, the earliest photos, ... the dresses of five years ago, [and] fashionable restaurants when the vogue has begun to ebb from them' (1978: 181). Through endorsement of a form of montage, Benjamin's surrealist *flâneur* sought to bring about a transformation of daily life that would constitute an implicit critique of the contemporary, including the restrictive morality of the Catholic Church and other facets of official culture (see Highmore 2002: 60–74). The adopted object served Benjamin's purposes well as it was seen as a mere extract from a particular moment in history that held no purchase over the present. If past objects could function in this way, it was implied, so would present objects in the future, a view that allowed detachment from the classic teleological understanding of temporal causality.

Gabriel's musical incorporations can easily be understood in Benjaminian terms, although a substantial proportion of listeners might not have recognized the song's musical allusions as such, especially in light of the song's markedly modern realization in term of its musical production. Visual reinforcement does, however, bring home a discrepancy between competing temporal planes. Notably, a stop-animated procession of antiquated everyday objects in the video's penultimate scene – a lamp-stand, a rocking chair, a drying frame, a chaise longue, a shabbily upholstered armchair, an A ladder, a candelabra, a circus monocyclist and an anthropomorphized stick figure composed from sledgehammers – conforms to Benjamin's vision of outmoded artefacts invested by the director/*flâneur* with a new lease of life.

Inverse to the surrealists' aversion to religious and state-endorsed morality was their preoccupation with sexuality, which Benjamin addresses indirectly through the concept of 'intoxication' (1978: 181, 190). Intoxication was something of a double-edged sword in Benjamin's conceptual arsenal: on the one hand, a symptom of distracted consciousness in modernity, on the other, a potential means of release from bourgeois morality. Whether induced by hashish, sexual ecstasy or reverie, this mode of consciousness was perceived as offering transformative potential that might be turned to subversive ends (Benjamin 1978). In 'Sledgehammer', sexual

---

[13]   The Kantian idea of the noumenal was later to occupy a central position in the writing of Roland Barthes, whose concept of the photographic 'punctum' – a small detail in a photograph that eschews the representational sphere – owes much to Benjamin (e.g., Barthes 1993: 79, 96, 107). For more on this concept, see Richardson (2007: 426–7).

intoxication is posited by Gabriel as a cathartic force that can be harnessed to bring about interpersonal realization, an aspect that has been recognized in the surrealists' writings on sexuality and love (Benjamin 1978: 181; Mundy 2001: 43–9). The inspiration for Gabriel's song sheds further light on this:

> There is a phrase by Nietzsche about what constitutes a good book, which he said should be 'Like an axe in a frozen sea'. That triggered me off to think of tools, not to put too fine a point on the word. Obviously there was a lot of sexual metaphor there. (Gabriel quoted in St Michael 1994: 48)

Nietzsche aside, there is plenty in this and other comments that resonates with the attitudes of the early surrealists toward sexual ethics, which although characterized by idealism, tended toward a permissive and politically egalitarian tenor (see, for example, Mundy 2001: 43–53).[14] The thematics of metaphor is another issue that strikes a chord with Benjamin's take on surrealism. As we have seen, the overly literal visual interpretation of the song's sexual content is a factor that illuminates conventional uses of language. In essence, the video works to bring about a separation of metaphor and image, an agenda that Benjamin recognized as integral to the surrealist project (1978: 191).

Humour in surrealism often takes a decidedly uncanny and grotesque turn, which can be seen in the images of dancing skinned and headless chickens in the song's instrumental break.[15] This scene coheres with the overall design of the video, insofar as it is concerned with animated objects rendered inanimate and vice versa. The opposition literally comes to a head in what is a prominent hook in the video, visually and musically. In the initial chorus, Gabriel's features are projected onto a sculpted head made from ice, which unmelts in accelerated reverse motion before being smashed to pieces by the song's main inanimate protagonist: a sledgehammer. The singer's real head remains steadfastly in place, however, symbolizing regeneration through ecstatic transfiguration. The second chorus finds Gabriel transformed into a plasticine caricature, a figure that will be subjected to multiple stop-motion transformations. The surrogate singer's

---

[14]   Brenda Schmahmann explores the gender implications of this video in her contribution to this volume (Chapter 5). While her reading resembles my own with respect to its attention to visual constructedness of the video, it is more concerned with the parodying of modernist art in the video and the question of gender performativity. It is beyond the scope of this essay to consider such matters in detail, although I do find her conclusions in both of these respects to be convincing.

[15]   There is a significant amount of inter-referentiality between symbolism in this song and 'The Family and the Fishing Net' (*Peter Gabriel IV*): in the lyrics 'Vows of sacrifice, headless chickens, Dance in circles, they the blessed'; and in the image of a 'pristine cage' (in 'Sledgehammer', a 'fruit cage') to invoke the female reproductive organs. Furthermore, in the video of 'Games Without Frontiers' (1980), a roasted headless chicken becomes the centrepiece in a scene depicting children dressed for dinner like upper-class adults.

plasticine arms morph into sledgehammers, which smash open his psyche to reveal the inner Gabriel (his Adam, complete with fig leaf), before multiple sexual symbols (from yin and yang to a wallpaper of sperm) yield to a constantly transforming gallery of quoted images. Here an element of pastiche takes over as the video's director surfs the history of Modernist art, with obvious allusions to the surrealist cubism of Picasso's *Guernica*[16] as well as Jackson Pollock's abstract expressionist drip paintings. Both images are rendered relatively harmless and child-like by their reworking in plasticine, in contrast to the shock value of the original paintings, which adheres to the subversive aesthetic of allusion discussed above. Deconstructive intent notwithstanding, it is possible to perceive an element of pedagogy in such conspicuous borrowings, a factor that obtains in much of Gabriel's work of this time, not least in his strong endorsement of Anne Sexton's poetry in 'Mercy Street', and in the gallery of contemporary and non-western art assembled in the printed programme for the *So* tour. There seems little doubt that Gabriel takes his role seriously as a mediator between 'high art' and 'the masses'. Perhaps this is inevitable in a mature artist – the desire to bridge generational and other cultural gaps and to bring to performances a larger slice of his accumulated experiences. The irony of this tactic is that the more conspicuously one dons the pedagogue's cap, the greater the risk of alienating a proportion of those you would wish to educate.

Coda: Toward a Genealogy of Surrealist Avant-pop

One reason for Gabriel's success in establishing a rapport with audiences that spans generations is his ability to incorporate stylistic markers from accredited musical styles. Always quick to adapt, Gabriel picked up on the expressive potential of New York's boundary-crossing new-wave scene sooner than many of his contemporaries – in particular, its cool, ironic, avant-gardish feel (see also Gendron 2002: 256–9; 291–6). This is apparent in the coda section, where the influence of performance artist Laurie Anderson and Talking Heads singer David Byrne is tangibly present. Here Gabriel adopts the ironic persona of a white-trash, bible-bashing preacher, confirmed by the appearance of an all-black gospel choir (see note 8). His jerky movements, nerdy sartorial style and declamatory vocal phrasing owe a considerable debt of gratitude to Byrne's persona in the video 'Once in a Lifetime' (1980). Laurie Anderson's performance art is invoked when

---

[16]   *Guernica* does not belong to Picasso's cubist period proper, although its reliance on geometric form invokes his earlier style. Elements from the toolbox section of the video that resemble this painting include: the presence of a head emerging from an open door on the right-hand side of the painting and the video; the wide eyes and open mouth of both Gabriel and the figure in the painting; the placement of radiant spherical object just to the left of and above each of the disembodied heads; the predominance of geometric (triangular) shapes and the essentially monotone colour schemes of both.

a cyborgian television is wheeled into shot, its screen inhabited by a large female mouth. Anderson had collaborated with Gabriel on the song 'Excellent Birds' (included on the CD version of *So*), so an influence from this direction is not unlikely. Both of these New York-based artists flirt with the posthuman imagery of the puppet and disembodied human forms in similar ways to Gabriel. Their influence provides audiences with obvious signposts that channel the artistic intent of the video.

Above all, this chapter has argued for a nuanced understanding of 'Sledgehammer' as historically rooted, locally marked but nevertheless bound up with transnational discourses of artistic and cultural production at the time of its making. The legacy of the song and video is impressive, not least in Gabriel's own subsequent work, including songs like 'Steam', 'Kiss that Frog' and 'The Barry Williams Show', where the songwriter audibly reproduces earlier successes. In live performances, moreover, Gabriel will often mimic the videos, including the use of a blacksuit adorned with stitched-in lights for performances of 'Sledgehammer' on the *Growing Up* tour. It seems likely that this video, more than any other, stimulated a renewed interest in animation in popular music, a line that extends to Daft Punk and Gorillaz (see Richardson 2005). The pace and density of the imagery in recent music videos has certainly increased, a tendency that could in part be attributed to the influence of animated forms (see Hawkins and Richardson 2007) as well as broader tendencies of intensification that have characterized recent audiovisual expression (see also Bordwell 2002). Moreover, popular performance at the time of writing, from the Scissor Sisters to the Flaming Lips, evidences an interest in the surreal that could be understood as extending the approaches discussed here. Not overtly political, 'Sledgehammer' nevertheless participated in a subtle politics of subversion that helped to define the nature of audiovisual fun at the end of second millennium and beyond.

Chapter 15

The Introspectionist: The Phonographic Staging of Voice in Peter Gabriel's 'Blood of Eden' and 'Digging in the Dirt'

Serge Lacasse

Introduction

In 1992, Peter Gabriel released *Us*, his sixth album as a solo artist (excluding live recordings and film music). According to Peter Gabriel's own words, this album is really about introspection: 'I started out with 23 different lyric ideas, on a range of subjects, but the personal stuff seemed to dominate the songwriting, as it had done in my life for the past five or six years. The whole look inside was central for me, and not to have written about it would have been a denial'. Indeed, Gabriel recorded the album after five years of therapy work with Robin Skynner:[1] 'Therapy taught me that it's always essential to be open about one's feelings and emotions, in order to get a grip on them' (Gabriel 2007).

In this chapter, I would like to uncover some of the strategies that Gabriel and his team brought into play for the expression of particularly intimate and introspective moments found in the album. More precisely, I will examine how the manipulation of voice through recording techniques can contribute to the mediation of such expressive moments. The artistic application of such techniques, which might include dynamics control, overdubbing or sound spatialization, helps make the voice (or any other sound source for that matter) sound 'larger than life'; it gives the voice some additional expressive power.[2] I propose to analyse the use of some of these effects in two songs featured on *Us*: 'Blood of Eden' and 'Digging in the Dirt'. As we shall see, even though the two songs are musically very different, the strategic use of specific effects contributes significantly to the expressive power of the voice in both songs. In order to explore these aspects of recorded music that are neglected too often despite their potential expressive power, I shall resort to

---

[1]   For more information about Skynner's therapy, see Skynner and Cleese 1993, among others.

[2]   Discussing the slap-echo effect heard in Elvis Presley's early Sun recordings, Richard Middleton writes that 'the effect is used largely to intensify an *old* pop characteristic – "star presence": Elvis becomes "larger than life"' (Middleton 1990: 89; his emphasis).

the concept of *phonographic staging*, which I would now like to briefly introduce before we go further in the analyses.

Phonographic Staging: The Model

Phonographic staging could be briefly defined as the way in which a recorded sound source presents itself to listeners, either following some electronic sound processing (reverberation, phasing effects, stereophonic location, etc.), or simply as the result of a given recording technique (types of microphone being used, their angle and distance from the source, the room in which the sound was recorded, overdubbing, etc.). Consequently, a given phonographic staging *effect* (or phonographic *setting*) will result from a specific configuration of these parameters. For instance, a sound source that has been recorded very close to the microphone, combined with heavy compression and a high sound level in the mix with little or no reverberation, is likely to produce an effect of sonic 'close-up'. Similarly, adding a lot of reverberation to a sound source whose higher frequencies have been previously lowered would make the sound source appear at a distance within the mix. As we'll see later, some of these techniques have been used in the songs under study.

Derived from the work of William Moylan (2002), the phonographic staging model aims to arrange these sound effects according to four main categories of sound perception: loudness, space, time and timbre (see Table 15.1). However, and in accordance with Allan F. Moore's (2001) epistemological stance, rather than describing the ways in which different sound effects are *produced* in the studio, the model aims to account for these effects mostly from the point of view of the listener: how do these effects alter the ways in which we *perceive* recorded sound sources? Table 15.1 is divided into four main columns: first, the 'Aspects of sound perception' column comprises the four large categories of loudness, space, time and timbre, which are in turn subdivided into subcategories. Loudness effects are categorized according to whether they occur at the level of the performance itself or at the level of the recording (once the performance has been recorded).[3] The table then distinguishes three types of spatial effects (stereo location, environment and distance). As far as time is concerned, the table lists only a few possible effects, including effects of repetition and simultaneity, as well as manipulations affecting our perception of chronology or speed (celerity). Finally, the category of timbre is divided into two main types: the alteration of pre-existing timbres or

---

[3]   The lighter shade of font in the table indicates that variations of dynamics produced during the actual performance (performance intensity) do not fall, strictly speaking, in the province of phonographic staging effects, since they do not result from the use of external technology. However, and as we will see shortly, they interact closely with other loudness effects that are produced electro-mechanically.

Table 15.1   Phonographic staging Effects

Aspects of Sound Perception		Parameters/Effects	Short Definitions	Reference Methods/Examples
Loudness	Performance	Performance Intensity	The level at which a given sound source was performed during the recording process. This expression refers to the traditional concept of *dynamics*.	- Description: *Soft, Louder than, etc./piano, forte, mp, fff. etc.* - Graph
	Recording	Dynamic Level	The level at which a sound source is heard in the context of a recording (within a mix).	
		PI *versus* DL	Ratio between performance intensity and the perceived dynamic level (includes effects such as fade-out and compression/limiting.)	
	Stereo Location	Position	Place occupied by a sound source on the left-right stereo array.	- Description: *Left, Right, Centre.* - Numeric scale: *−3* (left) to *+3* (right), *0*=centre - Graph
		Diffusion	Area that a given sound source appears to cover along the left-right stereo array.	- Description: *Point Source, Spread Source, Split Source (Bilateral)* - Graph
Space	Environment	Reverberation	Prolongation of a given sound event in time. Some characteristics of reverberation include reverberation time, level (envelope), frequency spectrum, etc. In most cases, reverberation effects are associated with spatial environments.	Expressions used to refer to common environments (reverb effects): *Gated Reverb, Concert Hall, Cathedral, Bathroom.* - Description (time): *Short, Long* - Numeric Value: *150 ms, 2 sec.* - Graph
	Distance	Resolution + others	Apparent location of a sound source along the front/back axis. Impression of distance is mostly the result of timbre resolution (influenced by other parameters, such as reverberation, dynamic level, equalization, etc.).	- Description: *Close, Far, Close Up, etc.* - Graph
Time	Autosonic Repetition	Echo	Regular repetition of a given sound event in time. Echo is mostly characterized by a usually fixed delay time between repetitions (≥ 50 ms), by the number of repetitions, and the dynamic level of repetitions (usually fading).	- Description - Graph
		Looping	Sound excerpt regularly repeated in time, usually in accordance to metre.	
		Reiteration	Irregular repetition of a given sound event in time.	
		Scratching	Repetition of a given sound event in time, usually accompanied by a typical vinyl scratch sound.	
	Simultaneity *(overdubbing)*	Doubling	Superimposition of two (or more) performances of a given musical part executed by the same sound source.	- Description - Graph
		Self-Harmonization	Harmonization of a given musical part performed by the same sound source.	
		Overlapping	Performance of a musical part by a given sound source that lies partly over another part performed by the same sound source.	
	Chronology	Backward playing	Performance heard in reverse.	- Description - Graph
		Chopping	Division of a sample in smaller units that are reconfigured in a new order.	
	Celerity	Acceleration	Noticeable speed variation of a given performance.	- Description - Graph
		Deceleration		
Timbre	Alteration	Equalization	Noticeable variation within the frequency spectrum of a given sound source.	- Description - Graph
		Saturation	Typical harsh sound following the saturation (distortion) of a given sound source.	
		Phasing Effects	Variation in time of the harmonic content of a given sound event. Includes effects such as phase shifting, flanging, chorus, etc.	- Description - Graph
	Electronic	*Others*	Sounds created with the help of electronic instruments, such as synthesizers, computers, etc.	

*Derived from William Moylan, *The Art of Recording: Understanding and Crafting the Mix*, 2nd edition. Focal Press, 2002.

the creation of new electronic timbres.[4] The second column of the table, entitled 'Parameters/effects', provides a list of phonographic effects (or of technological parameters responsible for these effects) for each of the four aspects of sound perception and their subcategories. The third column offers a definition of these effects and parameters. Finally, the last column, labelled 'Reference methods/ examples', presents possible way of referring to or representing these effects, in graphic, numeric or verbal forms.

Despite its apparent strict categorization, in no way is this proposed classification intended to be exclusive, for these aspects of sound are usually mutually intertwined. For example, reverberation, which is mostly responsible for spatial effects, also alters our perception of spectral and temporal characteristics of the original sound source. Moreover, it is more than common to find a single sound source affected by more than one effect at the same time. There are also effects that evolve in time, which can render their analysis even more difficult. The main reason for using such a classification system, really, is simply to help us orientate the examination process. Before concentrating on the Gabriel songs, and without going into too much detail, I will now briefly go through each of the four main categories, starting with loudness.

In the context of a sound recording, William Moylan (2002: 137–55) distinguishes between two kinds of loudness: first, 'performance intensity', which refers to the actual level at which a given sound event was performed during the recording process. This is different from 'dynamic level', which rather consists in the level of a sound event as heard in the context of a recorded mix independently from its original performance intensity. For example, in the context of a mix, a whispered voice (low performance intensity) might be heard at a much higher dynamic level than, say, a crashed cymbal. As our analysis will illustrate, this type of contradictory manipulation, often impossible to realize in everyday situations, might be used in expressive ways.

Still according to Moylan (2002: 173–219), our perception of space, in a stereo recording, results from the combination of three types of spatial information: stereo location, environment and distance.[5]

- *Stereo location* is defined by two parameters: first, the stereo *position* of a sound source on the stereo array; and, second, its *diffusion*, which refers to the area this sound source appears to cover along that array. For example, a hi-hat might seem to sound from a precise point on the left-hand side, while a voice might be more diffused and located centre. Of course, some

---

[4]   As in the case of performed dynamics, this last aspect of timbre does not constitute phonographic staging per se and is only mentioned in order to situate the borders of the model, hence the lighter font again.

[5]   Even though Moylan spends some space discussing surround sound, in the context of this chapter I am limiting my analysis to stereo sound, since this is the format in which *Us* was originally released.

effects, such as reverberation, might as well be described in terms of stereo position and diffusion. Conversely, reverberation might induce diffusion to the original sound source.

- *Environment* can be defined as the perceived space within which a source seems to be sounding in a recording. Usually, it is reverberation (or the absence of it) that is responsible for giving the impression of a given environment. We thus can find environmental characteristics ranging from relative dryness (little or no reverberation) to infinite (sustained) reverberation; not to mention special effects such as gated reverb. Again, one will also describe characteristics of such environments in terms of other parameters, such as timbre. For example, a given reverberation effect might be characterized by a very high level of high frequencies.

- *Distance* constitutes the third kind of spatial information. Still according to Moylan (2002), distance can be defined as the perceived location of a sound source along the depth of a recording's virtual sound stage. The sound source will be perceived as sounding from a given distance from the listener, within a given environment. Interestingly, although reverberation and loudness obviously contribute to our perception of distance, the fundamental parameter responsible for the perception of distance is the *timbral definition* of the perceived sound source – which points again to the porosity of the model's categories.

The third main aspect of sound perception that might be affected by phonographic staging parameters is time. Indeed, a large number of sound effects and editing techniques allow us to manipulate time characteristics of sound events. For example, overdubbing techniques allow us to superimpose or make overlap two performances by the same singer, which of course is not possible in the everyday.[6] Again, such techniques might lead to very expressive phonographic staging effects, including those described in the table and which we'll encounter in the following analyses.

Finally, a sound source's timbre (Moylan 2002: 157–72) might be altered in different ways, providing us with additional expressive effects. The table lists only a few of these effects, such as equalization, phasing and saturation. As mentioned earlier, the aim of the model is to try to provide the analyst with a tool for describing what is *heard* in recordings. Therefore, when mentioning equalization for example, I am referring to forms of filtering and EQ that are marked enough so

---

[6]   This example points once more to the model's porosity, since overdubbing might as well be associated with a modification of our perception of space: for example, in a case of a double performance of a single line by the same singer that has been overdubbed and distributed on the left and right tracks, we would have the same individual located at two different places performing simultaneously. Despite this spatial connotation, it still seems to me that the time dimension is somewhat prevalent, as illustrated by the fact that this multispatial performance occurs 'at the same time' or 'simultaneously'.

they become noticeable to listeners, such as the 'telephone' effect heard in CCR's 'Suzie-Q' (1968) or Annie Lennox's flanged voice in the bridge section of 'Money Can't Buy It' (1992), or the saturated voice in Gabriel's 'Darkness' (2002). It is with this brief overview in mind that we will now turn to the analyses, starting with an examination of 'Blood of Eden'.

The Analyses

'Blood of Eden'

Peter Gabriel is renowned for his creative use of technology.[7] Among the many examples found in his repertoire, I have chosen to discuss his use of loudness and reverberation in 'Blood of Eden'. According to Gabriel:

> On *Us*, what is primarily involved is communication and relationships between human beings in all possible shades. And what is involved is how you, as an individual, are seen by other people. The idea, then, is of 'us' and 'them'. As soon as a group of people are designated as 'them', a remoteness, a distancing, is created right from the outset. (Gabriel 2007)

In fact, in 'Blood of Eden', the characters (played by Gabriel and Sinéad O'Connor) seem to attempt to breach these barriers in a moment of intimacy:

> I wanted to use the biblical image in 'Blood of Eden' because it was the time when man and woman were in one body, and in a sense maybe in a relationship. In making love, that sort of struggle is to get some form of merging of boundaries; it's a really powerful union. And there are many obstacles to this. Sinéad O'Connor's voice means that musically there is something to set it off – two emotional, needy voices, in a way. We actually had quite a lot of trouble with the song. Initially, Daniel Lanois wasn't keen on this at all and it didn't settle down. I couldn't get the groove to work and it went through probably four or five different feels, and less became more in terms of the rhythm content because it verged on sounding trite. But there was also, in the central part of the song, musically and lyrically, a point of union, a breakthrough. So, emotionally, I feel close to this song. (Gabriel 2007)

---

[7]   As far as voice is concerned, Umberto Fiori (1987) describes a contrast between the singer's 'cold' attitude and the highly emotional lyrics in 'I Have the Touch', a contrast further enhanced by a vocal setting 'robotizing' Gabriel's voice. David Schwarz (1997: 87–99) also discusses Peter Gabriel's 'Intruder', notably in terms of the way the voice is phonographically staged.

In a sense, these explorations of distancing and rapprochement are illustrated and in part expressed by some phonographic staging effects. Reverberation, for example, contributes to create a sense of distance, not only at a concrete 'spatial level' but also, and perhaps especially so, on a metaphorical level, at least in two (related) ways. First, in the verses, we are faced with a subject who reflects on himself, and reverberation contributes to illustrate this situation. But the song is also rooted in 'biblical images', as Gabriel himself tells us.

In the song, the chosen environment enhances high frequencies, apparently in order to support what is expressed through the lyrics. Gabriel's 'Blood of Eden' presents an $A_1-A_2-B_1-A_3-A_4-B_1-C-A_5-B_1-B_2$ form (in which A_n stand for the verses, B_n for choruses and C for the bridge). Each section, represented by a letter, presents (at least) one specific vocal setting. For now, we will concentrate on the environment heard during the A sections, which is characterised by a high level of reverberation with reverb time of around two to three seconds. Furthermore, the reverb effect enhances high frequencies, and is thus triggered by most voiceless consonant sounds such as [s], [tʃ], [ʃ], [t], [k], [f], and so on.[8] Interestingly, the song lyrics are full of words displaying these sounds, most noticeably in the verse parts. For example, in A_1 (00:42–01:04)[9] we have 'I **c**aught **s**ight of my re**fl**e**ct**ion', 'I **s**aw the darkne**ss**', 'I **s**aw the **s**igns', etc. In A_2 (01:07–01:29) we find 'And the darkne**ss** **st**ill', '**S**o **s**e**c**ure', and so forth. There is even a line in A_5 (04:36–04:59) saying 'Wa**tch** ea**ch** one rea**ch** for **c**reature **c**omfort'. In fact, and right from the outset, there is an obvious relation between the idea of 'reflection' in the first line and the long reverberation following the word, a metaphor that is extended during the whole verse ('caught sight', 'saw', etc.). There is even some silence right after the word 'reflection' that helps put the last syllable and its reverberation in the foreground. This almost denotative relationship is further exploited in more symbolic terms in the beginning of A_3 (02:10–02:34) when Gabriel sings 'My grip is surely slipping'. Here again, reverb is clearly heard because of [ʃ] and [s] consonants coupled with the presence of a short silence, and again reverb helps support the image conveyed by the lyrics (the slipping, the emptiness). As I've suggested earlier, reverberation also largely contributes to evoking a religious or spiritual connotation. Of course, this relation between spirituality and love is not new. For example, the Orioles' 'Crying in the Chapel' (1953), a song renowned for its ambivalence between love and religious devotion (Garofalo 1997: 116), is also known for its use of reverberation, an obvious acoustic allusion to 'chapel'.[10]

But perhaps an even more powerful use of phonographic staging, despite its relative discretion, is to be found in the bridge section of 'Blood of Eden' (3:28–4:23). By its very nature, a bridge section is meant to be a contrast. Consequently,

---

[8]   Pronunciation symbols follow those used in Greenbaum 1996: xi.

[9]   When referring to sound excerpts from recordings I will be indicating time references in brackets (00:00–00:00). In the case of repeated lyric lines, I will refer to the first occurrence, unless otherwise specified.

[10]   See Lacasse 2002 for similar observations on Alanis Morissette's 'Front Row'.

elements belonging both to music and lyrics are used to create the desired effect. In 'Blood of Eden', many musical elements help in producing a contrast with what precedes. Interestingly, and as suggested by Gabriel's earlier quote, the bridge section has been mixed *separately* by a different sound engineer (Richard Chappell) and re-inserted afterwards within the song's final mix. As we will now see, this section is particularly expressive.

From the outset, we hear an interrupted cadence (V–vi) that already contributes to creating a contrasting atmosphere. The contrast is further enhanced by the relative thinness of the instrumental texture. Drums and percussion cease to play, the rhythm being only subtly outlined by the few remaining instruments, such as the bass and the fading-in and echoic guitar that are accompanied by a floating synthesizer pad. All these musical features help enhance another contrast, that of the specific vocal staging configuration heard during the bridge. Gabriel's voice suddenly seems much more present, just as if we were passing from middle distance within a rather large room to acoustic close-up. In addition to the changes in instrumentation just mentioned, the effect of distance contrast is created by the combination of a number of technical manipulations: besides the fact that Gabriel was manifestly recorded very close to the microphone, the voice is clearly louder, highly compressed, and with little reverberation, contrary to what is heard in the verses. Moreover, in the preceding chorus, while Gabriel's voice is mixed at a rather low dynamic level and intimately blended with Sinéad O'Connor's vocal line and other vocal parts, in the bridge, Gabriel's voice is completely isolated and foregrounded in the mix. When listening with headphones, it is almost as if Gabriel's voice was suddenly entering our head – or giving us access to the character's mind – being as close as it can be. Most important, perhaps, among these parameters is the contrast between Gabriel's performance intensity and the voice's dynamic level.

As already mentioned, performance intensity (PI) is defined as the level at which a given sound source was performed during the recording process. This is, so to speak, a 'natural' way of modifying one's loudness: playing or singing loudly or softly. Dynamic level (DL), on the other hand, refers to the level at which a sound source is heard in the context of a recording *regardless* of the sound source's original performance intensity. This ratio between performance intensity and dynamic level is illustrated in Figure 15.1, which presents a graphic representation of PI *versus* DL of the lead vocal in the bridge section. The graph is divided into two sections. The upper section of the graph displays my (subjective) tracing of Gabriel's original performance intensity. The lower section shows what I perceived as being the variation of the voice's dynamic level in that same portion of the mix. At the bottom of the graphs, we find a grid divided into bars, hence the 4/4 time signature at the beginning. In the present case, if we except the 2/4 bar signature just before 3:52, each short vertical line represents a four-beat bar – the slightly longer ones indicating larger formal divisions, such as a verse, chorus, and so on. Below the grid, there are time indications (as found on most CD players) as well as formal sections. Time indications are particularly helpful for musical sections without clear pulse, or for helping analysts not familiar with musical terminology. Still, any listener should quickly pick out larger divisions (illustrated by the longer vertical lines) simply by comparing the grid with the CD time indication while listening to the recording. As one can see on the graph, there are times where PI and DL are completely opposed, especially at 3:29, at the very beginning of the bridge section. At this point, even though Gabriel starts murmuring, his voice becomes the loudest sound source in the mix, giving rise to an effect of extreme proximity. When combined with the lyric's narrative, the resulting effect of intimacy is striking.

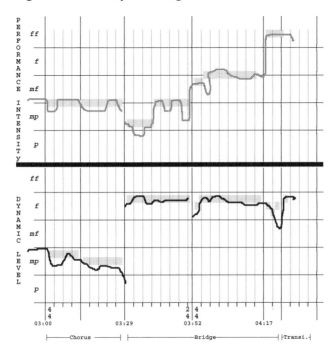

Figure 15.1 Performance intensity *versus* dynamic level (voice) in Peter Gabriel's 'Blood of Eden' (1992)

Contrary to what has been previously sung (more in the form of a descriptive narrative), the bridge section depicts an intimate and privileged moment as experienced by the character, most probably occurring in the context of sexual intercourse: '"Blood of Eden" is fairly obviously about the failure of a relationship and the moments of trying to work it through, making love in a moment of storm' (Gabriel quoted in O'Hagan 1992: 4–5). The character starts addressing his unheard partner who 'take[s] [him] in' at his own request. Time is suspended, 'Holding still for a moment'. The lack of rhythmical reference enhances this impression of suspended time as much as the voice foregrounding enhances the image of intimate fusion as experienced by the character-subject. In that example, it is thus in the context of 'A moment of bliss' that an effect of acoustic close-up is used. By contrast, phonographic staging effects heard in 'Digging in the Dirt' seem to express a different kind of interaction, one involving two antagonistic sides of the same character.

'Digging in the Dirt'

According to Gabriel (2007), '"Digging in the Dirt" was looking at the darker side of myself. ... I was looking at the way I'd been behaving – sort of passive-aggressive – looking at the bastard in me that I hadn't really acknowledged, and as I was writing, I was inter-weaving bits of myself.' Rather than expressing a moment of ultimate intimacy between two distinct beings, this song relates what seems to be a violent confrontation between two aspects of a single character. As soon as the track begins, musical arrangements point to a metaphorical 'digging' within the character's mind, notably illustrated by the gradual layering of elements: 'David Bottrill and Richard Blair have done some great stuff with the rhythm track. There are a lots of layers and the song is all about investigating the layers within yourself, like the layers of an onion – you come across something else each time and you try to peel it back and find out what lies underneath' (O'Hagan 1992: 4).

Indeed, the central sonic element around which are gradually superimposed the other rhythmical parts consists in a 'dirty' sampled loop. One could interpret this dirty loop as a musical metaphor for the repression of older psychological wounds, slowly and deeply buried within the character's mind. The whole point of a therapy, of course, becomes the unearthing of these wounds so they can eventually be healed. The whole song could be read against that loop around which is built the character's confrontation with himself. In that context, and as my analysis shall demonstrate, the phonographic staging of Gabriel's voice becomes a crucial aspect of the song. However, vocal staging is only one of many elements that contribute to suggesting the character's interior conflict. In that regard, another key aspect of the song is its formal structure.[11]

Interestingly, the unusual formal structure of the song already expresses the character's ambiguity, helping the articulation of the interior divide. After the introduction – during which the different elements are gradually 'burying' the loop – we hear the first two verses (V_1 and V_2), followed by a pre-chorus (PC) ('This time you've gone too far / I told you'). Then, this pre-chorus leads to what sounds to be an aggressive chorus C_1 ('Don't talk back / Just drive the car'), itself followed by what could be described as the 'real' chorus (C_2). Indeed, the lyrics of this second chorus include the title ('Digging in the dirt / Stay with me I need support'). Also, its accompaniment is much softer than what is heard in C_1. After the first occurrence of C_2, an instrumental transition leads to the repetition of the same formal structure (V_{3-4}–PC–C_1–C_2–Coda). In short, we have what looks like a

---

[11]   For a detailed analysis of text–music relationships in 'Digging in the Dirt', see Lacasse 1995.

traditional song form, except that we find two contrasting choruses, each of which seems to be associated with one of the character's two sides: C_1 corresponds to moments of anger as experienced by the character, while C_2 rather evokes periods of vulnerability while he is 'digging' in his wounds in order to find the source of the psychological pain. Approached from that perspective, the song structure becomes much clearer. In fact, when analysing all musical and textual features of the song with this structure in mind, one realizes that every single element contributes to the overall coherence of the song. In the following, I shall analyse section by section the phonographic staging of the voice.

In general, verses describe the character's discomfort and the difficulty he has in trying to identify its cause. In the verses, Gabriel sings in a low tone and his voice has been doubled and panned centre; moreover, and this is when it becomes interesting, most of the time, the two vocal tracks are not synchronized, sometimes with different intonation, making the voice blurred. In my opinion, this effect helps convey the ambiguity felt by the character when trying to find the source of the problem: 'Something in me / Dark and sticky / All the time is getting strong.' Moreover, the doubled voice also already suggests the two-sided character, who will eventually split himself in two in the choruses. In the third verse, the character confesses 'The more I look / The more I find / As I close on in / I get so blind'. Again, the blurred voice supports the character's difficulty in sublimating his interior conflict, just as if he were unable to 'visually' focus on the source of his ill-being. This whole feeling of ambiguity felt in the verses is of course also supported by other musical effects, such as the descending organ line that keeps oscillating between the major and minor modes.

In the pre-chorus, Gabriel's voice is also doubled (even tripled), but this time the performances are more synchronized.[12] This effect, widely used in recorded popular music, helps in thickening the sound source. In the context of the song, when the character shouts 'This time you've gone too far', the doubled voice does indeed sound richer and more aggressive. However, toward the end of the pre-chorus, when the character repeatedly shouts 'I told you, I told you, I told you, I told you', he is suddenly interrupted by what seems to be ... himself! We then can clearly hear an effect of vocal overlapping between the end of the pre-chorus and the beginning of C_1. Not only is this effect supporting the accumulation of tension that leads to the expression of anger in C_1, but the overlapping effect is denoted in the lyrics themselves, when the interrupting side of the character starts the 'aggressive' chorus by shouting 'Don't talk back' (see Figure 15.2).

As was the case in 'Blood of Eden', the sound of the words themselves are brought into play: for example, the use of successive crisp consonants, especially in C_1, contributes to an overall effect of anger ('I told you', 'Don't talk back', etc.), consonants that are also exaggerated by the synchronous double-tracking of the voice. Again, other musical parts, such as the distorted guitar, participate in the whole.

---

[12]   However, when listening closely, one can hear that the word 'time' is sustained separately by one of the voice-tracks.

⊢I to̦ld you⊣   ⊢I to̦ld you⊣   ⊢I to̦ld you⊣   ⊢I to̦ld you⊣

                                                    ⊢Don't talk back⊣

Figure 15. 2 'Digging in the Dirt'

Note: Vertical lines represent beats.

The tension is at its paroxysm when the character has to face reality at the end of C_1 ('This is for real'), when the last syllable is sustained in a harsh and doubled voice sound, leading to the second chorus. This time, in C_2, Gabriel's singing is much more gentle, making apparent a now fragile character asking for help ('Digging in the dirt / Stay with me I need support'). Here, the leading melodic line is harmonized by Gabriel himself (auto-harmonization), suggesting both a more euphonic and friendly environment. Other musical elements contribute to the chorus' ambience: for example, the stereo echoing clean guitar supports the harmonious environment, while the compound metre, with the insertion of a 2/4 bar, and its overall asymmetrical hypermetric structure, help convey a sense of instability in such a moment of vulnerability (see Figure 15.3).

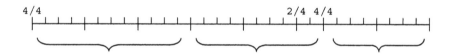

Figure 15.3   Hypermetric structure of C_2

Note: Each small vertical line represents a beat, while longer ones refer to the beginning of a bar. Braces, for their parts, indicate the hypermetrical grouping of bars.

But, in the end, what is indeed the source of the character's trouble? Musically, where does the whole structure of the song lead us? The answer is provided in the last verse, right in the middle of the song (2:40–2:45), again with the help of the phonographic staging of the voice. As I suggested earlier, in V_3 the character is unable to focus on the source of the pain. However, in V_4, he finally finds it: 'I feel it in my head / I feel it in my toes / I feel it in my sex / That's the place it goes'. Not that surprisingly perhaps, and as it seems to be often the case in therapy, the problem seems to lie in the character's sexuality. Interestingly, the sound level of the crucial line ('I feel it my sex') is significantly higher that before, and especially so on the word 'sex' whose sibilant sounds are at the same time exaggerated by the vocal doubling. When the next pre-chorus enters, then, it is enriched by this additional piece of information and leads to a new series of actions and emotive content, just as if the process was never entirely completed, as suggested by the rather long coda which ends in a fade-out (itself suggesting a never-ending process). Of course, and as I repeatedly mentioned earlier, many other musical parameters contribute to the song's narrative and emotional trajectory. However, Peter Gabriel's voice, and its phonographic staging in particular, are clearly playing an important role in the process. In fact, when listening to all his albums, one is astonished by the constant recourse to relevant and original phonographic staging effects, an artistic feature that should further be studied in detail as part of Gabriel's overall stylistic vocabulary.

Conclusion

In this chapter, I have attempted to illustrate the expressive power of phonographic staging effects when applied to the voice. Most analyses I have conducted so far significantly tend to demonstrate that phonographic staging contributes as much as other musical parameters to the aesthetic and symbolic aspects of recorded popular music.[13] In fact, more often than not, it is in 'concrete' parameters such as phonographic staging and vocal or instrumental performances that popular music richness is to be found, not (only) in abstracted parameters such as harmony. In the specific case of Peter Gabriel, there is no way that an analysis of any of his songs could account for its aesthetic potential value or possible symbolic content without considering with the greatest care phonographic staging effects and how they interact with all other parameters.

---

[13]   See especially Lacasse 2000.

Chapter 16

Turning the Axis: The Stage Performance Design Collaboration Between Peter Gabriel and Robert Lepage

Kimi Kärki

Introduction

> Peter wasn't just doing 'Shock the Monkey' and dancing around. He was also trying to be very intimate and saying very profound dark things, and that was quite a challenge, to be intimate in a huge unintimate place. (Robert Lepage in Bright 1999: 390)

Designing a powerful rock performance for large arenas is a demanding task. Canadian artist and stage designer Robert Lepage (born 1957) articulated clearly the central problem of presenting an ambitious theatrical and musical performances in big venues, namely the lack of intimacy for a performer who might want to do anything less bombastic than a succession of loud hit songs. Peter Gabriel has, throughout his musical career, been interested in mediating a broader range of emotions than what is provided by his crowd pleasers such as 'Sledgehammer', 'Steam', 'Solsbury Hill' or, indeed, 'Shock the Monkey'.

In this chapter I will focus on Peter Gabriel's collaboration with Robert Lepage. Their joint efforts produced spectacular shows, but also a 'secret' world of mechanics, lighting rigs, wires, road crew, and especially the world of ideas and meanings which links them all together. Peter Gabriel's two most recent big tours, *Secret World* (1993) and *Growing Up* (between 2002 and 2004, if we count the additional *Still Growing Up* shows) were ambitious audiovisual theatre, in many ways using the same imagery and ideas as his side projects, such as several multimedia products.[1] These tours were planned in close cooperation with Lepage, who had extensive experience in experimental theatre and opera as an actor, director and designer. The difference between the two tours was in the direction of movement. Whereas *Secret World* was horizontal, *Growing Up* was vertical;

---

[1]   I am working on a similar analysis as a part of a larger study on the stage design of stadium scale spectacles of Pink Floyd, U2 and The Rolling Stones. See for example Kärki (2005: 38). For earlier Gabriel shows, see for example Jeff Callen's chapter in this volume (Chapter 13).

basically they decided to turn the axis to meet the narrative demands of their newer concept. I will focus on the cultural and technological elements of creating these two tours, and explore the ideas and philosophies on which the actual stage designs were based, especially focusing on the idea that they *play* with different popular cultural elements and technologies.

In order to be intimate in a large arena one must understand the theatrical and technical issues involved. Peter Gabriel has always been interested in rock music performance as a form of theatre. His stage performances are famous for their theatrical innovations and experiments. When he was singing in the English progressive rock band Genesis in the first half of 1970s, he created weird roles, stories and costumes at the centre of their performances (see Kärki 2007: 46–7). In his early solo days, while trying to cast off the associations and reputation arising from Genesis, he consciously avoided these performative elements (Coburn 1994: unpaginated).

This changed in the early 1990s. He became hugely interested in the possibilities of multimedia, and had a plan to create a theme park around his audiovisual ideas. This led to two CD-ROMs, *Xplora* and *Eve*, and later the 20-minute-long Millennium Dome main show (and its soundtrack *Ovo*) in the year 2000, on which he worked with British architectural designer Mark Fisher, perhaps the world's best-known stadium rock stage designer, who had worked with the likes of Pink Floyd, The Rolling Stones and U2. Rather than as a musician, Gabriel preferred to be categorized as an 'experience designer', to signal that he was constantly trying to create more than just a rock show (Bright 1999: 371). His central objective was to collaborate with imaginative people who are experts in their respective fields:

> There's always excitement when you get interesting people from different disciplines throwing their minds and perspectives at a similar problem. So whether the park happens in a physical form, the process is one that I'm really enjoying, and I think as an artist, I'm still very attracted to trying to do art in that medium. (Gabriel quoted in Rubin 2007 unpaginated; see also Newby 2008: 8)

The suggested names for the planned theme park attractions speak for themselves: Minotaur Maze, Ride of Fears, The River of Life, Black Hole, Psyche Drama, Big Dipper Tripper, Hall of Digital Mirrors ... all this in the 'Real World Experience Park', once called 'Gabrieland' (Bright 1999: 3–5, 376). The idea in a theme park is that you *do* theme park instead of *being* there, and that the pleasure and fantasy become more real than the reality itself (Hjemdahl 2003: 132). Despite the fact that the theme park has not yet reached fruition, Gabriel was at least able to apply some of its ideas and technology to the *Secret World* tour and its promotion. One such innovation was a device called Mindblender, which was originally meant to be a flight simulator. The 'mobile simulation' trailer of Gabriel's 'Kiss That Frog' music video was presented to an estimated crowd of 300,000 people throughout 63 cities in the USA. The audience experienced a simulated journey down a frog's throat. The idea was that you could sit inside a simulator and feel part of the video (Bright 1999: 378, 380–81).

While pursuing these various multimedia projects Gabriel still had some time for what he has been best known for; that is, being a famous rock star who records and tours. But the urge to explore new technology and to collaborate with various experts in different fields remained a central feature of his activities. The ultimate motivation seems to be to bring the making of art back to people:

> It is assumed that you have to have talent to communicate in art and music, and a lot of people restrict themselves from that because they weren't given encouragement or don't believe that they have that means to do it. My hope is that the technology and some of the experiences that are going to be created at the park will encourage people to get inside the experience and take elements of other people's work that excite them, and that will give them a sense that they *can* be artists and musicians, that there isn't this barrier between creative and non-creative people. (Harrington 1993: unpaginated)

The two CD-ROMs which were products of Gabriel's Real World Multimedia company, *Xplora* and *Eve*, attempted exactly this. In particular *Eve* made it possible to create your own sophisticated versions of some Gabriel tunes, by enabling you to mix the material that was left over from the *Us* recording sessions (Bright 1999: 450).

Earlier, when starting to think about touring with *Us* album material, Gabriel already knew he wanted to communicate complex and existential subject matter and quiet songs to noisy and 'faceless' arena crowds. One of the ways to encourage people to actually listen and think further was by trying to renovate the idea of a rock show, and bring back the theatrical aspects he had to a certain extent neglected during his solo career. To achieve that Gabriel decided to ask creative stage designer Robert Lepage to design the *Secret World* tour concept with him. 'What I love about what he does is the sort of stunning use of very simple visual imagery. And I thought this could work very well with a rock show' (Gabriel in *Behind the Scenes* 2003: 2:00–2:16).

Lepage had actually seen Genesis live in Quebec when he was 12 years old, and this experience had a profound influence on him and his choice of profession, as he later claimed there was no other way he would ever have been introduced to theatre (Bright 1999: 387; Weatherford 2004: unpaginated). Knowing this, it is hardly surprising that his own works were inspired by the theatricality of rock groups like Genesis and Jethro Tull, who were telling stories, wearing costumes onstage and inhabiting the realm of mythological creatures and characters. Lepage saw Gabriel as one of his heroes because of his groundbreaking influence on rock theatre in the 1970s (Shewey 2001: unpaginated).

Gabriel and Lepage had been introduced by a mutual friend in December 1990, when Gabriel was working with Laurie Anderson and Brian Eno to develop theme park plans (Coburn 1994: unpaginated; Bright 1999: 372). Gabriel soon realized how useful a collaborator Lepage could be:

> There was a wonderful thing called Needles and Opium in London, which is a one-man show he did, basically around the lives of Miles Davis, Jean Cocteau and himself, and it's very simple in a way, but very strong. It was great use of visuals. So we began brainstorming, I got to know him and thought that he would be a great person for this, and I discovered in talking to him that he had been an old fan and seen a lot of my concerts in Montreal, so he knew my songs, probably better than I did, which was a good start. (Coburn 1994: unpaginated)

From the outset of what was clearly to become a fruitful collaboration, during the lengthy discussions while designing the *Secret World* tour concept, they discovered what they considered to be significant affinities in achieving creative results. They were fascinated to find that both of their names' values in numerology were seven. Quite bizarrely they also noted that the letters of their names, when they were making anagrams with *Scrabble* tiles, were the same save just one letter: an 'o' for an 'i'. Thus Robert Lepage became Peter Gabroel and Peter Gabriel became Ribert Lepage. Furthermore, both of them used the *I Ching*, the Chinese system of meditating and predicting future events, for years as a creative tool when designing shows. They immediately felt they were meant to work together and in a way they felt like each other's double (Bright 1999: 386–7). While all this suggests slightly eccentric minds, for Lepage these connections offered possibilities to enhance their joint creativity:

> I find this fascinating. It's not so much that I believe in it, but that it's kind of poetry that helps me to create. Maybe the connections are only made because we decide to give meaning to the games of numbers and forms. But even if we don't understand why they exist, these connections are nevertheless there. (Bright 1999: 387)

Getting hold of such background information is remarkable when we interpret rock shows, either as scholars or as rock fans, when we are giving meanings to what we observe and participate in during a concert or a mechanical reproduction. The joint effort of Gabriel and Lepage offers us an interesting case study on the usage of different cultural narratives and theatrical concepts in audiovisual rock performance.

The kinds of games they played to achieve creative results should be considered in a more methodological level. I argue that 'play' – or, quite synonymously, 'game' – is a central concept when we try to understand what is going on during these paradoxically vast and yet 'intimate' spectacles. I'd take this as far as arguing that this kind of play is central to the entertainment industry and artistic activity. This idea is now explored further.

Playing Games without Frontiers

> Just as when tribesmen make masks, disguise themselves as monsters, heap up
> disparate ritual symbols, invert or parody profane reality in myths and folk-tales,
> so do the genres of industrial leisure, the theatre, poetry, novel, ballet, film, sport,
> rock music, classical music, art, pop art, etc., *play* with the factors of culture,
> sometimes assembling them in random, grotesque, improbable, surprising,
> shocking, usually experimental combinations. (Turner 1982: 40, italics in the
> original)

Celebrated anthropologist Victor Turner's model of the universal role of play, and
how the playful element is manifested in the fields of industrial leisure, is usefully
applicable to the Peter Gabriel live shows. Even if the comparison between
tribesmen and rock stars is not exactly historically accurate, there are parallels
which also resonate with what French philosopher and founder of the Situationist
International movement Guy Debord (1931–94) argued about religious illusions
being replaced by material reconstructions (Debord 1995: 1.20). The triumph of
the spectacle is indeed evident throughout our culture, indeed our 'real world', or
as Debord wrote:

> The spectacle grasped in its totality is both the result and the project of the
> existing mode of production. It is not a supplement to the real world, an additional
> decoration. It is the heart of the unrealism of the real society. In all its specific
> forms, as information or propaganda, as advertisement or direct entertainment
> consumption, the spectacle is the present model of socially dominant life.
> (Debord 1995: 1.6)

In our spectacular culture, there are persistent elements which survive the pressures
of historical changes. One such element is the need for experiences which somehow
give meaning to our existence and/or give a feeling of reaching for something
beyond our everyday lives. I'd like to argue that, instead of religious illusions,
we now more often witness, experience and consume popular cultural illusions of
the entertainment industry, but they still play with similar needs. I find Debord's
ideas inadequate in the case of sonic phenomena, however, as their emphasis is
overwhelmingly visual. In the case of huge rock spectacles, which in my opinion
are some of the most conspicuous forms of audiovisual spectacle, we can find
equally powerful aural elements. But the spectacular forms of entertainment are
not always about bombastic and overpowering magnitude – there have to be
dynamics which offer intimate moments as well. These 'silences' are important,
and sometimes also the most emotionally touching parts of the arena events.

I am particularly interested in the methods, conditions and limits of such creative
design processes that aim to produce powerful and illusory events with dynamic
variation where theatre, technology and music intertwine to produce thrilling
audiovisual dreams. In the case of Gabriel there indeed seems to be an urge to go

beyond the idea of spectacle as a force which makes people just passive receivers – from time to time he tries to play with and even question the idea of the rock spectacle, to wake up the dreamers. Songs like 'Biko', 'Games Without Frontiers', 'Don't Give Up' and 'The Barry Williams Show', for example, offer realism and cultural critique in their narratives, instead of just pure entertainment.

In his influential book *Homo Ludens*, Dutch cultural historian Johan Huizinga (1872–1945) observed history through the idea that human beings are first and foremost players – for Huizinga 'play' precedes culture; it is something we share with the animals (Huizinga 1984: 5, 9, 12). Partly influenced by Huizinga's ideas, German philosopher Hans-Georg Gadamer (1900–2002) claimed that everyone interprets and 'plays' art from her or his own personal perspective. In this interpretation process art becomes a dynamic actor, a part of semiosis, where the meanings and acts are fused. The work of art thus only exists in its various changing interpretations. Gadamer chose the German word 'spiel' when talking about the interpretation process. 'Spiel', meaning game or more appropriately play, always has its own rules, its own space and its own time. For Gadamer 'spiel' relates to 'spiegel', a mirror. The art exists in its interpretations but it is greater than any of the interpreters that observe the work of art and any of the players of the play (Gadamer 1999: 101–110; 139–40).[2]

I'd like to argue that a rock spectacle is a useful subject for such an interpretative playing process, where those who made the rules, in this case Gabriel and Lepage, also participated in the play, just like the audience and even the researcher. I am also able to 'play' with these shows from other perspectives than that of a spectator of, and listener to, the live shows.[3] The sometimes unclear narrative meanings of the shows become available not only through the concerts and their audiovisual recordings but also through various interviews and biographical texts. The extra layers of meaning achieved that way are invaluable for the kind of research this chapter aims to present.

Certainly the playful elements combined with the serious and universal themes – such as birth, death and relationships – make *Secret World* and *Growing Up*

---

[2]   It is evident, however, that the past of the work of art is present in it, and thus understanding the work of art leads us to a deeper understanding of the past. Hence, a work of art transfers historical information. The nature of this transfer is dialogical: work of art as an act of play is a subject which hides meanings and is renewed in relation to each player (Linge 1977: xxiii).

[3]   I have witnessed Peter Gabriel live only once, in Bell Arena, Montreal, in summer 2003. This was a happy coincidence as I was there to participate in a conference. However, this live show I saw was not purely one of those *Growing Up* tour shows, it was a special hybrid event for the fans in Montreal. During this show Gabriel's organization combined elements both from *Secret World* and *Growing Up*. The stage was a traditional angular one at the other end of the hall, so it didn't utilize the round stage idea at all, an idea central to both concepts I'm dealing with in this chapter. But the actual tours were available for me in DVD format.

excellent subjects of interpretation for revealing the possibilities of theatrical and technological playing. As a matter of fact, Robert Lepage pays attention to Gabriel's ability to play, referring to him as *ludique*, French for 'playful character'. As Lepage says:

> That's one of the great qualities of Peter's genius, his playfulness, pun intended – play in the sense of theatre as a player, what he does comes out of playing [music] a lot, and the idea of playing. I think that's also why he got involved in this theme park thing, this idea that there's so much to be transmitted and communicated through playing. When he rehearses with the band you really have the impression that they are playing together in either sense of the word. So it was important that I got a chance to go to Real World and play with him and try things out and play around. So we invented a miniature playground for this show and I got to explore with him some of the ideas really early on. (Bright 1999: 388)

This kind of wide interpretation of playing, be it playing a concert, a game, or a miniature concert arena, makes the artistic processes evidently more fun, and this might be something that is revealed in the outcome. The designers of the play are sucked into it, they are able to play with their creation just like anyone else. This will be evidenced through descriptive analysis of the tours in question, to which I now turn.

Inside a Secret World

> I think the crew were very depressed when they saw the amount of dreams that we'd turned into solid lumps of material. During the show itself the crew were very busy. There's a lot of things that you don't see from the outside that are actually going on underneath in terms of preparing bits of props or music changes. So the odd numbers that I was under the stage it was quite interesting and quite fun to watch the other show. (Gabriel in *Behind the Scenes* 2003: 6:40–7:30)

Secret World, a concept based on Gabriel's *Us* album (1992), had a narrative of relationships and communication between men and women, in both a metaphorical and biographical sense (as the subject matter of *Us* was very much derived from Gabriel's personal relationships), and the design of the stage took the idea of symbolic masculinity and femininity further (Coburn 1994: unpaginated). As Gabriel and Lepage had envisioned it, two horizontal stages, rectangular masculine and round feminine, were connected by a pathway/treadmill, and moving from a square to a round environment symbolized a river, a road, a place of mental transformation. Besides the gender integration this structure also suggested other polarities, such as water/fire, man-made/organic, and yin/yang (Harrington 1993: unpaginated; Sandall 1993: unpaginated; Bright 1999: 389).

The original idea for the stage show was an 'all out video assault' with flying TV screens and a lot of visual action. Gabriel decided to change the focus after he heard about U2's *ZooTV*, a Mark Fisher design, and he actually went to see the U2 show five times, impressed by the 'strong visual intelligence' (Harrington 1993: unpaginated; Sandall 1993: unpaginated). He also had another idea which turned out to be too dangerous:

> Originally, I wanted a train thing – a little train set for a big boy, I guess – that would drive through stadiums, but the health and safety people wouldn't allow me to do that. So the central [second] stage and the conveyer belt seemed to be a good alternative. (Rubin 2007: unpaginated; see also Bright 1999: 389)

He and Lepage went in a more intimate direction, which probably serves the emotional narrative well. According to Lepage, Gabriel's method of working while planning the staging was similar to the way he works in the studio – that is, building things layer by layer, combining and mixing ideas without being too interested in whose idea was used, as long as it worked. One important aspect they agreed on was that the 360-degree revolving video screen, one of the central elements of the show, would feature Gabriel's face only when there were artistic reasons to do so – the standard procedure was to use video screens to enlarge the performer so that the people in the back of the arenas could achieve at least some contact. This idea of achieving contact through technology is certainly a paradox, as people in part watch a representation of the performer, not the live performance itself.[4] Instead of just screening Gabriel or his band, the screen featured, for example, the visual art images used in the *Us* booklet, and elements from Gabriel's music videos.

The revolving screen acted both as an aerial eye because of the cameras attached to it, and as a projection element of live and taped material (Moles 1993: 59). Gabriel and Lepage tried to keep the show as close to the people and as intimate as possible within the massive space. One of the ways to keep people interested was to let the staging reflect the aforementioned universal themes of Gabriel's lyrics. According to Lepage, 'People go to these big venues because they want to hear things that are very fundamental and mythical and universal' (Bright 1999: 389–390). But the tour featured a considerable amount of practical jokes as well, some of them visible to the audience – this becomes evident when reading the tour diary on Gabriel's Internet pages (see 'Secret World. Tales From the Understage').

The few weeks before the tour, in March and April 1993, were difficult for the tour crew, as the sheer complexity of the equipment developed for the show was

---

4   Here I come close to Philip Auslander's ideas in his excellent book *Liveness*. He claims most large-scale live events in general are hardly live any more because they are so heavily mediated (Auslander 1999: 27, 38, 83–5).

proving hard to handle. There were problems with lighting equipment arriving very late, with some people who had come from a theatre background trying to adjust to the tougher and heavier staging materials meant to last the strains of touring, and with the 60-foot walkway between the stages refusing to work at all during the rehearsal period. Finally, nine trucks were on the way for the first leg of European tour, 'hauling 60 feet of conveyor belt, two stages, an 8-foot tree, a red British telephone box, giant heads, 58 crew and a band party of 12, performing 36 shows in 32 different cities in 49 days' (Bright 1999: 391). Despite the technical problems and initially poor ticket sales, Gabriel ended up making some profit, and the show was seen by an audience of more than a million people on five continents (Bright 1999: 400).

The show, besides including an arsenal of special effects, also relied greatly on Gabriel's own theatrical habitus. He was able to move from messianic rock star gestures to showing his fractured face on video screens with a portable miniature camera, as done during the song 'Digging in the Dirt' (Gottelier 1993: 21). But the special effects were featured as a continuous sequence, from Gabriel's highly theatrical entrance, during the show opener 'Come Talk to Me', in a telephone box that rises from within the rectangular stage. Gabriel was inside, holding a telephone. Gabriel seemingly sang into the phone, a theatrical gesture, as he was already wearing a microphone headset. Standing on the round stage, backing vocalist Paula Cole was waiting and listening. Once the song reached its chorus Gabriel left the phone booth, and the phone cord became longer and longer – extending 60 feet in all – as he reached toward the round stage, where Cole joined him during the chorus, with a vocal harmony, both singing 'Oh please, come talk to me'. The central theme of the tour – communication between the sexes – was thus introduced as early as the opening number. But the real shift happens during 'Across the River', as Gabriel, holding a rain stick, 'rows' the band from square to round stage using the conveyer belt. Gabriel felt that this horizontal movement was a central idea for the show:

> You get this sense of transition. And in a sense it's also a discovery of the self and discovering the feminine nature, and that's where 'Digging in the Dirt' takes place. So it's designed in a way to have a narrative from start to finish. (*Behind the Scenes* 2003: 4:30–4:50)

Later on, during the song 'Blood of Eden', another binary opposition becomes evident; a tree rises from the depths of the round stage, to contrast with the earlier 'urban' telephone box (Gabriel and Girard 2003; Coburn 1994: unpaginated; Bright 1999: 396). The tree was, however, an anti-climax for Gabriel:

> When the tree arrived ... I was reminded of Spinal Tap for a moment, when Stonehenge arrived. Because I had in mind this grand tree that was going to dominate this circular stage. And what was actually practical for something that

we could get underneath the stage and have emerge, was the pint-sized version. (*Behind the Scenes* 2003, 3:30–3:50)

In the show's climax, before the encores, the whole band apparently 'disappeared' in a suitcase on the floor, going through a trap door to the sub-stage. The suitcase was then picked up by Gabriel who walked to the centre of the round stage and was covered by a huge oval 'Dome' or 'UFO' structure lowered from the ceiling (Gottelier 1993: 21; Gabriel and Girard 2003). This finale could be read either as a triumph of the feminine values or as a return to the womb. Either way, the escape from urban to rural milieu provided a visual feast.

For Gabriel it is extremely important that the visual side is in sync with the songs. This is why so much time and effort is devoted to getting the audiovisual experience as seamless and unified as possible:

> If you absorb the images as they come at you, hopefully some of them will have an afterlife, and resonate a little. The sense I've got back from people is that the music and the imagery have come from the same place, that they haven't been artificially stuck together. (Sandall 1993: unpaginated)

This would not be possible if the band playing (music) with Gabriel was not up to the challenge of the visual narratives offered. The very high level of musicianship is indeed one very important factor in Peter Gabriel tours. Utilizing such well-known musicians as Tony Levin, Manu Katché and David Rhodes provides a more organic feel of people jamming together, behind the usage of loops and samplers which are needed to bring the multilayered Real World Studio efforts alive. They were also given the best available technology to be able to play their parts in the visual sense, to be able to walk around and between the two stages. On this tour the whole band used personal in-ear monitoring, something which was cutting-edge technology at the time (Cunningham 1999: 34). Sound design was difficult for such an unusually shaped stage, but the problems were overcome by dividing the arenas into six inter-related zones. For the same reason the placement of the mixing console proved difficult, and it was agreed it would be in between the stages next to the treadmill, under the main PA system. Thus, they also needed some crew members in the audience who would report about sounds during the gig (Gottelier 1993: 20).

The required technological innovations were not cheap. Predicting the costs of such a tour proved to be incredibly difficult, as the production costs at the start of the tour were six million pounds, instead of the originally envisioned two. Gabriel summed up the problem: 'You want a piece of wood to solve a particular problem and you think it'll cost £10, but by the time you've flown it round the world, it's cost you £10,000' (Sandall 1993: unpaginated). One way to attempt to recover such tour costs is to release a live video. *Secret World* was soon released as a video, and later as a DVD, though it's hardly an 'authentic' record of a live performance, as Gabriel later emphasized: 'It took two and a bit nights, but they were both at the same place, in Modena, so we had a bit of time to do some pickup shots for the filming as well; and we also cheated a bit afterward, with some overdubs' (Coburn 1994: unpaginated; see also Bright 1999: 443–4).

Secret World remains an interesting tour de force in the history of theatrical stage design. Despite many bands attempting much bigger stadium-scale productions, Gabriel and Lepage were able to do something intimately theatrical in an arena environment. This is rare and certainly challenging. For Gabriel the real innovation was in communication between different traditions: 'It's an ongoing process developing the *Secret World*. And it's changed really each time we've gone out. Rock people and theatre people don't always talk the same language. We wanted to try and break some new ground and find a new territory' (*Behind the Scenes* 2003: 14:10–14:26). If we consider the combination of the *Secret World* stage and the songs performed on it, we can obviously call it a successful mixture of playful audiovisual elements with some more serious undercurrents. But it was hardly as innovative as one might expect, thinking about Gabriel's ideas on theme parks and multimedia which I discussed earlier. As a rock show, however, it worked well and was truly original. But how were they going to top that ten years later?

Growing up with Stage Technology

> Some of the things I enjoy doing the most now are brainstorming with interesting people. And doing a visual tour gives me a chance to do that, particularly with Robert. (Gabriel in Tillyer 2003: 1:50–2:04)

The idea of connected horizontality in *Secret World* was ultimately turned vertical. The *Growing Up* tour stage, which only had a round stage, but on two levels, upper and lower, thus formed 'heaven' and 'earth' parts respectively (Cumberbatch 2002: unpaginated). The 'earth' part had two sections, inner and outer. The outer annulus was able to revolve horizontally, which helped to create many of the special effects. To do a show completely in the round was the logical next step after Gabriel and Lepage found the *Secret World* round stage the more rewarding of the two. This solution was also preferred by the financial backers in order to sell more tickets (Kinnersley 2003: unpaginated).

Peter Gabriel's 2002 album *Up* was the outcome of a long process. Ten years or so after the *Us* album he came up with a complex and more universally themed album, but he still saw significant continuity between them:

> A lot of *Us* album was about relationships. This album is still from a personal perspective, but it probably looks at a bigger picture. I think a lot of what we see in life is what's just ahead of us; we forget what's above us or below us. … The moon and water were symbols for this record. They have a continuous unseen influence, and it's that unseen world I wanted to write about. (Gardner 2002: D.04)

But talking about tidal waves and menstrual cycles, for example, was not the whole story about the show, as the *Up* album had even more fundamental themes, ranging from birth to death. Gabriel was now dealing less with his usual middle-age subject matter: 'It felt like the lyrics have more to do with the beginning and end of life than the middle. I was surprised to see four or five songs talked about death in one way or another. That's not the normal pop subject!' (Cumberbatch 2002: unpaginated). At the same time, however, the element of childlike play was still present. Gabriel himself saw the paradox hidden in the tour name: 'Growing Up is the name of the tour, but actually, if you look at most adult musicians, grown-up is not the first word that comes to mind. And I look at us having fun on or off stage and it all seems very childlike' (Gabriel 2003: 31:55–32:10).

Even if the album was titled, rather optimistically, *Up*, it was indeed going beyond the trauma of mid-life crisis to look at the beginning and end of life. Or, as Gabriel stated when talking about the album: 'Our culture's so obsessed with youth that we don't look on our own mortality. As a society we try to pretend it's not there' (Spencer 2002: unpaginated).

The process of designing the *Growing Up* tour began with the usual discussions in expensive restaurants and sketches on tablemats. Lepage and Gabriel, who both collected art books, spent hours going through them to find the right feeling for the tour, and also went around talking with artists and sculptors about their ideas (Kinnersley 2003: unpaginated). The resulting ideas were ambitious. As the themes of the *Up* album involve life cycles and growing up, the egg shape was a natural choice for the projection screen. The images projected on to the egg were mostly watery in their nature: water plants and fluid shapes. The idea Gabriel and Lepage had was that the images would turn from water to drier elements and finally almost fiery before the egg gave birth to a giant transparent ball called a zorb (Kinnersley 2003: unpaginated).

Once the show was on the road, it was again just one stage structure touring (instead of the usual feature of really big tours where one identical stage was built, one was played on, and one dismantled, all this simultaneously in different cities). Although cost-effective, this meant problems with the schedules. Most of the time the whole stage production, 11 trucks in all, had to be constructed and taken down daily: 'The immense workload, combined with multiple back-to-back shows, meant that soundchecks were simply not possible on some days' (Frink 2003: unpaginated).

Growing Up was surprisingly physical: Gabriel performed suspended upside down, riding around on a tiny bicycle, and rolling around the stage inside the zorb ball (during 'Downside Up', 'Solsbury Hill' and 'Growing Up': Gabriel and Hamilton 2003). This could provide a field day for some critics, such as Fiona Shepherd, writing for *The Scotsman*:

> By the time he had penetrated a large, transparent beachball and begun marching around inside it to perform the Bowiesque Growing Up, it was beyond ridiculous
> – Beyond Thunderdome even. Only a certain venerable bearing separates

Gabriel from the Spinal Tap stage excesses of the Darkness. (Shepherd 2004: unpaginated)

The original idea behind the use of zorb ball was that Gabriel could go into the audience inside it, something which he had done in the 1980s without a ball. The joint weight of the ball and Gabriel, however, would 'be enough to sort of flatten the smaller members of the audience', so they decided to stay on stage (Tillyer 2003: 4:05–4:20; also Gabriel 2003: 14:05–14:15).

Because the stages changed gradually, as they underwent a progressive modification during the shows, there was a fairly strict order on the set list. While the hanging cloth in the shape of an egg that was suspended above the earth stage had indeed acted as a three-dimensional projection screen, it was lost when the zorb ball had been released, so songs designed with most of the video images had to appear earlier in the show. (Between 'Red Rain' and 'Growing Up': Gabriel and Hamilton 2003). In the later parts of the show the cloth connected the stages in the form of a cylinder, leaving drummer Ged Lynch inside of it, and again providing an element for projections.

During all this the road crew were making sure everything was working smoothly, and in fact they had been incorporated into the show, as noted by Fiona Shepherd in her review:

Everything about this presentation was precision-drilled. The men in the band were shorn and everyone wore sober black smocks and headsets, while his multi-media needs were served by a swarm of worker drones clad in bright orange overalls. Hypnotic images pulsated on imposing giant discs hung from the rafters. The audience were expectant onlookers in a futuristic amphitheatre. It was all very Logan's Run.[5] (Shepherd 2004: unpaginated)

Distinguishing the road crew by dressing them in orange was an interesting and creative idea that enabled them to become part of the show, rising from the depths of the stage through trap doors to make the adjustments and slight changes to the stage. This can also be seen as an alienation effect; in a way, this kind of deliberate emphasizing of the existence of the road crew can also remind the audience about the constructed nature of the magic they were witnessing. It could furthermore be seen as a 'class' distinction between artists and workers – the musicians themselves paid no attention to the gradual changes made by the orange-dressed crew; most of the time they were stationed around the centre of the stage, facing each other, giving a sense of intimate musical interaction. If the

---

[5]   *Logan's Run* (1967) is a dystopic novel by William F. Noland and George Clayton Johnson. Michael Anderson's film version was released in 1976. The main idea is that in the twenty-third century no one is allowed to live past their 30th birthday and the needs of the young people are taken care by automated machines. The reviewer obviously refers to the aesthetics of the film.

workers were really visible in their orange, the musicians were wearing as simple but perhaps less flashy 'uniforms'. Robert Lepage wanted the musicians to wear simple black costume: 'The theme – there's a lot of black, shiny black and matte black' (Gabriel 2003: 12:25–12:34).

Gabriel also wanted to comment on the Reality TV phenomenon during 'The Barry Williams Show', during which he directed a video camera into the audience (Gabriel and Hamilton 2003). Gabriel wanted to present a bit of media critique by performing as a satirical version of the Reality TV host. Thus he became 'Barry Williams', giving the audience a role by feeding their faces onto the circular cloth screen hanging from the 'sky' stage. The idea was to communicate his fears about the future of media culture: 'Sometimes, when we watch television, it's like a fix of junk food. You think you want it, you take it – and then you feel like throwing up. This is about the future of "Reality TV"' (Rubin 2002: unpaginated).

The two tours had a very similar pre-encore gimmick. While in *Secret World* the band disappeared into a suitcase, which Gabriel took into his hand before he was buried under a huge dome, this time the band disappeared while drummer Ged Lynch, encircled in the mentioned cylinder of fabric, played the last beats of 'Signal to Noise':

> As Lynch slammed away at his drums over pre-recorded strings, the band members began to disappear, one at a time, down through trap doors in the stage, until only Lynch remained. The second stage slowly lowered, hiding Lynch as the music ended. (Rubin 2002: unpaginated)

The audio technology was again top quality. The main PA speaker system was made of four clusters, each made of a dozen small speakers.

> Two of these, angled outward a few degrees, were aimed down the longer axis of the arena and were mirrored – with L/R channels reversed – on the opposite side of the center-floor stage. Twelve-box arrays of dv-DOSC units aimed at the arena's sides completed the stereo image, which could be detected throughout most of the venue. Six-box columns of E-V MTL quad-18 subs were flown at each side of the stage, providing even low-end coverage without causing bass build-up in the center. (Frink 2003: unpaginated)

The difficulties with unusual acoustic arrangement – that is, having the main speaker system in the centre of the arena and still wanting to achieve good audio surround – were therefore overcome by the careful placing of the speaker cabinets. It is not clear whether the technical crew was always able to calibrate the speaker positions when entering different arenas, as the arenas are hardly ever precisely similar, and the time limitations were really strict with only one stage construction used during the tour.

Nevertheless, the *Growing Up* tour was considered yet another landmark in stage design, with mostly very good press reviews. Building from the most successful elements of *Secret World*, Gabriel and Lepage were able to play with the expectations of the audience, and despite the ever increasing spectacular nature of competing entertainment products, even blow them away with the combination of high end audiovisual technology and strong narratives. But for Gabriel himself the social aspects became more and more important, and he felt that he had grown as a person:

> There's this sort of bonding that goes on just being in a group of people which you don't always notice until you get back. I think the unreal world of touring affects me much less now, at 54, than it did, say, at 20. It could go into your head and I think sometimes we would think we were much more important than we were. (Tillyer 2003: 8:55–9:20)

Thus, instead of the stardom egotrip, he now saw value in the tribal quality of the tour crew bonding. This was highlighted by the fact that Gabriel now brought his family with him, not just his wife and young son, but older children as well: daughter Melanie was singing and daughter Anna shooting a documentary film about the tour (see Gabriel 2003). This was yet another aspect to drive Gabriel to more intimate play in the arenas.

Conclusion: The Struggle for Intimacy

> There would be a knock on the door, and three or four whiz kids from Bristol would come in to demonstrate this new technology something. Then Peter would turn it around on its tail and make something more interesting with it, or ask the kind of questions artists ask. People obsessed with the technical aspect know that the way to push the edge is to brush with the artist who uses technology in a completely different way. (Shewey 2001: unpaginated)

Peter Gabriel's quest for intimacy, both on and off stage, has not always been a great success. As he seems to be constantly open to new people and ideas, he becomes easily distracted, often resulting in some kind of new enthusiasm. This has led to very long intervals between his studio albums, for example. Similarly, in the arena, when he is trying to focus on some more intimate and introverted song, there might be a drunken kid shouting for 'Sledgehammer'. In the most successful contemporary arena spectacles the visual narratives are carefully intertwined with the audio narratives and the lyrical content of the songs. Peter Gabriel takes great pains to achieve this. He is in a way a living paradox, because he goes to these huge arenas to say 'Shh, listen…' and performs a considerable number of introverted, emotionally vulnerable songs such as 'Secret World', 'Mercy Street', and 'I Grieve' among the more rocking songs.

Arena technology was partially developed to provide the means for a modern version of Wagnerian *Gesamtkunstwerk*, a complete work of art (Macan 1997:

11, 68). The technology connects the performer's theatrical gestures to wider, carefully planned thematic structures. This is what large venues and their disposable architecture are all about: connecting sound, light and material surfaces with popular imagery, and also with popular nostalgia, sometimes irony, and the historical references of the audiovisual narratives. But the audience also experiences shock and awe in front of overpowering technology.

Turning the axis of the stage, by moving from horizontal to vertical between the two Gabriel tours, might have changed the dynamics of the show a bit, but the purpose was the same, to entertain while striving for the intimate and meaningful. Despite this, Lepage was ready to confess the realities of dealing with arena crowds:

> There are 20,000 fans who want to listen to 'Sledgehammer'; you know it's the
> last song on the set list and you have to get them there. Whatever you do, it has
> to be playful and poetic enough for them to be mesmerized. (Kinnersley 2003:
> unpaginated)

By playing their staged multimedia games Gabriel and Lepage reveal the spectacular essence of our culture and society, sometimes by being subtle and intelligent, and sometimes by being grotesque and harsh. Struggling for intimacy has not always been the key element of their playing. In 2001 they collaborated on a play called *Zulu Time*, which wasn't performed publicly at the time. During the play an aeroplane was supposed to be blown up on the stage, and the big launch was going to be in New York. Three or four days before the planned opening was 11 September 2001, and the show was cancelled by a spectacle of much greater magnitude (Shewey 2001: unpaginated; Newby 2008: 16–17). At times, evidently, their art imitated life too well.

Bibliography

Note: Finnish readers will need to follow English rules of alphabetical order to find names containing ä and ö. All websites accessed in early 2009 unless separately mentioned.

Articles and Books

Ackroyd, Peter. 2002. *Dickens. Public Life and Private Passion.* London: BBC Worldwide Ltd.

Adorno, Theodor and Hans Eisler. 1994 (1947). *Composing for the Films.* London: The Athlone Press.

AdZe MiXXe. *StarBios Report for Peter Gabriel.* www.adze.com/Celebrities/PeterGabriel.htm.

Aletti, Vince. 1986. 'Tubemusic: Zap to the Beat', *Village Voice* 31:24, p. 43.

Altick, Richard D. 1973. *Victorian People and Ideas.* London: W.W. Norton & Co.

Angel, Johnny. 1994. 'Born to Lose: Fear and Self-Loathing in the Ostrich Generation', *San Francisco Bay Guardian*, 17 August, pp. 41–3.

Ansell, Gwen. 2004. *Soweto Blues: Jazz, Popular Music and Politics in South Africa.* New York: Continuum.

Apter, Emily. 1992. 'Masquerade', in Elizabeth Wright (ed.), *Feminism and Psychoanalysis: A Critical Dictionary.* Oxford and New York: Blackwell, pp. 242–4.

Attali, Jacques. 2006 (1985). *Noise. The Political Economy of Music.* Minneapolis: Minnesota University Press.

Auslander, Philip. 2005 (1999). *Liveness. Performance in a Mediatized Culture.* Abingdon: Routledge.

Ballantine, Christopher. 1993. *Marabi Nights.* Johannesburg: Ravan Press.

Balliger, Robin. 1995. 'Sounds of Resistance' in Ron Sakolsky and Fred Wei-han Ho (eds), *Sounding Off!: Music as Subversion/Resistance/Revolution.* New York: Autonomedia.

Barthes, Roland. 1977. *Image – Music – Text.* Trans. Stephen Heath. New York: Noonday.

Barthes, Roland. 1993. *Camera Lucida: Reflections on Photography.* London: Vintage.

Bellman, Jonathan (ed.) 1998. *The Exotic in Western Music.* Boston, MA: Northeastern University Press.

Benjamin, Walter. 1978. *Reflections.*Ed. Peter Demetz. New York: Schocken Books.

Bennett, Tony. 1986. 'Popular Culture and "the Turn to Gramsci"', in Tony Bennett, Colin Mercer and Janet Woollacott (eds), *Popular Culture and Social Relations*. Philadelphia, PA: Open University Press, pp. xi–xix.

Benzon, William. 2001. *Beethoven's Anvil: Music in Mind and Culture*. New York: Basic Books.

Bernstein, Hilda. 1978. *No. 46 – Steve Biko*. London: International Defence and Aid Fund for South Africa.

Biko, Steve. 1988. *I Write What I Like*. London: Penguin.

Bloustein, Gerry. 2004. 'Still Picking Children from the Trees? Reimagining Woodstock in Twenty-first Century Australia', in Andy Bennett (ed.), *Remembering Woodstock*. Aldershot: Ashgate, pp. 127–45.

Blumenfeld, Larry. 1995. 'My Week in the Real World', *Rhythm Music*, October, pp. 30–35.

Bohlman, Philip W. 2002. *World Music. A Very Short Introduction*. Oxford: Oxford University Press.

Bohlman, Philip. 1988. *The Study of Folk Music in the Modern World*. Bloomington: Indiana University Press.

Boone, Graeme. 1997. 'Tonal and Expressive Ambiguity in "Dark Star"', in John Covach and Graeme Boone (eds), *Understanding Rock: Essays in Musical Analysis*. New York and Oxford: Oxford University Press, pp. 171–210.

Boone, Graeme. 2008. '"Dark Star" Revisited, Revisited', unpublished paper delivered at the Grateful Dead Caucus of the 29th Annual Meeting of the Southwest/Texas Popular Culture and American Culture Association, Albuquerque, February.

Bordwell, David. 1985. *The Classical Hollywood Cinema. Film Style and Mode of Production to 1960*. New York: Columbia University Press.

Bordwell, David. 2002. 'Intensified Continuity: Visual Style in Contemporary American Film', *Film Quarterly* 55:3, pp. 16–28.

Born, Georgina and David Hesmondhalgh. 2000. 'Introduction: On Difference, Representation and Appropriation in Music', in Georgina Born and David Hesmondhalgh (eds), *Western Music and its Others. Difference, Representation and Appropriation in Music*. Berkeley and Los Angeles: University of California Press, pp. 1–58.

Borthwick, Stuart and Ron Moy. 2004. *Popular Music Genres*. Edinburgh: Edinburgh University Press.

Bourdieu, Pierre. 1977. *Outline of a Theory of Practice*. Cambridge: Cambridge University Press.

Bourdieu, Pierre. 1993. *The Field of Cultural Production*. Ed. Randal Johnson. New York: Columbia University Press.

Bowie, Andrew. 1998. *Hermeneutics and Criticism and Other Writings*. Cambridge: Cambridge University Press.

Bowler, Dave and Bryan Dray. 1992. *Genesis. A Biography*. London: Sidgwick & Jackson.

Bowman, Rob. 1997. *Soulsville, USA: The Story of Stax Records*. New York: Schirmer Books.

Bracewell, Michael. 1997. *England is Mine. Pop Life in Albion from Wilde to Goldie*. Glasgow: HarperCollins.

Bradley, Fiona. 1997. *Movements in Modern Art: Surrealism*. London: Tate.

Breton, André. 1960 (1928). *Nadja*. Trans. Richard Howard. New York: Grove Press Incorporated.

Bridger, John and Susan Nunziata. 1991. 'Real World Project Boasts Wide Universe of Talent', *Billboard*, 21 September, p. 41.

Bright, Spencer. 1988. *Peter Gabriel. An Authorised Biography*. London: Sidgwick & Jackson.

Bright, Spencer. 1989. *Peter Gabriel. An Authorised Biography*. London: Headline.

Bright, Spencer. 1999. *Peter Gabriel. An Authorized Biography* (updated). London: Sidwick & Jackson; New York: Macmillan.

Bristol Recorder No. 2, January 1981. Bristol: Bristol Recorder.

Brooman, Thomas. 1993. 'Peter Gabriel in Conversation', *RMM*, September, pp. 12–15.

Brown, T. 1980. 'Did Anyone Know his Name? Coverage of Steven Biko and the Black Consciousness Movement in South Africa by the *New York Times* and the *Washington Post*, 1969–1977', *Ecquid Novi* 1:1, pp. 29–49.

Bruzzi, Stella. 1997. 'Mannish Girl: k.d. lang – from Cowpunk to Androgyny', in Sheila Whiteley (ed.), *Sexing the Groove: Popular Music and Gender*. London and New York: Routledge, pp. 191–206.

Bryson, Norman. 1983. *Vision and Painting: The Logic of the Gaze*. New Haven, CT: Yale University Press.

Buckley, David. 2005. 'In An English Country Garden', *Mojo Classic. Pink Floyd and the Story of Prog Rock* (July), pp. 84–93.

Business Week. 2006. 'Capturing Human Rights Abuse', 1 February. This URL is no longer available. www.businessweek.com/bwdaily/dnflash/feb2006/nf200621_2292_db052.htm.

Butler, Judith. 1999 (1990). *Gender Trouble: Feminism and the Subversion of Identity*. New York and London: Routledge.

Byerly, Ingrid Bianca. 1998. 'Mirror, Mediator and Prophet: The Music *Indaba* of Late-Apartheid South Africa', *Ethnomusicology* 42:1, pp. 1–44.

Byerly, Ingrid Bianca. 2008. 'Decomposing Apartheid: Things Come Together. The Anatomy of a Music Revolution', in Grant Olwage (ed.), *Composing Apartheid*. Johannesburg: University of the Witwatersrand Press, pp. 255–80.

Carlson, Marvin. 2006 (1996/2004). *Esitys ja performanssi. Kriittinen johdatus*. (Performance: A Critical Introduction). Trans by Riina Maukola. Like: Helsinki.

Caufield, Catherine. 2005. *The Man Who Ate Bluebottles and Other Great British Eccentrics.* London: Icon Books.

Cavanagh, David. 2007. '"Blooming Marvellous": Exclusive Interview with Peter Gabriel', *Uncut*, 122, pp. 80–83.

Césaire, Aimé. 1972 (1955). *Discourse on Colonialism.* Trans. Joan Pinkham. New York: Monthly Review Press.

Chambers Encyclopedic English Dictionary. 1994. Editor-in-chief Robert Allen. Edinburgh: Chambers.

Chambers, Iain. 1994. *Migrancy, Culture, Identity.* London: Routledge.

Cheyney, Tom. 1990. 'The Real World of Peter Gabriel', *The Beat* 34:9/2, pp. 22–5.

Chion, Michel. 1990. *Audio-Vision: Sound on Screen.* Trans. Claudia Gorbman. New York: Columbia University Press.

Chion, Michel. 1994. *Audio-Vision: Sound on Screen.* New York: Columbia University Press.

Coburn, Bob. n.d. 'Peter Gabriel Interview'. This URL is no longer available. www.cs.clemson.edu/~junderw/pg/interviews/swl.html.

Coburn, Bob. 1994. 'Peter Gabriel. Secret World Live'. Transcribed from radio interview, fall, by Wendy Katz. Accessed in February 2007. This URL is no longer available. http://jnu.freeshell.org/~jnu/pg/interviews/swl.html.

Coetzee, Jan K. 2003. *Life on the Margin: Listening to the Squatters.* Grahamstown: Rhodes University.

Coetzee, John. M. 1996. *Giving Offense.* Chicago, IL: University of Chicago Press.

Colbert, Paul. 1992. 'So What about *Us*?', *Vox*, October, pp. 22–5.

Coleman, Nick. 1994. 'Electric Disneyland', *Mojo*, October, pp. 53–5.

Collis, Clark. 2001. 'Bloody Students', *Mojo*, March, pp. 70–82.

Comaroff, Jean and John Comaroff. 1991. *Of Revelation and Revolution: Christianity, Colonialism, and Consciousness in South Africa.* Chicago, IL: University of Chicago Press.

Conti, Jacopo. 2007. *Minimalismo, modalità e improvvisazione nella musica dei nuovi King Crimson.* Final dissertation, Università di Torino.

Cook, Nicholas. 1998. *Analysing Musical Multimedia.* Oxford and New York: Clarendon Press and Oxford University Press.

Cope, Julian. 1998. *The Modern Antiquarian.* Glasgow: HarperCollins.

Cope, Julian. 2004. *Megalithic European: The 21st Century Traveller in Prehistoric Europe.* Glasgow: HarperCollins.

Coplan, David. 1982. 'The Emergence of an African Working Class Culture' in Shula Marks and Richard Rathbone (eds), *Industrialisation and Social Change in South Africa: African Class, Culture and Consciousness, 1870–1930.* London: Longman, pp. 358–75.

Coronil, Fernando. 1992. 'Can Postcoloniality be Decolonized? Imperial Banality and Postcolonial Power', *Public Culture* 5:2, pp. 89–108.

Cosgrove, Stuart. 1988. 'Music Global Style?' *New Statesman & Society*, 9 September, p. 50.

Cumberbatch, Franklin. 2002. 'Peter Gabriel: Had a Nice Decade. New record, New Tour, Big Ideas, Same Old Genius', Interview for *vh1.com* on 27 September www.vh1.com/artists/news/1457838/09272002/gabriel_peter.jhtml.

Cunningham, Mark. 1999. *Live & Kicking. The Rock Concert Industry in the Nineties.* London: Sanctuary Publishing.

Dane, Cliff. 2001. *The UK Record Industry Annual Survey 2001.* Weston-Super-Mare: Media Research Publishing.

Danielsen, Anne. 2006. *Presence and Pleasure: The Funk Grooves of James Brown and Parliament.* Middletown, CT: Wesleyan University Press.

Davie, Lucille. 2008. 'Biko is at the Apartheid Museum', City of Johannesburg website, 21 January. www.joburg.org.za/content/view/2082/168.

Davis, Fred. 1993. 'I Want My Desktop MTV', *Wired*, July/August, pp. 4–11.

Debord, Guy. 1995 (1967). *The Society of the Spectacle* (orig. *La Société du spectacle*). Trans. Donald Nicholson-Smith. New York: Zone Books.

di Liberto, John. 1992. Peter Gabriel Interview by John di Liberto. *Morning Edition*, National Public Radio, 29 September.

Dibango, Manu. 1994. *Three Kilos of Coffee.* Chicago, IL: University of Chicago Press.

Dilberto, John. 1986. '*So*' (record review), *Down Beat* 53:10 (October), p. 30.

Dodd, Philip (ed.) 2007. *Genesis: Chapter and Verse.* London: Weidenfeld & Nicolson.

Douglas, Mary. 2002 (1966). *Purity and Danger: An Analysis of the Concept of Pollution and Taboo.* London and New York: Routledge & Kegan Paul.

Drewett, Michael. 1998. Interview with Jacobus Van Rooyen, Pretoria, 11 September.

Drewett, Michael. 2002. 'Satirical Opposition in Popular Music within Apartheid and Post-Apartheid South Africa', *Society in Transition* 33:1, pp. 80–95.

Drewett, Michael. 2004. *An Analysis of the Censorship of Popular Music Within the Context of Cultural Struggle in South Africa During the 1980s.* Unpublished PhD thesis, Rhodes University.

Drewett, Michael. 2005. 'Stop This Filth: The Censorship of Roger Lucey's Music in Apartheid South Africa', *South African Journal of Musicology* 25, pp. 53–70.

Drewett, Michael. 2007. 'The Eyes of the World are Watching Now: The Political Effectiveness of 'Biko' by Peter Gabriel', *Popular Music and Society* 30:1, pp. 39–51.

Drummond, Bill. 2000. *45.* London: Little, Brown and Company.

Duncan, Carol. 1982. 'Virility and Domination in Early Twentieth-Century Vanguard Painting', in Norma Broude and Mary Garrard (eds), *Feminism and Art History: Questioning the Litany.* New York: Harper and Row, pp. 293–314. Revised version of essay first published in *Artforum*, December 1973, pp. 30–39.

Duran, Lucy. 1989. 'Key to N'Dour: The Roots of the Senegalese Star', *Popular Music* 8:3, pp. 275–84.

Durkheim, Emile. 1984. *The Division of Labor in Society*. New York: Free Press.

Dyer, Richard. 2004 (1979). *Stars*. Supplementary Chapter by Paul McDonald. London: BFI Publishing.

Dyson, Michael Eric. 2004. *Mercy, Mercy Me: The Art, Loves and Demons of Marvin Gaye*. New York: Basic Civitas Books.

Eagleton, Terry. 1990. *The Ideology of the Aesthetic*. Oxford: Blackwell.

Edwards, Bob. 1990. Paul Simon Interview. *Morning Edition*, National Public Radio, 18 October.

Everett, Walter. 2002. 'Detroit and Memphis: The Soul of *Revolver*', in Russell Reising (ed.), *'Every Sound There Is': The Beatles' Revolver and the Transformation of Rock and Roll*. Burlington, VT: Ashgate, pp. 25–57.

Eyerman, Ron and Andrew Jamison. 1998. *Music and Social Movements*. Cambridge: Cambridge University Press.

Eyre, Banning. 1990. 'Bringing It All Back Home: Three Takes on Producing World Music'. *Option*, November, pp. 75–81.

Fabbri, Franco. 1984a. *Elettronica e musica. Gli strumenti i personaggi la storia*. Milan: Fratelli Fabbri Editori.

Fabbri, Franco. 1984b. '*You're pushing the needle to the red*, ovvero della prospettiva, arte dell'illusione', *Fare Musica* 38 (May), now in Fabbri 2002, pp. 170–72.

Fabbri, Franco. 1986. 'Diavolo d'un Gabriel?', *Fare Musica* 66 (September), now in Fabbri 2002, pp. 176–8.

Fabbri, Franco. 2002. *Il suono in cui viviamo*. Roma: Arcana.

Fairley, Jan. 2001. 'The 'Local' and the 'Global' in Popular Music', in Simon Frith, Will Straw and John Street (eds), *The Cambridge Companion to Pop and Rock*. Cambridge: Cambridge University Press, pp. 272–89.

Fanon, Frantz. 1968 (1961). *The Wretched of the Earth*. Trans Constance Farrington. New York: Grove Weidenfeld.

Feld, Steven. 1994. 'Notes on "World Beat"', In Charles Keil and Steven Feld, *Music Grooves: Essays and Dialogues*. Chicago, IL: University of Chicago Press, pp. 238–46.

Feld, Steven. 2000a. 'The Poetics and Politics of Pygmy Pop', in Georgina Born and David Hesmondhalgh (eds), *Western Music and its Others. Difference, Representation and Appropriation in Music*. Berkeley and Los Angeles: University of California Press.

Feld, Steven. 2000b. 'A Sweet Lullaby for World Music', *Public Culture* 30, pp. 145–72.

Fielder, Hugh. 2006. 'The Rael Thing', *Classic Rock*, February, pp. 38–43.

Fiori, Umberto. 1987. 'Listening to Peter Gabriel's "I Have the Touch"', *Popular Music* 6:1, pp. 37–43.

Fiori, Umberto. 2000 'Listening to Peter Gabriel's "I Have the Touch"' in Middleton, Richard. (ed.), *Reading Pop*. Oxford: Oxford University Press, pp. 183–91.

Fitzpatrick, Eileen. 1997. 'Animators take Low-tech Style Sky-high; Wallace and Gromit Creators on the Rise', *Billboard* 109:15 (12 April), pp. 51–2.

Forster, E.M. 1936. *Notes on English Character*. London: Penguin Books.

Foucault, Michel. 1984. *The Foucault Reader*. Ed. Paul Rabinow. New York: Pantheon.

Fricke, David. 1983. 'Peter Gabriel: The Ethnic Shocks the Electronic', *Musician* 51:1, pp. 20, 22, 27–8, 36.

Frink, Mark, 2003. 'Peter Gabriel's Growing Up Tour', *Mix Online*, 1 Jan. http://mixonline.com/livesound/tours/audio_peter_gabriels_growing.

Friskics-Warren, Bill. 2005. *I'll Take You There: Pop Music and the Urge for Transcendence*. New York: Continuum.

Frith, Simon. 1983. *Sound Effects: Youth, Leisure, and the Politics of Rock 'n' Roll*. London: Constable.

Frith, Simon. 1996. *Performing Rites. On the Value of Popular Music*. Oxford and New York: Oxford University Press.

Frith, Simon. 1997. 'The Suburban Sensibility in British Rock and Pop', in Roger Silverstone (ed.), *Visions of Suburbia*. London: Routledge, pp. 269–79.

Frith, Simon. 2000. 'The Discourse of World Music', in Georgina Born and David Hesmondhalgh (eds), *Western Music and its Others. Difference, Representation and Appropriation in Music*. Berkeley and Los Angeles: University of California Press. pp. 305–322.

Frith, Simon and Andrew Horne. 1987. *Art into Pop*. New York and London: Methuen.

Frith, Simon and Angela McRobbie. 1990. 'Rock and Sexuality', in Simon Frith and Andrew Goodwin (eds), *On Record: Rock, Pop, and the Written Word*. First published in *Screen Education* 29, 1978. London: Routledge, pp. 371–89.

Gabriel, Peter. n.d. *Us* website at Real World Records. This URL is no longer active. http://realworld.on.net.pg/tina/pgfaq4.html.

Gabriel, Peter. 1987. So *Tour Guide*. London: Cliofine.

Gabriel Peter. 1991. 'North and West Africa: Introduction', in P. Sweeney (ed.), *The Virgin Directory of World Music*. London: Virgin Books, pp. 1–3.

Gabriel, Peter. 1993. Liner notes to *Plus from Us*. Real World Carol 2327–2.

Gabriel, Peter. 2002. *Up* press pack notes.

Gabriel, Peter. 2007. 'All About ... *Us*'. Accessed in February 2007. This URL is no longer active. http://petergabriel.com/features/All_About.._Us.

Gadamer, Hans-Georg. 1999 (1960). *Truth and Method*. Trans Joel Weinsheimer and Donald G. Marshall (orig. *Warheit und Methode. Grundzüge einer philosophischer hermeneutik*). New York: Continuum.

Gallo, Armando. 1986. *Peter Gabriel*. London: Omnibus Press.

Gamson, Joshua. 1994. *Claims to Fame: Celebrity in Contemporary America*. Berkeley: University of California Press.

Gardner, Elysa. 1992. 'Peter Gabriel's *Us*', *Rolling Stone*, 17 September, p. 27.

Gardner, Elysa. 2002. Peter Gabriel looks 'Up', *Usa Today* 3, D.04 (Life).

Garofalo, Reebee (ed.), 1992. *Rockin' the Boat: Mass Music and Mass Movements*. Boston, MA: South End Press.

Garofalo, Reebee. 1997. *Rockin' Out: Popular Music in the USA*. Boston, MA: Allyn and Bacon.

Gendron, Bernard. 2002. *Between Montmartre and the Mudclub: Popular Music and the Avant-Garde*. Chicago: University of Chicago Press.

Gibson, Penny, Errol Norris and Peter Alcock. 1992. *Music: The Rock – Classic Connection*. Cape Town: Oxford University Press South Africa.

Giddens, Anthony. 1991. *Modernity and Self-Identity: Self and Society in the Late Modern Age*. Cambridge: Polity.

Gilbert, Jerry. 1972. 'Genesis doing the Foxtrot', *Sounds*, 9 September, www. rocksbackpages.com/article.html?ArticleID=8422 (accessed on 1 October 2010).

Gillett, Charles. 1972. *The Sound of the City*. New York: Dell.

Goldman, Erik. 1995. 'Ethnotechno: A Sample Twist of Fate', *Rhythm Music*, July, pp. 36–9.

Goldstein, Dan. 1986. 'Technology's Champion', *Electronics & Music Maker* 6:4 (June), pp. 52–7.

Goodwin, Andrew. 1992. *Dancing in the Distraction Factory: Music Television and Popular Culture*. Minneapolis: University of Minnesota Press.

Goodwin, Andrew. 1993. *Dancing in the Distraction Factory: Music Television and Popular Culture*. London: Routledge.

Goodwin, Andrew and Joe Gore. 1990. 'World Beat and the Cultural Imperialism Debate', *Socialist Review* 20:3, pp. 63–80.

Gottelier, John. 1993. 'The Secret World of Peter Gabriel. Jonathan Gottelier in Cyberspace', *Lighting and Sound International*, July, pp. 20–22.

Gow, Joe. 1992. 'Music Video as Communication: Popular Formulas and Emerging Genres', *The Journal of Popular Culture* 26:2, pp. 41–70.

Gracyk, Theodore. 2001. *I Wanna Be Me. Rock Music and the Politics of Identity*. Philadelphia, PA: Temple University Press.

Gramsci, Antonio. 1971. *Selections from the Prison Notebooks*. Ed. and trans. Quintin Hoare and Geoffrey Nowell Smith. New York: International.

Gray, John. 2002. 'Ulrika is a Sign that we've Got it All', *New Statesman* 28 October, pp. 28–30.

Greenbaum, Sidney. 1996. *The Oxford English Grammar*. Oxford: Oxford University Press.

Grossberg, Lawrence. 1996. 'On Postmodernism and Articulation: An Interview with Stuart Hall', in Dave Morley and Kuan-Hsing Chen (eds), *Stuart Hall: Critical Dialogues in Cultural Studies*. London: Routledge pp. 131–50.

Grundlingh, Albert. 2004. '"Rocking the Boat"? The 'Voëlvry' Music Movement in South Africa: Anatomy of Afrikaans Anti-Apartheid Social Protest in the

Eighties', *International Journal of African Historical Studies* 37:3, pp. 483–508.

Guttenberg, Steve. 2005. 'Peter Gabriel' (interview), *Home Theater*, September. www.hometheatermag.com/httalksto/905talks.

Guy, Rebecca. 2007. *Pipe Up The Volume: The Role of the Flute in Progressive Rock*. Doctoral thesis, University of Salford.

Hall, Stuart. 1979. 'Culture, the Media and the "Ideological Effect"', in James Curran, Michael Gurevitch and Janet Woollacott (eds), *Mass Communication and Society*. Beverly Hills, CA: Sage, pp. 315–48.

Hall, Stuart. 1991. 'The Local and the Global: Globalization and Ethnicity', in Anthony D. King (ed.), *Culture, Globalization and the World-System*. Binghamton, NY: Department of Art and Art History, State University of New York at Binghamton, pp. 19–39.

Hall, Stuart. 1996. 'Introduction: Who Needs Identity?', in Stuart Hall and Paul DuGay (eds), *Questions of Cultural Identity*. London: Sage, pp. 1–17.

Hammond, Ray. 1987. 'Peter Gabriel: Behind the Mask' *Sound On Sound* 2:3 (January), pp. 40–44.

Hannigan, Des. 2004. *Eccentric Britain. A Celebration of Britain's Bizarre Buildings, Peculiar Places and Offbeat Events*. London: New Holland Publishers.

Harrington, Richard. 1993. 'The Secret Tour. Genesis Founder Peter Gabriel Takes His Soul on the Road', *Washington Post*, 20 June. www.ingsoc.com/gabriel/articles/wash93.html.

Hashmi, Yasmin. 1989. 'Audio Tablet', *Studio Sound* 31:1 (January), pp. 30–31.

Hawkins, Stan. 1996. 'Perspectives in Popular Musicology: Music, Lennox, and Meaning in 1990s Pop', *Popular Music* 15:1 (January), pp. 17–36.

Hawkins, Stan and John Richardson. 2007. 'Remodeling Britney Spears: Matters of Intoxication and Mediation', *Popular Music and Society* 30:5, pp. 605–629.

Healey, Jack and Bob Guccione Jr. 1991. 'Living in the Real World', *Spin 7* (November), pp. 70–72, 74, 76.

Hebdige, Dick. 1979. *Subculture: The Meaning of Style*. London: Methuen.

Henke, James. 1988. *Human Rights Now! The Official Book of the Concerts for Human Rights Foundation World Tour*. London: Bloomsbury.

Highmore, Ben. 2002. *Everyday Life and Cultural Theory*. London: Routledge.

Hjemdahl, Kirsti Mathiesen. 2003. 'When Theme Parks Happen', in Jonas Frykman and Nils Gilje (eds), *Being There. New Perspectives on Phenomenology and the Analysis of Culture*. Lund: Nordic Academic Press, pp. 129–48.

Holm-Hudson, Kevin (ed.) 2002. *Progressive Rock Reconsidered*. New York and London: Routledge.

Holm-Hudson, Kevin. 2008. *Genesis and The Lamb Lies Down on Broadway*. Aldershot: Ashgate.

Hopkins, Pat. 2006. *Voëlvry: The Movement that Rocked South Africa*. Cape Town: Zebra Press.

Hornby, Nick. 2003. *31 Songs*. London: Penguin.

'Hot Shots: Peter Gabriel'. 1986–87. *Rolling Stone* 489–90, p. 20. http://rec.horus. at/music/gabriel/songs/comment.cgi?Biko

Howatson, Margaret (ed.) 1997. *The Concise Oxford Companion to Classical Literature.* Oxford: Oxford University Press.

Hudson, Mark. 1995. 'Praise Be!', *Guardian Weekend*, 30 September, pp. 26–31.

Huizinga, Johan. 1984 (1944). *Leikkivä ihminen. Yritys kulttuurin leikkiaineksen määrittelemiseksi* (orig. *Homo Ludens. Versuch einer Bestimmung des Spielelements der Kultur*). Trans. Sirkka Salomaa. Porvoo, Helsinki, Juva: WSOY.

Hutcheon, Linda. 1994. *Irony's Edge: The Theory and Politics of Irony.* London and New York: Routledge.

Hutchinson, John. 1986. 'From Brideshead to Shrunken Heads: Interview with Peter Gabriel', *Musician* 93:7, pp. 68–78.

Infusino, Divina. 1993. 'Singer Peter Gabriel Reveals His Inner Journey', *Christian Science Monitor*, 3 August, p. 13.

Iversen, Margaret. 1997. 'Visualising the Unconscious: Mary Kelly's Installations', in Margaret Iversen, Douglas Crimp and Homi K. Bhabha, *Mary Kelly*. London: Phaidon Press, pp. 32–85.

Jackson, Alan. 1987. 'Middle Class Hero', *New Musical Express*, 28 November, pp. 28–9, 49.

Jolliffe, John. 2001. *Eccentrics.* London: Duckworth.

Jowers, Peter. 1993. 'Beating New Tracks: WOMAD and the British World Music Movement', in Simon Miller (ed.), *The Last Post: Music after Modernism.* New York: Manchester University Press, pp. 52–87.

Kamin, Philip and Peter Goddard. 1984. *Genesis: Peter Gabriel, Phil Collins And Beyond.* New York: Beaufort Books.

Kaplan, E. Ann. 1987. *Rocking Around the Clock: Music Television, Postmodernism, and Consumer Culture.* New York and London: Methuen.

Kinder, Marsha. 1984. 'Music Video and the Spectator: Television, Ideology and Dream', *Film Quarterly* 38:1 (Autumn), pp. 2–15.

Kinder, Marsha. 1987. 'Phallic Film and the Boob Tube: The Power of Gender Identification in Cinema, Television and Music Video', *One Two Three Four: A Rock and Roll Quarterly* 5, pp. 33–49.

Kingsbury, Henry. 1988. *Music, Talent and Performance.* Philadelphia, PA: Temple University Press.

Kinnersley, Hannah. 2003. 'Up, Down and All Around', *Live Design Online*, 1 February. http://livedesignonline.com/mag/show_business_down_around.

Kivnick, Helen. 1990. *Where is the Way? Song and Struggle in South Africa.* London: Penguin.

Koopmans, Ruud. 2004. 'Protest in Time and Space: The Evolution of Waves of Contention', in David Snow, Sarah A. Soule and Hanspeter Kriesi (eds), *The Blackwell Companion to Social Movements.* Oxford: Blackwell, pp. 19–46.

Kot, Greg. 1992. 'Recordings: *Us*', *Rolling Stone* 640 (1 October), p. 63.

Kraidy, Marwan M. 2005. *Hybridity or the Cultural Logic of Globalisation*. Philadephia, PA: Temple University Press.

Kramer, Lawrence. 2002. *Musical Meaning: Toward a Critical History*. Berkeley: University of California Press.

Kristeva, Julia. 1982. *Powers of Horror: An Essay on Abjection*. First published in French in 1980. New York: Columbia University Press.

Kärki, Kimi. 2005. '"Matter of Fact it's All Dark": Audiovisual Stadium Rock Aesthetics in Pink Floyd's *The Dark Side of the Moon Tour* 1973', in Russell Reising (ed.), *Speak To Me. The Legacy of Pink Floyd's Dark Side of the Moon*. Aldershot: Ashgate, pp. 27–42.

Kärki, Kimi. 2007. 'Kun Gabriel laskeutui taivaalta. Mytologiat osana progressiivisen rockin lavaesiintymistä', *Musiikin suunta* 3, pp. 41–52.

Lacasse, Serge. 1995. *Une analyse des rapports texte-musique dans 'Digging in the Dirt' de Peter Gabriel*. Masters thesis, Université Laval, Quebec.

Lacasse, Serge. 2000. *'Listen to My Voice': The Evocative Power of Vocal Staging in Recorded Rock Music and Other Forms of Vocal Expression*. Doctoral thesis, University of Liverpool.

Lacasse, Serge. 2002. 'Vers une poétique de la phonographie: la fonction narrative de la mise en scène vocale dans "Front Row" (1998) d'Alanis Morissette', *Musurgia: analyse et pratique musicales* 9:2, pp. 23–41.

Lacasse, Serge. 2010. 'The Phonographic Voice: Paralinguistic Features and Phonographic Staging in Popular Music Singing', in Amanda Bayley (ed.), *Recorded Music: Society, Technology, and Performance*. Cambridge: Cambridge University Press.

Laing, Dave. 2003. 'Resistance and Protest', in John Shepherd, David Horn, Dave Laing, Paul Oliver and Peter Wicke (eds), *Continuum Encyclopaedia of Popular Music of the World*. London: Continuum, pp. 345–6.

Lakoff, George and Mark Johnson. 1980. *Metaphors We Live By*. Chicago, IL: University of Chicago Press.

Lambert, Stu. 1993. 'The Angel Gabriel', *New Statesman & Society*, 25 June, p. 34.

Laubscher, Leswin. 2005. 'Afrikaner Identity and the Music of Johannes Kerkorrel', *South African Journal of Psychology* 35:2, pp. 308–330.

Le Vay, Benedict. 2000. *Eccentric Britain. The Bradt Guide to Britain's Follies and Foibles*. Chalfont St Peter: Bradt Publications.

Legrand, Emmanuel. 2004. 'Gabriel's Music Clips get DVD Remix', *Billboard* 116:42 (16 October), p. 38.

Leja, Michael. 1993. *Reframing Abstract Expressionism: Subjectivity and Painting in the 1940s*. New Haven, CT, and London: Yale University Press.

Leonard, Marion. 2007. *Gender in the Music Industry: Rock, Discourse and Girl Power*. Aldershot: Ashgate.

Linge, David. 1977. 'Editor's Introduction', in Hans-Georg Gadamer, *Philosophical Hermeneutics*. Ed. and trans. David Linge. Berkeley: University of California Press, pp. xi–lviii.

Macan, Edward. 1997. *Rocking the Classics. English Progressive Rock and the Counterculture*. Oxford and New York: Oxford University Press.

Macan, Edward. 2006. *Endless Enigma: A Musical Biography of Emerson, Lake and Palmer*. Chicago, IL: Open Court Press.

Mäkela, Janne. 2004. *John Lennon Imagined. Cultural History of a Rock Star*. New York: Peter Lang.

McClary, Susan. 1991. *Feminine Endings: Music, Gender, and Sexuality*. Minneapolis: University of Minnesota Press.

McGuigan, Jim and Abigail Gilmore. 2002. 'The Millennium Dome: Sponsoring, Meaning and Visiting', *International Journal of Cultural Policy* 8:1, pp. 1–20.

Mencken, H.L. 1922. *In Defense of Women*. New York: Alfred Knopf Publishers.

Merrett, Christopher. 1994. *A Culture of Censorship*. Cape Town: David Phillip.

Meyer, David S. and Suzanne Staggenborg. 1996. 'Movements, Countermovements and the Structure of Political Opportunity', *American Journal of Sociology* 101, pp. 1628–60.

Middleton, Richard. 1990. *Studying Popular Music*. Milton Keynes: Open University Press.

Middleton, Richard. 2000. 'Approaches To Textual Analysis In Popular Music', in Richard Middleton (ed.), *Reading Pop*. Oxford: Oxford University Press, pp.104–121.

Milano, D. 1989. 'Peter Gabriel's Identity', *Keyboard Magazine* 15, pp. 32–8.

Mill, John Stuart. 2002 (1859). *On Liberty*. New York: Dover Publications.

Minà, Gianni. 2004. *Una vita da Maestro, intervista a E. Morricone*. www.andreaconti.it/morricon.html.

Mitchell, Tony. 1993. 'World Music and the Popular Music Industry: An Australian View', *Ethnomusicology* 37:3, pp. 309–338.

Moens-Haenen, Greta. 2001. 'Vibrato', in Stanley Sadie (ed.), *The New Grove Dictionary of Music and Musicians*. London: Macmillan. Vol. 26, pp. 523–5.

Moles, Steve. 1993. 'Big Time Lightning. LD Vince Foster Guides the Enormous Elements of Peter Gabriel's World Tour', *Lighting Dimensions*, September, pp. 56–9, 94.

Moore, Allan F. 1992. 'The Textures of Rock', in Rossana Dalmonte and Mario Baroni (eds) *Secondo convegno europeo di analisi musicale. Atti a cura di Rossana Dalmonte e Mario Baroni*. Trento: Università di Trento, pp. 341–4.

Moore, Allan F. 2001. *Rock: The Primary Text: Developing a Musicology of Rock*. Aldershot: Ashgate.

Moylan, William. 2002. *The Art of Recording: Understanding and Crafting the Mix*. Boston, MA: Focal Press.

Mulvey, Laura. 1989. 'Visual Pleasure and Narrative Cinema', in *Visual and Other Pleasures*. London: Macmillan. First published in *Screen* 16:3 (Autumn 1975), pp. 14–26.

Mundy, Jennifer. 2001. 'Letters of Desire', in Jennifer Mundy (ed.), *Surrealism: Desire Unbound*. London: Tate, pp. 10–53.

Myers, Daniel J. 2000. 'The Diffusion of Collective Violence: Infectiousness, Susceptibility and Mass Media Networks', *American Journal of Sociology* 106:1, pp. 173–208.

Negus, Keith. 1992. *Producing Pop: Culture and Conflict in the Popular Music Industry*. New York: Edward Arnold.

Negus, Keith. 1999. *Music Genres and Corporate Cultures*. London and New York: Routledge.

Nelson, Victoria. 2001. *The Secret Life of Puppets*. Cambridge, MA: Harvard University Press.

Nercessian, Andy. 2002. *Postmodernism and Globalisation in Ethnomusicology: An Epistemological Problem*. Lanham, MD and London: Scarecrow Press.

Newby, Julian. 2008. 'Peter Gabriel. MIDEM Personality Of The Year 2008', in *Personality Of The Year. MIDEM 2008. Peter Gabriel*. Paris: Reed MIDEM.

Nicholls, Dave. 2004. 'Virtual Opera, or Opera Between the Ears', *Journal of the Royal Musical Association* 129:1, pp. 100–142.

Nidel, Richard. 2004. *World Music: the Basics*. London and New York: Routledge.

Nzewi, Meki, Israel Anyahuru and Tom Ohiaraumunna. 2001. 'Beyond Song Texts: The Lingual Fundamentals of African Drum Music', *Research in African Literatures* 32:2, pp. 90–104.

O'Hagan, Sean. 1992. 'All About Us: Peter Gabriel Talks About the New Album', interview with Peter Gabriel, *The Box* 1, pp. 4–5.

O'Hagan, Sean. 1995. 'The Great White Hopes', *The Times Magazine*, 2 December, pp. 20–23.

Olwage, Grant (ed.) 2008. *Composing Apartheid: Music for and Against Apartheid*. Johannesburg: University of the Witwatersrand Press.

Palmer, Gareth. 1997. 'Bruce Springsteen and Masculinity' in Sheila Whiteley (ed.), *Sexing the Groove: Popular Music and Gender*. London and New York: Routledge, pp. 100–117.

Pareles, Jon. 1983. 'Music without Frontiers: Peter Gabriel', *Musician, Player & Listener*, September/October, pp. 40–44.

Pareles, Jon. 1986. 'Peter Gabriel Sings of Lost Ego', *New York Times*, 15 June. http://query.nytimes.com/gst/fullpage.html?res=9A0DE6D7173BF936A2575 5C0A960948260&sec=&spon=&pagewanted=1.

Pareles, Jon. 1992. 'For Peter Gabriel, This Time It's Personal', *New York Times*, 27 September, §H, p. 30.

Petridis, Alex. 2004. 'The Day the Music Dies', *The Guardian*, 4 February.

Pityana, N. Barney, Mamphela Ramphele, Malusi Mpumlwana and Lindy Wilson (eds). 1991. *Bounds of Possibility: The Legacy of Steve Biko and Black Consciousness*. Cape Town: David Phillip.

Plastino, Goffredo. 2003. 'Inventing Ethnic Music. Fabrizio De André's *Creuza de mä* and the Creation of *Musica mediterranea* in Italy', in Goffredo Plastino (ed.), *Mediterranean Mosaic. Popular Music and Global Sounds*. New York and London: Routledge, pp. 267–86.

Posner, Gerald. 2002. *Motown: Music, Money, Sex, and Power.* New York: Random House.

Pride, Dominic. 1993. 'WOMAD's Future Appears Wobbly', *Billboard*, 16 January, p. 87.

Qureshi, Regula Burkhardt. 1986. *Sufi Music in India and Pakistan: Sound, Context and Meaning in Qawaali.* Cambridge: Cambridge University Press.

Randall, Lucian and Chris Welch. 2002. *Ginger Geezer. The Life of Vivian Stanshall.* London: Fourth Estate.

Rattalino, Piero. 1982. *Storia del pianoforte. Lo strumento, la musica, gli interpreti.* Milan: Il Saggiatore.

Repsch, John. 2004. *Joe Meek. The Legendary Telstar Man.* London: Cherry Red Books.

Richards, Jeffrey. 1997. *Films and British National Identity. From Dickens to Dad's Army.* Manchester: Manchester University Press.

Richardson, John. 2005. '"The Digital Won't Let me Go": Constructions of the Virtual and the Real in Gorillaz' "Clint Eastwood"', *Journal of Popular Music Studies* 17:1, pp. 1–29.

Richardson, John. 2007. 'Double-voiced Discourse and Bodily Pleasures in Contemporary Finnish Rock: The Case of Maija Vikkumaa', in John Richardson and Stan Hawkins (eds), *Essays on Sound and Vision*). Helsinki: Yliopistopaino, pp. 401–41.

Ringer, Benjamin B. and Elinor R. Lawless. 1989. *Race-Ethnicity and Society.* New York: Routledge, 1989.

Riviere, Joan. 1986. 'Womanliness as a Masquerade', in Victor Burgin, James Donald and Cora Kaplan (eds), *Formations of Fantasy*. First published in *The International Journal of Psychoanalysis* 10 (1929). London and New York: Methuen, pp. 35–44.

Rose, Jacqueline. 1996. *The Haunting of Sylvia Plath.* London: Virago Press.

Rose, Jonathan. 2001. *The Intellectual Life of the British Working Classes.* London and New Haven, CT: Yale University Press.

Rothenberg, Jerome (ed.). 1972. *Shaking the Pumpkin: Traditional Poetry of the Indian North Americas.* Garden City, NY: Doubleday.

Rubin, Chris. 2002. 'Gabriel Back Up With Tour. After nearly ten years, Peter Gabriel returns to the stage', *Rollingstone.com*, 13 Nov. www.rollingstone.com/news/story/5935663/gabriel_back_up_with_tour

Rubin, Chris. 2007. 'Peter Gabriel: A Very Old Interview'. http://theesurientmanlistens.blogspot.com/2007/05/peter-gabriel-very-old-interview.html

Rushdie, Salman. 1996. 'In Defense of the Novel, yet Again', *New Yorker*, 24 June and 1 July, pp. 48–55.

Saccone, Teri. 1991. 'Manu Katché', *Modern Drummer* 15:8, pp. 20–24, 66–73, 75–6.

Said, Edward W. 1991. 'The Politics of Knowledge', *Raritan* 11:1, pp. 17–31.

Sandall, Robert. 1993. 'Peter Gabriel: Gawp Factor Ten', *Q*, July. www. rocksbackpages.com/article.html?ArticleID=1412

Schapiro, Mark. 1997. 'Wounds, Peak Experience, and the Vomit Theory of Art'. http://archive.salon.com/april97/21st/gabriel970403.html.

Schmahmann, Brenda. 2004. *Through the Looking Glass: Representations of Self by South African Women Artists*. Johannesburg: David Krut Publishing.

Schwarz, David. 1997. *Listening Subjects: Music, Psychoanalysis, Culture*. Durham, NC, and London: Duke University Press.

'Secret World. Tales From the Understage' in *www.petergabriel.com*. www. petergabriel.com/features/Secret_World_-_Tour_Tales.

Seidman, Steven A. 1992. 'An Investigation of Sex-role Stereotyping in Music Videos', *Journal of Broadcasting & Electronic Media* 36:2 (Spring), pp. 209–216.

Sexton, Anne. 1975. *The Awful Rowing Toward God*. Boston, MA: Houghton Mifflin.

Sexton, Anne. 1999. *The Complete Poems: Anne Sexton*, foreword by Maxine Kumin. New York: Mariner Books.

Sexton, Paul. 1994. 'WOMAD Back for 2nd US Tour; Western, World Music Acts Team Again', *Billboard*, 21 May, p. 1.

Sharma, Ashwani. 1996. 'Sounds Oriental: The (Im) Possibility of Theorising Asian Music Cultures', in S. Sharma, J. Hutnyk and A. Sharna, *Dis-Orienting Rhythms. The Politics of the New Asian Dance Music*. London: Zed Books, pp. 15–31.

Sharpe, Graham. 2005. *The Man Who Was Screaming Lord Sutch*. Bodmin: Aurum Press.

Shepherd, Fiona. 2004. 'Gabriel Rewards Devotees with a Show that's Out of this World', music review, *The Scotsman*, 7 June. http://living.scotsman.com/features/Gabriel-rewards-devotees-with-a.2535413.jp.

Shepherd, John. 1991. *Music as Social Text*. Cambridge: Polity Press.

Shewey, Don. 2001. 'Robert Lepage: A Bold Québécois Who Blends Art With Technology', *New York Times*, 16 September. www.donshewey.com/theater_articles/zulu_time_for_NYT.htm.

Shumway, David. 1999. 'Performance', in Bruce Horner and Thomas Swiss (eds), *Key Terms in Popular Music and Culture*. Oxford: Blackwell Publishers, pp. 188–98.

Sinclair, David. 1992. 'World Music Fests Flourish in UK', *Billboard*, 8 August, p. 12.

Sinclair, David. 1993. 'Peter Gabriel's Secret World', *Rolling Stone*, 19 August, p. 9.

Sitwell, Edith. 1971 (1933). *English Eccentrics. A Gallery of Weird and Wonderful Men and Women*. St Ives: Penguin Books.

Skynner, Robin and John Cleese. 1993. *Life and How to Survive It*. London: Methuen.

Small, Christopher. 1980. *Music Society Education*. London: John Calder.

Smit, Brendon. 1992. *Afrikaans Alternative Popular Music 1986–1990: An Analysis of the Music of Bernoldus Niemand and Johannes Kerkorrel.* B.Mus. thesis, University of Natal.

Smith, Sid. 2001. *In the Court of King Crimson.* London: Helter Skelter.

Smith, Suzanne E. 1999. *Dancing in the Street: Motown and the Cultural Politics of Detroit.* Cambridge, MA: Harvard University Press.

Snow, David and Pamela Oliver. 1994. 'Social Movements and Collective Behaviour: Social Psychological Dimensions and Considerations', in Karen Cook, Gary Fine and James House (eds), *Sociological Perspectives on Social Psychology.* Boston: Allyn & Bacon, pp. 571–99.

Soule, Sarah A. 2004. 'Diffusion Processes within and across Movements', in David Snow, Sarah A. Soule and Hanspeter Kriesi (eds), *The Blackwell Companion to Social Movements.* Oxford: Blackwell, pp. 294–310.

Spencer, Liese. 2002. 'Peter Grows Up', *The Scotsman*, 12 September. http://living.scotsman.com/features/Peter-grows-up.2360976.jp

St Michael, Mick. 1994. *Peter Gabriel: In His Own Words.* London: Omnibus Press.

Staiger, Janet, Kristin Thompson and David Bordwell. 1985. *The Classical Hollywood Cinema: Film Style & Mode of Production to 1960.* New York: Columbia University Press.

Stokes, Martin. 2003. 'Globalization and the Politics of World Music', in Martin Clayton, Trevor Herbert and Richard Middleton (eds), *The Cultural Study of Music. A Critical Introduction.* London, Routledge, pp. 297–308.

Strang, David and Sarah Soule. 1998. 'Diffusion in Organization and Social Movements: From Hybrid Corn to Poison Spills', *Annual Review of Sociology* 24, pp. 265–90.

Straw, Will. 1990. 'Characterizing Rock Music Culture: The Case of Heavy Metal', in Simon Frith and Andrew Goodwin (eds), *On Record: Rock, Pop, and the Written Word.* London: Routledge, pp. 97–110.

Street, John. 2001. 'Rock, Pop and Politics', in Simon Frith, Will Straw and John Street (eds), *The Cambridge Companion to Pop and Rock.* Cambridge: Cambridge University Press.

Stump, Paul. 1997. *The Music's All That Matters. A History of Progressive Rock.* London: Quartet Books.

Sullivan, Jim. 1980. 'Gabriel on Gabriel or Man vs. Record', *Trouser Press*, October, pp. 22–5.

Sutcliffe, John. 2003. 'Season of the Witch', *Mojo Magazine*, February, pp. 72–80.

Tarrow, Sidney. 1994. *Power in Movement: Social Movements, Collective Action and Politics.* New York: Cambridge University Press.

Taylor, Timothy D. 1997. *Global Pop. World Music, World Markets.* London and New York: Routledge.

Taylor, Timothy D. 2007. *Beyond Exoticism. Western Music and the World.* Durham, NC: Duke University Press.

Tenaille, Frank. 2002. *Music is the Weapon of the Future: Fifty Years of African Popular Music.* Chicago, IL: Lawrence Hill.

Thompson, Dave. 2005. *Turn it on Again: Peter Gabriel, Phil Collins & Genesis.* San Francisco, CA: Backbeat Books.

The Timelords. 1988. *The Manual (How to Have a Number One the Easy Way).* n.p.: KLF Publications.

Timpson, John. 1991. *English Eccentrics.* Norwich: Jarrold Publishing.

Toff, Nancy. 1996. *The Flute Book: A Complete Guide for Students and Performers.* New York: Oxford University Press.

Tomaselli, Keyan G. and Bob Boster. 1993. 'Mandela, MTV, Television and Apartheid', *Popular Music and Society* 17:2, pp. 1–19.

Toop, David. 1999. *Exotica. Fabricated Soundscapes in a Real World.* London: Serpent's Tail.

Townsend, Martin. 1994. 'Vision of Gabriel', *Vox*, February, pp. 22–5.

Turner, Victor. 1970 (1969). *The Ritual Process.* Chicago, IL: Aldine Publishing Company.

Turner, Victor. 1982. *From Ritual to Theatre. The Human Seriousness of Play.* New York: Performing Arts Journal Publications.

Unterberg, Richie. 1998. *Unknown Legends of Rock 'n' Roll.* San Francisco, CA: Backbeat Books.

Van Rooyen, Jacobus C.W. 1987. *Censorship in South Africa.* Cape Town: Juta.

Vernallis, Carol. 2004. *Experiencing Music Video: Aesthetics and Cultural Context.* New York and Chichester: Columbia University Press.

Volkov, Solomon. 1979. *Testimony: The Memoirs of Dimitri Shostakovitch as Related to and Edited by Solomon Volkov.* Trans. Antonina W. Bouis. New York: Proscenium Publishers.

Walser, Robert. 1993. 'Forging Masculinity: Heavy-Metal Sounds and Images of Gender', in Simon Frith, Andrew Goodwin and Lawrence Grossberg (eds), *Sound and Vision: The Music Video Reader.* London and New York: Routledge, pp. 153–81.

Walters, Barry. 1986. 'Hit Me', *Village Voice* 31:28, p. 67.

Watrous, Peter. 1992. 'The Pop Life', *New York Times*, 23 September, §C, p. 14.

Weatherford, Mike. 2004. 'Renaissance Man: Balancing Act', *Review-Journal*, 7 November. www.reviewjournal.com/lvrj_home/2004/Nov-07-Sun-2004/living/25065557.html.

Weber, Max. 1958. *The Rational and Social Foundations of Music.* Trans. and ed. Don Martindale, Johannes Riedel and Gertrude Neuwirth. Carbondale: Southern Illinois University Press.

Weeks, David and Jamie James. 1995. *Eccentrics.* London: Weidenfeld & Nicolson.

Welch, Chris. 1998. *The Secret Life of Peter Gabriel.* London: Omnibus.

Wells, Paul. 1997. 'Body Consciousness in the Films of Jan Svankmajer', in Jayne Pilling (ed.), *A Reader in Animation Studies.* Sydney: John Libbey, pp. 177–94.

'What Peter Gabriel songs mean to us'. Site accessed in June 2003, this URL is no longer available.

Whiteley, Sheila. 1997. 'Little Red Rooster v. The Honky Tonk Woman: Mick Jagger, Sexuality, Style and Image', in Sheila Whiteley (ed.), *Sexing the Groove: Popular Music and Gender*. London and New York: Routledge, pp. 67–99.

Williamson, Nigel. 2006. 'Welcome to the Family', *Songlines*, September/October, pp. 20–23.

Wilson, Lindy. 1991. 'Bantu Stephen Biko: A Life', in B. Pityana, M. Ramphele, M. Mpumlwana and L. Wilson (eds), *Bounds of Possibility: The Legacy of Steve Biko and Black Consciousness*. Cape Town: David Phillip.

'WOMAD'. 1996. *WOMAD* (promotional brochure). Wiltshire: WOMAD.

Young, Jon. 1986. '*So*' (record review), *Musician* 93:10, pp. 96, 98.

Zak, Albin J. III. 2001. *The Poetics of Rock: Cutting Tracks, Making Records*. Berkeley: University of California Press.

Zoglin, Richard. 1987. 'MTV Faces a Mid-Life Crisis', *Time*, 29 June. www.time.com/time/magazine/article/0,9171,964805-1,00.html.

Discography

Artists United Against Apartheid. 1985. *Sun City*. EMI. Re-released Razor and Tie Music CD RE2007, 1993.

Baez, Joan. 1987. *Recently*. Gold Castle Records 171 004-1.

Brand, Dollar (Abdullah Ibrahim). 2003. 'Mannenburg', *Amandla! A Revolution in Four-part Harmony: Original Soundtrack*. CD. New York. ATO 54997925.

Collins, Phil. 1981. 'In the Air Tonight', *Face Value*. WEA International 2292-54939-2.

De André, Fabrizio. 1984. *Creuza de mä*. Dischi Ricordi CDMRL 6308.

De André, Fabrizio. 1996. *Anime salve*. BMG Ricordi TCDMRL 392352.

Dibango, Manu. 1994. *Wakafrika*. Giant Records CD 9 24566-2.

Du Plessis, Koos. 1979. 'Kinders van die Wind', *Skadus teen die Muur*. LP. Warner Bros. Records. OCLC 60785265.

Eno, Brian and David Byrne. 1981. *My Life in the Bush of Ghosts*. E.G. Records 2311 060.

Ethnotechno: Sonic Anthropology. 1994. Vol. 1. Wax Trax! Records TVT 7211-2.

Fripp, Robert. 1979. *Exposure*. E.G. Records 2310 661.

Fripp, Robert. 1980. *God Save The Queen/Under Heavy Manners*. Polydor 2311005.

Gabriel, Peter. 1977. *Peter Gabriel* (a.k.a. 'Car'). Atco 36-147-2. Charisma CDS 4006. CD 1983 Virgin PGCD 1.

Gabriel, Peter. 1978. *Peter Gabriel* (a.k.a. 'Scratch', 'Slash' or 'Fingernails'). Atlantic 19181-2. Charisma CDS 4013. CD 1987 Virgin PGCD 2. Charisma Records 9124 025.

Gabriel, Peter. 1980. *Peter Gabriel* (a.k.a. 'Melt'). Mercury SRM-1-3848. *Peter Gabriel*. Charisma Records 9124 054.

Gabriel, Peter. 1982. *Peter Gabriel* (a.k.a. *Security* in US release). Geffen GHS 2011-2. Charisma Records 6302 201.

Gabriel, Peter. 1986. *So*. Charisma Records PG 5. Geffen GHS 24088-2. Virgin CD PGCD 5.

Gabriel, Peter. 1987. *Book of Memories* (bootleg). Heartland ZP 234878.

Gabriel, Peter. 1989. *Passion: Music for The Last Temptation of Christ*. Real World/Virgin RWCD 1. Geffen Records M5G 24206.

Gabriel, Peter. 1992. *Us*. Geffen GEFD 24473-2. PGCD 7. Itunes 2002 Virgin PGCDR7.

Gabriel, Peter. 2002. *Up*. Geffen 069493388-2. Virgin/Real World PGCD11.

Gabriel, Peter. 2010. *Scratch My Back*. Real World PGCDX 12.

Gabriel, Peter. n.d. *Slowburn* (a.k.a. *Live USA*; bootleg). Imtrat 900.014.

Gaye, Marvin. 1983. *Compact Command Performances*. Tamla TCD06069TD.

Genesis. 1969. *From Genesis to Revelation*. Decca SKL 4990. CD 1996 Disky 86 3092. (2005: 2 CD deluxe edition). Edsel MEDCD721.

Genesis. 1970. *Trespass*. Charisma CAS 1020. CD 1985 Virgin/Charisma CASCD 1020. MCA MCAD 1653.

Genesis. 1971. *Nursery Cryme*. Charisma CAS 1052. CD 1985 Virgin CASCD-1052.

Genesis. 1972. *Foxtrot*. Charisma CAS 1058. CD 1985 Charisma CASCD-1058.

Genesis. 1973. *Selling England by the Pound*. Charisma CAS 1074. CD 1985 Virgin CASCD-1074.

Genesis. 1974. *The Lamb Lies Down on Broadway*. Atlantic 82677-2. Charisma CGS 101. CD 1986 Virgin CGSCD-1.

Genesis. 1977. *Seconds Out*. Charisma GE 2001. itunes 1994 Virgin GECDX 2001.

Genesis. 1990. *The Lamb Woke Up Again* (bootleg). Stonehenge 2008/2009.

Genesis. 1994. *Besides the Silent Mirror* (bootleg). Alternative Recording Co. ARC 012.

Genesis. 1998. *Genesis Archive 1967–1975*. Virgin CDBOX6.

Genesis. 1999. *Rare Tapes* (bootleg). MIL Productions 616.

Kerkorrel, Johannes en Die Gereformeerde Blues Band. 1990. *Eet Kreef*. CD. Shifty Records. OCLC 66517790.

Khan, Nusrat Fateh Ali. 1990. *Mustt Mustt*. Real World 0777 7862212 3.

Khan, Nusrat Fateh Ali. *Night Song*. Real World 8406832.

King Crimson. 1969. *In the Court of the Crimson King: An Observation by King Crimson*. Island ILPS 9111. CD 1999. Virgin CDVKC1.

King Crimson. 1974. 'Fracture', *Red*. Island ILPS9308.

King Crimson. 1981. *Discipline*. E.G. Records 2311 103.

King Crimson. 1982. *Beat*. E.G. Records 2311 156.

King Crimson. 1984. *Three of a Perfect Pair*. E.G. Records 817 882-1.

Lanois, Daniel. 1989. *Acadeie*. WEA/Warner Bros. 7599 25969 2.

Lanois, Daniel. 1993. *For the Beauty of Wynona.* WEA/Warner Bros. 7559 45030.

Lucey, Roger. 1979. 'Thabane', *The Road is Much Longer.* LP. 3rd Ear Music. 3EE 7004.

Mursal, Maryam. 1998. *The Journey.* Real World CAR 2370-2.

N'Dour, Youssou. 2000. *Joko: From Village to Town.* Columbia COL 4897 18-2.

N'Dour, Youssou. 1989. *The Lion.* CD. Virgin Records. CDV2584.

Patti and the Dep Band (UB40). 1986. 'Biko'. Important Records TAN 11.

Paxton, Tom. 1978. 'The Death of Stephen Biko'. Vanguard Recording Society VS 5009.

Simon, Paul. 1990. *The Rhythm of the Saints.* Warner Bros. 9 26098-2.

Simon, Paul and Ladysmith Black Mambazo. 1986. *Graceland.* CD. Warner Bros. Records. OCLC:14565137. W2-25447.

Simple Minds. 1989. *Street Fighting Years.* Virgin Records CD MINDSCD1.

Steel Pulse. 1979. 'Biko's Kindred Lament', *Tribute to the Martyrs.* LP. Island Records. 162-539 568-2.

Stevens, Cat. 1970. *Mona Bona Jakon.* Island ORL 8488. Itunes Island Masters IMCD 35.

Various Artists. 1988. *Voëlvry.* 1988. CD. Shifty. SHIF 001.

Various Artists. 1989. *Passion – Sources.* Real World RWCD2.

Various Artists. 1991. *Bringing it all Back Home.* BBC CD 844.

Various Artists. 2001. *Spirit of Africa.* Real World CDR W97.

Various Artists. 2002. *Voëlvry: Die Toer.* CD. Sheer Records. SHIF 002.

Various Artists. 2008. *Big Blue Ball.* Real World. USCDR W150.

Vilakazi, Strikes. 1994. 'Meadowlands', *From Marabi to Disco: 42 Years of Township Music.* CD. Gallo Music Productions. OCLC 47795279.

Wilson, Ray. 2002. *Live and Acoustic.* Inside Out Music IOMACD 2042.

Wyatt, Robert. 1984. 'The Wind of Change', 12-inch single featuring Robert Wyatt with the SWAPO singers. Rough Trade Records. RTT 168.

Wyatt, Robert. 1985. 'Biko', 7-inch single. Rough Trade Records. RTT 149.

Zukie, Tapper. 1978. 'Tribute to Steve Biko', *Peace in the Ghetto.* CD. Virgin Records. FL25.

Films and Videos

All about Us. 1993. Geffen GEFV 39544.

Behind the Scenes. Peter Gabriel's Secret World. 2003. On Peter Gabriel and François Girard. *Secret World Live.* Widescreen. Digitally re-mixed and re-mastered. DVD. Real World / Geffen 0694935949.

Carruthers, Bob (Director). 2004. *Inside Genesis – The Gabriel Years 1970–1975: An Independent Critical Review.* Classic Rock Productions. CRP1728.

Douglas, Mitchell (Director) and Michael Drewett (Producer). 2002. *Stopping the Music.* Video Documentary. Cutting Grooves.

Gabriel, Anna. 2003. *Peter Gabriel. Growing Up On Tour A Family Portrait. A Film By Anna Gabriel.* DVD. Real World, PGDVD01 180030000 15 4.

Gabriel, Peter. 2004. *Play. The Videos.* DVD. Real World/Warner Strategic Marketing R2 970396. 5050467-5681-2-9.

Gabriel, Peter. 2004. 'Introduction' in *Peter Gabriel Play: The Videos.* Compilation of music videos by Peter Gabriel with surround mixes by Daniel Lanois and Richard Chappell. Real World Music Ltd.

Gabriel, Peter and François Girard. 2003. *Secret World Live.* Widescreen. Digitally re-mixed and re-mastered. DVD. Real World / Geffen 0694935949.

Gabriel, Peter and Hamish Hamilton. 2003. *Growing Up Live.* DVD. Real World / Warner Music 5050466-8596-2-4 / Real World 02498 61143 2.

Thomson, Hugh (Director and Series Producer). 1993. *Dancing in the Street: A Rock and Roll History.* BBC and WGBGH co-production. Episode 3 entitled *Respect.*

Tillyer, York. 2003. 'The Story of Growing Up. A Film by York Tillyer'. On Peter Gabriel and Hamish Hamilton, *Growing Up Live.* DVD. Real World / Warner Music 5050466-8596-2-4.

Index

Aardman Animations 5, 57, 61, 195, 204
Afro Celt Sound System (ACSS) 145 n4,
    153, 154
'Ain't That Peculiar' 48–9, 51, 187 n6
Amnesty International 6, 7, 37, 108–10,
    128, 137, 146, 152
Anderson, Ian 11, 35, 161, 163, 165
Anderson, Laurie 179 n3, 189 n9, 191,
    209, 227
apartheid 6, 7, 37, 99, 100, 102, 103, 105,
    106, 107, 108, 109, 110, 113, 114,
    115, 116, 118, 119, 120, 122, 123,
    124 n 20, 125 n21, 127, 128, 129,
    186
Artists United Against Apartheid 6, 106
Atlantic soul 43, 203

Babacar Faye Drummers 133, 134, 145
bagpipes 101–3, 127, 134, 136, 178, 179
    n4
Banks, Tony 2, 43, 45, 162
Beatles, the 38, 184, 187 n7
Benjamin, Walter 198, 206–8
Betjeman, John 34, 35
Big Blue Ball 12, 153
'Biko' 5, 6, 7, 23, 24, 26, 99, 101–11, 113,
    114, 115 n3, 116, 118, 120, 122,
    124, 125–30, 178–9, 186, 187, 188,
    230,
Biko, Stephen 6, 7, 99, 100–1, 102–5, 106,
    107, 108, 109, 110, 111, 114–5,
    122, 125, 126–7, 129, 130, 186
'Big Time' 27, 41, 195
Birdy (1985) 3, 18 n7, 192
Black People's Convention 100, 107, 115
    n6
Blake, William 15, 17, 35, 38
Blind Boys of Alabama 143, 144
'Blood of Eden' 1, 12, 211, 216–9, 221,
    233

Bonobo Great Apes 41, 149
Bowie, David 15, 48, 50, 117, 191, 192,
    195, 196, 236
Brand, Dollar 117, 119
Brook, Michael 147, 150, 153
Brothers Quay 5, 57, 61, 195, 201 n5
Brown, James 53, 54, 66, 203 n8
Bush, Kate 22, 36, 186 n3, 191
Byrne, David 173, 189, 191, 192, 209

Camel 44, 159
Carroll, Lewis 33, 38
censorship 7, 105, 106, 107 n7, 116
Charisma label 2, 3, 35, 38, 44
Charterhouse School 2, 5, 38, 43, 44, 161,
    162
claymation 11, 63, 65, 66, 196, 197, 200,
    203, 204, 206
Clementi, Muzio 181, 182
collaboration 5, 10, 12, 43, 101 n3, 109,
    120, 136, 138, 143, 145, 146, 147,
    148, 177, 195, 225, 228
Collins, Phil 2, 43, 50, 167, 176, 178
'Come Talk to Me' 28, 49, 133, 134–6,
    144–5, 146, 233
Coyote 48, 50
Cropper, Steve 51–2, 53, 54
Cry Freedom 110, 115 n5, 186 n4
cymbals 52, 175–6, 178, 182, 187

'D.I.Y.' 26, 47, 185
Dalí, Salvador 117, 205–6
Dansette 5, 43
De André, Fabrizio 173–4
'Digging in the Dirt' 28, 45, 49, 86 n28,
    211, 220, 222, 233
'Don't Give Up' 27, 36, 192, 195, 230
doudouk (duduk) 133, 134, 143, 144

Ekome Dance Company 186 n4, 188 n8

Emerson, Lake and Palmer 16 n1, 44, 161
Englishness 18, 23, 25, 27, 29, 31, 33, 34,
    35, 36, 37, 205
Eno, Brian 173, 177 n2, 179, 189, 191,
    192, 227,
Erhard Seminar Training (EST) 22, 148
Eve 3, 226, 227
'Excuse Me' 21, 26, 39, 47, 124, 185

Fairlight Computer Musical Instrument
    (CMI) 11, 22, 152, 175, 178–80,
    181, 186, 189
'Family Snapshot' 22, 25 n19, 26, 186, 188
Fast, Larry 177, 178, 180 n5, 182, 185,
    187, 189
'Firth of Fifth' 159, 167
Fisher, Mark 3, 226, 232
Foxtrot 2, 4, 16, 20, 29, 61, 161, 165
Fripp, Robert 102 n5, 177, 185, 187 n6
From Genesis to Revelation 2, 44, 161

gamelan 92, 177
'Games Without Frontiers' 26, 104, 154,
    186, 208 n15, 230
Gaye, Marvin 48, 49, 50, 51, 54
Genesis 2–3, 4, 5, 8, 9, 10, 11, 12, 15, 16,
    17, 18, 20, 23, 29, 33, 34, 35, 37–9,
    41, 43, 44–7, 48, 49, 55, 59 n7, 61,
    123, 153, 159–71, 173, 183, 184–5,
    189, 192, 195, 205, 226, 227
Genesis Archive 1967–1975 46, 164, 169
globalization 132, 152, 155
Graceland 120, 133 n4
Grahamstown 100, 102 n4
Growing Up 1, 12, 54, 210, 225, 230 n3,
    235–6, 238

'Here Comes the Flood' 21, 26, 47, 48,
    124, 169. 177
hi-hat 23 n14, 49, 176, 178, 182, 203, 214
'Home Sweet Home' 22, 26, 40
human rights 3, 5, 6, 7, 8, 9, 12, 40, 99,
    109, 122, 146, 149, 152
'Humdrum' 21, 22, 26, 185, 187 n6, 190
hybridity 145, 148, 149, 150, 155

'I Don't Remember' 22, 23, 26, 40, 179 n4,
    188, 190

'I Have the Touch' 1, 22, 24, 25 n19, 27,
    188, 190, 216 n7
'I Heard It Through the Grapevine' 49,
    51, 54
'I Know What I Like (In Your Wardrobe)'
    39, 166
'I Talk to the Wind' 162–3
IASPM 1, 148
'In the Court of the Crimson King' 161,
    162
'In the Midnight Hour' 50, 51–2, 53
'In Your Eyes' 27, 28, 47, 146, 182, 195
indaba 113, 116, 118–21, 123, 124 n19,
    129
'Intruder' 23, 24, 25 n19, 26, 176, 179 n4,
    186, 190, 216 n7

jazz 10, 91 n38, 118, 142, 149, 150, 160,
    162–3, 165, 166, 185
Jethro Tull 11, 35, 159, 163, 165, 171, 227
Johnson, Stephen R. 5, 57, 61, 195, 197,
    200, 201, 202
Jung, Carl 23, 24, 39, 40, 66 n16, 148, 190

Kabuki 40, 46
Katché, Manu 27, 52, 134, 182, 234
King Crimson 44, 161, 162, 163, 177, 185
King, Jonathan 2, 44, 161, 171
'Kiss of Life' 24, 27
'Kiss That Frog' 28, 58 n5, 210

Lacan, Jacques 59, 63, 66
Lanois, Daniel 133, 134, 200, 216
'Lay Your Hands on Me' 22, 24, 27, 189,
    190–1
'Lead a Normal Life' 22, 179
Lear, Edward 33, 35
Lepage, Robert 1, 12, 225, 227–8, 230–2,
    235, 236, 238, 239, 240
Levin, Tony 54, 134, 185, 189 n8, 200,
    203, 234
Linn Drum Computer 50, 175, 178, 179
London Millennium Dome 3, 150, 226
Lucey, Roger 101 n2, 117, 119 n11, 122
    n17

Mahurin, Matt 5, 58, 72, 73, 77–8, 96
Mandela, Nelson 7, 108, 115 n6, 121

marimba 22, 23, 177
Martha and the Vandellas 50, 53
Memphis Horns 43, 53, 57, 200 n4
'Mercy Street' 4, 5, 27, 58, 71–96, 206
    n12, 209, 239
Milesi, Piero 173–5
Minassian, Levon 134, 143, 144
Monty Python 16, 205
'Moribund the Burgermeister' 21, 22, 26,
    39, 48, 185
Morricone, Ennio 174, 175
'Mother of Violence' 26, 124
Motown 5, 43, 46, 48, 49, 50, 51, 52, 53,
    54, 57 n2, 199
Mozo 4, 48, 50
MTV 11, 50, 57, 58, 59, 69, 72, 189, 195,
    196
MUDDA 3, 41
Mulvey, Laura 59, 62, 63
music hall 34, 38, 46, 184
musique concrète 187, 191
My Life in the Bush of Ghosts 173, 191

N'Dour, Youssou 6, 7, 28, 29, 141, 143,
    146, 147, 152
'No Self Control' 22, 23, 26, 28, 40, 177,
    178, 179, 185
Nursery Cryme 2, 38, 166, 167
Nusrat Fateh Ali Khan 143, 144, 146, 167,
    153, 154

O'Connor, Sinéad 108, 134, 135, 216, 218
'On the Air' 22, 25 n19, 26
Ovo (2000) 3, 148, 226

Passion (1989) 3, 8, 18 n7, 24 n18, 133,
    134, 153, 169
Peter Gabriel (1977), 'Car' 3, 18, 20, 21,
    26, 47, 124, 185
Peter Gabriel (1978), 'Scratch' 3, 25 n19,
    26, 28 n20, 39, 124, 177, 185,
Peter Gabriel (1980), 'Melt' 3, 6, 11, 21–3,
    25 n19, 26, 28, 36, 49, 50, 52, 99,
    124, 173, 174, 175–9, 185–6, 180,
    185, 188
Peter Gabriel (1982), 'Security' 3, 11, 19
    n8, 21 n12, 24 n17, 27, 40, 46 n3,

    48, 49, 50, 52, 183, 184, 185, 186,
    187, 188–91, 192
Peter Gabriel Plays Live (1983) 3, 18 n7,
    46 n3, 49, 183 n1, 193
Phillips, Anthony 2, 38, 162, 171
Picasso, Pablo 65, 150, 209
Pickett, Wilson 51, 53
Pink Floyd 39, 184, 195, 196, 225 n1
Playtime 1988 11, 183, 192
Pokrovsky, Dmitry 134, 135, 143
politics 5, 6, 9, 33, 109, 114, 115 n3, 129,
    132, 187 n6, 205 n11, 210
Pollock, Jackson 65, 66, 209
polyrhythms 146 n4, 177, 190, 192
polystylistic polyphony 101, 133, 134
Port Elizabeth 100, 102 n4, 128
postcolonialism 132, 155
progressive (prog) rock 2, 4, 10, 11, 15–7,
    18, 19, 20, 22, 23, 24, 25, 26, 28,
    29, 33, 35, 38, 44, 47, 48, 55, 59
    n7, 86 n28, 159, 160–3, 165, 167,
    168, 170–1, 173, 177, 183, 184,
    185, 186, 195, 226
protest 6, 7, 33, 99, 100, 107, 108, 111,
    113–5, 116, 118–20, 122–3, 125,
    127–8, 130,

R&B 43, 44–5, 46, 53
Rael 17, 168, 184
Real World 3, 6, 10, 12, 24, 41, 91 n38,
    101 n3, 137, 141–2, 143, 145 n4,
    146, 147, 149, 150, 152, 153–4,
    146, 147, 149, 150, 152, 153, 154,
    156, 180, 226, 227, 231, 234
'Red Rain' 27, 28 n20, 182, 192, 237
Redding, Otis 5, 43, 44, 47, 51, 53, 57, 68,
    147, 200 n4
Reich, Steve 187, 191
reverberation 45, 51, 76 n9, 83, 84, 126,
    163, 164, 174, 175, 176, 199, 212,
    214, 215, 216, 217, 218
Rhodes, David 53, 54, 102 n5, 134, 144.
    189 n8, 203
ritual 10, 11, 24, 35, 44, 63, 74, 88, 187,
    189, 190, 191, 192, 239
Robinson, Smokey 48, 49
Rolling Stones, the 44, 225 n1, 226
Rutherford, Mike 2, 161

Scorsese, Martin 3, 18 n7, 143, 144, 169
'Secret World' 18, 29, 169
Secret World Live (1994) 3, 12, 54, 225–6, 227, 228, 230, 231, 234–5, 238, 239
Selling England by the Pound 3, 20, 29, 159 n1, 161, 166, 167, 168
Sexton, Anne 5, 58, 71, 72, 73, 74, 75 n 8, 76, 78 n14, 79, 80 n15, 81 n16, 82 n18, 83 n20–21, 84 n22, 85 n26, 86, 87 n29, 88 n32–3, 91 n38–9, 95, 96, 209
sexuality 5, 17, 37, 48, 59 n7, 60, 207, 208, 222
shakuhachi 52–3, 54, 169 n7, 199, 205 n11
shaman 10, 183, 189
'Shock the Monkey' 27, 40, 50, 51, 188, 189, 225
Simon, Paul 81, 108, 133 n4, 189, 191
'Sledgehammer' 3, 4, 5, 11, 27, 28 n20, 41, 43, 44, 48, 49, 50–1, 52–3, 54, 57–9, 61–9
So (1986) 3, 4, 11, 18, 21 n12, 24 n17, 27, 28, 40, 42, 43, 49, 50, 52, 55, 57, 58, 146, 148, 169 n7, 174, 175, 181, 182, 192, 195, 205, 209, 210
'Solsbury Hill' 19–21, 22, 24, 26, 29, 47, 48, 124, 190, 225, 236
soul music 4–5, 12, 27, 43–5, 46–7, 48, 49–50, 53–4, 55, 57–8, 199–200, 203, 205 n11
South Africa 6, 7, 43, 99, 100, 103, 104–5, 106–7, 108, 109, 110, 113–7, 119 n11, 121–3, 125 n21, 126 n23, 127–8, 129–30, 141, 153, 178, 186
South Bank Show 175, 178, 179, 180
Stax 5, 43, 45, 50, 51–4, 57, 68, 200
'Steam' 5, 28, 50, 51, 53–4, 58, 210, 225
Stewart, Chris 2, 162
Sting 6, 191
Stockhausen, Karlheinz 187 n7, 191
Sun City Project 6, 7, 106
'Supper's Ready' 4, 16, 17, 18, 29, 39, 46, 47 n4, 165
surdo 74, 76, 83, 84, 87 n30, 88, 90, 91 n38, 92 n42, 94, 95
surrealism 12, 19, 67, 195, 205–8
Synclavier 152, 180

synthesizer pad 82, 83, 84, 90, 92 n41

Talking Heads 191, 192, 197, 209
tambourine 46, 51, 53, 170, 199
'That Voice Again' 27, 49
'The Barry Williams Show' 40, 42, 58 n5, 230, 238
'The Family and the Fishing Net' 27, 178, 190, 280 n15
'The Knife' 46, 159, 162, 163
The Lamb Lies Down on Broadway 3, 11, 17, 20, 39, 47, 159 n1, 160, 168, 184
The Last Temptation of Christ 3, 18 n7, 133, 143, 147, 153, 169
The Long Walk Home 143–4, 148
'The Musical Box' 38, 39, 46, 167
'The Rhythm of the Heat' 22, 23, 27, 40, 148, 180, 184, 188, 190
Trespass 2, 11, 38, 45, 46, 159, 160, 163, 166, 184, 259

U2 6, 225 n1, 226, 232
Un chien andalou 205–6
Up (2002) 3, 4, 40, 55, 147, 148, 182
Us (1992) 3, 4, 8, 12, 18, 19, 25, 28, 29, 49, 52, 53, 55, 133– 8, 144, 169, 174, 182, 211, 214 n5, 216, 227, 231, 232, 235

van Zandt, (Little) Steven 6, 7, 105–6, 108, 114
vibrato 164, 165–6, 167, 169, 171, 181

Wallace and Gromit 12, 203, 204
'Wallflower' 22, 27, 40
'We Do What We're Told (Milgram's 37)' 27, 28 n20, 40, 148
Wexler, Jerry 51, 52
Witness 3, 7, 8, 109, 122, 149
WOMAD 3, 6, 8, 24, 101 n3, 137, 141, 142, 143, 147, 149, 150, 151, 153, 156, 186 n4, 188 n8
Wonder, Stevie 50, 53
world music 2, 3, 6, 8, 9, 15, 24, 91 n38, 101 n3, 131, 137, 141–56, 169, 180, 189, 191, 205

Xhosa 103, 113 n2, 127
Xplora 226, 227

Yes 44, 161

Zappa, Frank 184, 196, 197
zorb ball 236–7